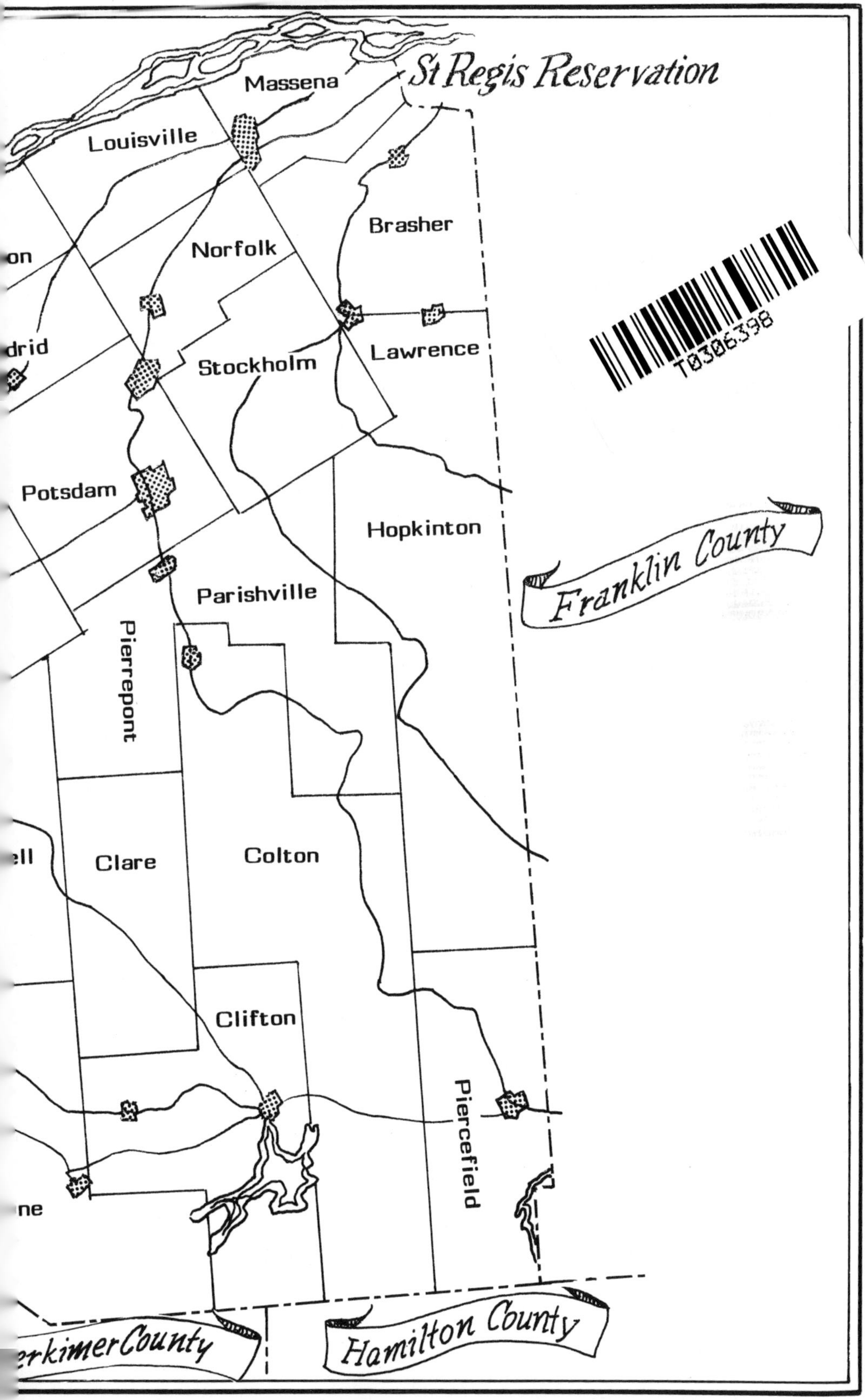
St Regis Reservation
Massena
Louisville
Brasher
Norfolk
Lawrence
Stockholm
Potsdam
Hopkinton
Franklin County
Parishville
Pierrepont
Clare
Colton
Clifton
Piercefield
Hamilton County

CLAIMS TO NAME:

Toponyms of St. Lawrence County

Kelsie B. Harder
Mary H. Smallman

North Country Books, Inc.
Utica, New York

CLAIMS TO NAME:
Toponyms of St. Lawrence County

edited by
Kelsie B. Harder
Mary H. Smallman

ISBN 0-925168-09-2

Library of Congress Cataloging-in-Publication Data

Claims to name: toponyms of St. Lawrence County / edited by Kelsie B. Harder, Mary H. Smallman.
p. cm.
ISBN 0-925168-09-2 ISBN 0-925168-10-6
1. Names, Geographical—New York (State)—Saint Lawrence County. 2. Saint Lawrence County (N.Y.) —History, Local. 3. Cities and towns—New York (State)—Saint Lawrence County—History.
I. Harder, Kelsie B. II. Smallman, Mary H., 1919-
F127.S2C57 1992
917.47'56'0014—dc20 92-43036
CIP

Published by
North Country Books, Inc.
PUBLISHER—DISTRIBUTOR
18 Irving Place
Utica, New York 13501
315-735-4877

Foreword

Someone once told me that St. Lawrence County is the largest county east of the Mississippi River. This at the time seemed impossible and still does. Couldn't Long Island fit two or three times into St. Lawrence County? How about the five boroughs of New York City? The county probably covers their total area ten times over. Those other places seem larger in size because of their reputations. You don't realize just how big St. Lawrence County is until you take a car ride from Somerville to Massena, or from Canton to Childwold.

Growing up in this county made you feel different from New Yorkers portrayed on television or from the people who run the state in Albany. A feeling is held in your heart for years that you're not much different from folks living in Minnesota or Wisconsin. But if you go away from this place and come back, you begin to wonder if the people here are more like their Southern cousins in Alabama or Georgia. The conservative views and values of Northern Republicans don't appear to be in contrast to those of Southern Democrats.

To understand our people, you must get beyond political labels or demographic generalizations. The long, hard winters have tempered the inhabitants of this county. The climate and the often unyielding soil return a small measure of the farmer's toil. Maybe living here makes you skeptical of one good harvest or a beautiful summer's day, knowing that next year could be a disaster. To an outsider, people in St. Lawrence County might seem laconic and hesitant. In this place, it isn't acceptable to poke fun at another's mother for a cheap laugh. A cold exterior guards the big and embracing North Country heart.

And this is the North Country, with apologies to those Canadians from our county's boundary to the North Pole. The North Country doesn't start just north of the Bronx. Maybe it starts just outside of Syracuse or Watertown. It is probably easier to say what St. Lawrence County is not.

The Adirondack foothills start in the eastern part of the county, but this is not the Adirondacks. The St. Lawrence River passes to the north, but there are no great ports like Chicago to be found here. The draw for tourists is not as great as it is to the south and west in the Thousand Islands. Lately, St. Lawrence County has had the dubious distinction of being one of the counties with the highest unemployment and lowest per capita income. This isn't really too hard to swallow, considering the county has less than 150,000 people and can barely muster one official city, Ogdensburg. Through boom and bust years, this county remains with its stagnant economic outlook. Its mines are in slow decline; major manufacturers threaten with their exodus; old dairy farms are being paid to liquidate; and its young leave for brighter shores. Why does anyone settle here?

With all of its pitfalls, this county provides some sort of stability to raise a family. It still has a rural attitude, a certain work ethic, and a spirit to endure. It isn't a county in Mississippi, Montana, Michigan, or Maine; it is a part of New York. No matter how much is said about how much money goes south, this county benefits from its affiliation with the rest of the state. It may not be the destination for people in the Northeast, but the cities of the Northeast and eastern Canada are within its grasp. Sure, it's isolated from great cultural and financial centers, but it is good enough for some to be called home.

–Daniel P. Vining

Preface

By an act of the Legislature on May 5, 1786 the following ten townships were approved for public auction to be held July 10, 1787 in the City of New York. The townships were established by a formal resolution of the commissioners of the land office on September 10, 1787.

1. Louisville	6. Canton
2. Stockholm	7. Dekalb (DeKalb)
3. Potsdam	8. Oswegatchie
4. Madrid	9. Hague
5. Lisbon	10. Cambray

Hague later was changed to Morristown and Cambray to Gouverneur. Thus, St. Lawrence County began as a jurisdictional unit in the State of New York, although the county was not legally established until March 3, 1802.

The number of towns has expanded since 1787, now including in total Brasher, Canton, Clare, Clifton, Colton, DeKalb, DePeyster, Edwards, Fine, Fowler, Gouverneur, Hammond, Hermon, Hopkinton, Lawrence, Lisbon, Louisville, Macomb, Madrid, Massena, Morristown, Norfolk, Parishville, Piercefield, Pierrepont, Pitcairn, Potsdam, Rossie, Russell, Stockholm, and Waddington.

The names of the first ten townships were consciously selected, but we do not know by whom. Perhaps they were chosen in committee, but someone had to have outlined the way the names were selected and made suggestions for them. The argument can be imagined as the chair of the committee presented a list of names. Certainly trade-offs occurred, for the list is a mixed one, with famous cities of the world represented, as well as an Amerindian name, the name of a Revolutionary War hero from a foreign country, a commemoration of a king of France, and a romantic and exotic name for Wales (Cambray), the latter probably insisted upon by a member of the committee who was of Welsh descent. The Surveyor General of the State was Simeon DeWitt, but we do not know how much influence he had in the naming of the townships. Supreme Court Justice Michael W. Duskas claims that seventh graders in his day were taught that a clerk (in the Surveyor General's office?) who watched ships coming into Albany port from exotic places suggested the names of the foreign capitals.

And this is the beginning of naming in St. Lawrence County, and also the last of the selective process. All other names came about the way naming has occurred in the United States, haphazardly and accidentally. Still, out of this seemingly onomastic anarchy, patterns do appear. First, the Europeans had a chance to name a new territory. The fact that the features (streams, mountains, lakes, plains) already had Amerindian names made no difference. The attitudes and the languages were too divergent to matter much. The Europeans with greater war-making power dominated and named as they needed names. Occasionally, however, Amerindian names, usually of streams and mountains, were retained or translated into one of the European languages, either French or English in St. Lawrence County.

The first names were usually descriptive, such as **Trout Lake**, for the presence of the fish, **Mud Pond, The Plains, Sharp Top Mountain, Big Swamp, Snake Island**, and **Sand Hill**. Then as property was accumulated, ownership, possessive, or proximity names began to appear. Among these would be **Abbots Swamp, Dickinsons Landing, O'Neil Road, Campbell Cemetery**, and **Wheeler Mountain**. Others were commemoratives, celebrating a person of respect or one of national or international stature, such as **Washington Street, Lincoln Place, Morristown**, or **Massena**.

More recent names came from housing developers, persons working in the highway department, land developers, and county and town officials. Such names reflect the views of the namers. Developers tend to search out names that have good connotations, sometimes nostalgic and patriotic, or rural and rustic, as **Ridgewood Avenue, Hillcrest Avenue, Prospect Circle**, or **Heritage Place**, or a set of transfer names from England, such as **Coventry Street, Windsor Road, Churchill Avenue, Dover Street**, or a set of college names, including **Cornell Avenue, Colgate Avenue, Clarkson Avenue**, and **Amherst Road**.

In recent years, all rural roads have been given names. Any county that wishes to make use of the 911 emergency telephone system has named all roads so that the drivers of the emergency vehicles can locate places. All the roads in the county have now been named, many of them given by workers for the Highway Department. Usually, the name of a family living on the road will be chosen, such as **Daly Road, O'Neil Road, Cutler Road**. Other factors contribute to such naming, often in reference to a feature in the area, such as **Eel Weir Road, Gravel Road, Mine Road**, or **Spruce Road**.

St. Lawrence County can be classified as a place with conservative names. Few names deviate from standard practices of naming for possession, flora and fauna, and commemoration. Only a few names are derived from other than traditionally English and European ones. **Adirondack, Chippewa, Oswegatchie, Hannawa, Wanakena**, and **Iroquois** are the few Amerindian names that appear.

Furthermore, very few of the names are exotic enough to attract much attention, although some do exist: **Arab Mountain, Army, Atlantis Island, Babylon Road, Ballybean, California Road, Childwold, Cracker Box Road, Mount Alone, Mount Pisgah, Slab City,** and **Jingleville Road.**

This does not mean, however, that naming was taken lightly. The names of the original ten townships were consciously given and no doubt represented a microcosm of the attitudes and aspirations of the namers, citizens of a new country that took pride in the repetition of great names and the celebration of one Amerindian name. Offsetting the public names are the ones dedicated to private interest. Soon after the lands were placed for public sale, speculators began buying the land. Some of the great names of the county reflect the early land investors: Macomb, Rensselaer, Morristown, Gouverneur, Parishville, DePeyster, Fine, Clarkson, Raymondville, and many others, all noted in the glossary along with historical information. A particularly interesting cluster of names involves the Ogdens. Ogdensburg was named for Samuel Ogden, who married Euphemia Morris, sister of Gouverneur Morris. Joshua Waddington married Gertrude Gouverneur Ogden in 1804, thereby cementing the families of Waddington, Ogden, and Morris.

—Kelsie B. Harder
Mary H. Smallman

Explanatory Notes

The glossary contains entries on all townships, places of habitation (townships, city, villages, hamlets, corners, and some buildings), all land features (rivers, bays, brooks, creeks, lakes, bogs, ponds, mountains, hills, plains), all man-made features (roads, streets, and highways). We have tried to record all the place names, although we know that complete coverage is probably impossible. We have also tried to obtain the origin of all the names, but in this task we learned that many origins still are unknown. The user will note that many origins are missing from many names, especially road and street names. We hope to fill in many of these in a second edition, if users will provide us with the information.

The entries are controlled by a main name, under which many names may be listed, each one located by township or in a few cases by village or city. If several names appear under one entry (see **Adams** as an example), the different names are separated by a slash /, and within the boundaries of each slash will be the information pertaining to that name. The references may contain additional material, although much of the search for name origins was done without the aid of printed sources, especially road and street names. We have relied on informants, town historians, our own interviews, and whatever printed sources and maps available. (See our list of sources.)

Ample use has been made of research by Thomas Perrin, who laboriously recorded each name that appeared on maps provided by the United States Geological Survey. Entries have been keyed to the maps wherever necessary. This may appear cumbersome, but the records are then available for anyone who wishes to do further research. Many names also have a reference to an article or articles in *The Quarterly*, a publication by the St. Lawrence County Historical Association (see **Abigail Island** for an example). Whenever a printed source was available, we listed it in our sources: **Abbot Hill**, for instance, is referenced to *Sketches of Parishville*. Abbreviations are used to avoid excessive repetition. At first glance, readers may find these difficult and pedantic, but after a few moments they should become clear. A few examples illustrate the method:

Bancroft Road: r., t. Edwards, n. Earl Bancroft (1861-1925), attorney. Freeman, 33.

Bancroft Road is the name listed on county highway maps. The entry identifies it as a road (r.) in the town (t.) of Edwards, named for (n.) Earl Bancroft (1861-1925), attorney. Freeman, 33, refers to the bibliographical source as Freeman, LaVerne H., **Edwards on the Oswegatchie**.

Colgate Drive: s., v. Massena, n. Colgate University.

Colgate Drive is the name listed on village maps. The entry identifies it as a street (s.) in the village (v.) of Massena, named for (n.) Colgate University.

If several places have exactly the same name, the different entries will be separated by a semicolon rather than a slash. See **Catherine** and **Cemetery Road** for examples.

With only a few exceptions, we have not indicated pronunciation, since most of the names will be known to the users of the glossary. The speech of residents of the county does differ from our neighbors south and west of us in New York, but it is insignificant for our purposes, at least not enough to warrant a pronunciation key.

We have held technical terms to a minimum, but two need to be illustrated: specific and generic. In a name such as **Lawrence Avenue**, **Lawrence** will be the specific, with **Avenue** as the generic. **Farnsworth School** would have **Farns-worth** as the specific, with **School** as the generic. **Creek School** would appear to have two generics, but in this case **Creek** would be the specific and **School** the generic. In **Lawrence Avenue School**, **Lawrence Avenue** would be the specific and **School** the generic. A list of abbreviations appears below, with the exceptions of months and states, which appear with currently accepted abbreviations:

Adm	Administrative	OE	Old English
alt.	altitude	p.	page
b.	born	pm	postmaster
c.	city	p. o.	post office
ca	circa	poss.	possibly
desc.	descriptive	pp.	pages
el.	elevation	prob.	probably
est.	established	Quad	Quadrangle
ety.	etymology	r.	road
ft.	feet	Rte.	Route
ff.	following	s.	street
h.	hamlet	St.	Saint
inc.	incorporated	SUC	State University College
m.	mile, miles	svc.	service
n.	name, names, named, named for	t.	town, towns
		trib.	tributary
no.	number	USGS	United States Geological Survey
npn	no page number	v.	village

Although we encountered many problems in entering the names, we need here to mention only two, both affecting the user. The spelling of **Grass(e)** and **Racquette** (or **Raquette**) cannot be settled with certainty; hence, we accept the divided usage in the spelling of the two names. The editors have experienced the problem outside our work here and have finally concluded, after looking at whatever evidence is available, that the users will have to decide for themselves which they prefer. We have listed **Grass(e)** as it is written here in our entries (see **Grass(e)**). **Racquette** or **Raquette** appears in the written sources with different spellings, including the early **Racket** (see entry). We cannot be certain when the French form appeared. Because it is our preference to do so, we have used **Racquette** as the spelling except in the entries for **Racket** and **Raquette**.

Additions and corrections are welcome and will be acknowledged. Send or give to Kelsie B. Harder, State University College, Potsdam, NY 13676, telephone (315) 265-8644 or (315) 267-2044; Mary H. Smallman, RFD 1, P. O. Box 171, Hermon, NY 13652, telephone (315) 347-3221. When a second edition is published, we will incorporate all the changes and eliminate errors we've unwittingly made.

Here I wish to thank three of my former students who have devoted much time to this project: Daniel Vining, who supervised the computer work and edited many entries; Thomas Perrin, who collected all the map names; and Christopher Blocher, who designed the book and prepared the camera-ready copy. And, above all, I wish to thank my mentor in St. Lawrence County history, Mary H. Smallman, co-author, whose contributions to the project and to the county exceed any acknowledgements.

–Kelsie B. Harder

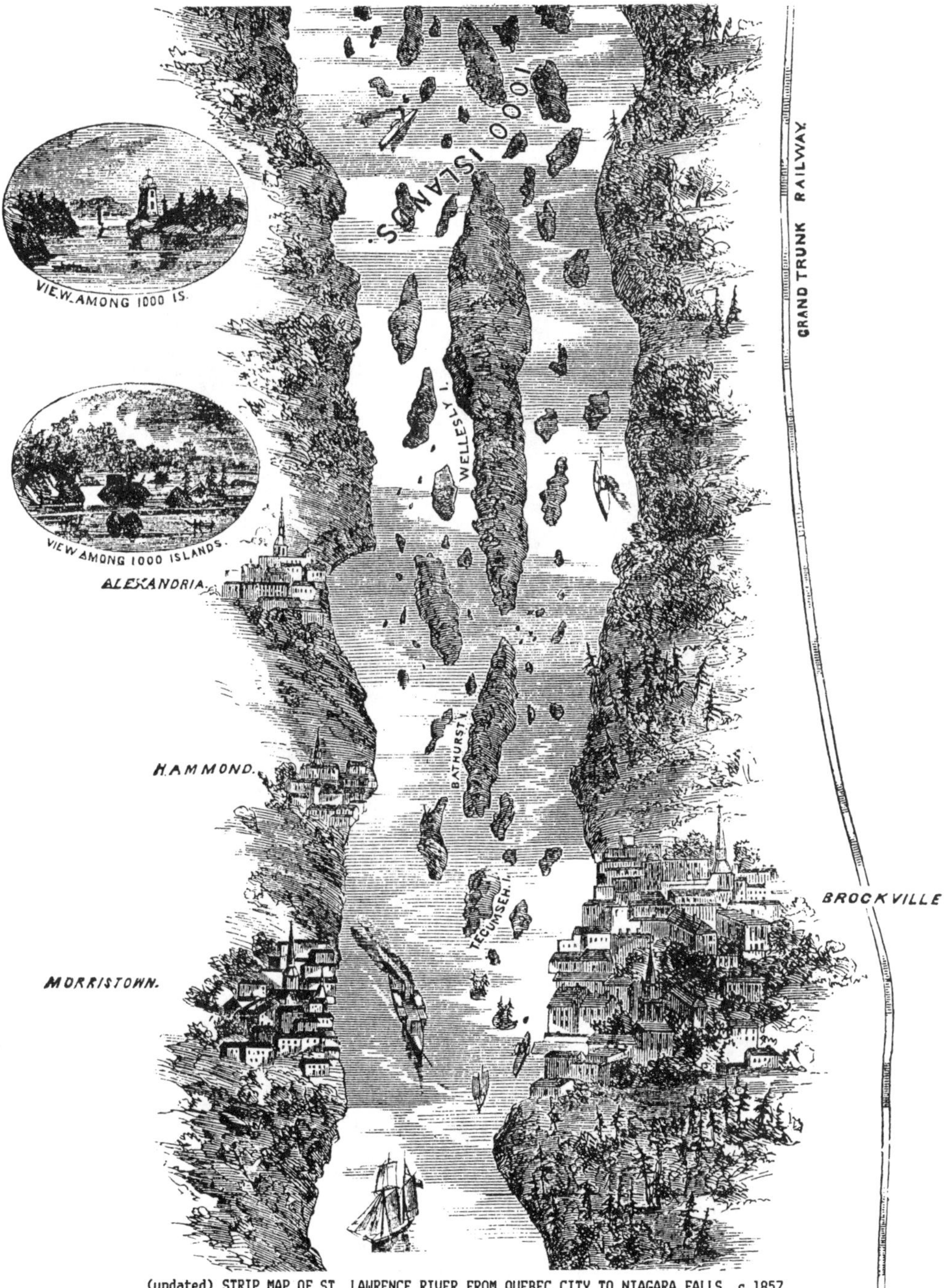

(undated) STRIP MAP OF ST. LAWRENCE RIVER FROM QUEBEC CITY TO NIAGARA FALLS c 1857
drawn by Alfred R. Waud Eng'd by John Andrew Boston US

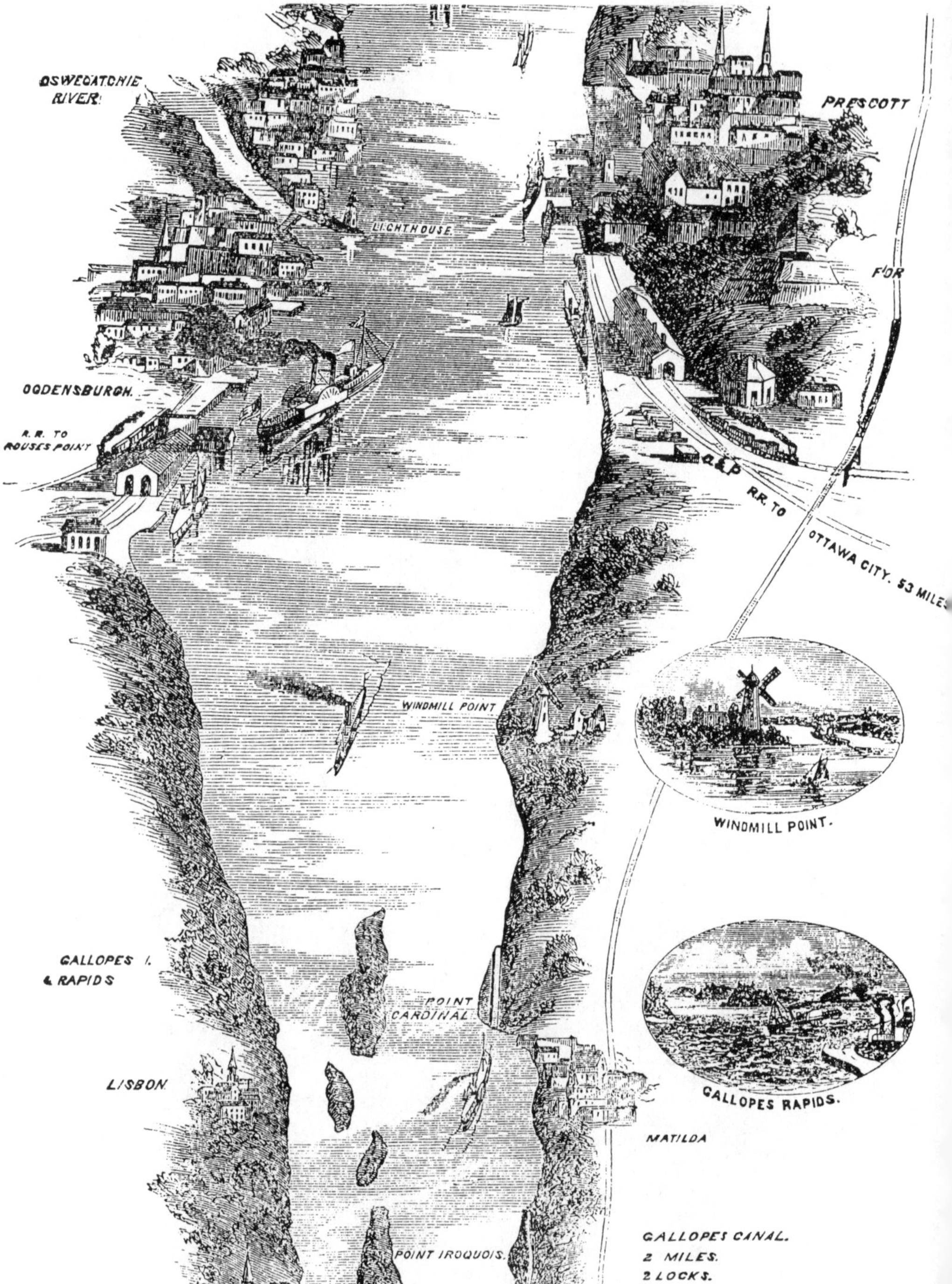
OSWEGATCHIE RIVER
PRESCOTT
LIGHTHOUSE
FOR
OGDENSBURGH.
R. R. TO ROUSES POINT
O&P
R.R. TO
OTTAWA CITY. 53 MILES
WINDMILL POINT
WINDMILL POINT.
GALLOPES I. & RAPIDS
POINT CARDINAL
GALLOPES RAPIDS.
LISBON
MATILDA
GALLOPES CANAL.
2 MILES.
2 LOCKS.
POINT IROQUOIS.
RAPID

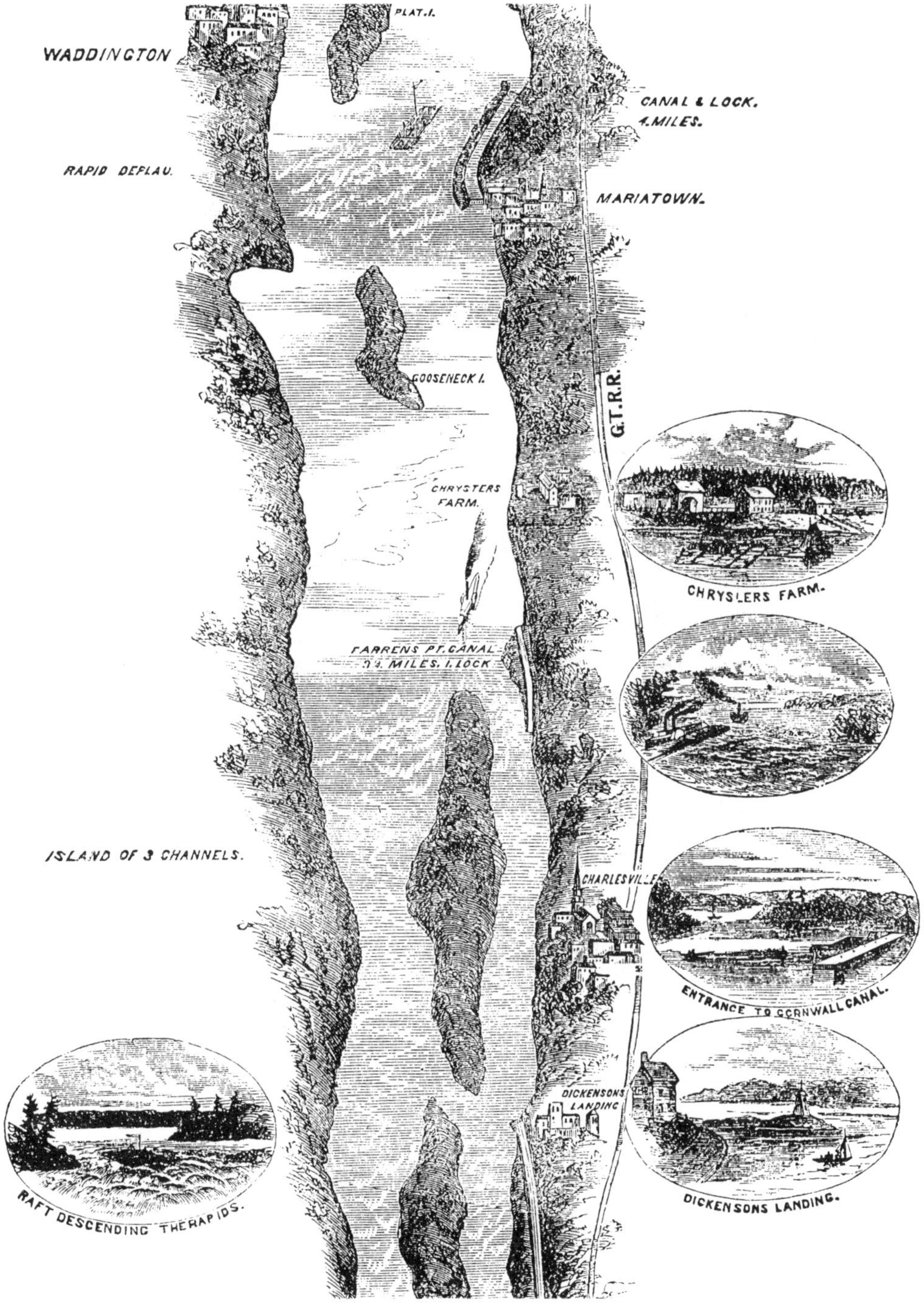
WADDINGTON
PLAT. I.
CANAL & LOCK.
4 MILES.
RAPID DEPLAU.
MARIATOWN.
GOOSENECK I.
G.T.R.R.
CHRYSTERS
FARM.
CHRYSLERS FARM.
FARRENS PT. CANAL
MILES. 1. LOCK
ISLAND OF 3 CHANNELS.
CHARLESVILLE
ENTRANCE TO CORNWALL CANAL.
DICKENSONS
LANDING
DICKENSONS LANDING.
RAFT DESCENDING THERAPIDS.

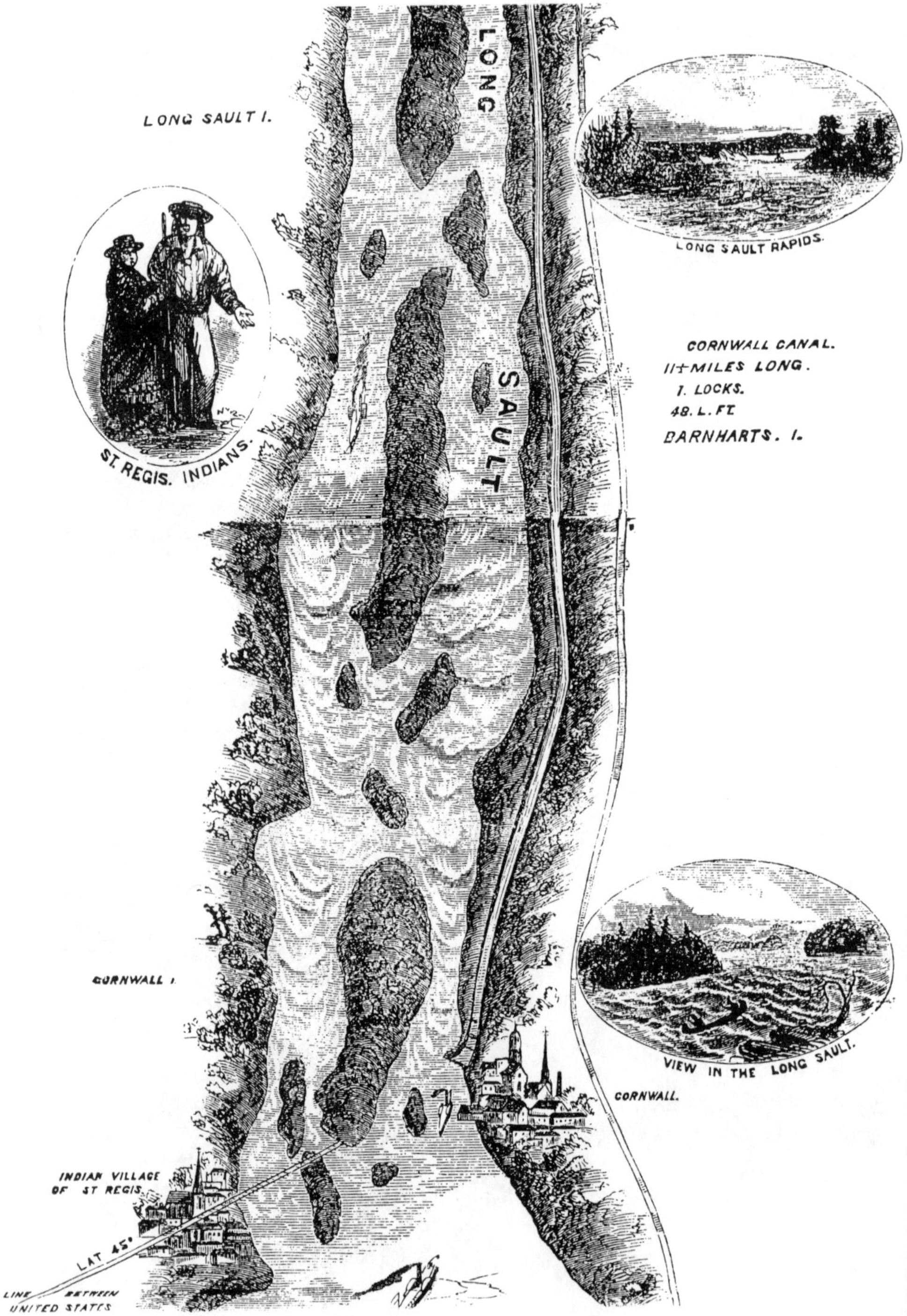
LONG SAULT I.
LONG
SAULT
LONG SAULT RAPIDS.
ST. REGIS. INDIANS.
CORNWALL CANAL.
11½ MILES LONG.
7. LOCKS.
48. L. FT
BARNHARTS. I.
CORNWALL I.
VIEW IN THE LONG SAULT.
CORNWALL.
INDIAN VILLAGE
OF ST REGIS.
LAT 45°
LINE BETWEEN
UNITED STATES

A

A. Barton Hepburn Hospital: in Ogdensburg, n. the benefactor, born in Colton, but became wealthy as superintendent of the Banking Department of New York State. / **A. Barton Hepburn Library**: Libraries in Edwards, Hermon, Colton, Madrid, Lisbon, Norfolk, and Waddington.

A. R. C. Building Entrance: s., v. Norwood.

Abbot Hill: in Picketville, t. Parishville, n. Benjamin Abbot, colorful early settler, "reticent and unsociable," who lived in "Abbot's Mansion," a home so large that Abbot could drive "an ox team into the basement, turn it around and drive out." See *Sketches of Parishville*.

Abbots Swamp: t. Fowler, n. Abbott family, early settlers along the Oswegatchie River. E. W. Abbott was Supervisor in 1852. Hough, p. 302. 1956 USGS Gouverneur Quad.

Abigail Island: in Trout Lake, t. Hermon, n. Abigail Cole, by Elsie Evans. *Quarterly*, 16 (1971), no. 2, p. 22.

Academy Place: s., c. Ogdensburg, n. because it is beside the Ogdensburg Free Academy.

Academy Street: s., v. Hammond, site of early high school.

Acres School: no. 2, common school, t. DeKalb, n. Acres family, especially for Haze and Collins Acres. 1956 USGS Bigelow Quad.

Adams: surname used as a specific: **Adams Island**: in Trout Lake, t. Hermon, n. owner, Charles Adams, physician. Formerly **Carpenter Island**. *Quarterly*, 16 (1971), no. 1, p. 10. / **Adams Road**: r., t. Potsdam, n. Adams family. / **Adams Road**: r., t. Norfolk, n. Samuel Adams from VT. / **Adams Street**: s., c. Ogdensburg, n. John Adams (1735-1832), 2nd president of the United States.

Adelia Street: s., v. Gouverneur, n. Mrs. Adelia Smith.

Adirondack: for an Algonquian tribe, called "bark-eaters" by their enemies, as first recorded by Roger Williams, who confused the tribe with the Mohawks. The meaning of the n. has been lost, but a semblance of the sound form has been perpetuated in the current spelling. / **Adirondack Preserve**: forest lands once distinct from the state park (see **Forest Commission Report, 1893**). / **Adirondack State Park**: partially in St. Lawrence County; the largest wilderness area, more than six million acres, east of the Mississippi.

Administration Building Road: r., t. Massena, n. the administrative building of the Seaway.

Akwasasane: See **St. Regis.** Variant spellings: **Akwesasne, Aghquis-**

sasne, Mohawk meaning, "where the partridge drums."

Alamogie School: t. Hammond; details not available. Variant of **Alamogin**.

Alamogin (pronounced al-a-moó-gee): (1) "Algonquian, probably meaning 'inward,' with reference to a pond isolated in the hills. Located in the hills near Rossie." (2) r., t. Hammond, no origin noted. *Quarterly*, 10 (1965), no. 4, p. 14. Variants: **Alamogin, Alamogie, Allemogen, Alamagien, Alamoogen**. In t. Hammond, a p. o. est. Sept. 8, 1898, George A. Monk, pm, closed Nov. 1, 1899, but p. o. never in operation.

Albany Road: the road from Albany to St. Lawrence River, t. Fine. *Quarterly*, 11 (1966), no. 4, p. 15. It was begun in 1811 as an inducement to settlement as a buffer against the British in Canada and to move goods from Albany to St. Lawrence River. Since the road was never completed, it was called a "paper road." / **Albany Street**: s., v. Ogdensburg, now **Albany Avenue**, n. for **Albany Road**, but also for the state capital.

Albert Marsh Hill: t. Clare, Colton, n. Albert Marsh who first bought land in Fine in about 1895. 1921 USGS Stark Quad.

Alcoa Park: v. Massena, n. Alcoa (Aluminum Corp. of America), which has a plant in the v. / **Alcoa Road**: s., v. Massena.

Alden Street: s:, v. Massena, n. William S. Alden who came from Vergennes, VT in 1834.

Alder: n. the tree of the genus *Alnus*. Since alders are plentiful, many features carry the n. as a specific: **Alder Brook**: t. Clare, stream, trib. Middle Branch Grass(e) River. 1915 Russell Quad; 1921 Stark Quad; 1902 Blankman; 1896 New. / **Alder Brook**: t. Colton. / **Alder Brook**: t. Hopkinton, trib. Long Pond Outlet. 1896 New; 1902 Blankman; 1912 Stoddard; 1919 USGS Nicholville Quad; 1964 USGS Lake Ozonia Quad. / **Alder Brook**: See **Alder Meadow Brook**. / **Alder Meadow Brook**: t. Parishville, n. the tree and meadow; trib. West Branch St. Regis River, n. the tree. ca 1840 Brodhead; 1858 **Alder Brook** Rogerson; 1873 **Alder Brook** Hamilton Child; 1908 Adm; 1908 USGS Potsdam Quad; 1964 USGS Rainbow Falls Quad.

Aldous Road: r., t. Pierrepont, originally part of Route 101 when road was straightened, n. Stephen E. Aldous family; claim is also made for Bob Aldous, early settler.

Aldrich: h., t. Fine, on the Carthage and Adirondack Railroad, n. from a member of the firm of Weston, Dean, and Aldrich. *Quarterly*, 11 (1966), no. 1, p. 16; 26 (1981), no. 2, p. 12; p. o. est. Feb. 25, 1903, Fred A. Maxwell, pm, closed Apr. 29, 1905, opened again May 16,

1905, Peter Yousey, pm, closed Feb. 28, 1921. 1916 USGS Oswegatchie Quad. / **Aldrich Pond**: t. Fine. 1916 USGS Oswegatchie Quad. / **Aldrich School**: t. Fine, Dist. 12. Reynolds, 199. / **Aldrich School**: no. 8, common school, t. Pierrepont, n. Caleb Aldrich from VT.

Alger School: see **Oswegatchie School.**

All Saints Mission Cemetery: on Barnhart Island, t. Massena. The bodies were removed to Pine Grove Cemetery, Cook St., Massena, at the time of the Seaway Expansion.

Allen: common surname used as a specific: **Allen Brook**: t. Brasher, trib. Trout Brook. 1964 USGS North Lawrence Quad; t. Clare, trib. South Branch Grass(e) River. 1915 USGS Russell Quad; t. Fine, trib. Little River. 1916 USGS Oswegatchie Quad. / **Allen Falls**: in West Branch St. Regis River, t. Parishville. David Parish built his house here; n. William Allen, a settler from CT. *Quarterly*, 4 (1959), no. 2, p. 3. 1858 Rogerson; 1898 EGB map; 1902 Blankman; 1908 Adm; 1908 USGS Potsdam Quad; 1964 USGS Parishville Quad. Variant: **Allens Falls**, used locally. / **Allen Falls Reservoir**: in East Branch St. Regis River, t. Parishville. 1964 USGS Parishville Quad. / **Allen Falls Road**: r., t. Parishville. / **Allen Pond**: pond, t. Clare, alt. 1,195 ft. 1880 Ely; 1896 New; 1902 Blankman; 1915 Russell Quad; 1921 Stark Quad. / **Allen Pond Outlet**: t. Clare, trib. South Branch Grass(e) River. 1915 USGS Russell Quad. / **Allen Road**: r., t. Fine; r., t. Pierrepont, n. David Allen. / **Allen Street**: s., c. Ogdensburg, one block connecting Covington and Main Streets west of Adams Avenue, n. Elijah Ball Allen (1791-1869), Amerindian agent in Michigan, fur trader, moved to then Ogdensburgh Village in 1827 and became a merchant, shipper, and landowner. / **Allen Street North**: s., v. Massena, prob. n. Ebenezer Allen. / **Allen Street** South: s., v. Massena; see **Allen Street North**.

Allens: possessive of **Allen**: / **Allens Corners**: t. Madrid, n. Jonathan Allen, a fence-viewer for t. Durant, 277. 1964 USGS Chase Mills Quad. / **Allens Corners-Raymondville Road**: r., t. Norfolk. / **Allens Falls**: t. Parishville. p. o. est. Jan. 29, 1892, William N. Crouch, pm, closed Dec. 31, 1914. Also **Allen's Falls**, n. John, Elizabeth, Harriet, and George Allen. Formerly, **Whittakers Falls**, n. Elias Whittaker, who operated a sawmill near the falls. / **Allens Falls Road**: r., t. Parishville. Also **Middle Road**. / **Allens Point**: on St. Lawrence River, t. Hammond, n. for either W. Allen or R. Allen. 1958 USGS Chippewa Quad. / **Allens Falls School**: no. 3, common school, t. Parishville.

Allison: surname used as a specific: **Allison Island**: see **Murphy Island**. 1941 USGS Murphy Island Quad. / **Allison Road**: r., t. Waddington, n. James or William Allison.

Allomogin School: no. 13, common school, t. Hammond. See **Alamogin**.

Alms House: built in 1826 to house the poor of the county. It was on an 80-acre site on the (Old) DeKalb Road, known as the Nathan Walker lot. The place was not satisfactory and was superseded by the **County Home**, which see; also known as the **Poor House**.

Alpine Road: r., t. Pitcairn, to Alpine Forge in Diana.

Aluminum City: see **Massena**.

Alumni Memorial Gymnasium: on Clarkson University Campus, n. alumni who helped fund it.

Alvern Avenue: s., v. Massena.

Alverson Road: r., t. Hermon, n. Alverson family, in particular for Almanson Alverson (1807-1879), early settler.

Amber: n.-color (yellowish brown): **Amber Lake**: t. Lisbon. / **Amber Lake**: t. Hopkinton, alt. 1,536 ft. 1853 HMC; 1858 Rogerson; 1860 Merrit; 1865 Beers; 1873 Hamilton Cahil; 1878 Durant & Pierce; 1896 New; 1902 Blankman; 1908 Adm; 1912 Stoddard; 1920 USGS Childwold Quad.

Ames: surname used as a specific: **Ames Road**: r., t. Canton, prob. after Joseph and/or William Ames, pioneer settlers. Lot 1, Range 6, Durant, p. 208, col. 2; r., t. Potsdam, n. Ames family; r., t. Edwards. / **Ames School**: t. Morristown, n. Jeremiah Ames. / **Ames Street**: s., v. Massena, prob. n. Fisher F. Ames.

American Island: adjacent to United States-Canadian Boundary, in St. Lawrence River, t. Morristown. 1963 USGS Morristown Quad.

Amherst Road: s., v. Massena, prob. n. Amherst, NH, but claimed also for a General Amherst, from War of 1812.

Amish Cemetery: t., Norfolk.

Amo Street: s., h. Star Lake, origin n. unknown.

Amolotte Drive: s., h. Hannawa Falls, origin n. unknown.

Anderson: surname used as a specific: **Anderson Creek**: t. DeKalb, trib. Oswegatchie River, n. Joseph Anderson, landowner, juror (1806), elector as of Dec. 2, 1807. Hough, 288. 1956 USGS Bigelow Quad. / **Anderson Road**: r., t. Pierrepont, n. Darius and George Anderson, brothers, early settlers; r., t. Potsdam, prob. n. William Anderson. / **Andersonville**: See **Fine**, n. Joseph Anderson, owner of an oar factory. See **Two Towns**, p. 5.

Andrew S. Schulter Building, on Clarkson University campus, n. trustee (1978-1983), a vice president of Sunshine Biscuits, Inc.

Andrews: surname used as a specific: **Andrews School**: no. 3, common school, t. Pierrepont, n. Erastus Andrews. Also, **Crarytown School, Brick School**. *Quarterly*, 7 (1962), no. 1, p. 16; and 11 (1966), no. 1, p. 6. / **Andrews Ridge**: t. Massena (Durant, 110, 407), n. John Charles Andrews and his parents, A. H. and Esther Andrews. *Quarterly*, 12 (1967), no. 3, p. 18. / **Andrews Street**: s., v. Massena, n. John B. Andrews, who came in 1810 from Claremont, NH.

Ann: Feminine first n., usually the spouse or daughter of the one who n. the place: **Ann Drive**: s., v., Massena. / **Ann Street**: s., v. Morristown; s., v. Norfolk.

Annas Lake: t. Colton, unidentified. 1896 New; 1902 Blankman.

Annette Street: s., v. Heuvelton.

Anshe Zophen Cemetery: t. Oswegatchie, n. means "People of the North," Jewish congregation. 1963 USGS Ogdensburg East Quad, noted incorrectly as **Zophen Cemetery.**

Anthony Street: s., c. Ogdensburg, probably n. Anthony C. Brown, lawyer, landowner, whose son, William C. Brown, became the first mayor of Ogdensburg. A claim, which has no merit, is made for "Mad" Anthony Wayne (1745-1796), famous American general in the Revolutionary War.

Anton House: on Clarkson University campus, n. for a Dr. Anton, who owned the house before it became property of the school.

Apple Island: peninsula, on Black Lake, t. Macomb, n. Apple family. 1961 USGS Hammond Quad.

Apple-Knocker: nickname of the Rochester line of the Northern Railroad. *Quarterly*, 7 (1962), no. 4, p. 7.

Appleton Arena: on St. Lawrence University campus, n. Charles W. Appleton, a trustee and corporate officer.

Arab Mountain: t. Piercefield, alt. 2,500 ft. 1860 Merrit; 1880 Ely; 1883 Ely-Wallace; 1896 New; 1902 Blankman; 1908 Adm; 1954 USGS Tupper Lake Quad.

Arbuckle: n. H. Arbuckle who lived near the pond in 1853 (Rogerson), but a claim is also made for William A. Arbuckle: **Arbuckle Lane**: t. Colton, n. pond. / **Arbuckle Pond**: t. Colton, n. **Clear Pond** before becoming **Arbuckle**. 1858 **Clear Pond** Rogerson; 1896 New; 1902 Blankman; 1908 **Clear Pond** Adm; 1908 USGS Potsdam Quad; 1964 USGS Colton Quad.

Areguna: see **Tupper Lake**.

Arena Drive: s., h. Louisville.

Armstrong Corners: crossroads, t. Stockholm. 1964 USGS Potsdam Quad.

Army: t. Macomb, on Black Lake, official p. o. est. May 14, 1898, Albert N. Barnes, pm, closed Nov. 30, 1900, Albert N. Barnes, pm. Known as Barnes Post of the Grand Army of the Republic, Gouverneur, *Quarterly*, 2 (1957), no. 4, npn.

Arnold: surname used as specific: **Arnold Road**: r., t. Oswegatchie, n. Arnold family. / **Arnold School**: no. 2, common school, t. Oswegatchie, n. Arnold family. / **Arnold Street**: s., c. Ogdensburg, n. Jacob Arnold, a brigadier general during the War of 1812, also a second cousin of Nathan Ford and husband to his niece, Anna Maria Spencer Ford.

Arquett Pond Pass: var. of **Arquette**, t. Hopkinton. 1919 USGS Nicholville Quad; 1964 USGS Lake Ozonia Quad.

Arquette Pond: t. Hopkinton, n. Chauncey T. Arquette. 1896 New; 1908 Adm; 1912 Stoddard; 1919 USGS Nicholville Quad.

Asbury Street: s. in Terrace Park, t. Morristown, n. Francis Asbury (1745-1816), first Methodist bishop in America.

Ash: n. the tree of the genus *Fraxinus americana*, a popular tree and the n. for many places and features: **Ash Pond**: t. Clifton, alt. 1,817. 1919 USGS Cranberry Lake Quad. / **Ash Ridge**: t. Fine. / **Ash Street**: s., v. Massena.

Ashbury Place: s., v. Massena, origin n. undetermined.

Ashley Street: s., v. Norwood, n. Ashley family.

Ashton Road: r., t. Parishville, n. John Ashton.

Atlantis Island: in Chippewa Bay, t. Hammond, n. for the lost continent. *Quarterly*, 16 (1971), no. 3, p. 11. 1958 USGS Chippewa Quad.

Atherton: t. Piercefield, a survey township, origin n. undetermined.

Atwood: surname used as a specific: **Atwood Hall**: houses the Department of Education on St. Lawrence University campus, n. Atwood family of Canton. / **Atwood Road**: r., t. Morristown, n. Anthony Atwood from VT.

Atwater Street: s., v. Norfolk, n. family.

Augsbury Physical Education Center: on the St. Lawrence University campus, n. by the benefactor, Frank A. Augsbury, Jr., trustee, in memory of his parents.

Aults Island: t. Louisville, formerly **Loux Island**. Also, **Ault Island**.

Austin: surname used as specific: **Austin Lounge**: in College Union on State University College, Potsdam, campus, n. David P. Austin, a graduate of the college and assistant in the college union. / **Austin Road**: r., t. Edwards, n. Albert Austin. / **Austin Ridge Road**: r., t. Potsdam, n. Phineas Austin, early settler from NH. / **Austin School**: no. 20, common school, t. Potsdam; **Austin Street**: s., v. Gouverneur, n. Isaac Austin, early settler ca 1805 who came with Dr. Richard Townsend to the area. Webster, 11. / **Austins Corners**: t. Pierrepont, n. Austin family. 1915 USGS Russell Quad.

Averell Street: s., v. Gouverneur, n. James G. Averell III, who with his brother William J. Averell, and Charles Anthony were proprietors of a "private banking-house" (est. Oct. 1, 1860). Durant, 342. Beers, 33, shows a residence near the present Averell Street marked "Averell & Anthony." The Averells of Ogdensburg also donated the triangular piece of land in the middle of the v. as a park. Durant, 342. See also Webster, 50. **Averills**: possessive of **Averill**: **Averills Brook**: trib. Racquette River, t. Piercefield. 1896 New. / **Averills Rapids**: in Racquette River, t. Piercefield. In 1860 Merrit notes **Averill's Camp**, n. H. Averill, a guide who lived at the foot of the bog. Merrit also lists misspelled form **Arrils**; 1880 Ely; 1883 Ely-Wallace; 1896 New.

Ayres Road: r., t. Pierrepont, n. Horace C. Ayres, of Crary Mills.

B

Babcock Street: s., v. Gouverneur. Also **East and West Babcock Street**. Poss. n. Pardon Babcock, one of the first settlers (1806) of the v. Durant, 335-6. He was an assessor and also the first blacksmith in the v. Webster, 16-17. "Dozens of Gouverneur's residents today can trace their ancestry directly to Isaac Austin, Willard Smith, Pardon Babcock, or Eleazer Nichols, the pioneer settlers," Webster, 15.

Babylon Road: r., t. Stockholm.

Bach Circle: s., h. Star Lake, n. William Bach from Michigan, one of the early officials at Jones & Laughlin Steel Corporation.

Back Hannawa Road: r., t. Colton and Potsdam, n. on west side of Racquette River, r. known as the back way to Hannawa Falls from Potsdam.

Backus: surname used as a specific: **Backus**: railroad crossing, t. Pitcairn, n. Backus family, English settlers. Backus was known as an English settlement. 1958 USGS Harrisville Quad. / **Backus Hill**: t. Russell, n. Cornelius S. Backus. 1915 USGS Russell Quad. / **Backus Road**: r., t. Pitcairn, n. Backus family.

Bacon's Crossing: on Carthage & Adirondack Railroad, t. Pitcairn, n. early settler.

Baerman Road: s., v. Richville; also called **Cole Road**.

Bagdad Road: s., v. Potsdam; r., t. Potsdam, one of the handful of completely undiscovered mystery roads; local spelling, **Bagdad**, not **Baghdad.**

Baily: surname used as a specific: **Island**: in Black Lake, t. Morristown, n. Charles Baily. 1961 USGS Pope Mills Quad. / **Baily Road**: r., t., Massena, n. Baily family.

Bailey's Mills: n. Bailey family, or for one of the following: Joseph, Benjamin, Ansel, or Moses Bailey. See **Slab City**.

Baken Family Cemetery: t. Rossie, on Oxbow Road.

Baker: surname used as a specific; possessive is **Bakers: Baker Road**: r., t. Lisbon; r., t. Potsdam. / **Bakers Corners**: t. Hermon. n. Baker family. / **Bakers Corners-Barnum School Road**: r., t. Hermon, n. Sayre or Stephen Baker and Ossian Barnum.

Balantine Road: r., t. Lisbon, n. Balantine family.

Bald Mountain: see **Baldface Mountain**.

Baldface: desc., usually of a hill or mountain: **Baldface Hill**: t. Pitcairn, alt. 1,030. 1961 USGS Harrisville Quad. / **Baldface Mountain**: t. Colton, alt. 1,875 ft. 1896 **Bald Mountain** New; 1902 **Bald Mountain** Blankman; 1921 USGS Stark Quad.

Baldwin: surname used as specific: **Baldwin Acres**: v. Norwood. / **Baldwin Avenue**: s., v. Massena. / **Baldwin Avenue**: s., v. Norwood, n. Baldwin family, prominent early settlers. / **Baldwin Branch**: trib. Little River, t. Russell. 1964 USGS Pierrepont Quad. / **Baldwin Road**: r., t. Hopkinton. Same as **Beebe Road.**

Ballybeen: t. Russell, one of the survey townships, n. for the home (in Ireland) of Daniel McCormick. Durant, 77. This township became **Russell**, although McCormick wished that it retain the n. of his native place. Durant, 426.

Balmat: h., t. Fowler, n. Jean de Balmat (also, John D. Balmat), who married daughter of Major Godden, an officer accompanying Lafayette in 1777; site of St. Joseph Lead Co., a mining community with many citizens of French descent. *Quarterly*, 10 (1965), no. 4, p. 8; also see *Quarterly*, 17 (1972), no. 4, p. 15; p. o. est. June 2, 1930, Mrs. Stella G. Hood, pm., existing, ZIP 13609. 1956 USGS Gouverneur Quad. / **Balmat-Fowler Road**: r., t. Fowler. / **Balmat School**: no. 2, common school, t. Fowler.

Balsam Brook: t. Hopkinton, trib. Stony Brook, n. balsam fir (*Abies balsamea*). 1896 **Harper Brook** New; 1902 Blankman; 1908 Adm; 1912 Stoddard; 1919 USGS Nicholville Quad; 1964 USGS Sylvan Falls Quad. Also **Balsam Creek.** / **Balsam Cemetery**: in Russell v. / **Balsam Pond**: t. Colton. 1921 USGS Stark Quad.

Bancroft Road: r., t. Edwards, n. Earl Bancroft (1861-1925), attorney. Freeman, 33.

Banford Elementary and Junior High School: v. Canton. See **Frances Sheard Banford Elementary and Junior High School.**

Bank Street: s., v. Norfolk.

Barber Point: t. Clifton. 1919 Cranberry Lake Quad.

Barbour Hill: t. Clare, n. early settler. 1915 Russell Quad.

Barclay Street: s., v. Potsdam, n. Barclay family.

Barkley Pond: See **Sterling Pond.**

Barnage Road: r., t. Lawrence, northwest corner.

Barns: See **Barnes Road.**

Barnes: surname used as specific: **Barnes Corners**: t. Canton, n. Truman Barnes, early settler. Also, **Barns Corners.** / **Barnes Post**: Grand Army of the Republic at Gouverneur, club house at Mineral Point on Black Lake; n. for Edwin H. Barnes. *Quarterly*, 7 (1962), no. 4, p. 14. See **Army.** / **Barnes Road**: r., t. Canton. n. prob. Truman Barnes and also school district #9, later **Martyn.** Lot 4, Range 9, settled 1810. 1865 Beers, as Barnes. Durant, p. 208, with lot desc. p. 205. Also **Barns.** / **Barnes Road**: r., t. Potsdam, prob. n. Daniel Barnes from MA. / **Barnes Street**: s., v. Gouverneur, poss. n. (Capt.) Rockwell Barnes (1788-1869), who settled in 1808. He is described as "a man of enterprise, who did much to advance the prosperity of the town." Durant, 336. Webster, 24, writes, "He owned the village's largest sawmill, was justice of the peace, and a pioneer founder of the Presbyterian Church in the village. In his day Rockwell Barnes was a carpenter of exceptional ability, and it was he who erected many of the houses and buildings of early Gouverneur."

Barney: surname used as a specific: **Barney Pond**: t. Parishville. 1858 **Trout Pond** Rogerson; 1873 **Trout Pond** Hamilton Child; 1896 **Bolton Pond** New; 1898 **Bolton Pond** EGB map; 1902 **Bolton Pond** Blankman; 1908 **Bolton Pond** Adm; 1912 **Bolton Pond** Stoddard; 1921 USGS Stark Quad. / **Barney Street**: s., v. Gouverneur. Also **East Barney** and **West Barney**. Poss. n. Milton Barney, town Supervisor of Gouverneur, 1853, 1857-1859 and owned a chair factory, purchased from Rockwell Barnes. A claim is also made for either Albert M. Barney (Civil War officer) or James Barney, marble dresser. Durant, 337, 343.

Barnhart Island: in St. Lawrence River, t. Massena; n. for William George Barnhart, Sr., who leased the island in 1795 from the St. Regis Indians for 999 years at a yearly rental of $30.00 a year. In 1805 the lease was renegotiated and Barnhart agreed to pay $60.00 a year for a perpetual lease. During the Revolutionary War, Barnhart was loyal to the English. In 1804, William George Barnhart, Jr., became the first settler on the island. He was ejected by the Ogdens in 1849. When the Seaway expansion occurred, the bodies of the Barnhart dead were removed to Old Pine Grove Cemetery. See Durant, 411, for a history of the family. See, Dumas, 19, for the many spellings of the n.: **Bernhart**, **Barnardt**, **Bernard**, and others. Dumas, 19, gives a slightly different version of the lease arrangement with the Indians. Also, **Barnhart's Island**. French n.: **Isle les Têtes**, on 1779 map. Amerindian n.: **Niionenhiasekowane**, "big stone." 1942 USGS Barnhart Quad; 1964 USGS Racquette River Quad. Now, **Robert Moses State Park**. / **Barnhart Island School**: no. 9, common school, on the island, t. Massena. / **Barnhart Road**: s., v. Massena, n. Barnhart family of Barnhart Island.

Barnharts: on Barnhart Island, p. o. est. May 4, 1900, Frank A. Barnhart, pm, closed Apr. 29, 1905, Frank A. Barnhart, pm, reopened Mar. 13, 1906, Harvey P. Barnhart, pm, closed Nov. 15, 1912.

Barnum School: no. 9, common school, later **Beaver Meadow School**, t. Hermon, prob. n. Ossian Barnum family. 1915 USGS Gouverneur Quad.

Barraford School: t. Edwards, Dist. 2, n. Barraford family. Freeman, 16. 1915 USGS Russell Quad. Same as **Creek School**.

Barre Street: s., c. Ogdensburg, poss. n. Isaac Barre (1726-1802), British soldier and politician who defended the rights of American colonists.

Barrett Road: r., t. Stockholm and Hopkinton, n. Barrett family.

Barrington: Thomas Barrington, a former president of SUC, Potsdam campus: **Thomas Barrington Student Union**: on SUC, Potsdam, campus, known locally as **Student Union.** / **Barrington Drive**: s., SUC, Potsdam campus.

Barry T. Leithead Field House: on St. Lawrence University campus, n. Barry T. Leithead, trustee.

Barter Hill: t. De Peyster, n. Barter family. 1963 Heuvelton Quad.

Bartlett Drive: s., v. Gouverneur, n. Bartlett family.

Barton Brook: t. Parishville, trib. West Branch St. Regis River. ca 1840 Brodhead; 1908 USGS Potsdam Quad; 1964 USGS Rainbow Falls Quad; 1964 USGS Parishville Quad.

Basley Road: r., t. Lisbon; connects Sand and Murphy Roads.

Bassett's Woods: t. Canton, n. Bassett family. Also **Woodmere**. *Quarterly*, 13 (1968), no. 3, p. 8.

Bassout: surname used as a specific: **Bassout Creek**: t. Clifton. / **Bassout Pond**: Cranberry area, t. Clifton. *Quarterly*, 17 (1972), no. 2, p. 12.

Basswood Ridge Road: r., t. Lisbon, n. the tree, a variety of linden, a wood that has strong fibers.

Battle: n. occurs either because of an incident or as a surname: **Battle Hill**: t. Fowler, Gouverneur, Hermon, alt. 610 ft., n. difficult to go over it, "uphill battle to conquer." Also, a claim is made for two women fighting over who had the best farm. *Quarterly*, 11 (1966), no. 3, p. 9. 1956 USGS Gouverneur Quad. / **Battle Hill**: t. Hammond, poss. n. James Battle/Battell, but more apt because of the difficulty, "a battle," to get to the top. Now known as **Marvin Hill.** / **Battle Hill Road**: r., t. Fowler, Gouverneur. Hermon. / **Battle Hill School**: no. 10, common school, t. Hermon.

Baxter: surname used as a specific: **Baxter Cemetery**: t. Norfolk. / **Baxter's Island**: See **Croil's Island**.

Bay: a body of water indenting a shore line: **Bay Island**: in Rollway Bay, Black Lake, t. Morristown. 1961 USGS Pope Mills Quad. / **Bay Pond**: extension of Massawepie Lake, t. Piercefield. 1880 Ely; 1883 Ely-Wallace; 1896 New. / **Bay Road**: r., t. Fowler; r., t. Colton, in Higley Flow area; r., h. Hailesboro. / **Bay Street**: s., v. Morristown, to bay in St. Lawrence River., then along the river; s., v. Potsdam, n. bay of water formed by the Racquette River, formerly, **Water Street**, which extended from the present Water Street to Pierrepont Avenue.

Baycroft Island: in St. Lawrence River, t. Lisbon. 1906 USGS Red Mills Quad.

Bayley Road: s., v. Massena, n. Ariel K. Bayley.

Bayleys Inn: t. Massena, n. Elijah Bayley.

Bayside Cemetery: v. Potsdam. 1943 USGS Potsdam Quad.

Beach Street: s., v. Massena, n. Beach family.

Beal Street: s., v. Potsdam, n. Beal family.

Beaman: surname used as a specific, here a family n.: **Beaman Road**: r., t. Gouverneur. / **Beaman School**: no. 5, common school, t. Brasher.

Bear: Many places are n. for the bear, still rather plentiful in St. Lawrence County: **Bear Brook**: t. Hopkinton, trib. Jordan River. 1896 New; 1920 USGS Childwold Quad. / **Bear Brook**: t. Hopkinton, trib. Racquette River. 1898 Blankman. Also **Bear Creek.** / **Bear Brook**: t. Piercefield, trib. Racquette River. 1896 New; 1902 Blankman. / **Bear Brook**: t. Piercefield, trib. Bog River. 1860 **Jenkins Brook** Merrit shows that a Jenkins lived in the bog between Warren Point and Paradise Point; 1873 **Jenkins Brook** Hamilton Child; 1896 **Jenkins Brook** New; 1902 Blankman; 1908 Adm; 1912 Stoddard; 1954 USGS Tupper lake Quad. Jenkins was the only settler at Tupper Lake, 1860, Street (published 1860), pp. 234-235. / **Bear Creek**: t. Clare and Colton, trib. Middle Branch Grass(e) River. 1921 USGS Stark Quad. / **Bear Creek**: see **Bear Brook**, t. Hopkinton. / **Bear Lake**: t. Fine, alt. 1,298 ft. On Carthage and Adirondack Railroad. *Quarterly*, 11 (1966), no. 1, p. 16. / **Bear Lake Road**: r., t. Fine. / **Bear Mountain**: t. Clifton, alt. 2,250 ft. 1896 New; 1883 Ely-Wallace; 1908 Adm; 1880 Ely; 1902 Blankman; 1912 Stoddard; 1919 Cranberry Lake Quad. / **Bear Mountain**: t. Colton, alt. 2,525 ft. 1902 **Little Bear Mountain** Blankman (identification not certain, most likely **Little Mountain**); 1954 USGS Tupper Lake Quad. / **Bear Mountain**: t. Hopkinton, alt.

1,700 ft. 1919 USGS Nicholville Quad; 1964 USGS Sylvan Falls Quad. / **Bear Mountain Pond**: bay in Cranberry Lake, t. Clifton. 1896 New. / **Bear Pond**: see **Beaver Pond**, t. Colton.

Beaver: The beaver inhabits all the streams of St. Lawrence County and is a popular n. for water features: **Beaver Creek**: t. Macomb and Oswegatchie, trib. Oswegatchie River. 1898 Blankman. 1963 USGS Rensselaer Falls Quad. / **Beaver Creek State Forest**, # 29, t. DePeyster; 32, 37, t. Gouverneur. / **Beaver Dam Brook**: see **Spangler Brook**, t. Piercefield. / **Beaver Lake**: pond, t. Edwards. alt. 784 ft. 1951 USGS Harrisville Quad; 1956 USGS **Bonner Lake** Edwards Quad. / **Beaver Meadow**: t. Russell. 1915 USGS Russell Quad. / **Beaver Meadow**: t. Hermon. / **Beaver Meadow Pond**: t. Colton. 1902 Blankman. / **Beaver Meadow School**: no. 9, common school, t. Hermon, n. Beaver Meadow. / **Beaver Pond**: t. Colton. 1858 **Bear Pond** Roberson; 1865 **Bear Pond** Beers, p. 86; 1873 **Bear Pond** Hamilton Child; 1878 **Bear Pond** Durant & Pierce; 1883 **Bear Pond** Ely-Wallace; 1896 New; 1902 Blankman; 1908 Adm; 1912 Stoddard; 1921 USGS Stark Quad.

Beckwith Street: s., v. Gouverneur, n. Rev. Baruch B. Beckwith, pastor of the Presbyterian Church, 1843-66. He was also the president of the Riverside Cemetery Association when it was founded in 1857. Durant, 345-6. Beckwith Street appears to have been called **Sterling Street** at one time. Beckwith lived near the corner of East Main Street and Sterling, now Beckwith. Beers, p. 33.

Beebe: surname used as a specific, here a family n.: **Beebe Pond**: t. Fine. 1908 Adm; 1912 Stoddard. / **Beebe Road**: r., t. Fine. Also **Baldwin Road**.

Beech: n. tree of the genus *Fagus*: **Beech Grove Cemetery**: t. Russell, n. trees at Putnam's Corner, juncture of **Woods Bridge Road** and **Pyrites-Russell Road**. / **Beech Grove School**: no. 2, common school, t. Russell. Also, **Gibbs School**. / **Beech Plains**: t. Pierrepont. / **Beech Plains Cemetery**: t. Pierrepont. / **Beech Plains Road**: r., t. Canton and Pierrepont. Also **Plains Road**. / **Beech Street**: s., v. Waddington.

Beechertown: n. John Beecher: / **Beechertown**: crossroads, t. Stockholm, n. John Beecher; p. o. est. Oct. 3, 1901, Ellsworth B. Adams, pm, closed Aug. 13, 1904. 1964 USGS Parishville Quad. / **Beechertown School**: no. 18, common school, t. Stockholm, n. the crossroads.

Beeliner: n. train, last passenger train into Massena, 1946.

Belker Road: r., t. Lisbon, connects Tracy and Moran roads.

Bell: schools seem to have the n. naturally, but they usually derive from a personal n.; sometimes the n. represents beauty: **Bell Brook**: t. Brasher, stream, tributary St. Regis River. 1964 Brasher Falls Quad. / **Bell School**: no. 13, common school, t. DeKalb, n. Bell family. 1915 USGS Gouverneur Quad. / **Bell School**: no. 5, common school, t. DePeyster, n. Bela Bell. / **Bell School**: t. Lisbon, n. Bell family. 1906 USGS Ogdensburg Quad. Not listed in 1896 list of common schools. / **Bell Isle**: in Trout Lake, t. Hermon, n. Bell family. *Quarterly*, 16 (1971), no. 1, p. 10.

Belle: usually translated from French as "beautiful," although its French meaning is "a woman celebrated for her beauty and charm." The meaning has been somewhat modified as noted in the features entered here: **Belle Island**: in Black Lake, t. Morristown, "beautiful." 1961 USGS Pope Mills Quad. / **Belleville**: "beautiful place," t. Russell. / **Belleville Cemetery**: t. Russell. / **Belleville Road**: r., t. Russell. / **Belleville School**: no. 15, common school, t. Russell, *Quarterly*, 19 (1974), no. 2, p. 20. 1915 USGS Russell Quad.

Bellevue Street: "beautiful view," s., v. Gouverneur

Belmont Street: s., v. Massena, probably personal n.

Benedict Island: in St. Lawrence River, t. Lisbon, prob. n. Thomas B. Benedict, early military leader and general in War of 1812. 1963 USGS Red Mills Quad.

Benham Brook: t. Hopkinton, trib. St. Regis River, n. Napoleon B. Benham. 1964 USGS Nicholville Quad.

Bennett: surname used as a specific: **Bennett Brook**: t. Fowler, trib. West Branch Oswegatchie River, n. Bennett family. 1956 USGS Edwards Quad. / **Bennett School**: no. 7, common school, t. Edwards, n. Bennett family.

Benson Mines: h. t. Fine, on Carthage and Adirondack Railroad. *Quarterly*, 11 (1966), no. 1, p. 16; p. o. est. July 18, 1890, Harry E. Esler, first pm, closed Aug. 15, 1942. The area became known as the Benson Ore Body, with mining begun in 1889 by the Magnetic Iron Company which became the Benson Mines Company in 1908.

Jones & Laughlin Steel Corporation acquired the holdings in 1946. Of feature interest is that Bob Fitzsimmons, boxer, fought his last fight here, with Jim Paul, whom he knocked out. Lee N. Fuller, *Quarterly*, 14 (1969), no. 1, p. 5. 1886 New; 1916 USGS Oswegatchie Quad; 1919 USGS Cranberry Quad. Mines are now abandoned. See **Chaumont Ore Body**; also, Reynolds, 107, 116. Some derived n. include: **Benson Mines-Newton Falls Road**: r., t. Clifton and Fine, Route 50. / **Benson Mines School**: no. 3, common school, t. Clifton.

Benson Road: r. t. Parishville, n. Seth Benson.

Benton Road: r., t. Stockholm, n. Wareham Benton.

Berg Road: r., t. Edwards, off Route 58 in Pleasant Valley, western part of t., n. Berg family.

Berkley: usually a surname used as a specific: **Berkley Mountain**: t. Colton, alt. 2,350. 1896 **Long Mtn.** New; 1902 **Long Mtn.** Blankman; 1908 **Long Mt.** Adm; 1954 USGS Tupper Lake Quad. / **Berkley Pond**: t. Parishville. See **Ormsbee Pond.** / **Berkley Drive**: s., v. Potsdam.

Bernard Avenue: s., v. Norwood.

Berry Brook: t. Clare, trib. Orebed Creek, prob. n. berries. 1915 Russell Quad.

Bertrand H. Snell Lock: see **Snell Lock.**

Best School: no. 16, common school, t. Oswegatchie, n. Best family, particularly James and John W. Best.

Bewkes Science Hall: on St. Lawrence University campus, n. Dr. Eugene Garrett Bewkes, President of the University from 1945 to 1963.

Bicknell: surname used as a specific: **Bicknell**: mill area, n. Amos Bicknell, who built mills on the west branch of the St. Regis River. Also, **Bicknellville** (nickname, **Bickneyville**). See **West Stockholm.** / **Bicknell School**, no. 7, common school, t. Parishville, n. Ralph Bicknell from Canaan, NH, 1826. / **Bicknell Street**: s., v. Norwood, n. Bicknell family.

Big: A popular American size-n. that describes a geographical feature larger than is expected. Sometimes it is contrasted with **Little**: **Big Bay**: in Black Lake, t. Morristown, Hammond. 1961 USGS Hammond Quad. / **Big Brook**: t. Colton, trib. Pleasant Lake Stream. 1921 USGS Stark Quad. / **Big Cold Brook**: see **Cold Brook**, t. Colton. / **Big Creek**: t. Fine.

/ **Big Creek**: t. Pitcairn, trib. West Branch Oswegatchie. 1865 Beers, p. 72; 1951 USGS Harrisville Quad. / **Big Curve**: on Canton-Ogdensburg Road, opposite former County Home. *Quarterly*, 16 (1971), no. 4, p. 6. / **Big Hornet Pond**: See **Hornet Ponds**. / **Big Hollow Brook**: t. Hopkinton, trib. St. Regis River. 1864 USGS Nicholville Quad. / **Big Inlet**: see **Cranberry lake Inlet**. / **Big Island**: in St. Lawrence River, t. Hammond, n. because it is larger than islands nearby. 1958 USGS Chippewa Quad. / **Big Island**: in Black Lake, t. Morristown. 1961 USGS Pope Mills Quad. / **Big Lake**: t. Fine; now **Star Lake**. *Quarterly*, 5 (1960), no. 1, npn. See **Robbin Lake**. / **Big Marsh**: t. Clare. 1915 Russell Quad. / **Big Pine Pond**: t. Colton. See **Pine Pond**. / **Big Pool**: at Brown's Falls, t. Fine. / **Big Sink**: on Carthage and Adirondack Railroad, halfway between Harrisville and Kalurah, the place where a work train sank into the mud at a swampy crossing. *Quarterly*, 11 (1966), no. 1, p. 16. / **Big Sucker Brook**: t. Macomb, trib. St. Lawrence River, n. suckers (fish of the family *Catostomidae*) which ran in spring. 1898 Blankman. / **Big Sucker Brook**: t. Lisbon, n. fish. Also **Big Sucker Creek**. / **Big Swamp**: t. Clare. 1915 Russell Quad. / **Big Trout Pond**: see **Trout Pond**, t. Piercefield. / **Big Tupper Lake**: see **Tupper Lake**. / **Big Woods**: The Adirondacks. Also, name for the forest near the upper St. Regis River (*Sketches of Parishville*, p. [6]).

Bigelow: surname used as a specific: **Bigelow**: h., t. DeKalb, p. o. est. May 3, 1880, Levi A. Totman, pm, closed Nov. 30, 1953; n. William H. Bigelow (1826-1899), a descendant of one of the early families. "Mr. Felt, another old settler, gave the name Bigelow, after some of his relatives who ran a pump house near the depot to supply the trains with water." Quoted from *Quarterly*, 11 (1966), no. 3, p. 18. Includes by custom **Bishops Corners**, **Bishop's Corners**. Also **Richville Station/Depot**, the main settlement. 1956 USGS Bigelow Quad. / **Bigelow School**: no. 9, common school, t. DeKalb, at Bishops Corners, n. William H. Bigelow. / **Bigelow School**: t. Macomb, n. Bigelow family. 1949 USGS Hammond Quad. / **Bigelow Street**: s., c. Ogdensburg, n. Bigelow family.

Bilberry Island: in St. Lawrence River, t. Hammond, n plant of the genus *Vaccinium*. 1858 USGS Chippewa Quad.

Billings: surname used as a specific: **Billings Cross Road**: r., t. Gouverneur, intersects with Maple Ridge

Road in the west and the Rock Island Road in the east. Beers, p. 31, shows an A. B. Billings living near the Rock Island Road intersection. / **Billings School**: no. 10, common school, t. Gouverneur. Beers, p. 31, shows School No. 15 near the residence, south, of A. B. Billings. 1915 USGS Gouverneur Quad; 1956 USGS Richville Quad.

Bilow Road: r., t. Gouverneur. Beers, p. 31, shows M. Bylow (Marquis de Lafayette Bilow, 1849-1918) living on this road.

Bingo Road: r., t. Edwards, south off Route 58, west-central part of t. The story is that many people attempted to farm there and all failed in a short time, and Bingo! they were gone.

Birch: n. tree of the *Betula* genus, *Betulaceae* (birch) family, indigenous to St. Lawrence County and northeastern United States. The n. is used often for places and geographical features: **Birch Brook**: t. Russell, trib. Stammer Creek. 1915 USGS Russell Quad. / **Birch Creek**: t. Macomb, trib. Fish Creek. *Quarterly*, 6 (1961), npn. 1898 Blankman; 1961 USGS Pope Mills Quad. / **Birch Island**: in Cranberry Lake, t. Clifton. 1896 New; 1902 Blankman; 1919 Cranberry Lake Quad. / **Birch Point**: on St. Lawrence River, t. Morristown. 1963 USGS Morristown Quad. / **Birch Road**: r., t. Pierrepont. / **Birch Street**: s., v. Rensselaer Falls, developed only a short way, never laid out. [Hartman] / **Birchwood Drive**: s., v. Gouverneur.

Bird Street: s., v. Canton, n. Bird, owner of a carding machine, ca 1827, later owned by Hodskin. Durant, p. 216. Poss. n. Thomas B. Bird (1787-1833).

Bishop: surname used as a specific: **Bishop Avenue**: s., v. Massena. / **Bishop Hall**: on SUC, Potsdam, campus, n. Franklin H. Bishop, a professor of music. / **Bishop Road**: r., t. Macomb; r., t. Oswegatchie. / **Bishop School**: no. 3, common school, t. Potsdam. / **Bishop's Corners**: now **Bigelow**. *Quarterly*, 11 (1966), no. 3, p. 19. / **Bishop's Old Log Hotel**: See **Cranberry Lake Inn**. *Quarterly*, 3 (1958), no. 4, p. [6].

Bixby Cemetery: v. Norfolk, n. Parry C. Bixby.

Black: n. applied to any feature that has real or imagined darkness, prob. the commonest of all color desc.; sometimes a translation from an Amerindian n.; and occasionally a personal n.: **Black Bay**: in Black

Lake, t. Hammond. 1961 USGS Hammond Quad. / **Black Bay**: in Tupper Lake, t. Piercefield. 1860 Merrit; 1896 New; 1902 Blankman; 1908 Adm; 1954 USGS Tupper Lake Quad. / **Black Brook**: t. Clifton, trib. Oswegatchie River. 1896 New; 1902 Blankman. / **Black Brook**: t. Russell, trib. Grass(e) River. 1915 USGS Russell Quad. / **Black Creek**: t. Fine. / **Black Creek**: rises in Jefferson Co., flows through t. Hammond and Rossie, trib. Black Lake. 1865 Beers, p. 27; 1898 Blankman; 1958 USGS Redwood Quad; 1961 USGS Hammond Quad. / **Black Creek**: t. Pitcairn, trib. West Branch Oswegatchie River 1951 USGS Harrisville Quad. / **Black Creek**: t. Hermon, becomes Tanner (see 1896 map). / **Black Dock Hole**: bay in Cranberry Lake, t. Clifton. 1896 New. / **Black Lake**: Stretches across t. Hammond, Macomb, DePeyster, and Oswegatchie. (1) Mohawk, **chegwaga**, "in the hip"; (2) Bogardus, 121, writes "**O-tsi-kwa-ke** is the Indian name. It means 'where the ash tree grows with large knots for making clubs.'" The water is dark because of the drainage of peaty swamps. The first settlement on Black Lake was begun in 1796 by John Davies. He was the first sheriff and a county judge. William Davies, a lineal descendant of the family, still owns the property. See *Quarterly*, 17 (1972), no. 1, p. 10, for proposal to change the n. to **Roosevelt Lake**, after Theodore Roosevelt. 1963 USGS Edwardsville Quad. / **Black Lake**: t. Oswegatchie, p. o. est. Dec. 18, 1850, William H. Davies, pm, closed June 3, 1858, reopened June 23, 1892, Hobart A. Morse, pm, changed to **Blacklake**, Dec. 1895, Hobart A. Morse, pm, closed Aug. 15, 1899. / **Black Lake Cemetery**: on Route 63, west of Edwardsville, t. Morristown. Also **Lutheran Church Cemetery**. 1961 USGS Hammond Quad. Bogardus, 233. / **Black Lake Road**: r., t. Macomb, Morristown, Oswegatchie, Hammond, from Hammond, through Edwardsville and to Ogdensburg along scenic Black Lake. Now known as **Lake Road**. Also, once known as **Klock Road**. / **Black Lake Toll Bridge**: at Edwardsville. *Quarterly*, 1 (1956), no. 4, npn, / **Black Lake-Brier Hill Road**: r., t. Morristown. / **Black Point**: on Tupper Lake, t. Piercefield. 1954 USGS Tupper Lake Quad. / **Black Pond**: t. Piercefield. 1860 Merrit; 1883 Ely-Wallace; 1896 New; 1902 Blankman; 1908 Adm; 1912 Stoddard; 1954 USGS Tupper Lake Quad. / **Black River**: now **Grass(e) River**. *Quarterly*, 6 (1961), no. 4, p. 13. / **Black Rock Island**: in St. Lawrence River, t.

Hammond. 1958 USGS Chippewa Quad.

Blacklake: See **Black Lake**.

Blackmer Road: r., t. Russell, n. Blackmer family.

Blackstone Bay: in St. Lawrence River, t. Morristown, n. Calvin Blackstone. 1963 USGS Morristown Quad.

Blair School: no. 8, common school, t. Hopkinton, n. Blair family.

Blake: surname used as a specific, here n. family or person: **Blake**: h., t. Parishville, p. o. est. Feb. 3, 1902, Charles G. Blake, first pm, closed June 30, 1917. / **Blake Cemetery**: t. Parishville. / **Blake Falls**: See **Blake Falls Reservoir**. / **Blake Falls Dam Road**: r., t. Parishville. / **Blake Falls Reservoir**: in Racquette River, t. Parishville. 1964 USGS Sylvan Falls Quad. / **Blake School**: see **Blake's Mills School**. / **Blake Settlement**: t. Parishville. / **Blake's Mills School**: no. 4, common school, t. Hopkinton, n. Azro L. Blake. / **Blake's Point**: on St. Lawrence River at Oak Point, n. Wainwright Blake, owner.

Blanchard: surname used as a specific: **Blanchard Avenue**: s., v. Norwood. / **Blanchard Hill**: t. Russell, n. Alex Blanchard. 1915 USGS Russell Quad. / **Blanchard Hill Road**: r., t. Russell; also **Palmerville Road**; r., t. Potsdam; r., t. Norfolk, n. William Blanchard with Charles, John, and Samuel from MA. / **Blanchard School**: no. 19, common school, t. Russell, n. Alex Blanchard family.

Blandin Road: r., t. Hermon, n. Blandin families who lived along the road.

Blind: n. state of being hidden: **Blind Bay**: in St. Lawrence River, t. Hammond. "This tiny bay has one inlet which is small and very difficult to see from the river." It is also hidden by an island. 1958 USGS Chippewa Quad. / **Blind Crossing Road**: r., t. Stockholm, n. railroad crossing. / **Blind Pond**: t. Hopkinton, alt. 1,079 ft. 1919 USGS Nicholville Quad; 1964 USGS Nicholville Quad. / **Blind Pond Outlet**: t. Hopkinton. 1919 USGS Nicholville Quad.

Blink Bonny: t., DeKalb, p. o. est. Dec. 2, 1850, closed Feb. 7, 1852, William Cleghorn, Jr., pm; Scottish n., origin unknown.

Bloodough Road: r., t. Oswegatchie, n. Peter Bloodough from Herkimer Co., with sons Peter and John Bloodough, b. Jefferson Co.

Bloomfield: a survey township, t. of **Fine** now.

Bloomfield School: t. Fine.

Blue: a color-n. often applied to mountains which have a haze that appears to be blue: **Blue Mansion Avenue**: v. Heuvelton, n. home of J. A. Van den Heuvel, built 1824, painted blue. Now **John Street**. / **Blue Mountain**: t. Fine, alt. 1,388 ft. 1916 USGS Oswegatchie Quad. / **Blue Mountain**: a railroad tract of land on which the Hollywood Club was located. See **Little Blue Mountain**. / **Blue Mountain**: see **Mount Matumbla**, t. Piercefield, n. color. / **Blue Mountain Stream**: t. Colton, trib. Middle Branch Grass(e) River. 1902 **Mud Creek** Blankman; 1921 USGS Stark Quad. / **Blue Pond**: t. Colton. 1896 New; 1902 Blankman; 1908 Adm; 1912 Stoddard; 1921 USGS Stark Quad.

Bluff Island: see **Dark Island**. 1958 USGS Chippewa Quad., t. Hammond, n. feature. A fifty-foot hill occupies half of the island.

Boat House: built in 1972, used for canoe storage on Clarkson University campus.

Bob Power Road: t. Lisbon, now **Fisher Road**.

Bog: a generic n. for a wet, spongy place, the n. occurs fairly often in St. Lawrence County: **Bog, The**: *Quarterly*, 13 (1968), no. 4, p. 19; p. o., est. as **Bog** Apr. 30, 1884, Caroline A. Munger, pm, changed to **Stark** May 12, 1884. / Also listed as **The Bog** / **Bog Falls**: in Racquette River, t. Colton. 1860 Merrit (1/2 m. from **Little Bog**); 1883 **Bag Falls** (misprint) Ely-Wallace. May be the same as **Carry Falls**. / **Bog Falls**: [Bog River], t. Piercefield. 1860 **Bog River Falls** Street, p. 234; 1860 **Falls** Merrit; 1902 Blankman. / **Bog Lake**: also **Robin Lake**. *Quarterly*, 14 (1969), no. 1, p. 22. / **Bog Mountain**: near Carry Falls, t. Colton, alt. 1,600 ft, n. nearby bog. 1896 New; 1902 Blankman; unrecorded on USGS maps. / **Bog Outlet, The**: see **The Bog Outlet**. / **Bog River**: flows into Tupper Lake. *Quarterly*, 18 (1973), no. 3, p. 23. / **Bog River Falls**: *Quarterly*, 19 (1974), no. 1, p. 13, n. river. See **Bog Falls**. / **Bog River Flow**: lake, t. Colton, Clifton, n. river. 1919 USGS Cranberry Lake Quad.

Bogardus Island: in St. Lawrence River, t. Morristown, n. Bogardus family. 1963 USGS Morristown Quad.

Boggs Cemetery: t. Lisbon. Noted on 1963 USGS Ogdensburg Quad, but not otherwise identified.

Boice: former settlement, t. Lisbon, Waddington, p. o. est. Mar. 10, 1891, closed Nov. 15, 1902, Clara N. Boice, pm, svc. Lisbon Center, n. pm. Also, **Boyce**.

Boiling Spring: t. Fine, n. descriptive. 1919 USGS Cranberry Lake Quad.

Boland: see **Borland**.

Bolton: surname used as a specific: **Bolton Pond**: t. Parishville. / **Bolton School**: no. 6, common school, t. Gouverneur, n. Bolton family. / **Bolton School**: no. 16, common school, t. Macomb.

Bombay-Helena Road: r., t. Brasher. **Bombay**, Franklin County, n. Bombay, India, by Mrs. Michael Hogan, who once lived there. Hough, 482. See **Helena**.

Bondy Pond: t. Fine, behind Twin Lakes, about two miles from Star Lake, n. Colonel Bondy from Syracuse who also owned **Twin Lakes**, which now belong to the Scott Paper Company. Also **Bundy Pond**.

Boni Road: r., t. Fine, n. Boni family.

Bonner Lake: t. Edwards, n. Joseph M. Bonner, early settler. Freeman, 4. Formerly, **Beaver Lake**. 1956 USGS Edwards Quad.

Bonno Road: r., t. Pierrepont, n. Bonno family.

Boot Tree Pond: see **Boottree Pond**.

Booths Island: in Black Lake at Edwardsville, n. Emmett R.(or H.) Booth, ferryman. *Quarterly*, 1 (1956), no. 4, npn. Also **Booth's Island**, not listed in *Quarterly*. Official spelling in 1963 **Booths Island** USGS Edwardsville Quad. Also, **Booth's Island**.

Boottree Pond: t. Piercefield. 1880 Ely; 1883 Ely-Wallace; 1896 **Boot Tree Pond** New; 1908 **Boot Tree Pond** Adm; 1912 Stoddard; 1954 USGS Tupper Lake Quad.

Borland: surname used as a specific: **Boland Cave Creek**: trib. Oswegatchie River, t. DeKalb, n. Charles Borland; note spelling error. Also **Boland Creek**. The Beers map (1865) shows **Portland Creek**, misprint for **Borland**. 1956 USGS Richville Quad. / **Boland Road**: r., t. Hermon, n. William G. Borland family; error for **Borland**.

Bostwick Creek: t. Rossie, trib. Black Lake, n. William B. Bostwick, supervisor in 1858. 1961 USGS Hammond Quad.

Bouck Road: r., t. Lisbon, n. John Bouck family.

Boundary Street: s., v. Heuvelton.

Boutwell Cemetery: t. Russell, n. Enos E. and Martin M. Boutwell. Also, **South Russell Cemetery**.

Bow: bend in Oswegatchie River, t. Gouverneur. Also, **Little Bow**.

Bowers Street: s., v. Massena, n. Bowers family.

Bowker School: no. 5, common school, Potsdam, n. Thomas and John Bowker.

Bowling Court: s., v. Waddington.

Bowman: surname used as specific: **Bowman Island**: in Black Lake, t. Morristown, n. Bowman family. 1961 USGS Hammond Quad. / **Bowman Hall**: residence and dining hall on SUC, Potsdam campus, n. Horace Bushnell Bowman, teacher of music.

Boyd: surname used as a specific: **Boyd Pond**: t. Russell, n. William E. Boyd, early justice of the peace. Copper was once mined here. 1915 USGS Russell Quad. / **Boyd Pond Road**: r., t. Russell, n. William E. Boyd. / **Boyd Road**: r., t. Canton, Boyd family. Also **Meade Road**.

Boyden Brook: t. Canton, trib. Grannis Brook, n. W. D. Boyden, landowner. Also, see *Quarterly*, 16 (1971), no. 1, p. 1. 1964 USGS Pierrepont Quad.

Boynton: settlement, t. Massena, p. o. est. July 7, 1896, rescinded July 30, 1896, George A. Deans, pm. / **Boynton Street**: s., v. Massena, Luke Boynton.

Bradford: surname used as specific: **Bradford Island**: in St. Lawrence River, t. Louisville, n. Bradford family, especially Joseph and his son Samuel, settlers in 1802. 1964 USGS Louisville Quad. / **Bradford Point**: on Bradford Island, St. Lawrence River, t. Louisville. 1964 USGS Louisville Quad. See **Bradford Island**. / **Bradford School**: no. 15, common school, t. Louisville.

Bradish Road: r., t. Pitcairn, n. Bradish family. Also, **Durham Road**.

Bradley Drive: s., v. Potsdam, n. Bradley farm.

Brady Road: r., t. Madrid, n. Brady

family. Also **Braddy Road** (error).

Brainerd Hall: on SUC, Potsdam campus, n. for Asa Brainerd, preceptor (principal) of St. Lawrence Academy, 1828-1847. *Quarterly*, 11 (1966), no. 3, p. 11.

Branch Brook: t. Russell, trib. Little River. Now **Baldwin Brook**. 1915 USGS Russell Quad.

Branch School: t. Clifton, n. school at branching of Plum (or Plumb) Brook.

Brandy: surname used as a specific: **Brandy Brook**: rises in Lilypad Pond, t. Colton, trib. Cranberry Lake. 1858 Rogerson; 1865 Beers; 1873 Hamilton Child; 1880 **Brandy Creek** Ely; 1883 **Brandy Creek** Ely-Wallace; 1896 New; 1902 Blankman; 1908 Adm; 1912 Stoddard; 1919 USGS Cranberry Lake Quad. / **Brandy Brook**: t. Colton, trib. South Branch Grass(e) River. 1919 USGS Cranberry Lake Quad. / **Brandy Brook**: rises in t. Lisbon, flows through t. Waddington, trib. St. Lawrence River. 1964 USGS Waddington Quad. / **Brandy Brook Flow**: inlet, Cranberry Lake, t. Clifton. 1919 USGS Cranberry lake Quad. / **Brandy Brook Junction:** four m. east of Cranberry Lake, t. Colton. *Quarterly*, 3 (1958), no. 4, [6]. / **Brandy Brook Road**: r., t. Lisbon. / **Brandy Brook School**: no. 3, common school, t. Oswegatchie. / **Brandy Creek**: see **Brandy Brook**, t. Colton. / **Brandy Road**: t. Hammond, n. Frederick Brandy, landowner. *Quarterly*, 10 (1965), no. 4, p. 9. / **Brandy Road**: same as **Brandy Brook Road.**

Brannon School: no. 2, common school, t. Louisville. n. Brannen family, with spelling change.

Brasher: pron. /bray-zher/. northeastern corner and borders with Franklin Co. t. formed from Massena, April 21, 1825 and organized Apr. 25, 1825. Petitioners first wanted Helena, n. for daughter of Joseph Pitcairn, as the n., but the senate altered it in favor of Philip Brasher, of Brooklyn, landholder and member of the legislature. (Durant, p. 412). 1964 Hogansburg Quad. Many n. derive from **Brasher**: **Brasher and Stockholm High School**: no. 18, common school, t. Brasher. / **Brasher Cemetery**: Roman Catholic, t. Brasher. / **Brasher Center**: h. in t. Brasher, three m. below the falls on St. Regis River. Settled in 1832; p. o. est. June 8, 1893, Nancy E. Clark, pm, closed Feb. 15, 1907. See Durant, 414. 1964 Brasher Falls Quad; 1873 Hamilton Child, p. 90. / **Brasher Center Road**: r., t. Brasher. / **Brasher Center School**: no. 13, common school, t. Brasher. / **Brasher Falls**: v. in t.

Brasher, "on both banks of St. Regis River about a mile below the junction of its branches." Durant, 416. Improvement in the area began in 1826; p. o. est. Apr. 22, 1840, Calvin T. Hulburd, pm, existing, ZIP 13613. Amerindian n.: **tiohionhoken**, "place where the river divides." Also, **Brashers Falls, Brasher's Falls**. 1964 Brasher Falls Quad; 1873 Hamilton Child, p. 90. / **Brasher Falls-Helena Road**: r., t. Brasher. / **Brasher Falls School**: no. 11, common school, t. Brasher. / **Brasher Flats School**: no. 15, common school, t. Brasher. / **Brasher Forest**: county forest, t. Brasher. / **Brasher Iron Works**: h. in t. Brasher, on Deer River, 2-1/2 m. above Helena. Begun Sept., 1835, by Stillman Fuller, p. o. est. July 14, 1849, Isaac W. Skinner, pm, closed Apr. 15, 1909. Formerly **Fullerville**. Durant, 414. Also **Brasher Iron-Works**. 1964 **Brasher Iron Works** Hogansburg Quad; 1873 **Brasher Iron Works**, Hamilton Child, p. 90. Amerindian n.: **Tsitkarestonni**, "where they make iron." / **Brasher Iron Works School**: no. 12, common school, t. Brasher. / **Brasher State Forest**, #1, 5, 6, 10, 7-17, t. Brasher.

Brasie: n. members of Brasie family: **Brasie Corners**: t. Macomb; p. o. est. Jan. 21, 1879, Alonzo B. Brasie, pm, closed June 29, 1935. 1961 USGS Pope Mills Quad. See *Quarterly*, 7 (1962), no. 4, p. 14, for incidental information, some incorrect. / **Brasie Corners-Rossie Road**: r., t. Rossie and Macomb. / **Brasie Corners School**: no. 4, common school, t. Macomb.

Bray Road: r., t. Norfolk, n. Bray family.

Brayton Road: r., t. DeKalb, n. Asa Brayton, Jr., family, first settlers to arrive in Edwards, 1812, but later moved.

Bread Rocks: on shore of Trout Lake, t. Hermon, n. shape. *Quarterly*, 16 (1971), no. 1, p. 9.

Bresett Road: r., t. Fowler, n. Bressett family.

Brewer: surname used as specific: **Brewer Road**: r., t. Canton, family n.; s. v. Massena, n. Nathaniel Brewer.

Brewers Creek: t. Massena. Noted as **Breser's Creek**, Dumas, 40.

Brice Road: r., t. DeKalb, n. Andrew Brice (1st settler) family, residents to the fourth generation.

Brick: building material: **Brick Barn**: t. Parishville, landmark building at

Allen's Falls; in 1959, destroyed to make way for a new road. Built by David Parish, it was known as the Sheep Barn because Parish tried to raise Spanish Merino sheep on the land. *Quarterly*, 4 (1959), no. 4, p. 11. / **Brick Chapel**: h., t. Canton, n. an early brick chapel, 1835. 1964 Pierrepont Quad. / **Brick Chapel Cemetery**: t. Canton. / **Brick Chapel School**: no. 5, common school, near Brick Chapel, t. Canton. / **Brick School**: t. Pierrepont, Dist. 3. See **Andrews School**. / **Brick School House School**: no. 3, common school, t. Hammond; , on Wooster Road, school #3, only brick school in t. Also, **Wooster School**.

Bridge: n. manmade feature spanning streams, railroads, etc., that extends as a specific n. to the whole stream or feature spanned. The n. is very popular, even where the bridge is not necessarily important: **Bridge Brook**: pond, t. Hopkinton. **Bridge Brook**: trib. Tupper Lake, t. Piercefield. 1912 Stoddard; 1954 USGS Tupper Lake Quad. / **Bridge Brook Bay**: in Tupper Lake, t. Piercefield. 1883 Ely-Wallace; 1896 New. / **Bridge Brook Pond**: t. Piercefield. 1858 **Bridge Pond** Rogerson; 1860 Merrit; 1865 **Bridge Pond** Beers, p. 86; 1873 Hamilton Child; 1880 Ely; 1883 Ely-Wallace; 1896 New; 1902 Blankman; 1908 Adm; 1954 USGS Tupper Lake Quad. / **Bridge Cemetery**: t. Canton, south of U. S. 11, east of v., n. E. and George Bridge family. 1964 USGS Canton Quad. / **Bridge Pond**: see **Bridge Brook Pond**. / **Bridge Road**: r., t. Fine. / **Bridge Street**: r., t. Canton, n. George and E. Bridge; s., h. Madrid; s., h. Nicholville; s., c. Ogdensburg, also called **East Lake Street**, just east of the "Iron" (Lake Street) bridge; r., t. Hopkinton; r., t. Pitcairn; s., v. Massena, now **Main Street**; s., h. Pyrites, from Pelton's Store across the Grass(e) River, t. Canton. Edward J. Austin, *Quarterly*, 10 (1965), no. 3, p. 12; s., h. Russell.

Bridges: surname: **Bridges Avenue**: s., v. Massena, n. Wilson Bridges from VT, father of prominent doctors and lawyers in the county. One son, Zina B. Bridges (1826-1893), practiced in Ogdensburg, was superintendent of schools, and president of the state medical society. / **Bridges Place**: s., v. Massena, n. John O. Bridges.

Brier Hill: h. in t. Morristown, p. o. est. Mar. 6, 1851, David Griffin, first pm, changed to **Brierhill**, Dec. 1895, Loren H. Harder, pm, changed to **Brier Hill**, Dec. 1905, Elijah A. Barney, pm; still existing, ZIP 13614: Abner Swain kept a tavern at the time of the windfall (1845). The place where the tavern was grown up in briers. Brier Hill is on the route of old Indian Trail that was used by people from Ogdensburg, Morristown, Hammond, and Rossie. 1963 USGS Morristown Quad. Derived names: **Brier Hill Cemetery**: on main street, Brier Hill, t. Morristown. Bogardus, 233. / **Brier Hill School**: no. 5, common school, t. Morristown. Bogardus, 60. / **Brier Hill Station**: former railroad station, no longer existing, t. Morristown. / **Brier Hill-Longs Corners Road**: r., t. Morristown. Same as **Potato Street**.

Briggs: h., t. Fine; p. o. est. Mar. 17, 1904, Leslie W. Davis, pm, closed Aug. 13, 1904; n. Charles and William Henry Briggs, but Brandy Briggs and J. Briggs also mentioned, all from Canada, settled back of Oswegatchie h. 1916 USGS Oswegatchie Quad. See **Briggs Switch**. / **Briggs Road**: r., t. Fine. See **Briggs**. / **Briggs School**: no. 19, common school, t. Lisbon, n. Briggs family. / **Briggs Switch**: t. Fine, on Carthage and Adirondack Railroad. *Quarterly*, 9 (1964), no. 2, p. 13; 11 (1966), no. , p. 16. See **Briggs**.

Brighton Street: s., v. Massena, n. Brighton family.

Bristol Road: r., t. Gouverneur, n. Bristol family.

Bristol's Settlement: t. DePeyster, n. Samuel Bristol, first settler. When the area was incorporated into a t. on Mar. 14, 1825, it was proposed to n. the place Stilwell, in honor of Smith Stilwell, prominent citizen. He declined. **Punchlock** is a nickname because the punchlock gun was manufactured there. The n. survives affectionately. See **DePeyster**.

Broad Street: descriptive, s., c. Ogdensburg; s. v. Potsdam.

Broadway Street: s., h. Pyrites, from Pelton's Store to past the former school site, t. Canton, n. desc. and in imitation of Broadway, NY City, to mean, in derision, the "main drag." See **Bridge Street**, Pyrites.

Brockville Rock: rocks, on St. Lawrence River, t. Morristown. 1963 USGS Morristown Quad.

Brodie School: no. 8, common school, t. Edwards, n. Joseph Brodie, an early settler and town supervisor (1855-1857, 1860, 1868). Freeman, 16, 30. 1915 USGS Gouverneur Quad.

Bromaghan Road: t. Oswegatchie. New York State Atlas. Durant, 157. See **Bromaghim**.

Bromaghim Settlement: n. for Francis Bromaghim (also spelled **Bromaghin**,

Brummigan, and others) and brothers, Dutch setters from Mohawk Valley, in t. Oswegatchie. *Quarterly*, 10 (1965), no. 4, p. 14. The n. forms are hopelessly confused in documents.

Bromley Brook: rises in Dillon Pond, flows through t. Clifton, trib. South Branch Grass(e) River. 1896 New; 1898 Blankman.

Bronson Hill: t. Parishville, "a mile out of town out George Street from Bronson," n. first settlers, Asa and D. Bronson.

Brookdale: desc. and commendatory: **Brookdale**: h., t. Stockholm; known locally as **Scotland**; p. o. est. Jan. 14, 1876, Daniel Tryon, pm, closed Dec. 14, 1903. Durant, 392. 1964 USGS Norfolk Quad. / **Brookdale Cemetery**: t. Stockholm. / **Brookdale Road**: r., t. Norfolk and Stockholm. / **Brookdale School**: no. 17, common school, t. Stockholm. / **Brookdale-Jenkins Corners Road**: r., t. Stockholm.

Brookfield Cemetery: t. Waddington. 1964 USGS Waddington Quad. Also, **Brookside**.

Brooklyn: "on the other side of the river," as in Brooklyn, NY, from which the n. is borrowed: **Brooklyn Road**: r., t. Lawrence, so-called "section across the river – Nicholville." / **Brooklyn School**: no. 4, common school, t. Canton. / **Brooklyn Street**: s., v. Gouverneur. Former n. of **West Main Street**, which was divided as Brooklyn Street and Somerville Road. Beers, 33, where it appears as **Brooklin**. Webster, 54, claims that Main Street in the "West Side, over the river," was known as **Brooklyn**.

Brooks: surname used as a specific: **Brooks Hall**: on Clarkson University campus, n. John Pascal Brooks (1861-1957), who came to the institution as Director of the School of Technology in 1911, and under the amended charter of 1913 became President of the College, serving until 1928 when he retired, but returned as "Acting President," 1932-1933. / **Brooks Point**: on St. Lawrence River, t. Morristown, n. Brooks family, early owner. 1961 USGS Edwardsville Quad.

Brookside Cemetery: location n., t. Waddington.

Brookview Drive: desc. n., s., v. Waddington.

Brothers: Either for a close group or for siblings: **Brothers Ponds**: three ponds, n. metaphorically as brother ponds, t. Clifton. 1896 **Middle**

Brother Pond, North Brother Pond, South Brother Pond New; 1898 same EGB [E. G. Blankman], p. 28; 1908 same Adm; 1912 same Stoddard; 1902 same Blankman; 1921 **Brothers Ponds** USGS Stark Quad. / **Brothers Road**: r., t. Norfolk and Stockholm, n. Brothers family.

Brough School: no. 10, common school, t. Morristown, n. Peter Brough family. Bogardus, 61.

Brouse Road: r., t. Norfolk, n. Jacob and Wesley Brouse from Canada.

Brouses Corners: t. Clare, n. Brouse family. 1915 Russell Quad.

Brown: usually a family n., but sometimes a color: **Brown Bay**: in Black Lake, t. Morristown. 1961 USGS Pope Mills Quad. / **Brown Church Road**: r., t. Waddington. / **Brown Falls**: t. Colton, n. an early settler. Also **Browns Falls**. / **Brown Falls Dam**: on Oswegatchie River. *Quarterly*, 11 (1966), No. 4, p. 15. / **Brown Road**: r., t. Lisbon. Also **Cline Brown Road**; r., t. Potsdam and Canton. Also **Wilkinson Road**. / **Brown School**: no. 4, common school, t. Colton; no. 5, common school, t. Hopkinton; no. 5, common school, t. Rossie. / **Brown Street**: s., c. Ogdensburg, n. Jonathan Brown, who with Selick Howe built in 1808 and 1809 two schooners, **Experiment** and **Collector**. The **Experiment** was launched on July 4, 1809, with the **Collector** later.

Browning Road: r., t. Louisville, n. Sam and Barney Browning.

Browns: possessive of **Brown**, sometimes written **Brown's**: **Brown's Bay**: in Jo(e) Indian Pond, t. Parishville, n. Horace Brown, Sr., resident and surveyor. See *Sketches of Parishville*. / **Brown's Bridge**: over Racquette River at Pierrepont, possibly n. Samuel C. Brown from England. Also, **Browns Bridge**. / **Browns Bridge**: bridge, t. Parishville, n. David and Horace Brown, Jr., prominent residents. 1921 USGS Stark Quad. Also **Brown's Bridge**. See *Sketches of Parishville*. / **Browns Bridge**: settlement, t. Pierrepont. 1964 USGS Colton Quad. / **Browns Bridge Road**: r., t. Pierrepont. / **Browns Falls**: t. Parishville, n. Horace Brown. / **Browns Falls**: t. Fine, n. Amasa I. Brown, the third settler to enter the area. / **Browns Falls Road**: r., t. Fine, n. the falls. / **Browns Falls School**: t. Fine, Dist. 10, begun in the 1840s. Reynolds, 199. Also, **Brown's Falls School**. / **Browns Island**: in Trout Lake, t. Edwards, n. J. S. Brown.

Brownville School: no. 16, common school, on Woods Bridge Road, t. Russell, near Hermon, n. James B. Brown, early settler from VT, shoemaker. 1915 USGS Russell Quad **Brownsville.**

Brunner: surname used as a specific, here n. family: **Brunner Falls**: t. Hopkinton, in West Branch St. Regis River. 1919 USGS Lake Ozonia Quad; 1964 USGS Sylvan Falls Quad. / **Brunner Hill**: t. Colton, alt. 1,700. 1921 USGS Stark Quad.

Brush Island: in Chippewa Bay, St. Lawrence River, t. Hammond, n. dense thicket. *Quarterly*, 16 (1971), no. 3, p. 11.

Buck: an extremely popular American specific n., that of the male deer; often associated with an incident, such as the sighting or killing of a male deer, after which the place named is extended to the whole stream or feature. Occasionally, a personal n.: **Buck Avenue**: r., t. Stockholm, n. Asahel Buck. / **Buck Brook**: t. Pierrepont. / **Buck Brook**: t. Clare, trib. North Branch Grass(e) River, n. male deer. 1915 USGS Russell Quad. / **Buck Brook**: t. Fine, trib. Oswegatchie River. 1916 USGS Oswegatchie Quad; 1919 USGS Cranberry Lake Quad. / **Buck Brook Road**: r., t. Clare. / **Buck Hill**: t. Hopkinton, alt. 1,780 ft. 1964 USGS lake Ozonia Quad. / **Buck Island**: in Cranberry Lake, t. Clifton. 1896 New; 1902 Blankman; 1908 Adm; 1912 Stoddard; 1919 USGS Cranberry Lake Quad. / **Buck Mountain**: t. Clifton, alt. 1,900 ft. 1896 New; 1902 Blankman; 1908 Adm; 1912 Stoddard; 1919 USGS Cranberry Quad. / **Buck Mountain**: t. Piercefield, alt. 2,321 ft. 1908 Adm; 1912 Stoddard; 1954 USGS Tupper Lake Quad. / **Buck Pond**: t. Fine, alt. 1,770 ft. 1902 Blankman; 1908 Adm; 1912 Stoddard; 1919 USGS Cranberry Lake. / **Buck Pond**: t. Hopkinton, alt. 1,533 ft. 1858 **Marsh Pond** Rogerson; 1860 **Marsh Pond** Merrit; 1865 **Marsh Pond** Beers; 1873 **Marsh Pond** Hamilton Child; 1880 **Marsh Pond** Ely; 1882 **Marsh Pond Ely-Wallace**; 1896 New; 1908 Adm; 1912 Stoddard; 1920 USGS Childwold Quad. / **Buck Pond**: t. Pierrepont. 1915 USGS Russell Quad. / **Buck Pond**: t. Potsdam, probably for Isaac Buck. / **Buck Pond Road**: r., t. Pierrepont, n. **Buck Pond.** /**Buck Road**: r., t. Madrid, n. a Mr. Buck. / **Buck Road**: r., t. Waddington, n. Isaac Buck. / **Buck Street**: s., v. Canton, n. Lemuel Buck, supervisor of Town of Canton, 1836-40. Durant, p. 210. Beers Atlas shows L. Buck living near the present street. / **Buck's Bridge**: see **Bucks Bridge**. / **Bucks Bridge**: in western corner of t. Potsdam, n. Isaac Buck, from Shoreham, VT, who built a sawmill on the site in 1806; p. o. est. Mar. 30, 1836, noted as **Buck's Bridge**, closed Oct. 29, 1856, Owen Buck, first pm; reopened Nov. 11, 1884, changed to **Bucks Bridge**, Dec. 1894, Alfred G. Buck, pm; **Bucks Bridge**, p. o. began Dec. 1894, changed Dec. 1895 to **Bucksbridge** (which see). New York Postal History. Durant, 239; *Quarterly*, 9 (1964), no. 3, p. 10. Also known as **Buck's Bridge**. 1964 USGS Morley Quad. / **Bucks Bridge Cemetery**: t. Potsdam. / **Buck's Corners**: t. Stockholm, two m. south of h. Stockholm. n. for Asahel Buck. Durant, 392. Also **Bucks Corners**.

Buckhorn: usually n. presence of antlers: **Buckhorn Creek**: t. Fine, trib. Mink Creek, t. Diana (Lewis Co.). / **Buckhorn Ridge**: t. Colton, alt. 1,700 ft. 1921 USGS Stark Quad.

Bucksbridge: p. o. changed Dec. 1895 from **Bucks Bridge**, closed Apr. 30, 1920, Charlotte Lawrence, pm, svc. Madrid. See **Bucks Bridge**. / **Bucksbridge School**: no. 10, common school, t. Potsdam. See **Bucks Bridge**.

Buckton: crossroads, t. Stockholm; p. o. est. May 27, 1890, Henry Burroughs, pm, closed July 30, 1904. New York Postal History. *Quarterly*, 10 (1965), no. 1, p. 14. 1964 USGS Parishville Quad. / **Buckton Cemetery**: t. Stockholm. / **Buckton Road**: r., t. Stockholm. / **Buckton School**: no. 9, common school, t. Stockholm. / **Buckton State Forest**, #31, t. Stockholm.

Buells Mill: h. Newton Falls, t. Fine, n. Augustus Buell. Reynolds, 101.

Buffham Road: r., t. Potsdam, n. Wesley Buffham family living at Bucks Bridge.

Bull Run Road: r., t. Lisbon.

Bullard Street: s., v. Gouverneur, n. Ezekiel Bullard; listed as Bullet Street in 1915 Census.

Bullhead: n. fish of the genus *Cotus*: **Bullhead Island**: in Black lake, t. Hammond. 1961 USGS Hammond Quad. / **Bullhead Point**: on Cranberry Lake, t. Clifton, n. fish. 1880 Ely (identification uncertain); 1883 Ely-Wallace; 1896 **Lone Pine Point** New. / **Bullhead Pond**: t. Clare. 1915 USGS Russell Quad. / **Bullhead Pond**: t. Pitcairn. 1951 USGS Harrisville Quad.

Bullis Island: in Grass(e) River, t. Canton, n. Bullis family. Several members of the family are buried in the Silas Wright Cemetery.

Bullock Creek: t. Russell, trib. Carncross Creek, n. Bullock family. 1915 USGS Russell Quad.

Bulson: n. Ogden Bulson: **Bulson Road**: r., t. DeKalb. / **Bulson School**: no. 10, common school, t. DeKalb, n. Bulson family.

Bundy Pond: t. Fine; see **Bondy Pond**. 1916 USGS Oswegatchie Quad.

Bunnell Road: r., t. Russell, n. Jesse and Enos Bunnell, first settlers, Jesse in 1805 and Enos in 1807.

Burnett Road: r., t. Hopkinton. Also **Meacham Road**.

Burnap Memorial Library: on Clarkson University campus, n. Harriet Call Burnap, "thanks to the generosity of Frank P. Burnap," her husband.

Burney Avenue: s., v. Massena, n. Thomas Burney, died at Andersonville Prison during the Civil War.

Burnham: surname used as a specific: **Burnham Corners**: crossroads, t. Potsdam. 1964 West Potsdam Quad. / **Burnham Corners-Norwood Road**: r., t. Potsdam.

Burns Flat: flatland, t. Russell and t. Clare, possibly n. Darius Burns family from VT. 1915 USGS Russell Quad.

Burnt: n. something destroyed or partially destroyed by fire or burned over: **Burnt Bridge Pond**: see **Burntbridge Pond**. / **Burnt Island**: in Racquette River, t. Piercefield, n. desc. of the burned area. 1920 USGS Childwold Quad. / **Burnt Island Rapids**: in Racquette River, t. Piercefield, n. **Burnt Island**. 1920 USGS Childwold Quad. / **Burnt Rock**: t. Colton, n. desc. of a rock in a burn area. 1954 USGS Tupper Lake Quad. / **Burntbridge Outlet**: stream, trib. South Branch Grass(e) River, t. Colton. 1912 Stoddard; 1954 USGS Tupper Lake Quad. / **Burntbridge Pond**: t. Colton, alt. 1,607. 1896 **Burnt Bridge Pond** New; 1902 **Burnt Bridge Pond** Blankman; 1908 **Burnt Bridge Pond** Adm; 1912 Stoddard; 1954 USGS Tupper Lake Quad.

Burts Falls: n. Charles H. Burt who owned land in h. Russell adjacent to the scenic falls on Grass(e) River.

Burpee Lane: s., v. Massena, n. Sparhawk/Sparahawk Burpee. Dumas, 57.

Bush: usually surname used as a

specific: **Bush Road**: r., t. Fine. n. John Bush. / **Bush School**: no. 18, common school, t. Lisbon, n. Bush family.

Butler: surname used as a specific, here n. family: **Butler Road**: r., t. Hammond, goes to Rossie; r., t. Louisville, n. Butler family. / **Butler School**: no. 19, common school, t. Brasher.

Butterfield Mills: see **Little River**, t. Canton. Beers Atlas shows h. there with the n. Butterfield occurring in area. Shown also as **Butterfields Mills**. Elisha Clark built the first saw- and gristmills there. Durant, p. 209. I. Butterfield and A. Butterfield, lot. 4, range 10, noted in Beers, p. 11. Durant, p. 209 notes the Bridge Cheese Factory, owned by Butterfield and Sons.

Butternut: n. tree (*Juglans cinerea*) of the walnut tree family that bears an edible oily nut: **Butternut Island**: in St. Lawrence River, t. Lisbon. 1906 USGS Red Mills Quad. / **Butternut Ridge**: t. Pierrepont. / **Butternut Ridge Road**: r., t. Pierrepont. Also **Ridge Road**. / **Butternut Ridge School**: no. 7, common school, t. Pierrepont.

Buys Biology Laboratories: on St Lawrence University campus in the Bewkes Science Hall, n. Dr. John L. Buys, long-time chairman of the Biology Department.

Byrns Road: r., t. Fowler, n. Byrns family. Also **Shantyville Road**.

C

C & A: see **Carthage & Adirondack Railroad**.

Cady Street: s., h. Madrid.

Calaboga: t. Hammond. *Quarterly*, 10 (1965), no. 4, p. 14. a student at SUC, Potsdam campus wrote, "Area between South Hammond and St. Lawrence River. This is an old Scottish name for a stone quarry. A bogie was a type of cart used to haul stones. 'Call a bogie,' was a frequent term used until the area became known as Calaboga. This is pronounced Calabogie." Another version is that it was n. for Caleb Bogue, a mill owner in the hills. Also, Amerindian, "large mouth fish." The origin is still in doubt. / **Calaboga School**: no. 6, common school, to. Hammond. Also, **Calliboga School**.

Caldwell Street: s., v. Canton. Now **Church Street**. Listed as Caldwell in Beers Atlas, p. 13. Poss., n. Theodore Caldwell, "prominent businessman," and on the committee that formed what is now St. Lawrence University. Durant, p. 125, col. 1.

Caledonia: n. Scotland, the country: **Caledonia**: t. Gouverneur, Rossie. / **Caledonia Mines**: near Gouverneur. Also **Caledonia Mine**. / **Caledonia Road**: r., t. Rossie, n. **Caledonia**. All the settlers were from Scotland.

California: n. state, believed to be a place of wealth and romance: **California Road**: r., t. Macomb. "Family announced that it was going to 'Californy,' but didn't. In derision the road on which they lived was called California Road." *Quarterly*, 10 (1965), no. 4, p. 9; t. Pitcairn, Fowler. A different road from the one in Macomb. / **California School**: no. 15, common school, t. Fowler, n. the road. 1913 USGS Lake Bonaparte Quad; no. 13, common school, t. Macomb. 1949 USGS Hammond Quad. / **California Road State Forest**, #21, t. Fowler, Pitcairn.

Calliboga School: see **Calaboga School**.

Calnon: a family n.: **Calnon Road**: r., t. Canton; r., t. Stockholm.

Calvary: n. hill where Jesus was crucified: **Calvary Cemetery**: on bank of Grass(e) River, t. Massena. 1964 USGS Massena Quad; t. Potsdam, near v. Norwood. 1943 USGS Potsdam Quad.

Campbell: surname used as a specific: **Campbell Cemetery**: n. John Campbell, who owned land bordering the cemetery. Also, **Flackville Cemetery**. *Quarterly*, 16 (1971), no. 2, p. 15. / **Campbell Cemetery Road**: r., t. Lisbon. Also **Cemetery Road**. / **Campbell Road**: r., t. Gouverneur. Beers, 46, shows a G. A. Campbell living on this road in the bordering town of Macomb. Modern maps show this section of land as being in Gouverneur; at Trout Lake, r., t. Hermon and Edwards; r., t. Waddington, n. Campbell family. / **Campbell School**: no. 14, common school, t. Macomb. / **Campbell Point Road**: r., t. Colton.

Cambray: one of original ten towns, p. o. est. Sept. 23, 1807, n. Cambria, meaning "co-landers," poetic for Wales; Richard Townsend, first pm, changed to **Gouverneur**, Oct. 28, 1818. Also **Cambrai**. / **Cambray Street**: s., v. Gouverneur, n. Cambray, former name of **Gouverneur**.

Cameron Road: s., h. Hannawa Falls.

Camp: n. gathering place or military grouping area: **Camp Island**: in St. Lawrence River, t. Lisbon. / **Camp Jolly**: at Cooper Falls; an area in the falls where at one time dances were held, and candy and ice cream were sold. After the place was blasted in 1914 to benefit nearby farm land, "Camp Jolly" disappeared. *Quarterly*, 12 (1967), no. 3, p. 12. / **Camp View Island**: in St. Lawrence River, t. Lisbon. / **Camp Wheeler**: c. Ogdensburg, n. William Almon Wheeler (1819-1887) of Malone, attorney, U. S. Representative, and Vice President of the U. S., who sponsored a training site for Civil War soldiers at Ogdensburg. See J. Karlton Dewey, "Vestiges of Camp Wheeler Still Remain," *Quarterly*, 6 (1961), no. 2, p. 9. Also see **Wheeler**.

Campus Road: s., h. Star Lake, n. SUC, Potsdam, Star Lake campus.

Canada: n. nation: **Canada Circle**: s., c. Ogdensburg. / **Canada towns**: the ten townships. Durant, 77.

Canal: n. presence of canal: **Canal Street**: s., c. Ogdensburg; s., v. Potsdam.

Canton: one of the first ten townships, n. Canton, China. Surveyed in 1799 by Amos Lay, assisted by Reuben Sherwood and Joseph Edsall. (Hough, 273-274); t. formed from Lisbon, Mar. 28, 1805. 1964 Morley Quad. / **Canton**: v., t. Canton; p. o. est. Apr. 1, 1804, as **New Cairo**, Daniel W. Sayre, pm (Hough, 574), changed to **Canton**, July 1, 1807, Stillman Foote, first pm, p. o. in existence, ZIP 13617. On Jan. 28, 1828, Canton was made the county seat. The New York State Constitution stipulates that a county seat shall be no more than a day's buggy ride away. Canton was more centrally located than was Ogdensburg, the former county seat. The first settler in Canton was Stillman Foote, who built the first sawmill and grist mill and also the first inn. The v. inc. May 14, 1845. 1964 Canton Quad. / **Canton Academy**: v. Canton, private school est. 1831, coeducational 1839, and in 1868 the name was changed to **Union Free School**, with support from town, county, and state. Stillman Foote, Jr., son of the first permanent settler of Canton, was the first graduate. Mary Joanne Lawrence, "Education in Canton," *Quarterly*, 9 (1964), no. 2, pp. 3-4, 18. / **Canton-Chester Road**: Begun April 1, 1808 (see Everts), with appropriations made in 1810 and 1814, and opened under the direction of Russell Attwater. Called the **Albany Road**, it was little used; on June 19, 1812, directed to be opened to foot of sloop navigation, Albany, and in 1815 a tax was levied to make the road passable for teams. See also

Russell Turnpike. / **Canton College of Technology**: v. Canton, on west side of Grass(e) River, is a State University of New York (SUNY) state-operated college, est. in 1906 as a New York State School of Agriculture. It was a part of St. Lawrence University until 1925 when it became state operated entirely. In 1940 its name was changed to Canton Agricultural and Technical College. Later it was granted its present name. / **Canton Falls**: See **Tateville.** *Quarterly*, 11 (1966), no. 1, p. 3; 6 (1961), no. 1, p. 11. Now **Rensselaer Falls.** / **Canton Farm**: clearing, t. Clare. 1921 Stark Quad. [1896] on Blankman's map, a place is marked Canton Lumber Co's Farm; however, this is on the South Branch Grass(e) River, t. Clifton. / **Canton Grammar School**: v. Canton, built in 1883, now disappeared. / **Canton High School**: no. 1, common school, v. Canton, built in 1908 near the old Academy buildings, now replaced by county buildings. / **Canton-Madrid Road**: r., t. Canton and Madrid. / **Canton, Morley and Madrid Plank-Road**: see **Plank Roads.** / **Canton Plank-Road**: see **Plank Roads.** / **Canton-Potsdam-Madrid Road**: r., t. Canton, Potsdam, Madrid. / **Canton-Pyrites Road**: r., t. Canton. / **Canton Street**: s., v. Potsdam, on SUC, Potsdam campus; s., c. Ogdensburg, r. leads to Canton (Route 68); s., v. Hermon, n. t. Canton, road leads to Canton; s., v. Rensselaer Falls, road leads to Canton. / **Canton to Chester** (Warren Co.) **Road**: *Quarterly*, 3 (1968), no. 1, p. 6.

Capell Street (pronounced. kay-pull): s., v. Parishville, n. Capell family. Also noted on some maps as **Chapell**, a misprint. See *Sketches of Parishville*.

Caravan Road: r., t. Louisville, where itinerant gypsies were allowed to camp.

Carey Road: r., t. Massena, n. Carey family.

Carncross Brook: *Quarterly*, 19 (1974), no. 2, p. 19. See **Carncross Creek.** / **Carncross Creek**: t. Russell, trib. Elm Creek, near Palmerville, n. Randall Carncross. 1915 USGS Russell Quad. Also, **Carncrose.**

Carnegie Hall: on St. Lawrence University campus, n. Andrew Carnegie, benefactor.

Carney Place: s., v. Massena, n. Carney family.

Caroline Street: feminine, given name, usually for the daughter of a prominent person: **Caroline Street**: s., h. DeKalb

Junction; s., v. Gouverneur; s., h. Madrid; s., v. Morristown; s., c. Ogdensburg, n. daughter of Nathan Ford.

Carpenter: family n.: **Carpenter Island**: in Trout Lake, now **Adams Island**, t. Hermon. *Quarterly*, 16 (1971), no. 1, p. 10. Origin of n. unknown. / **Carpenter Brook:** *Quarterly*, 19 (1974), no. 2, p. 19.

Carr Pond: t. Fine, small body of water behind Fine h., alt. 1,139 ft., n. Carr family. 1915 USGS Russell Quad.

Carrier School: no. 27, common school, t. Lisbon, n. Carrier family.

Carrs Point: on St. Lawrence River, t. Louisville. 1942 USGS Murphy Island Quad. Also, **Carr's Point**, Tedford, 52.

Carry: n. portage around a falls or difficult area: **Carry, The**: foot route est. by Amerindians from head of Black Lake at Hammond-Morristown lines over present present Irelan Road to Chippewa Creek, then to St. Lawrence River, often safer than weather-dangerous Ogdensburg-to-Chippewa river. / **Carry Falls**: on Racquette River, near Hollywood, t. Colton. 1896 New; 1902 Blackman; unrecorded on USGS maps. See **Bog Falls**. / **Carry Falls Road**: r., t. Colton, n. falls.

Carson Hall: on SUC, Potsdam, campus, n. William R. Carson, who served on the College Council from 1953 to 1974. A physician, he played an important role in the development of the St. Lawrence County Mental Health Clinic and its location on the campus.

Carter: surname used as specific: **Carter Creek**: t. Edwards, trib. Huckleberry Lake, n. Cornelius Carter (1816-1906). 1956 USGS Edwards Quad. / **Carter Creek**: enters Tanner Creek, t. Hermon. Tanner Creek is outlet of Trout Lake.

Carthage & Adirondack Railroad: known as the **C & A**, built in the 1880s, ran from Carthage to Newton Falls. *Quarterly*, 11 (1966), no. 1, p. 16.

Carvill Cemetery: t. Brasher.

Cary Hill: t. Colton, alt. 1,675 ft. 1921 USGS Stark Quad.

Casey Corners: crossroads, t. Potsdam. 1964 USGS Morley Quad.

Cassidy: surname used as a specific, here n. family: **Cassidy Road**: r., t.

Hopkinton; r., t. Russell.

Castle: surname used as a specific: **Castle Cemetery**: t. Hopkinton, n. Merriman Castle family. / **Castle Drive**: s., v. Potsdam, n. Dorothy Castle, who built a stone house in the area. / **Castle School**: no. 7, common school, t. Hopkinton, n. Merriman Castle family.

Cat: n. usually involving the sighting or killing of a wild cat. Sometimes found as a translation of French **chat** or from an Amerindian animal n.: **Cat Island Shoal**: in St. Lawrence River, t. Louisville, n. translated from French **chat**, "cat," for shape of island. 1964 USGS Louisville Quad. / **Cat Mountain**: t. Clifton, alt. 2,261 ft., southwest St. Lawrence County. *Quarterly*, 16 (1971), no. 2, p. 11. 1896 New; 1902 Blankman; 1908 Adm; 1912 Stoddard; 1919 USGS Cranberry Lake Quad. / **Cat Mountain Pond**: t. Clifton, alt. 1,715 ft, n. mountain. 1896 New; 1898 EGB, p. 27; 1902 Blankman; 1908 Adm; 1912 Stoddard; 1919 USGS Cranberry Lake Quad. / **Cat Pond**: see **Catamount Pond**, t. Piercefield.

Catamount, short for **cat of the mountain**, indicates an early n., usually 18th and early 19th centuries, and also connotes some kind of wildcat: **Catamount Hills**: see **Catamount Mountain.** / **Catamount Island:** in Cranberry Lake, t. Clifton. Now, **Sears Island** (which see). / **Catamount Mountain**: t. Colton, near Hollywood, alt. 1,825 ft. See, also, *Quarterly*, 13 (1968), no. 3, p. 19; 16 (1971), no. 2, p. 11. 1860 **Catamount Hills** Merrit; 1896 New; 1902 Blankman; 1908 Adm; 1912 Stoddard; 1921 USGS Stark Quad. / **Catamount Peak**: see **Catamount Mountain.** / **Catamount Pond:** t. Hopkinton. / **Catamount Pond**: near Childwold, t. Piercefield, alt. 1,517 ft. *Quarterly*, 16 (1971), no. 2, p. 11. 1858 Rogerson; 1860 **Cat Pond** Merrit; 1865 Beers, p. 86; 1880 Ely; 1883 Ely-Wallace; 1896 New; 1902 Blankman; 1908 Adm; 1912 Stoddard 1920 USGS Childwold Quad. / **Catamount Ridge**: t. Stockholm. / **Catamount Ridge Road**: r., t. Stockholm.

Catfish Rock: island in Oswegatchie River, t. DeKalb, n. fish of the genus *Nematognathi*, sometimes confused with the bullhead. 1963 USGS Rensselaer Falls Quad.

Catherine: feminine, given n., usually for daughter of prominent citizen: **Catherine Street**: s., v. Hermon, n. Catherine Ames, who lived in the first house built on the street until she died in 1891; s., c. Ogdensburg, n. a daughter of Nathan Ford; s., v. Parishville; s., h. Star Lake.

Catherineville: a survey township, t. Hopkinton. 1964 USGS Parishville Quad. See *Sketches of Parishville*. / **Catherineville State Forest**, #8, t. Hopkinton.

Catholic Cemetery: t. Potsdam; t. Waddington; Massena (**St. Peters**).

Caty's Rift: also **Keaton's Rift**. Durant, 147.

Cayey Road: r., t. Colton, n. Cayey family.

Cecil Avenue: s., v. Massena.

Cedar: n. the coniferous tree, genus *Cedrus*, of the pine family, noted for fragrance of the wood; very popular American n. for features, even ones with few cedars or perhaps only one present. The n. also is religiously influenced by "the cedars of Lebanon": **Cedar Bay**: t. Clifton. in Cranberry Lake. 1896 New; 1908 Adm. / **Cedar Brook**: t. Hopkinton, trib. Cold Brook. 1920 USGS Childwold Quad. / **Cedar Cliff on the St. Lawrence**: t. Morristown. A group of buildings that included a cavalry school. Bogardus, 91. / **Cedar Islands**: in Chippewa Bay, St. Lawrence River, t. Hammond, n. the white cedars. *Quarterly*, 16 (1971), no. 3, p. 11. 1907 7th Report for Fish-Game Commerce, p. 77; 1958 USGS Chippewa Quad. / **Cedar Lake**: t. Edwards, Hermon. / **Cedar Rapids**: in Grass(e) River, t. Russell. / **Cedar Spring**: t. Clare. 1915 Russell Quad. / **Cedar Street**: s., v. Massena; s., v. Norwood; s., c. Ogdensburg, n. the tree in a section of tree names, Ward 2; s., v. Potsdam. / **Cedar Swamp**: adjacent Cranberry Lake, t. Clifton. 1858 Rogerson. / **Cedars, The**: stage stop and h. on Black Lake, also school district, t. Morristown. *Quarterly*, 2 (1957), no. 4, npn; 7 (1962), no. 4, p. 14; p. o. est. Dec. 8, 1892, Oscar D. Moore, pm., closed Aug. 15, 1899. Also **Cedars** and **Cedars on Black Lake**. 1961 USGS Hammond Quad. / **Cedars School**: no. 4, common school, t. Morristown. Bogardus, 60. / **Cedars School**: no. 19, common school, t. Stockholm.

Cemetery Road: common and prosaic name for roads that pass by or lead to a cemetery: s., v. Norwood. Same as **Lakeshore Drive**; r., t. Colton; r., t. Lawrence; r., t. Lisbon; r., t. Norfolk; r., t. Potsdam. Also **Lakeshore Drive**; r., t. Potsdam; r., t. Russell; r., t. Morristown; r., t. Stockholm.

Centennial Terrace: c. Ogdensburg, residence for senior citizens, dedicated 1965.

Center: usually for a middle point: **Center Pond**: t. Colton. 1880 **Centre Pond** Ely; 1883 **Centre Pond** Ely-Wallace; 1896 New; 1908 Adm; 1912 Stoddard; 1954 USGS Tupper Lake Quad. / **Center Pond Mountain**: t. Colton, alt. 2,450 ft., n. pond. 1912 Stoddard; 1954 USGS Tupper Lake Quad. See **Edgar Mountain**. / **Center Road**: r., t. Morristown and Oswegatchie, between Morristown and Morristown Center h. / **Center School**: no. 12, common school, t. Morristown, at junction of Center and Charlesworth Roads. Bogardus, 60. / **Center Street**: s., v. Massena. West Center and East Center Streets are divided by Harrowgate Street.

Central School: designates a consolidated school at a convenient location: v. Hammond. 1961 USGS Hammond Quad; v. Morristown. 1963 USGS Morristown Quad.

Centre Pond: see **Center Pond**.

Cessna Drive: s., h. Star Lake, located on a new development on what was the Kerr Brothers Airport; n. Ralph Kerr's plane, a Cessna.

Chain: description of a series of features: **Chain Ponds**: see **Lows Lake**. / **Chain Ponds**: t. Clifton. Possibly includes **Clear, Slender**, and **Tamarack**. 1883 Ely-Wallace.

Chair Rock: descriptive of shape of feature: **Chair Rock Bay**: in Cranberry Lake, t. Clifton. 1896 New. / **Chair Rock Creek**: t. Clifton, trib. Cranberry Lake. 1880 Ely; 1882 Ely-Wallace; 1896 New; 1902 Blankman; 1908 Adm; 1919 USGS Cranberry Lake Quad. / **Chair Rock Flow**: t. Clifton, south end of Cranberry Lake. / **Chair Rock Island**: in Cranberry Lake, t. Clifton. 1919 USGS Cranberry lake Quad.

Chamberlain Corners: t. Waddington, n. Anson Chamberlain who built the Chamberlain House, which gave the locality its name. Tedford, 31; *Quarterly*, 16 (1971), no. 4, p. 18. 1964 USGS Chase Mills Quad. Derived names include: **Chamberlain Bridge**, t. Waddington. / **Chamberlain Corners Cemetery**: t. Waddington. / **Chamberlain Corners-Norfolk Road**: r., t. Madrid and Waddington. / **Chamberlain Corners School**: no. 6, common school, t. Waddington. / **Chamberlain House**: See **Chamberlain Corners/ Bridge**. Also, known as the **Temperance Tavern**. The house was also an underground railroad station for slaves escaping from the South. / **Chamberlain Road**: s., v. Massena, n. Martin J. Chamberlain.

Chambers School: no. 14, common school, t. Lisbon, n. Chambers family.

Champlain Street: s., c. Ogdensburg, n. Champlain family.

Champlin Island: in Grasse River, Canton, n. George Champlin. *Quarterly*, 25 (1980), no. 4, p. 4.

Chandler Pond: in Jamestown area, t. Colton, alt. 1,437 ft., n. Chandler family. 1896 New; 1908 Adm; 1912 Stoddard; 1920 USGS Childwold Quad.

Chaney Dining Center: on SUNY Canton College of Technology campus, n. Mary Adele Chaney, former head of the Home Economics Department.

Chapel: usually for a nearby church, but occasionally a surname: Chapel Hill: t. Parishville, n. because the Congregational church was built here, the first one in the t. See *Sketches of Parishville*. / **Chapel Hill Cemetery**: Parishville, n. hill. 1964 USGS Parishville Quad. / **Chapel Hill Road**: r., t. Parishville. / **Chapel Road**: r., t. Lisbon. / **Chapel Street**: s., v. Canton, n. church on corner.

Chapell Street: see **Capell Street**.

Chapman: surname used as a specific: **Chapman Point**: on Black Lake, t. Hammond and Morristown, n. Chapman family. 1961 USGS Hammond Quad; 1963 USGS Morristown Quad. / **Chapman Street**: s., v. Morristown, n. Augustus Chapman (1786-1860), merchant, town supervisor, banker, founder of the present Norstar Bank of Ogdensburg. He came to Morristown in 1820 and purchased the Samuel Stocking House, now the Chapman House, a Greek Revival style mansion. Bogardus, 43 ff.

Chapp Hill: t. Colton, alt. 1,325 ft. 1921 USGS Stark Quad.

Charles Street: s., h. Parishville.

Charlesworth Road: connects Scotch Bush and Center Roads, t. Morristown, n. Charlesworth family.

Charlton: n. Lawrence Charlton, a leader of the Irish group: **Charlton District**: t. Waddington, the "**Irish Settlement**" area. / **Charlton School**: no. 2, common school, t. Waddington.

Chase Mills: h., t. Waddington, n. Alden Chase, sawmill builder, p. o. est. Nov. 19, 1853, as **Chase's Mills**,

Thomas J. Wheeler, first pm; changed to **Chase Mills**, Feb. 21, 1894, Frank P. Fobare, pm, existing, ZIP 13621. Formerly, **Chase's Mills, Chases Mills, Crow-Crow, Cracko** or **Croco.** The latter three are nicknames: "The neighbors in the area would gather in their yards and shout back and forth, sounding like a flock of chattering crows." Tedford, 36; 1964 USGS Chase Mills Quad. Derived n. include: **Chase Mills Cemetery**: t. Louisville. / **Chase Mills Inn**: hotel in Chase Mills, also known as **Mary-George Inn**, for Mary and George Lenney, owners in 1941. The building now has Historical Building Register status. / **Chase Mills-Louisville Road**: r., t. Louisville. / **Chase Mills Road**: r., t. Madrid. / **Chase Mills School**: no. 12, common school, t. Louisville. / **Chase Street**: s., v. Massena, n. Hiram Chase.

Chateau: n. home of the Corrigans on Dry Island, t. Waddington.

Chateaugay Trail: Lake Champlain to St. Regis River, very important to settling of northern New York by New Englanders; later Old Military Turnpike. *Quarterly*, 15 (1970), no. 1.

Chat's Island: in St. Lawrence River, t. Louisville. French, "cat."

Chaumont: a survey township, now incorporated into **Clifton**; from family name of J. D. LeRay; place n. in France, home of the LeRays. Durant, 77: **Chaumont Ore Body**: reportedly found in 1810 by engineers surveying the area in preparation for military road from Albany to Ogdensburg, it was first recognized as an ore body about 1839 by the New York State Geologist. Reynolds, 107. / **Chaumont Pond**: t. Clifton, alt. 1,423. 1896 New; 1898 EGB; 1902 Blank-man; 1908 Adm; 1912 Stoddard; 1919 USGS Cranberry Lake Quad.

Cheel Campus Center: on Clarkson University campus, n. Helen Snell Cheel, who made a major gift commitment to the building of the center. Her father was the late North Country Congressman Bertrand H. Snell, a longtime Clarkson trustee.

Cherry: n. the wild cherry tree, much valued in American culture, with the n. occurring often, especially in street n., but occasionally a personal n.: **Cherry Hill Road**: s., h. Star Lake and r., t. Fine. **Cherry Island**: in St. Lawrence, t. Hammond. / **Cherry Patch Pond**: see **John Pond**, t. Colton, n. grove of cherry trees. / **Cherry Patch Road**: in Hollywood, t. Colton. *Quarterly*, 13 (1968), no. 3, p. 19. See **Cherry Patch Pond** / **Cherry Street**: s., v.

Massena; s., c. Ogdensburg, n. Samuel Cherry, a captain in the War of 1812, who in early 1809 commanded a company of troops stationed in Ogdensburg to protect the citizens. According to Hough, 618, the troops "are represented as the worst set of men that ever lived," causing the people of Ogdensburg to organize their own patrol for protection. Eventually, the troops were withdrawn but not without some nasty incidents between them and the ones they were ostensibly to protect; s., v. Potsdam.

Chester to Russell Road: from Chester in Washington Co. *Quarterly*, 13 (1968), no. 1, p. 6.

Chesterfield: a survey township, p. o. est. Sept. 5, 1808, Joseph St. Clair, pm, closed in 1816; now **Lawrence**. Also see *Quarterly*, 14 (1969), no. 4, p. 20. The origin of the n. is undetermined but poss. English place n. in Derbyshire; ety., OE **ceaster** "[Roman] fort" + OE **feld** "open country."

Chestnut: n. presense of the tree: **Chestnut Street**: s., v. Massena; s., v. Potsdam.

Chevrolet Road: r., t. Massena, n. the General Motors Plant.

Childs Road: r., t. DeKalb, n. Childs family.

Childwold: n. by Addison Child, from Boston, in 1878: "'Child' for my name and 'wold,' which means 'high rolling ground.'" His tract of land lay near Massawepie Lake. First p. o. est, Apr. 1, 1884, as **Childwood**, a mistake by the postal officials in Washington; changed Apr. 22, 1884, to **Childwold**, with Child as first pm, closed Mar. 15, 1905, reopened, Mar. 25, 1905, Thomas McKizer, pm, existing, ZIP 12922. See also Beulah Dorothy, "How Childwold Got Its Name," *Quarterly*, 6 (1961), no. 4, p. 11. 1883 Ely-Wallace; 1896 New; 1902 Blankman; 1908 Adm; 1920 USGS Childwold Quad, t. Hopkinton, Piercefield. Derived n.: **Childwold Park**: h., t. Piercefield. 1896 New; 1902 Blankman; 1920 USGS Childwold Quad. The park itself was a fish and game preserve and summer resort, including Lake Massawepie and six smaller lakes and ponds, covering 5,109 acres, all owned by Addison Child. See **Massawepie**; also **Forest Commission Report, 1893**, p. 191. / **Childwold School**: common school, t. Piercefield. 1920 USGS Childwold Quad. Formerly, no. 15, t. Hopkinton. / **Childwold Station**:

Quarterly, 3 (1958), no. 4, p. [6].

Chilton School: no. 18, common school, t. Russell, n. Thomas and Alex Chilton.

Chimney: n. presence as a landmark: **Chimney Island**: in St. Lawrence River, t. Lisbon. *Quarterly*, 1 (1956), no. 3, npn; 11 (1966), no. 4, p. 3. Formerly, **Oraquointon, Oraconenton,** an Amerindian n. meaning unknown. The island was the scene of a battle between the English and the French in 1760. See **Point Airy**. 1963 USGS Ogden East Quad. / **Chimney Point**: on St. Lawrence River, t. Oswegatchie. 1963 Ogden East Quad.

Chipman: h., t. Waddington, n. for Samuel Chipman, 1801 settler, p. o. est. June 3, 1897, E. Jane Rutherford, pm, closed Oct. 14, 1903. See also *Quarterly*, July 1961. Tedford, 44; 1964 USGS Waddington Quad. Derived n.: **Chipman Road**: r., t. Lisbon, Waddington, Madrid. / **Chipman School**: h. Chipman, the building still standing. / **Chipman-Waddington Road**: t. Waddington.

Chippewa: "Properly known as Ojibway, for a large Indian tribe of Algonquian linguistic stock. There are 160 islands and shoals adjacent to Hammond, where a group of river pirates made river travel risky around the time of the War of 1812. The bandits robbed a British scow headed for Kingston which was loaded with supplies and money. The thieves hid the boat and money up Chippewa Creek." Folk tradition collected by a student informant at SUC, Potsdam. Derived n.: **Chippewa Bay:** h. in t. Hammond, p. o. est. Aug 3, 1880, Alexander Allen, first pm, existing, ZIP 13623. 1865 Beers, p. 37; 1958 USGS Chippewa Bay Quad. Also **Chippewa Village.** / **Chippewa Bay School**: no. 11, common school, t. Hammond. / **Chippewa Cemetery**: outer Sand Street, three m. from Brier Hill, t. Morristown. Bogardus, 233. Also, **Chippewa Street Cemetery**. / **Chippewa Creek**: t. Oswegatchie and Hammond, flows through center of t. Morristown into St. Lawrence River. 1865 Beers, p.17; 1958 USGS Chippewa Quad; 1963 USGS Edwardsville Quad. / **Chippewa Point**: on St. Lawrence River, t. Hammond. 1865 Beers, p. 27; 1858 USGS Chippewa Quad. / **Chippewa Road**: see **Chippewa Bay**. / **Chippewa Village**: see **Chippewa Bay**, h.

Chisholm Road: r., t. Rossie, n. Chisholm family.

Chittenden School: no. 5, common

school, t. Stockholm, n. Carlos Chittenden family.

Chokeberry Island: in Chippewa Bay, St. Lawrence River, t. Hammond, n. plant of the genus *Aronia*. 1958 USGS Chippewa Quad.

Chub Lake: t. Fowler, alt. 578 ft., n. the fresh water fish of the genus *Coregonus*. *Quarterly*, 16 (1971), no. 1, p. 9. 1956 USGS Edwards Quad. / **Chub Lake Road**: r., t. Hermon.

Church: n. associated with the presence of a house of worship, but occasionally a personal n.: **Church Brook**: t. Canton, flows into State Wetlands Swamp, n. Church family. 1964 Canton Quad. / **Church Mill Road**: t. Morristown, n. Daniel Whipple Church, early settler and adjutant in War of 1812, participating in many skirmishes in the area, later mill owner and influential citizen in Morristown. Bogardus, 19, 22, 96-7. / **Church Mills**: t. Rossie. / **Church Mills**: t. Colton. See **Church Pond**. Also **Church's Mills**. / **Church Pond**: t. Colton, alt. 1,548 ft.; head of branch of Grass(e) River, n. Dan W. Church, pioneer settler and premier mill builder. *Quarterly*, 13 (1968), no. 3, p. 19. 1858 Rogerson; 1860 Merrit; 1873 Hamilton Child; 1880 Ely; 1883 Ely-Wallace; 1896 New; 1902 Blankman; 1908 Adm; 1912 Stoddard; 1921 USGS Stark Quad. / **Church Road**: r., t. Lisbon; r., t. Pierrepont, from Highway 56 to River Road; r., t. Pierrepont, from Post Road to Ridge Road; r., t. Waddington. / **Church Street**: r., t. Lawrence; s., v. Canton, poss. n. Daniel W. Church from VT, who helped Stillman Foote settle in Canton and also built first sawmill (Durant, pp. 207, 215, 269), but churches near the street may be the reason for the n.; s., h. Brasher Falls; r. and s., t. and h. Colton; s., h. DeKalb Junction; s., v. Edwards; r., t. Fine; s., v. Gouverneur; s., h. Hannawa Falls; s., v. Hermon; r., t. Lawrence; s., h. Madrid; s., h. North Lawrence, all churches being on it; s., v. Massena, n. Nathan and Harvey Church.

Churchill: surname used as a specific: **Churchill Avenue**: s., v. Massena / **Churchill Street**: s., h. Pyrites, t. Canton, ran from Pelton's Store up past Kelly's Store, n. O. B. Churchill, carpenter and house builder. See **Bridge Street**, Pyrites.

Circle: shape n.: **Circle Drive**: s., v. Potsdam. / **Circle Road**: r., t. Hopkinton.

Claflin: n. Abel Claflen, with change

in spelling: **Claflin School**: t. Pierrepont, Dist. 10, n. Abel Claflen. Also **Cleflen School**. / **Claflin's Corners**: t. Pierrepont, n. Abel Claflen. Also **Claffins Corners**.

Clare: a survey township, south of central St. Lawrence County, t. formed Dec. 2, 1880, taken from **Pierrepont**; n. for county in Ireland. Madame de Stael, famous French author, owned part of the survey through the recommendation of Gouverneur Morris, a close acquaintance. Hough, 429. 1915 Russell Quad; 1921 Stark Quad. / **Clare**: h., t. Clare, p. o. est. June 27, 1881, Abbie Dewey, first pm, closed June 30, 1919. Clarke, 27, lists Isabel Van Brocklin as first pm. Derived n.: **Clare School**: no. 3, common school, t. Clare, served community around Gleason's Mills, closed around 1912. Also **Clare Mills School**. 1921 USGS Stark Quad. / **Clare Road**: r., t. Clare. / **Clare Town Line- Pierrepont Center Road**: r., t. Pierrepont.

Claremont Avenue: s., v. Massena.

Clark: common surname used as a specific: **Clark Bridge**: across St. Regis River, nine m. north from Brasher Falls. / **Clark Cemetery**: t. Canton, north of Pink Schoolhouse Road, n. many Clark families who lived in the area. 1964 USGS Canton Quad. / **Clark Point**: on St. Lawrence River, t. Waddington. 1964 USGS Waddington Quad. Also, **Clarks Point**. / **Clark School**: no. 10, common, t. Potsdam, n. Clark family. / **Clark Street**: s., v. Canton. n. prob. Dr. Darius Clark, long-time physician of Canton, between 1824 and 1876, also one-time inspector of state prisons. Durant, p. 218 ff.; s., v. Massena; s., v. Norwood, poss. n. Joseph Clark family who had manufacturing interests in the Norwood-Norfolk area. See *Quarterly*, 6 (1961), no. 1, p. 12; s., c. Ogdensburg, n. Edwin Clark, early merchant, son-in-law of Louis **Hasbrouck**; s., v. Parishville, n. S. L. Clark, who owned a sawmill.

Clarks: possessive of **Clark**: **Clark's Crossing**: "one of the first co-operative settlements in the United States." V. M. Ingram, Jr., *Quarterly*, 5 (1957), [p. 1]. / **Clarks Corners**: t. Russell, n. Clark family. 1915 USGS Russell Quad.

Clarksboro: h., t. Clare, n. Lucian C. Clark, New York City, one of the promoters and "money men" for Clifton mines. *Quarterly*, 1 (1956), no. 4, npn; 14 (1969), no. 2, p. 3; p. o. est. Jan. 18, 1869 as **Clarksborough**, Elisha Burnham, first pm, closed Oct. 31, 1892, reopened Nov.

23, 1892, and on Dec. 1893 changed to **Clarksboro**, Alvah H. Allen, pm, closed Dec. 15, 1914. 1915 Russell Quad. / **Clarksboro School**: no. 5, common school, t. Clare.

Clarkson: n. members of the Clarkson family, founders of Clarkson University or for the university. The Clarkson family acquired the Town of Potsdam in 1802 and can legitimately be said to be the founders, through their agent Benjamin Raymond: **Clarkson Avenue**: s., v. Massena; s., v. Potsdam, n. Clarkson family. / **Clarkson Hall**: on Clarkson University campus, n. Robert Livingston Clarkson, a trustee and honorary president of the Board of Trustees, holder of the positions of Chairman of the Board of the American Express Company and President of the Chase National Bank of New York. / **Clarkson 7 Springs**: t. Parishville, south side of French Hill Road. Area for sports and acting; owned by Clarkson University. / **Clarkson University**: in Potsdam, founded as a "school of crafts" and named in 1896 as **Thomas S. Clarkson Memorial College of Technology**, n. Thomas S. Clarkson (1837-1894), by his sisters (Frederica, Elizabeth, and Lavinia). One account claims it was given by David M. Clarkson, a member of the Clarkson family of Potsdam. Thomas S. Clarkson died in an accident at a quarry. Many articles and books are available on the prominent Potsdam family.

Clary Street: s., v. Massena, n. J. E. Clary.

Clear: n. often a desc. for transparent, pure water, free from cloudiness or muddiness; sometimes commendatory whether the water is clear or not: **Clear Creek**: t. Fine; t. Pitcairn, trib. West Branch Oswegatchie River. 1865 Beers, p. 37; 1951 USGS Harrisville Quad. / **Clear Lake**: t. Clare, alt. 1,025 ft. 1915 Russell Quad; t. Edwards, alt. 800 ft. 1956 USGS Edwards Quad. / **Clear Pond**: near Hollywood Club, t. Colton, Clifton, alt. 1,575. 1880 Ely; 1883 Ely-Wallace; 1896 **Hedge Hog Pond** New; 1908 Adm; 1912 Stoddard; 1919 USGS Cranberry Lake Quad; t. Colton and Clifton, alt. 1,453 ft. 1858 Rogerson; 1865 Beers, p. 86; 1896 New; 1902 Blankman; 1912 Stoddard; 1921 USGS Stark Quad; see **Arbuckle Pond**; south of Cranberry Lake, t. Clifton, alt. 1,691 ft. *Quarterly*, 17 (1972), no. 2, p. 12. 1896 New; 1898 EGB; 1908 Adm; 1912 Stoddard; 1919 USGS Cranberry lake; Irving Bacheller, in a letter to mapmaker Blankman, claimed that "Clear Pond is now Lake Ann." See *Quarterly*, 14 (1969), no. 1, p. 22. See **Lake Ann**. / **Clear Pond Road**: r., t. Hopkinton, n. the pond.

Cleared Island: See **Manzanita Island**.

Cleaveland Street: s., v. Canton, n. Frank Nash Cleaveland. *Quarterly*, 13 (1968), no. 4, p. 5.

Cleflin School: no. 10, common school, t. Pierrepont.

Clifton: formerly a survey township, now t.; organized Apr. 21, 1868, combining t. of Clifton and Chaumont; n. taken from Clifton Iron Co., but according to Hough (255) was named for a city in England. Durant, 79, 452. / **Clifton Falls**: *Quarterly* 1 (1956), no. 4, npn.

Cline: surname used as a specific: **Cline Road**: r., t. Louisville; r., t. Potsdam. / **Cline Brown Road**: r., t. Lisbon. / **Clines Bay**: at end of Long Sault Island, n. William and John Cline, vessel owners. Also, **Cline's Bay**.

Clinton: all the streets were n. DeWitt Clinton (1769-1828), graduate of Columbia College, lawyer, state assemblyman, U. S. Senator, mayor of New York City, and governor of New York (1817-21, 1825-28): **Clinton Street**: r., t. Norfolk; s., v. Gouverneur; s., v. Heuvelton; s., v. Norfolk; s., v. Potsdam, but a claim is made for Norman Clinton, one of the first deacons of the First Baptist Church; s., v. Waddington.

Clintsman School: no. 4, common school, t. Fine, probably n. Henry Clintsman family. Also, **House School**. Reynolds, 199.

Clock Street: see **Klock Street**.

Cloe Road: r., t. Pierrepont, n. Cloe family.

Clohosy School: no. 12, common school, t. Pierrepont, n. Clohosy family.

Close: usually a family n.: **Close Pond**: t. Colton. 1908 Potsdam Quad; 1912 Stoddard; 1964 USGS Rainbow Falls Quad. / **Close Road**: r., t. Stockholm, probably n. Close family.

Clough Street: s., v. Potsdam, n. Clough family, with members still living on the street.

Club Road: r., t. Stockholm.

Coakley Road: r., t. Canton, n. family of merchants.

Coal Hill: t. Rossie, n. apparently for

the mineral. The hill, however, is near a lead mine.

Cobble Road: r., t. Parishville, n. type of stones.

Cobbles: county forest, t. Parishville,

Coffee Mountain: t. Hopkinton, alt. 1,480 ft., Coffee family. 1964 USGS Sylvan Falls Quad.

Coffin: n. W. S. Coffin: **Coffins Mill**: t. Fine, on Carthage and Adirondack Railroad. *Quarterly*, 11 (1966), no. 1, p. 16, n. W. S. Coffin of Carthage who started a sawmill here. Reynolds, 94. Also **Coffin Mills, Coffin's Mills**./ **Coffin Mills Road**: r., t. Fine, n. mill.

Coggswell: surname used as a specific: **Coggswell School**: no. 7, common school, t. Madrid. Also **Cogswell School**. / **Cogswell Corners**: t. Madrid, n. Seth Cogswell. 1964 USGS Waddington Quad. / **Cogswell Corners Road**: r., t. Madrid.

Cold: often desc. of fresh water according to the sensation of the tester; very popular American place n.: **Cold Brook**: t. Colton, trib. Racquette River. 1853 HMC; 1858 Rogerson; 1860 Merrit; 1865 **Big Cold Brook** Beers, p. 17; 1873 Hamilton Child; 1880 Ely; 1882 **Gold Brook** (misprint) Ely-Wallace; 1896 **Big Cold Brook** New; 1902 **Big Cold Brook** Blankman; 1908 **Big Cold Brook** Adm; 1912 **Big Cold Brook** Stoddard; 1921 USGS Stark Quad. / **Cold Brook**: t. Piercefield, trib. Tupper Lake. 1880 Ely; 1883 Ely-Wallace; 1896 New; 1902 Blankman; 1912 Stoddard; 1954 USGS Tupper Lake Quad. / **Cold Brook**: t. Clare, Middle Branch Grass(e) River. 1915 Russell Quad. / **Cold Brook**: t. Hopkinton, in Hollywood area, trib. Racquette River. / **Cold Brook**: t. Potsdam. / **Cold Brook Road**: r., t. Colton. / **Cold Brook School**: no. 3, common school, t. Colton. 1921 Stark Quad. / **Cold Hill Brook**: t. Hopkinton, trib. Hopkinton Brook, n. feature. 1964 USGS Nicholville Quad. / **Cold Pond**: t. Colton. 1921 USGS Stark Quad. / **Cold Spring**: 1/4 m. above barracks of Ogdensburg. *Quarterly*, 16 (1971), no. 2, p. 11. / **Cold Spring Creek**: trib. Big Creek, t. Pitcairn. 1916 USGS Oswegatchie Quad. / **Cold Spring School**: see **Cold Springs School**. / **Cold Spring State Forest**, #18, t. Pitcairn. / **Cold Springs**: on Grass(e) River, near Canton. *Quarterly*, 13 (1968), no. 3, p. 8; 25 (1980), no. 4, p. 4. / **Cold Springs School**: no. 23, common school, t. Lisbon, n. springs. / **Cold**

Springs Road: r., t. Lisbon.

Cole: surname used as a specific: **Cole Road**: r., t. DeKalb; s., v. Richville, also **Baerman Road**; r., t. Russell, n. Whitlock Cole from NH. / **Cole School**: no. 16, common school, t. Gouverneur. / **Cole's Creek**: t. Waddington and Louisville, n. family. See **Coles Creek**. / **Cole's Creek School**: no. 1, common school, t. Louisville. / **Coles Creek**: t. Louisville, n. Levi Cole. Durant, 397. 1964 USGS Louisville Quad. / **Coles Creek Campground and Marina**: t. Louisville, but near v. Waddington. / **Coles Creek Campsite Road**: r., t. Waddington.

Colgate Drive: s., v. Massena, n. Colgate University.

College: n. presence of a school of higher education: **College Court**: s., v. Canton, n. St. Lawrence College, now St. Lawrence University. / **College Park Road**: s., v. Potsdam. / **College Street**: s., v. Canton, n. St. Lawrence College, now St. Lawrence University.

Collins: surname used as a specific: **Collins**: h. t. Pitcairn, on Carthage & Adirondack Railroad; no longer exists. / **Collins Road**: r., t. Potsdam.

Colony Road: r., t. Edwards, off Route 58 to Fine, n. Alvin B. Colony, but a claim is also made for Harlow Colony. Also, **Coloney**.

Colton: t. southeastern corner of the county and stretch- ing far into the interior; n. from middle name of Jesse Colton Higley, landowner; t. formed from Parishville, Apr. 24, 1843 (Hough, 284, gives Apr. 12 as the date), the 27th t. in St. Lawrence County. Early petitioners wanted **Springfield** for the n. Higley proposed his own name, but he was very unpopular. However, it was agreed that if Higley would furnish powder for July 4 celebration, opposition to the place being named for him would be dropped. He did; they did. Situated on both sides of Racquette River, the t. contains 155,520 acres, the largest t. in New York. Durant, 453; Hough, 284-286; *Quarterly*, 9 (1964), no. 2, p. 6. The philanthropist A. Barton Hepburn was born in Colton. 1873 Hamilton Child, 104; 1908 Potsdam Quad; 1964 USGS Colton Quad. / **Colton**: formerly **Matildaville**, h. in t. Colton; p. o. est. June 19, 1851. as **Matildaville**, Israel C. Draper, pm, existing, ZIP 13625. See **Colton**. Also formerly **High Falls**. / **Colton Cemetery**: t. Colton. / **Colton Creek**: t. Russell, n. Colton family. 1915 USGS Russell Quad. / **Colton Hill**: t. Fine, n. "the numerous"

Colton family. / **Colton Hill School**: no. 3, common school, t. Fine, n. hill. Reynolds, 199. / **Colton Lane**: s., h. Star Lake / **Colton Road**: r., t. DeKalb, n. Luther Colton; r., t. Russell. / **Colton School**: no. 1, common school, t. Clare, n. Colton family. / **Colton Village School**: no. 1, common school, h. Colton.

Columbia: patriotic n., first used in a poem by Philip Freneau, 1775, as the n. for the new nation and spread to many places: **Columbia**: now h. of **Madrid**, p. o. est. Nov. 9, 1809, Asa Lord, first pm, changed to **Madrid**, Mar. 1, 1826. / **Columbia Road**: s., v. Massena, n. Columbia University. / **Columbia Street**: s., v. Morristown. / **Columbia Village**: now **Madrid**. See Hough, 344-348, 715, for information on this village.

Columbian Road: s., h. Cranberry Lake, t. Clifton, n. Columbian Hotel.

Columbiaville: See **Madrid**.

Colvin: n. Verplank Colvin, surveyor: Colvin Pond: t. Colton, n. Verplank Colvin, surveyor. 1880 Lake Colvin Ely; 1896 Colvin Lake; 1902 Colvin Lake Blankman; 1908 Colvin lake Adm; 1919 USGS Cranberry Lake Quad.

Commerce: n. business enterprises: **Commerce Drive**: s., v. Massena. / **Commerce Street**: s., v. Heuvelton. / **Commerce Street**: s., c. Ogdensburg.

Community Cemeteries: t. Louisville. 1964 USGS Louisville Quad.

Coney Island: summer camp, t. Pierrepont. n. Coney Island, New York City ocean front, south of Brooklyn. 1964 USGS Colton Quad.

Congdon: Dr. Randolph Congdon, principal of the Potsdam Normal School from 1919 to 1939: **Congdon House**: on Clarkson University campus. The Normal School was housed in what is now **Congdon Dormitory**. / **Congdon Campus School**: on SUC, Potsdam campus, used as a primary school and also for teacher education purposes, also known as the **Research & Demonstration Center**.

Conger: surname used as a specific: **Conger Bay**: in Black Lake, t. Morristown, n. Gerrit Conger. 1961 USGS Pope Mills Quad. / **Conger Road**: r., t. Hammond, n. several Conger families live along the road; r., t. Canton, n. possibly the J. J. Conger family; r., t. Macomb, n. Squire Conger.

Congress: Usually relating in a commendatory manner to the United

States Congress, but sometimes for a church group: **Congress Street**: r., t. Brasher; s., h. Brasher Falls; s., c. Ogdensburg; s., v. Rensselaer Falls, n. perhaps because Henry Van Rensselaer was a member of Congress and owned most of the land in the area. [Hartman]

Conifer: h., t. Piercefield. *Quarterly*, 3 (1958), no. 4, p. [6]: "A committee was set to name the place [submit a name for a new p. o.] but could not. A member looked out the window and observed the cones on the fir trees," hence the name. Founded by Emporium Lumber Co., which owned the mill, the workers' houses, the schools, and stores. *Quarterly*, 8 (1963), no. 4, p. 16; also, **At Your Leisure**, "Conifer Remembered," Nov. 18, 1984, p. 3; p. o. est. Feb. 24, 1912, William J. Snyder, first pm, changed to rural branch, Tupper Lake, Mar. 26, 1965; ZIP 12925; discontinued, May 10, 1972. 1954 USGS Tupper Lake Quad. / **Conifer Lake**: t. Piercefield. / **Conifer Road**: r., t. Piercefield, from Piercefield Village to Conifer.

Conkey: n. family: **Conkey Branch**: t. Clare, trib. Buck Brook. 1915 Russell Quad. / **Conkey School**: no. 13, common school, t. Canton, n. Conkey family, particularly Asa, Jacob, Thomas, and Joshua.

Conlin School: no. 12, common school, t. Hopkinton, n. John Conlin family.

Connell Preserve: t. Fine, n. D. C. Connell of New York City, owner of the 8,266 acre tract. See **Forest Commission Report, 1893**, p. 200.

Connie Woods Road: r., t. Waddington.

Connor Road: r., t. Parishville, n. Connor family.

Converse: corners, t. Stockholm, n. Elijah Converse, born 1792, Middlesex, VT. early settler in t. Parishville; p. o. est. Feb. 27, 1896, Levi R. Nye, pm, closed July 14, 1904. 1964 USGS Parishville Quad. / **Converse Road**: r., t. Stockholm, Hopkinton, n. Parker and Susannah Converse.

Cook: common surname used as a specific: **Cook Corners**: t. Clifton, n. John Cook. USGS Cranberry Lake Quad. 1898 **Cook's Hotel** New. 1902 Blankman's map lists a **Cook Hotel** on the corners. *Quarterly*, 7 (1962), no.1, p. 9. Also **Cooks Corners**. / **Cook Creek**: stream, trib. Natural Canal and Indian Creek, t. Canton. 1898 Blankman; 1964 Rensselaer

Falls Quad. / **Cook Hall**: on SUNY Canton College of Technology campus, n. Director (President) of School of Agriculture, 1908-1917. / **Cook Pond**: t. Clifton, alt. 1,471 ft. 188 **Deer Pond** Ely (misplaced); 1882 **Cooks Pond** Ely-Wallace; 1896 New; 1902 Blankman; 1908 Adm; 1912 Stoddard; 1911 USGS Cranberry Lake Quad. / **Cook Pond Outlet**: t. Colton, trib. South Branch Grass(e) River. 1921 USGS Stark Quad. / **Cook Road**: r., t. Hammond. n. Henry P. Cook, who resided on the road and was an inspector of schools in 1818; r., t. Hermon, n. Ellis Cook; s. v., Massena; r., t. Norfolk; r., t. Parishville, n. Cyrus and Libeus Cook from NH; r., t. Russell; r., t. Stockholm, n. Chester Cook. / **Cook School**: no. 15, common school, t. Pierrepont, n. G. and E. Cook families. See **Cooks Corners**. / **Cook Street**: s., v. Massena.

Cookham: a survey township, t. Parishville; origin of n. undetermined, but poss. English place n. from Berkshire; ety., OE **cocc** "hill" + OE **hamm** "meadow."

Cooks: possessive of **Cook**, surname: **Cooks Corners**: t. Pierrepont. / **Cooks Corners Cemetery**: t. Pierrepont. / **Cooks Corners School**: t. Pierrepont, Dist. 15. See **Cook School**. / **Cooks Pond**: R. R. Kerr, "Lumbering in the Adirondack Foothills," *Quarterly*, 9 (1964), no. 2, p. 13. See **Cook Pond**.

Coolen School: see **Coulin School**.

Coon: n. family: **Coon Hill Road**: r., t. Fine. / **Coon Road**: r., t. Parishville; r., t. Pierrepont, n. John Coon family, "a numerous line."

Cooper: surname used as a specific: **Cooper Falls**: See **Coopers Falls**. / **Cooper Hill**: t. Pitcairn, alt. 1,010 ft. 1951 USGS Harrisville Quad. / **Cooper Road**: r., t. Macomb, n. George Cooper from Scotland. / **Cooper Street**: s., v. Massena. / **Cooper's Falls**: see **Coopers Falls**. / **Coopers Corners**: t. Russell. 1915 USGS Russell Quad. / **Coopers Falls**: settlement, t. DeKalb. n. Judge William Cooper, father of James Fenimore Cooper, novelist. Judge Cooper, for whom DeKalb was first named, erected a grist mill at the falls (1803), one m. below DeKalb h. Durant, 356; *Quarterly*, 5 (1960), no. 3, npn. In 1848, The DeKalb Works at Cooper Falls organized and was incorporated in 1854 as the Cooper Falls Iron Works. By 1904, it was a ghost town. 1963 USGS Rensselaer Falls. Now, **Cooper Falls**. / **Coopers Falls School**:

no. 6, common school, t. DeKalb. Also, **Cooper's Falls School.** / **Cooper Service Complex**: on SUNY Canton College of Technology campus, n. William Cooper, former Vice President for Administration.

Copeland Oil Dock: t. Massena, formerly **Richards Landing**.

Copper Falls: in South Branch Grass(e) River, t. Clifton, n. for the metal. 1858 Rogerson.

Corbin School: no. 11, common school, t. Gouverneur, n. Corbin family. 1915 USGS Gouverneur Quad.

Corcoran Road: r., t. Pierrepont, n. Corcoran family.

Corduroy, The: log road 1/4 m. long, t. Edwards. *Quarterly*, 16 (1971), no.1, p. 9.

Cornell Avenue: s., v. Massena, n. Cornell University.

Cornelia Street: s., v. Rensselaer Falls, n. for a daughter of Henry Van Rensselaer.

Corrigan's Island: in St. Lawrence River, t. Waddington, n. Mr. Corrigan, millionaire owner of the island, who received it from Rebecca Ogden in 1859. Tedford, 52.

Costos: h., t. Clifton. 1916 USGS Oswegatchie Quad. Not otherwise identified except as noted on map by USGS.

Cotey's Corner: crossroads, t. Lawrence, n. Cotey family. 1964 USGS North Lawrence Quad.

Cottage: commendatory n., connoting rural setting; sometimes for a dwelling of any kind: **Cottage Road**: r., t. Colton, Higley Falls area, off Gulf Road. / **Cottage Street**: s., v. Norwood; s., v. Potsdam.

Cotter Road: r., t. Brasher, n. Cotter family.

Coughsagrage: The land north of the Totten's and Crossfield purchase is described as "beaver-hunting country of the Six Nations" and "deer-hunting ground of the Iroquois." Durant, 69-70. See **Irocoisia**.

Coulin: a family n., variant spellings include **Coulon**, **Coolen**: **Coulin Cemetery**: t. Parishville, private cemetery in Jo Indian Pond section. Listed on 1964 USGS Sylvan Falls Quad as **Coulch Cemetery**, a misprint. / **Coulin School**: no. 10, common, t. Parishville.

Country Club Road: r., t. Fowler; also a s., h, Hailesboro.

County: n. belonging to or pertaining to St. Lawrence County: **County Farm Road**: r., t. Canton. / **County Home**: built in 1869 to house the poor, a brick structure, designed by S. W. Lincoln, located on the bend of the Grass(e) River, 2 miles downstream from Canton. Also known as **Alms House**, **County Poor House**, and **Poor House**. Ordered to be destroyed in 1976 when the Social Services Unit of the county was moved to Harold B. Smith Office Building in Canton. See Dickinson and Crane. / **County Home Cemetery**: t. Canton, near the site of the former county home, on bank of Grass(e) River. 1964 USGS Canton Quad. / **County Island**: see **County Line Island**. / **County Line Island**: t. Piercefield, in Tupper Lake, between Piercefield (St. Lawrence Co) and Altamont (Franklin Co.). 1860 **County Island** Merrit; 1860 (?) **Long Island** Street, p. 189; 1883 Ely-Wallace; 1896 1902 Blankman; 1908 Adm; 1954 USGS Tupper Lake Quad. / **County Line Mountain**: t. Hopkinton (St. Lawrence Co.) and t. Waverly (Franklin Co.), alt. 2,122 ft. Also, **St. Lawrence Summit**. 1896 **County Line Mts** New; 1902 **County Line Mts.** Blankman; 1908 Adm; 1919 USGS Nicholville Quad; 1964 USGS Lake Ozonia Quad. Consists of four closely spaced peaks, only one of which is in St. Lawrence County. / **County Line Road**: r., t. Fowler. / **County Poor House**: see **County Home**.

Court: presence of a courthouse or for a surname: **Court Street**: s., v. Canton, n. county courthouse on the street; s., v. Edwards, prob. a surname.

Cousintown: prob. n. Thomas Cousin (or Cousins): **Cousintown**: t. Canton. Also sometimes **Cozens**. / **Cousintown Road**: r., t. DeKalb, Canton. / **Cousintown School**: no. 14, common school, t. Canton. Edward J. Austin, *Quarterly*, 10 (1965), no. 3, p. 13.

Cove: a valley or sheltered area; generic here used as specific: **Cove Creek**: t. Macomb, trib. Indian River. 1898 Blankman. / **Cove Road**: r., t. Colton, Higley Flow area.

Coventry Street: s., v. Massena.

Covey Road: r., t. Parishville, n. Sidney L. Covey and other family members from NH.

Covington Street: s., c. Ogdensburg,

n. Leonard Covington, general in War of 1812, wounded at the battle of Chrysler's Field.

Cow Horn Pond: see **Cowhorn Pond**.

Cowan Road: r., t. Canton. Same as **Cowen Mansion Road**.

Cowen Mansion Road: east of Canton. For Helen Cowen and John K. Cowen, railroad attorney and acting president of the Baltimore and Ohio Railroad. He built the mansion in late 1890s. *Quarterly*, 15 (1970), no. 1, p. 8.

Cowhorn Pond: t. Clifton, south of Cranberry Lake, alt. 1,740. *Quarterly*, 17 (1972), no. 2, p. 12. n. two inlets shaped like horns with main body resembling a cow's head. 1896 New; 1898 EGB, p. 27; 1902 **Cow Horn** Blankman; 1908 Adm; 1912 Stoddard; 1919 USGS Cranberry Lake Quad.

Cow Meadow: t. Parishville. 1908 USGS Potsdam Quad.

Cox's Mills: n. in 1838 for Gardner Cox (1794-1878). Cox arrived from Windsor Co., VT in 1813; moved to Hannawa, 1817, and est. several factories and mills. Now **Hannawa Falls**. *Quarterly*, 7 (1962), no. 3, p. 13; 6 (1961), npn.

Crab Island: in Black Lake, t. Morristown. 1961 USGS Pope Mills Quad.

Crabb Street: s., v. Norfolk, n. Crabb family.

Cracker Box Road: r., t. Russell, Fine, Clare, n. house shaped like old-time cracker box at end of road. At one time was a movie house. The house is still standing and used for public gatherings. *Quarterly*, 11 (1966), no. 4, p. 15. Also **Degrasse-Fine Road**.

Cracko: See **Chase Mills**.

Craig: n. family: **Craig Drive**: s., v. Canton. / **Craig School**: no. 7, common school, t. Lisbon.

Craig's Mills: t. Canton, p. o. est. Sept. 17, 1849 from **South Canton**, Truman Hunt, pm, changed to **Crary's Mills**, Dec. 10, 1849, to correct error by postal officials, who read **Crary's Mills** as **Craig's Mills**.

Cranberry Lake: lake, south St. Lawrence Co., t. Clifton, alt. 1,485 ft., n. the floating bogs covered with cranberry bushes (*Viburnum*). 1853 **Cranbery Lake** (misprint) HMC; 1873 Hamilton Child; 1878 Durant & Pierce; 1919 USGS Cranberry Lake Quad. / **Cranberry Lake**: h. in t. Clifton. 1896 **Harewood** New; 1908

Adm; 1912 Stoddard; 1919 USGS Cranberry Lake Quad. **Harewood** was changed to **Cranberry Lake** after the dam was built; p. o. changed to **Harewood**, Mar. 13, 1891, Samuel Bancroft, pm, closed May 11, 1893; reopened as **Cranberry Lake**, Aug. 26, 1902, Samuel Bancroft, pm; still existing, ZIP 12927. / **Cranberry Lake Dam**: Cranberry Lake is not a natural lake but was developed as a reservoir. In 1854, the New York State Legislature passed a bill that declared the Oswegatchie River a public highway and that improvements would be made in it for commercial purposes. By an act passed on April 21, 1865, companies and water users were empowered to build a dam to control the flow of water through the Oswegatchie. A dam was completed in 1867 and three succeeding ones since. Clara McKenney, "The Cranberry Lake Dam," *Quarterly*, 10 (1965), no. 4, 6-7, 19. / **Cranberry Lake Inlet**: t. Fine. 1880 **Big Inlet** Ely; 1883 **Big Inlet** Ely-Wallace; 1896 **Oswegatchie River** New; 1902 Blankman; 1908 Adm; 1912 Stoddard; 1919 USGS **Oswegatchie River** Cranberry Lake Quad. See **Oswegatchie River**; **Inlet Flow**, t. Clifton. / **Cranberry Lake Inn**: owned and operated by the Emporium Forestry Co. Formerly, **Bishop's Old Log Hotel**. *Quarterly*, 3 (1958), no. 4, p. [6]. / **Cranberry Lake School**: became Union Free School, District 2. Reynolds, 9. / **Cranberry Pond**: t. Clare. 1896 New; 1902 Blankman; 1921 USGS Stark Quad. / **Cranberry Pond**: on t. Edward and t. Pitcairn line. Now, **Pine Hill Pond**.

Crandallville: for Crandall family. Now, **Howardville**.

Crane: n. the bird; also often a surname: **Crane Pond**: t. Clifton. n. the bird of the family **Gruidae**. 1896 New; 1908 Adm; 1912 Stoddard; 1919 USGS Cranberry Lake Quad. / **Crane Road**: r., t. Stockholm. / **Crane School**: no. 15, common school, t. Canton, n. Olvison O. Crane family, prominent benefactors in Pyrites. / **Crane School**: no. 9. common school, t. Parishville, n. William and Polly Crane, who owned a house opposite the school. See *Sketches of Parishville*. / **Crane School of Music Center**: on campus of SUC, Potsdam, n. Julie Etta Crane, who taught music at the then-Normal School from 1884 to 1926. *Quarterly*, 11 (1966), no. 3, p. 12.

Crary: surname used as a specific: **Crary Drive**: s., v. Canton, n. Crary family. See **Crary Mills**. / **Crary Gap**: t. Clare, n. Crary family. / **Crary Mills**: h., t. Potsdam, n. Edward Crary who built a gristmill on the site. p. o. est., Dec. 10, 1849, as **Crary's Mills**, change from **Craig's Mills**, with Truman Hunt, first pm. In 1894, the apostrophe was dropped in all names on the authority of the Post Office Department. On Mar. 11, 1984, n. changed to **Crary Mills**, Nellie Witters, pm, closed Jan. 31, 1928. Also see *Quarterly*, 17 (1972), no. 3, p. 11. 1964 USGS Pierrepont Quad. / **Crary Mills Cemetery**: t. Canton, Pierrepont, and Potsdam. / **Crary Mills-Langdon Corners Road**: r., t. Canton. / **Crary Mills- Canton Road**: r., t. Potsdam. / **Crary Mills State Forest**, #48, t. Potsdam. / **Crary Road**: r., t. Pierrepont, n. Crary family. / **Crary School**: no. 13, common school, t. Pierrepont. / **Crary's Mills**: see **Crary Mills**. / **Crary's Mills School**: no. 13, common school, t. Potsdam.

Crarytown School: no. 3, common school, t. Pierrepont, Also, **Brick School, Andrews School** (until June 1958).

Crapser Island: n. John Crapser. See **Ogden Island**. *Quarterly*, 1 (1956), no. 3, npn.

Cream of the Valley Road: r., t. Gouverneur, n. cheese factory.

Creek: n. a stream: **Creek, The**: h., t. Rossie, no longer existing. Laura Gillett, "Spragueville Had a Busy Past," *Quarterly*, 6 (1961), no. 1, p. 7. / **Creek School**: no. 2, common school, t. Edwards., Dist. 2. Freeman, 16. Leah Noble, "Edwards Pioneers," *Quarterly*, 7 (1962), no. 2, pp. 8-9, 15-16. Also, **Barraford School**. / **Creek School**: no. 8, common school, t. Fowler. / **Creek Settlement**: 2-1/2 m. southeast of Edwards. Durant, 444.

Crescent: n. shape: **Crescent Street**: s., v. Canton; s., v. Norwood; s., c. Ogdensburg, n. shape along river. Also, **The Crescent**.

Crobar Road: r., t. Lisbon, n. Crobar family.

Crocker: settlement, t. Massena, p. o. est. Mar. 8, 1867, Thomas Crocker, pm, changed to **Massena Springs**, Mar. 19, 1867.

Crofton: t. Hermon, p. o. est. Jan. 6, 1898, n. Fred M. Croft, pm, closed July 31, 1903.

Croil's Island: in St. Lawrence River, t. Louisville, n. William Croil, who came from Glasgow, Scotland, in 1835. He bought Stacy island, renamed it for himself. His home on the island was called Kelvin Grove. His sons John who named his farm and home **Archerfield** and William who called his **God's Acre** succeeded him. A brother, John, lived at Aultsville and named his home Sunnyside. Previous names were **Ile au Chamailles** (French); **Tsiiowen-okwakarate** (Mohawk), "high island"; **Baxter**, for Asa Baxter, who owned the island in 1812 when it belonged to England and who refused to fight for the English in the War of 1812 and lost his title (See Durant, 200); **Stacy**, for the owner who succeeded Baxter; and then Croil. Also, **Grand Eddy Island** on 1779 map; and **Upper Long Saut** (Burr's map). Also, **Croils Island.** / **Croil Islands**: three islands in St. Lawrence River, t. Louisville. 1964 USGS Massena Quad. / **Croil's Island School**: no. 14, common school, t. Louisville.

Crooked: n. twisting shape or flow: **Crooked Creek**: rises in Jefferson Co., flows through t. Hammond into Chippewa Bay, St. Lawrence River, n. because very crooked near mouth. 1898 Blankman; 1958 USGS Chippewa Quad. / **Crooked Lake**: t. Colton, alt. 1,405. 1858 **Croked Pond** (misprint) Rogerson; 1860 **Crooked Pond** Merrit; 1865 **Crooked Pond**; 1873 **Crooked Pond** Hamilton Child; 1880 **Crooked Pond** Ely; 1883 **Crooked Pond** Ely-Wallace; 1896 **Crooked Pond** New; 1908 Adm; 1912 Stoddard; 1920 USGS Childwold Quad. / **Crooked Pond**: t. Colton, near Hollywood area. *Quarterly*, 13 (1968), no. 3, p. 19. See **Crooked Lake**, t. Colton.

Crosbie Road: r., t. Potsdam. Same as **Daily Ridge Road**.

Cross: usually for a road or street that intersects: **Cross Street**; s., v. Edwards, between Island and New Streets; s., t. Madrid, between Main and North Streets.

Crossing, The: early name for h. **Oswegatchie**, t. Fine.

Crossover Island: t. Hammond, in St. Lawrence River, near Oak Point; a lighthouse was erected on it in 1847. The island served as a marker where down river ships crossed from the American to the Canadian side. Early ferry from Oak Point to Canada touched there. Nickname, **Stony Lonesome**. 1958 USGS Chippewa Quad.

Crowley Road: r., t. Parishville, n. Crowley family.

Crow's Nest: island in St. Lawrence River, t. Hammond, at Oak Point. 1963 USGS Morristown Quad.

Crow-crow: See **Chase Mills**.

Crumack: t. Brasher, Irish survey township; ety. Irish **cromoge**, but derived from British **crumbo-** "crooked,' a river name, "crooked river."

Crumb Library: on the SUC, Potsdam campus, n. Frederick W. Crumb, president from 1946 to 1967.

Crump Road: r., t. Stockholm, n. Crump family.

Crusher Road: r., t. Canton, prob. n. use of stone crusher on road.

Crysler: surname used as a specific: **Crysler Island**: in St. Lawrence River, t. Louisville. / **Crysler Island Shoal**: in St. Lawrence River, t. Louisville. 1964 USGS Louisville Quad.

Crystal Lake: pond, t. Fine, n. clear water. *Quarterly*, 1 (1956), npn. 1916 USGS Oswegatchie Quad.

Cubley: Frank L. Cubley (1870-1960), native of Potsdam, had a long career as an attorney, president of the local Board of Education and of Potsdam Hospital (for 30 years), and trustee of Clarkson University from 1907 to his death: **Cubley Hall**: on Clarkson University campus. / **Cubley Park**: at corner of LeRoy Street and Lawrence Avenue.

Cummings Street: s., v. Massena.

Cunnie Woods Road: r., t. Waddington. Tedford, 52. Also, **Connie Woods Road**.

Cunningham Road: r., t. Canton, n. Isadore Cunningham. Also **Old Forest House Road**.

Curran Road: r., t. Louisville, n. Curran family.

Curtis: surname used as a specific: **Curtis Avenue**: s., v. Massena. / **Curtis Hall**: at St. Lawrence State Hospital, n. Newton Martin Curtis, an assemblyman who gave active support to est. the hospital. *Quarterly*, 11 (1966), no. 4, p. 19. / **Curtis Plains**: t. Russell. Clarke, 28. / **Curtis Pond**: t. Colton. 1883 Ely-Wallace; 1896 New; 1902 Blankman; 1912 Stoddard; 1919 USGS Cranberry Lake Quad. / **Curtis Road**: r., t. Russell, n. Ashbel Curtis; r., t. Stockholm, n. Henry A. Curtis.

Customs House: c. Ogdensburg, the oldest continuously government-owned building operated by the General Services Administration. *Quarterly*, 11 (1966), no. 1, p. 10.

Cutler Road: r., t. Hopkinton, n. Cutler family.

Cutry Lane: s., v. Massena, n. Cutry family.

Cutting Preserve: t. Hopkinton, a private forest and hunting preserve, n. Frank A. Cutting of Boston, MA. See **Forest Commission Report**, 1893, p. 192.

D

Dailey Ridge Cemetery: n. the Dailey family, t. Madrid. *Quarterly*, 22 (1977), no. 2, p. 9. Also **Daily**, *Quarterly*, 6 (1961), npn.

Daily: surname used as a specific: **Daily Ridge Road**: r., t. Potsdam. Same as **Crosbie Road.** / **Daily Ridge School**: no. 14, common school, t. Potsdam, n. Daily family. Also **Dailey** on 1896 Blankman. / **Daily Road**: r., t. Gouverneur. H. Daily shown living on present road, Beers, 31. Also L. Dailey is listed as being on the Seavey Road intersecting on the north. On some maps, the name is **Dailey**, which may be the correct spelling. Homer W. Dailey, son of Henry Dailey, b. 1861, lived on the Tuthill Road. Cent. Souv., 304. Tuthill may be Tuttle, since Beers, 31 shows S. P. Tuttle and G. P. Tuttle living on the same road as H. Daily. Also **Dailey Road.** / **Daily School**: no. 9, common school, t. Lisbon, n. James Dayley. with spelling change.

Dains: see **Danes.**

Dale Road: s., v. Gouverneur.

Dalton Crossing: railroad crossing, t. Waddington, n. Dalton family. 1964 USGS Chase Mills Quad.

Daly Road: r., t. Brasher.

Dam Road: s., h. Piercefield.

Damon Hall: on Clarkson University Campus, n. on June 1, 1963, to honor Ralph Shepard Damon (1897-1956), chairman of Board of Trustees from 1945 to 1955, also held positions as president of Curtiss-Wright Airplane Company, American Airlines, Inc., Republic Aviation Corporation, Trans World Airlines, Inc., and director of many corporations.

Dan Forth Place: see **Danforth Place.**

Dan Wright Brook: t. Hopkinton, trib. Trout Brook. 1964 USGS Parishville Quad.

Dana: surname. **Dana Hill**: t. Russell, n. Harvey Dana family of numerous sons. "Judson Hamilton married Lottie Dana of Dana Hill." Eugene Hatch, "Orchards of Hamilton Hill," *Quarterly*, 16 (1971), no. 4, p. 8. 1915 USGS Russell Quad. / **Dana Hill Road**: r., t. Russell. See **Dana Hill.** / **Dana Physical Education Complex**: on SUNY Canton College of Technology campus, n. Evan Dana, Professor of Agriculture and Coach, 1935-1971. / **Dana Point**: on St. Lawrence River, t. Hammond, n. Theodore Dana family of many river men. Also, **Daney Point**, the spelling reflecting local pronunciation. 1958 **Daney Point** USGS Chippewa Quad. / **Dana Street**: s., v. Massena. Also, **Dane Street.**

Dandy Road: r., t. Lisbon, n. Dandy family.

Dane Road: r., t. Gouverneur.

Danes: n. James Dane: **Danes Corners**: crossroads, t. Russell. 1915 USGS Russell Quad. Also **Dains Corners.** / **Danes School**: t. Russell. Also **Dains.**

Daney Point: see **Dana Point.**

Danforth Place: s., v. Massena, n. James Danforth. Also misspelled **Dan Forth.**

Dark Island: in St. Lawrence River, t. Hammond, n. the dark grove of trees on a 7-acre island, now called **Jorstadt Island. Dark Island Castle** (now **Jorstadt Island Castle**) was built from 1904-06 for Frederick G. Bourne, president of Singer Sewing Machine Company. Designed by Ernest Flagg, it was constructed of native granite quarried on nearby Oak Island. Property also contains icehouse, boathouses, caretaker's cottage, tennis and squash courts. The island is now owned by the Rev. George Martin, who holds non-denominational services here in the summer. 1958 USGS Chippewa Quad. See **Twilight Island.** Also once n. **Bluff Island**, descriptive of the 50-foot hill that occupies 1/2 of the island.

Darning Needle Pond: t. Clifton, desc. for shape, "lies along one of the forks of north-flowing Chair Rock Creek, which becomes Chair Rock Flow at the south end the lake [Cranberry Lake]." See Walter B. Gunnison, "In Search of John Cheever's 'Cranberry Lake'," Sunday Weekly, *Watertown Daily Times*, Sept. 2, 1990, p. 5.

Dashnaw: n. family: **Dashnaw Road**: r., t. Oswegatchie. / **Dashnaw Street**: s., h. Richville.

David: masculine first name: **David Street**: s., c. Ogdensburg / **David Street, East**: s., c. Ogdensburg.

Davies Cemetery: t. Oswegatchie, large private family cemetery on Black Lake between Stone Church Road and McCormick Road. 1963 USGS Edwardsville Quad.

Davis: n. family: **Davis Road**: s., h. Richville and r., t. DeKalb, n. Davis family, early Welsh settlers. / **Davis Road**: r., t. Pierrepont, poss. n. James Davis. / **Davis Street**: r., t. Waddington.

Dawley: n. family: **Dawley Hill**: t. Edwards. h. Talcville. Freeman, 9. / **Dawley School**: no. 15, common school, t. Lisbon.

Day: surname used as a specific: **Day School**: no. 7, common school, t. Hermon, n. John Day from Herkimer. 1915 USGS Gouverneur Quad **Days School**. / **Day's Mill Road**: r., t. Hopkinton, now Route 72. *Quarterly*, 15 (1970), no. 2, p. 18. Also **Days Mill Road**. / **Days Mill**: t. Hopkinton, 3 mi. southeast of Nicholville, near Franklin Co. line, n. a Mr. Day. 1919 USGS Nicholville Quad. Also **Day's Mill**.

Dayton Road: r., t. Potsdam. / **Dayton School**: no. 26, common school, t. Potsdam. Origin n. not determined.

De Kalb: see **DeKalb. De Kalb** is the USGS official spelling, but the editors here have opted for the **DeKalb** spelling as more traditional and in current usage.

De Peyster: see **DePeyster. De Peyster** is the USGS official spelling. The editors have chosen the **DePeyster** spelling because it is traditional and in current usage.

Dead: n. applied to a body of water that has little if any current; sluggish: **Dead Brook**: see **Sterling Pond Outlet**. / **Dead Brook**: t. Louisville, trib. Grass(e) River. 1898 Blankman. / **Dead Brook**: t. Parishville. See **Dead Creek** (t. Parishville), official USGS name. / **Dead Creek**: t. Fine, trib. Cranberry Lake. 1896 New; 1919 USGS Cranberry Lake Quad. See **Dead Creek Flow**, t. Clifton. / **Dead Creek**: t. Parishville, trib. Racquette River. 1896 New; 1898 EGB map; 1908 Adm; 1964 USGS Sylvan Falls Quad. Also **Dead Brook**. / **Dead Creek**: t. Piercefield, trib. Racquette River. 1858 Rogerson; 1860 Street, p. 267; 1860 Merrit; 1880 Ely; 1883 Ely-Wallace; 1896 New; 1908 Adm; 1954 USGS Tupper Lake Quad. /

Dead Creek: t. Colton, trib. Racquette River. 1853 HMC; 1858 Rogerson; 1908 USGS Potsdam Quad; 1912 Stoddard; 1964 USGS Rainbow Falls Quad. / **Dead Creek**: t. Clifton, trib. South Branch Grass(e) River. 1873 Hamilton Child; 1878 Durant & Pierce; 1896 New; 1908 Adm; 1921 USGS Stark Quad. / **Dead Creek Flow**: inlet, Cranberry Lake, t. Clifton. 1896 New; 1902 **South Inlet** Blankman; 1908 **South Inlet** Adm; 1912 **South Inlet** Stoddard; 1919 USGS Cranberry Lake Quad. / **Dead Creek Flow**: flows into Lake Ozonia. *Quarterly*, 25 (1980), no. 3, p. 5. / **Dead Creek Road**: t. Colton.

Dean: n. family: **Dean Brook**: trib. Van Rensselaer Creek, t. Pierrepont. 1915 USGS Russell Quad. / **Dean High School** gift of Myra Dean and daughters Jennie and Cora in 1914; : now **Gouverneur Central School**. / **Dean Road**: r., t. Clare. Also **Middle Branch Road**. / **Deans Corners**: t. Pierrepont, at intersection of Stone School House Road and Eells Road, n. Dean family. 1915 USGS Russell Quad.

Dean-Eaton Hall: on St. Lawrence University campus, n. Emily Eaton Hepburn and Cora and Emily Dean.

Dearborn Street: s., c. Ogdensburg, n. Henry Dearborn (1751-1829), American Revolutionary War hero and general.

Debra Drive: s., v. Potsdam.

Deer: Because the animal is so numerous in the United States, many places carry the n., usually associated with a sighting or an incident involving the deer: **Deer Island**: in Hamlin Bay, Tupper Lake, t. Piercefield. 1896 New. / **Deer Lick Brook**: t. Russell, trib. Little River. 1915 USGS Russell Quad. / **Deer Pond**: t. Piercefield. 1880 Ely; 1883 **Egg Pond** Ely-Wallace; 1896 New; 1902 Blankman; 1908 Adm; 1912 Stoddard; 1954 USGS Tupper Lake Quad. / **Deer Pond**: see **Silver Lake**. / **Deer Pond**: see **Cook Pond**. / **Deer Pond**: t. Fine. *Quarterly*, 5 (1960), no. 1, npn. / **Deer Pond**: t. Hopkinton, alt. 1,506 ft. 1860 Merrit; 1880 Ely; 1896 New; 1896 Adm; 1912 Stoddard; 1920 USGS Childwold Quad. / **Deer River**: t. Stockholm. *Quarterly*, 14 (1969), no. 4, p. 20. Also, t. Brasher, trib. St. Regis River. 1964 Hogansburg Quad; 1873 Hamilton Child, p. 89. / **Deer River Road**: r., t. Brasher. / **Deer-hunting grounds of the Iroquois**: country north of the Totten's and Crossfield's Purchase. Durant, 69.

Deerlick Rapids: n. for place where deer find salt, in South Branch Grass(e) River, t. Clifton. 1921 USGS Stark Quad. / **Deerlick Rapids Club**: noted on 1896 New.

Deerskin Creek: stream, trib. Middle Branch Grass(e) River, t. Clare and Colton; flows into Grass(e) River, n. incident involving the skin of a deer. 1921 Stark Quad; 1912 **Mud Creek** Stoddard; 1902 **Mud Creek** Blankman; 1896 **Mud Brook** New. / **Deerskin Pond**: t. Colton. 1921 USGS Stark Quad.

Degrasse: h., t. Russell, est. June 5, 1882; n. Comte de Francois Joseph Paul de Grasse (1722-1788), the French officer who played a decisive role in the Yorktown campaign when Cornwallis surrendered. His efforts contributed strongly to the winning of American independence; and in appreciation, the U. S. Congress gave him four captured cannon from the Yorktown battlefield. These were destroyed at his home in France by a mob in 1834. He was related by marriage to Theodosius Fowler; p. o. est. as **DeGrasse**, June 5, 1882, Abner H. Armstrong, first pm, changed to **Degrasse**, Apr. 7, 1894, Eneas Ingerson, pm; terminated in 1980s. Also **De Grasse, DeGrasse**. Formerly, **Monterey**. / **Degrasse-Fine Road**: r., t. Fine. Also **Cracker Box Road**. / **Degrasse-Russell Road**: r., t. Russell. / **DeGrasse State Forest**, #13, t. Russell.

DeKalb: west of center of the county, one of the ten original t., formed Feb. 21, 1806 from Oswegatchie; t. bought by William Cooper, father of James Fenimore Cooper, the novelist, in 1803 from Samuel Ogden; n. Johann Kalb, known as Baron Johann de Kalb, Revolutionary War hero, killed while commanding the Maryland division of the Southern Army at Camden, NJ, in 1780. *Quarterly*, 21 (1976), no. 1, p. 12. 1873 **Dekalb** Hamilton Child, p. 107; 1956 USGS **De Kalb** Bigelow Quad; 1963 USGS **De Kalb** Rensselaer Falls Quad. The n. has three spellings used locally: **DeKalb** (the most often used), **Dekalb**, and **De Kalb** (the USGS official spelling). / **DeKalb:** h. Now known as **Old DeKalb**. Formerly **Cooper's Village**. Durant, 351 ff. Formerly, **Williamstown**, n. after **William** Cooper; p. o. est. Apr. 1, 1807, William Cleghorn, first pm, changed to **Dekalb**, Dec. 1895 (day unknown), Asa J. Moore, pm, closed Nov. 15, 1902. In New York Postal History, the pm are noted as William Claghorn and Ara J. Moore, in error.

/ **DeKalb-Hermon Railroad** (spur): After mines at Stellaville abandoned, the Syracuse contractor, Abe Cooper, bought rails, mill equipment, and 3.61 miles of track in 1926. The Adirondack and St. Lawrence Railroad of the St. Lawrence Pyrites Company prior to 1905 operated a spur at Stellaville for hauling ore. In 1905 the company extended the line to Hermon for general freight and passengers, continuing until 1926. / DeKalb-Depeyster Road: r., t. DeKalb. / **DeKalb Junction**: h. at junction of main line of the Rome, Watertown & Ogdensburg Railroad; p. o. est. Dec. 1, 1863, Israel D. Smith, first pm, changed to **Dekalb Junction**, Dec. 1895, Arthur L. Hemenway, pm, changed Dec. 1905 to **DeKalb Junction**, Allerton C. Farr, pm; p. o. existing, ZIP 13630. Also see Durant, 357. 1873 **DeKalb Junction** Hamilton Child, p. 107; 1963 USGS **De Kalb Junction** Rensselaer Quad. / **DeKalb Junction-Rensselaer Falls Road**: r., t. DeKalb, Canton. / **DeKalb Junction- Richville Road**: r., t. DeKalb. / **DeKalb Junction Road**: r., t. DeKalb. / **DeKalb Junction-Russell Road**; r., t. DeKalb, Hermon, Russell. / **DeKalb Junction School**: no. 22, common school, t. DeKalb. / **DeKalb Road**: s., v. Canton to Old DeKalb. / **DeKalb School**: no. 4, common school, t. DeKalb.

Delack Point: on St. Lawrence River, t. Morristown, n. Delack family. 1963 USGS Morristown Quad.

Delaney: surname used as a specific: **Delaney Island**: t. Massena, slightly west of Long Sault Island, in St. Lawrence River, n. Thomas Delaney. Dumas, 30. / **Delaney Road**: r., t. Oswegatchie, n. Delaney family. /**Delaney Woods**: borders Black Lake. *Quarterly*, 10 (1965), no. 1, p. 8. / **Delany Shoal**: in St. Lawrence River, t. Massena. 1964 USGS Massena Quad; see **Delaney Island**.

DeMott Road: r., t. Morristown, n. Isaac De Mott, first settler on the road. Also **DeMot Road**, a misspelling of the original.

Denner Road: r., t. Hammond, n. Henry and Joseph Denner and descendants, later colorful law officers, said to have been "pirates" in early years, on the "other side of the law."

Dennis Road: r., t. Madrid, n. Dennis family.

Dennison Road: r., t. Massena, n. Dennison family. Also **Denison**.

Denny Street: s., c. Ogdensburg, n.

Denny family; also **St. Denny**.

Denton Road: r., t. Lawrence, n. Denton family.

DePau: t. Hermon, est. as t. formed from Edwards and DeKalb, April 17, 1830, n. Francis (or Francois) DePau of New York, who was involved in the French Purchase in Jefferson County (Durant, 435). Because of the similarity with Depauville in Jefferson County, the n. was changed to **Hermon**, Feb. 28, 1834. **DePau** is the historically correct spelling, but variants have crept in writings over the years. Also see *Quarterly*, 8 (1963), no. 4, p. 16. Also **Depau**.

DePeyster: t. formed from Oswegatchie and DeKalb, Mar. 24, 1825, to take effect on Apr. 1, 1825. The first name proposed was **Stilwell**, for Smith Stilwell, prominent citizen and first supervisor. Then it was n. for Frederick De Peyster of New York, a shipping merchant, who owned the portion of the town that had been a part of DeKalb. Durant, 366, wrote, "He contributed to the building of Bethel Union Church, and his son made a present of a bell for it. De Peyster never visited the place." See also *Quarterly*, 5 (1960), no. 4, p. 9; Hough, 293-294. Formerly, **Bristol's Settlement**. 1963 USGS Edwardsville Quad. / **DePeyster**: h. on Old State Road; p. o. est. Sept. 10, 1827, Smith Stilwell, pm (Hough, 574), changed to **Depeyster**, Dec. 1895, Ada L. Ward, pm, changed to **DePeyster**, Dec. 1905, Thaddeus P. Day, pm; p. o. existing, ZIP 13633. Also **Depeyster, De Peyster, Depeysster**. **Punch Lock** (or **Punchlock**) is an affectionate nickname. 1873 **DePeyster** Hamilton Child, p. 113; 1963 USGS **De Peyster** Heuvelton Quad. / **DePeyster Corners**: t. Depeyster. / **DePeyster-DeKalb Road**: r., t. DeKalb. / **DePeyster- Heuvelton Road**: r., t. DePeyster. / **DePeyster School**: no. 1, common school, t. DePeyster.

Depot: n. road or street leading to a railway station. Now only freight trains pass through, and all the depots have either been razed or turned into other types of buildings: **Depot Boulevard**: s., h. Madrid. / **Depot Street**: s., v. Edwards; s., v. Gouverneur, from Pooler Street to East Main Street; s., h. Hammond; s., h. Madrid; s., v. Massena; s., v. Norwood; s., v. Potsdam; s., v. Richville, also **Richville-Bigelow Road**.

DePue Road: r., t. Canton, n. DePue family.

Derbys Corners: t. Russell, n. Capt.

Hiry Derby, officer in Mexican War, superintendent of schools of St. Lawrence County, school teacher, Civil War officer, merchant. Durant, 434. 1915 USGS Russell Quad.

Desmond: n. Patrick Desmond: **Desmond Road**: r., t. Lawrence. / **Desmond Street**: s., h. North Lawrence.

Devillers Street: s., c. Ogdensburg, n. Louis C. A. de Villers, who came to America from France with Count Le Ray de Chaumont to serve in the Revolutionary War. His son-in-law was George N. **Seymour**.

Devils Elbow: dangerous bend in the road: r., t. Russell. 1915 USGS Russell Quad; r., t. Macomb.

Devine Road; r., t. Canton, from Rice Road towards Route 11, n. Devine family.

Devoy's Landing: see *Quarterly*, 10 (1965), no. 1, p. 8.

Dewey: n. family: **Dewey Avenue**: s., h. Piercefield. / **Dewey School**: no. 2, common school, t. Clare, poss. n. Chester Dewey family.

Dewitt: formerly a survey township, but now part of t. Pierrepont, Russell; n. Simeon DeWitt, surveyor-general of New York.

Dexter Street: s., v. Gouverneur.

Dezell Road: r., t. Lisbon, n. Dezell family.

Dickinsons Landing: on Barnhart Island, t. Massena. Dumas, 27. A Dickinsons Landing is also on the Canadian side of the St. Lawrence River.

Dies Street: s., v. Canton, n. George Dies.

Dilcox School: no. 24, common school, t. Lisbon, n. Dilcox family.

Dillabough: r., t. Pierrepont, n. Dillabough family.

Dillon Pond: t. Clifton, alt. 1,498 ft., n. Dillon family. 1880 Ely (misplaced); 1883 Ely-Wallace; 1896 New; 1902 Blankman; 1908 Adm; 1919 USGS Cranberry Lake Quad.

Dishaw: n. family: **Dishaw**: h., t. Louisville. 1964 USGS Chase Mills Quad. / **Dishaw Road**: r., t. Louisville, Norfolk.

Dismal Swamp: t. Clifton and Colton, n. either a gloomy place or a generic, translated from an Indian language, "swamp." See Stewart, p. 138. 1921 USGS Stark Quad.

Division: n. separation of areas: **Division Street**: s., c. Ogdensburg, two-block long street between Washington and Ford Streets, no longer existing; s., v. Potsdam.

Dixon: surname used as a specific: **Dixon Corners**: crossroads, t. Madrid, n. Dixon family. 1964 USGS Chase Mills Quad. / **Dixon Corners Cemetery**: t. Madrid. / **Dixon Island**: in St. Lawrence River, t. Lisbon. 1906 USGS Red Mills Quad. / **Dixon School**: no. 3, common school, t. Madrid, n. Dixon family.

Doane Road: r., t. Fowler, n. Doane family.

Dobbs Road: r., t. Pitcairn, n. Dobbs family.

Dodds: n. family: **Dodds Creek**: t. Rossie, trib. Indian River, n. Dodds family from Scotland. 1961 USGS Muskellunge Lake Quad. / **Dodds School**: no. 3, common school, t. Gouverneur, n. Dodds family from Scotland. 1915 USGS Gouverneur Quad.

Dodge: surname used as a specific: **Dodge Creek**: t. Massena, trib. Massena Power Canal, n. Thomas Dodge, a major in the Revolutionary War and early settler. 1964 USGS Massena Quad. / **Dodge Grove**: t., Gouverneur, n. Dodge family. / **Dodge Landing**: on St. Lawrence River, t. Massena, n. Samuel Dodge from Fairlee, VT. Also, **Dodges Landing.** / **Dodge Place**: s., v. Gouverneur, n. Judge Edwin Dodge (1801-1877), who settled in 1829 as an agent of Gouverneur Morris. He was pm from 1830-1849, trustee of the Gouverneur Wesleyan Seminary, president over the proceedings to incorporate the v. in 1850, and president of the v. 1872-76. Durant, 337-342. Beers, 33, shows an E. Dodge living near where the present street is. / **Dodge Pond**: t. Fine, on private land near Cracker Box Road. *Quarterly*, 5 (1960), no. 1, npn. / **Dodge Street**: s., v. Massena, n. Thomas Dodge. / **Dodgeville** : h., t. Fowler. See **Dodge Place**.

Dog: n. shape or for an incident involving dogs: **Dog Pond**: t. Colton, n. shaped like a dog's head. *Quarterly*, 13 (1968), no. 3, p. 19. 1880 **Trout Pond** Ely; 1883 **Trout Pond** Ely-Wallace; 1896 New; 1902 Blankman; 1908 Adm; 1912 Stoddard; 1954 USGS Tupper Lake Quad. / **Dog Pond Mountain**: t. Colton, alt. 2,450. 1896 New; 1902 **Dog Pound Mountain** (misprint) Blankman; 1954 USGS

Tupper Lake Quad. / **Dog Street School**: t. Edwards, Dist. 7. Freeman, 16. Also, **Fullerville School**.

Donald Avenue: s., h. Hammond, n. Donald family.

Dollar Road: r., t. Oswegatchie, Lisbon, n. Dollar family.

Donahue: surname used as a specific: **Donahue Hall**: on Clarkson University campus, n. Timothy S. Donahue, popular student adviser and director of Clarkson residences from 1958 to 1966. / **Donahue Road**: r., t. Massena, n. A. F. Donahue.

Donald M. Young Memorial Park: t. Parishville, n. a town supervisor, 1973; on outer Catherine Street on West Branch of St. Regis River.

Donovan School: no. 12, common school, t. Lawrence, n. Donovan family.

Doolittle Hill: t. Russell, n. Nelson Doolittle, who purchased the Russell Atwater House in Russell from Elihu Phelps on Nov. 1, 1844.

Doran: n. family: **Doran Cemetery**: t. Madrid. Also **Doren.** / **Doran Road**: r., t. Clifton, and s., h. Star Lake. / **Doran School**: no. 9, common school, near Bucks Bridge, t. Madrid, n. Leonard Doran.

Dorwin: s., v. Gouverneur, prob. n. Gustavus Dorwin.

Doud: n. family: **Doud Brook**: t. Louisville. / **Doud School**: no. 17, common school, t. Oswegatchie, also, **Dowd Road**.

Douglas: common surname used as specific: **Douglas Road**: s., v. Massena. Formerly, **Douglass Road**, n. Douglass family. Spelling has been changed through usage. / Douglas Rock: t. Colton, alt. 1,850. 1954 USGS Tupper Lake Quad. / **Douglas School**: no. 7, common school, t. Colton, n. John Douglas and his numerous offspring. / **Douglas Street**: s., v. Gouverneur, n. Douglas family.

Douglass Ridge: t. Norfolk, n. William Douglass (1831- 1904), settler, from Earl Hill, England. Susan C. Lyman, "Douglass Farm," *Quarterly*, 12 (1967), no. 1, p. 16. Now, **Tiernan Ridge**. / **Douglass Road**: see **Douglas Road**.

Dove School: no. 22, common school, t. Potsdam, n. Dove family.

Dover Street: s., v. Massena.

Dowd Road: see **Doud**.

Dowling Road: r., t. Fine, n. Dowling family.

Downerville: h., t. Russell, 1-1/2 m. off Russell Turnpike to east. to dead end near t. Clare line, n. Norman and Tarsius Downer, believed to be first settlers. *Quarterly*, 9 (1964), no. 2, p. 11. The school was no. 7, common, t. Russell. Derived names are **Downerville Cemetery / Road / School.** The road is mistakenly noted as **Donnerville** on some maps. / **Downerville State Forest**, #26, t. Clare, Russell.

Downeys Landing: on Racquette River at Marsh Ponds, t. Piercefield. 1860 **Downys Landing** Merrit; 1880 Ely; 1883 **Downey's Landing** Ely-Wallace; 1896 **Downey Landing** New. Also **Downey Landing, Downys Landing.**

Draffin School: in Ogdensburg, t. Oswegatchie, n. Draffin family. No longer exists.

Draime Hall: on SUC, Potsdam campus, n. Anna Patten Draime, a dean from 1906 to 1927.

Drew School: no. 9, common school, t. Waddington, n. Drew family.

Drews Corner: t. Waddington, n. Drew family. 1964 USGS Waddington Quad.

Driscoll Road: r., t. Lawrence, n. Driscoll family.

Drum Road: r., t. Rossie, n. Donald Drum.

Drumlin Drive: s., v. Potsdam.

Drury Point: on Black Lake, t. Morristown, n. Drury family. 1961 USGS Pope Mills Quad.

Dry: n. place without water either intermittently or permanently: **Dry Bridge Road**: r., t. Oswegatchie, n. bridge over railroad; s., v. Norwood, n. bridge over railroad, also **Norwood-Knapp Station Road.** / **Dry Island**: in St. Lawrence River, t. Waddington. See, **Corrigan's Island.** 1942 USGS Murphy Island Quad. / **Dry Timber Island**: t. Fine. 1916 USGS Oswegatchie Quad. / **Dry Timber Lake**: t. Fine.

Dublin Avenue: s., h. Hailesboro, n. Dublin, Ireland.

Duck Cove: bay in St. Lawrence River, t. Hammond, n. presence of ducks. 1958 USGS Chippewa Quad.

Dugway Hill: t. Parishville, n. road built up the hill, first finished in 1912, restructured in 1966-1967, as road from Potsdam to Parishville.

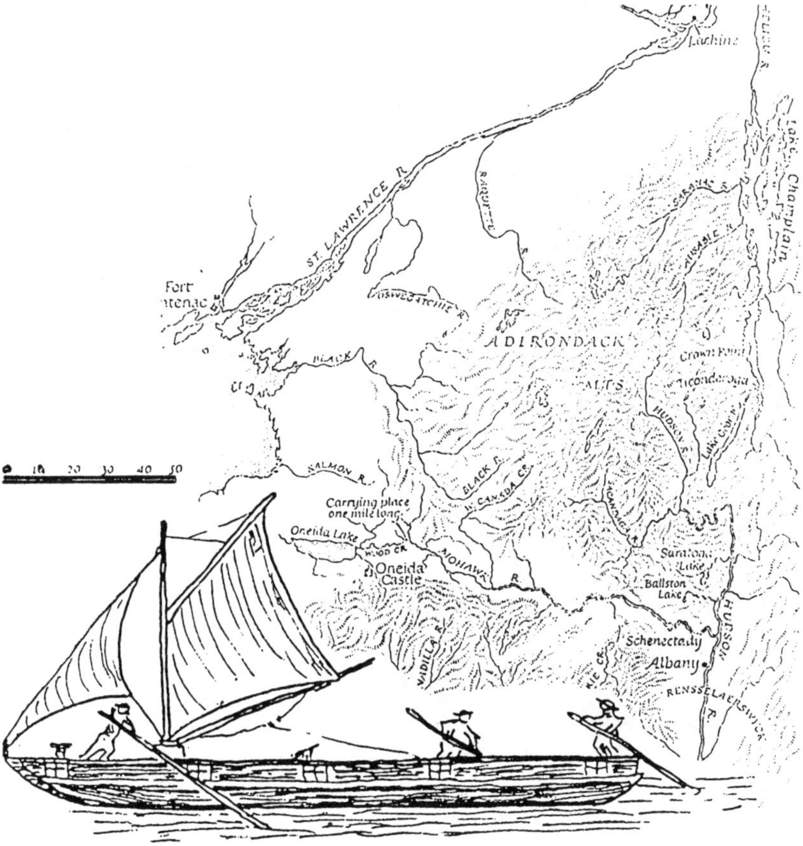

The first white settlers came to Ogdensburg in 1796 by Durham boat from Schenectady by way of the Mohawk River, Wood Creek, Oneida and Ontario Lakes, down the St. Lawrence River.

STONE ARCH BRIDGE ON ELM CREEK, HERMON VILLAGE

From up stream, built 1875

From down stream side

Bridge updated in 1920s by Mr. McBrier, copied from one he saw in Italy.

Dukie's Bridge: a truss iron bridge, nearly 200 feet long, over Oswegatchie River, two miles above Gouverneur, n. Rufus "Dukey" Blackburn. Also **Dukey's Bridge.** *Quarterly*, 5 (1960), no. 1, npn. "Blackburn, a well-to-do French Canadian, lived at the north end of the bridge for several years. The town line between Gouverneur and Fowler bisects the bridge diagonally almost in its center. This makes Gouverneur township responsible for the northern end to the middle; and Fowler township for the southern half. Gouverneur established the five tons limit, and Fowler the four tons limit. Some tales are told of teamsters arriving at the 'five ton' end, having to unload part of their consignment in order to avoid a penalty at the south end. There may be a suggestion of the wag in this part of the bridge history." Later, Fowler raised its limit to five tons. Contributed by Julius Bartlett, Gouverneur Village Historian.

Dullea Road: r., t. Stockholm, Brasher, n. Dullea family.

Dump Road: to a dumping area: r., t. Gouverneur; r., t. Massena; r., t. Oswegatchie; r., t. Piercefield; r., t. Russell.

Dunbar Road: r., t. Waddington, n. Dunbar family;

Dunkle Road: r., t. Potsdam, named for either Hazekial or Ebenezer Dunklee (note change in spelling).

Dunn: Dunn Hall: on SUC, Potsdam campus, n. E. Roger Dunn, history and social science teacher. / **Dunn Street**: s., v. Hammond, n. Dunn family.

Durham: either for n. family or county in England: **Durham Road**: r., t. Pitcairn, n. Durham family. Also **Bradish Road.** / **Durham Street**: s., v. Morristown, n. County of Durham, England.

Dutton Road: r., t. Russell, n. Dutton family.

Dwight D. Eisenhower Lock: in the St. Lawrence River, n. for the president when the lock was opened in 1956.

E

E. Hugh Williams Senior High School: v. Canton.

Eagers Bay: in St. Lawrence River, t. Morristown, n. Charles Eager from NH and Marshal Eager from VT.

1963 USGS Morristown Quad.

Eagle: n. either for presence of the bird or for the symbolism as the national bird for the United States: **Eagle Crag**: t. Piercefield. / **Eagle Crag Lake**: t. Piercefield, alt. 1,684, n. crag. 1865 Long Pond Beers, p. 86; 1873 **Long Pond** Hamilton Child; 1880 **Long Pond** Ely; 1883 **Long Pond** Ely-Wallace; 1896 **Long Pond** New; 1902 **Long Pond** Blankman; 1908 **Long Pond** Adm; 1912 **Long Pond** Stoddard; 1954 USGS Tupper Lake Quad. / **Eagle Island**: in Cranberry Lake, t. Clifton. 1896 New; 1902 **Gull Island** Blankman; 1908 Adm; 1912 **Gull Island** Stoddard; 1919 USGS Cranberry Lake Quad. / **Eagle Mill**: in v. Canton, symbolic n. Originally erected by Henry Van Rensselaer in 1842 as **Eagle Mills**, a grist mill built on the west bank of the Grass(e) River "close to the junction of the Gouverneur and Ogdensburg main highways." It was also operated by Lasell and Jewett, ca 1871. Durant, p. 216, col. 1. See also Bette Limpert Mayhew, "The Eagle Mill," *Quarterly*, 7 (1962), no. 3, p. 5. / **Eagle Rock**: near Nicholville, a high rock near the river. *Quarterly*, 14 (1969), no. 4, p. 22. / **Eagle Wing Island**: in St. Lawrence River, t. Hammond, n. shape of wing. 1958 USGS Chippewa Quad.

Eamon Road: r., t. Brasher, south of Maple Ridge, n. Eamon family, but all homes now gone.

Earl Island: in Grass(e) River, t. Edwards, n. Guy Earle, early settler. Freeman, 4. See *Watertown Daily Times*, Apr. 19, 1989, Sec. C, p. 1. 1915 USGS Russell Quad.

Earls Creek: t. Massena, trib. Squeak Brook. 1964 USGS Racquette River Quad.

East: a direction-n. and contrast with **West**: **East Avenue**: s., v. Massena. / **East Babcock Street**: s., v. Gouverneur. / **East Barney Street**: s., v. Gouverneur. / **East Bay**: see **East Inlet**. / **East Branch**: now **Heuvelton**. Also see **Fordsburgh**. / **East Branch Bridge**: over Oswegatchie River at Heuvelton, t. Oswegatchie. / **East Branch Hopkinton Brook**: t. Hopkinton, trib. Hopkinton Brook. 1919 USGS Nicholville Quad. / **East Brook**: t. Hopkinton; see **Jordan River**, t. Colton; see **East Creek**, t. Colton; see **Lake Ozonia Outlet**. / **East Brook Creek**: see **Lake Ozonia Outlet**. / **East Brook School**: t. Hopkinton. / **East Canton School**: no. 19, common school, t. Canton. / **East Center Street**: s., v. Massena. / **East Creek**: rises in Oakham, flows through t. Colton, trib. Cranberry Lake. 1880 **East Brook** Ely; 1883 **East**

Brook Ely-Wallace; 1896 New; 1908 Adm; 1912 Stoddard; 1919 USGS Cranberry Lake Quad. / **East Creek Mountain**: see **East Mountain.** / **East David Street**: see **David Street, East.** / **East DeKalb**: t. DeKalb, est. 1853, 2-1/2 m. southwest of DeKalb Junction; p. o. est. July 14, 1851, as **East De Kalb**, John H. Bartlett, first pm, closed Dec. 6, 1877. New York Postal History; Hough, 574; Durant, 357; *Quarterly*, 7 (1962), no. 4, p. 7. Baseball team of 1892 nicknamed **Clippers.** 1873 **East Dekalb** Hamilton Child, p. 107; 1956 USGS **East De Kalb** Bigelow Quad. USGS official spelling, **De Kalb.** / **East DeKalb Cemetery**: t. DeKalb. / **East DeKalb Road**: r., t. DeKalb, Hermon. / **East DeKalb School**: no. 1, common school, t. DeKalb. / **East Drive**: s., v. Canton; s., v. Potsdam. / **East Hall**: on St. Lawrence University campus, residence hall. / **East Hatfield Street**: s., v. Massena. / **East High Street**: s., v. Norfolk. / **East Hill Road**: r., t. Colton. / **East Inlet**: in Cranberry Lake, t. Clifton, Colton. 1896 **East Bay** New; 1908 Adm; 1919 USGS Cranberry Lake Quad. / **East Higley Flow Road**: r., t. Colton, in Higley Flow area. / **East Main Street**: s., v. Gouverneur. / **East Mountain**: t. Colton, alt. 2,325. 1896 **East Creek Mountain** New; 1902 **East Creek Mountain** Blankman; 1919 USGS Cranberry Lake Quad. / **East Orvis**: s., v. Massena. See **Orvis Street.** / **East Part**: t. DePeyster. / **East Part**: t. Stockholm. 1964 USGS Brasher Falls Quad. /**East Part Cemetery**: t. DePeyster. Also **East Road Cemetery.** / **East Part School**: near East Part, t. Stockholm. 1964 USGS Brasher Falls Quad. / **East Pierrepont**: p. o. est., Aug. 31, 1831, Joseph Dimick, Jr., first pm, closed July 3, 1861, changed to **Ellsworth**; now **Hannawa Falls.** / **East Pitcairn**: h., t. Pitcairn, p. o. est. Jan 15, 1850, Charles H. Bowles, first pm, closed July 15, 1905 and changed to **Ellsworth.** 1865 Beers, p. 72; 1915 USGS Oswegatchie Quad. / **East Pitcairn Cemetery** h. **East Pitcairn** / **East Pitcairn School**: no. 3, common school, t. Pitcairn / **East Pitcairn-South Edwards Road**: r., t. Pitcairn. / **East River Street**: s., c. Ogdensburg. / **East Road**: settlement, t. Russell, p. o. est. Dec. 11, 1900, Chauncey L. Moore, pm, closed Apr. 15, 1905. Baseball team in 1892 nicknamed **East Road Boys.** / **East Road**: r., v. Heuvelton; r., t. DePeyster; r., t. Russell, toward Canton on east side of h. Russell. / **East Road Cemetery**: t. DePeyster, east of h. 1963 USGS Heuvelton Quad. Also **East Part Cemetery.** / **East Road School**: no. 6, common school, t. DePeyster, Russell. / **East Road School**: no. 8, common school,

t. Russell. / **East Side School**: t. Gouverneur. 1956 USGS Gouverneur Quad. Not in 1896 listing. / **East Street**: s., h. Balmat; s., v. Rensselaer Falls, n. direction, only the right side developed, runs parallel to Congress Street. / **East Stockholm**: see **Stockholm.** / **East Stockholm School:** no. 1, common school, t. Stockholm. / **East Village**: in 1817, changed to **Nicholville.**

Eastbourneville: now, **Hermon** v. 1818 Lays map.

Eastman School: no. 2, common school, t. Parishville, n. Eastman family.

Eastview Heights: s., v. Norfolk.

Eastville: h. Nicholville, p. o. est. Mar. 16, 1829, Clemens C. Palmer, pm, changed to **Nicholville**, Jan. 9, 1831.

Eastwood: building at S. Lawrence State Hospital. *Quarterly*, 11 (1966), no. 4, p. 19.

Eben: railway station, t. Potsdam, n. Eben Holden, a character in a Bacheller novel. 1964 USGS West Potsdam Quad. / **Eben Road**: r., t. Potsdam. See **Eben.**

Echo Lake: see **Grass Pond.**

Ecklock Road: r., t. Rossie.

Eckman Street: s., v. Gouverneur, n. Lewis (or Louis) Eckman, an upholsterer and business partner in the Gouverneur Marble Co. with Alonzo J. Van Duzee, son of Stephen Brown Van Duzee. The business burned in 1877. Eckman and his partner also owned a furniture store in Watertown. Durant, 342, 350 ff.

Eddy: crossroads. Eddy Section, t. Canton, n. Eddy family, in particular Lula A. Eddy and John Eddy; p. o. est. Oct. 1, 1900, Lettie A. Stafford, pm, closed May 31, 1911. Also, see *Quarterly*, 10 (1965), no. 3, p. 12. 1964 USGS Canton Quad. / **Eddy Cemetery**: t. Canton. / **Eddy-Pyrites Road**: r., t. Canton. Also, **Lincoln Road**. / **Eddy Road**: r., t. Fine, probably n. John Eddy.

Edenton: t. DePeyster, n. origin unknown; p. o. est. June 13, 1850, Benjamin F. Partridge, pm (Hough, 574; Durant, 368), closed Aug. 31, 1909. / **Edenton School**: no. 8, common school, t. DePeyster.

Edgar Mountain: t. Colton. 1880 Ely; 1883 Ely-Wallace. see **Center Pond Mountain.**

Edgewater Park: t. Morristown, n.

desc., on St. Lawrence River. 1963 USGS Morristown Quad.

Edith Street: s., v. Gouverneur, n. Edith Waid, granddaughter of Josiah Waid.

Edmond Brook: t. Russell, trib. Grass(e) River, prob. n. Edmond Wood. 1915 USGS Russell Quad.

Edward John Noble University Center: on St. Lawrence University campus, n. Mr. Noble, a trustee and chairman of the University foundation. / **Edward John Noble Hospital**: v. Gouverneur.

Edwards: a survey township, now t. See **Edwards** v. for origin. 1873 Hamilton Child, p. 115; 1956 USGS Edwards Quad; t. patented in Mar., 1795. Formed as t. Apr. 27, 1827, becoming the 22nd t. in St. Lawrence County. Asa and Eunice Brayton were the first to arrive and settled on Pork Creek in 1812. Durant, 442. 1956 USGS Edwards Quad. / **Edwards**: v., t. Edwards, southeastern interior of the county; v. began in 1814 as **Sheads Mills** and **Sheads Corners**, n. Orra Shead, when gristmill was built; p. o. est. Nov. 16, 1827, George Allen, first pm; p. o. existing, ZIP 13635. Hough, 574, writes that p. o. est. Jan. 4, 1828, Orra Shead, pm; n. Apr. 27, 1827, Edward McCormick, sea captain in East India trade and brother of Daniel McCormick. Durant, 77, 444; *Quarterly*, 5 (1960), no. 4, p. 9; Leah Noble, "Edwards Pioneers," *Quarterly*, 7 (1962), no. 2, pp. 8-9, 15-16 / **Edwards Central School**: t. Edwards. Freeman, 16. / **Edwards High School**: in v., t. Edwards, now **Edwards-Knox Central School**. 1956 USGS Edwards Quad. / **Edwards- Kents Corners Road**: r., t. Hermon. / **Edwards Road**: r., t. Pitcairn. / **Edwards-Russell Road**: r., t. Russell. / **Edwards School**: no. 1, common school, t. Edwards, known as **Village School**, Dist. 1. Freeman, 16.

Edwardsville: h, on Black Lake, t. Morristown, n. Jonathan S. Edwards, first pm, the p. o. est. at **The Narrows**, the narrowest part of Black Lake. Mar. 22, 1837, closed Aug. 15, 1925. Formerly **Marysburgh**. Durant, 373. 1963 USGS Edwardsville Quad. / **Edwardsville Cemetery**: t. Morristown. / **Edwardsville- Hammond Road**: r., t. Hammond, Morristown. / **Edwardsville School**: no. 2, common school, t. Morris- town. Bogardus, 60.

Eel: n. elongated, snakelike fish, either eel or lamprey: **Eel Pond**: t. Stockholm, n. presence of eels. / **Eel Pond Road**: r., t. Stockholm, n. pond.

/ **Eel Weir State Park**: t. Oswegatchie, n. feature (dam) in Black Lake outlet for catching eels. The n. has been transferred to other places: **Eel Weir Cemetery**: see **Pine Hill Cemetery**. / **Eel Weir Road**: r., t. Oswegatchie. / **Eel Weir Picnic Area**: in State Park, t. Oswegatchie

Eells: several families n. Eells in Pierrepont area: **Eells Road**: r., t. Pierrepont. / **Eells School**: no. 19, common school, t. Pierrepont. Also, **Ells**, misprint.

Egg Pond: all ponds noted here n. shape: t. Piercefield, see **Deer Pond**. / t. Piercefield, see **Pine Pond**. / t. Colton. 1919 USGS Stark Quad; 1954 USGS Tupper Lake Quad. / t. Hopkinton. 1896 New; 1902 Blankman; 1908 Adm; 1912 Stoddard; 1919 USGS Nicholville Quad; 1964 USGS Sylvan Falls Quad.

Eisenhower Lock: see **Dwight D. Eisenhower Lock**.

Ekey Road: r., t. Madrid, n. Ekey family.

Elderkin Street: s., v. Potsdam, n. Noble Strong Elderkin.

Eldridge Road: r., t. Brasher, n. Eldridge family.

Elgin Avenue: s., v. Massena.

Elizabeth: feminine given n.: **Elizabeth Island**: in Black Lake, t. Morristown, reason n. unknown. / **Elizabeth Street**: s., v. Parishville, n. daughter of David Parish; s., c. Ogdensburg, n. a daughter of Nathan Ford; s., v. Rensselaer Falls, n. wife and daughter (both were named Elizabeth) of Henry Van Rensselaer.

Ellerslie: home of Gouverneur and Charlotte Ogden, west of the v. Waddington, n. "estate and house of the medieval Scottish hero, William Walklace, and figures prominently in Jane Porter's widely read romance **Scottish Chiefs** (1810). The name was chosen for its Scottish and romantic associations." Quoted from Tedford, 20. Built in 1829, the home was destroyed by fire, March 1, 1843.

Elliott: n. family: **Elliott Road**: r., t. Potsdam; r., t. Stockholm, Hopkinton.

Ellis: surname used as a specific: **Ellis Brook**: t. Piercefield, trib. Racquette River. 1860 Merrit; 1880 Ely; 1883 Ely-Wallace; 1896 New; 1902 Blankman; 1908 adm; 1912 Stoddard; 1920 USGS Childwold Quad. / **Ellis Cemetery**: t. Stockholm. 1943 USGS Potsdam Quad. / **Ellis Road**: r., t. Potsdam, n. Ellis family. / **Ellis**

School: no. 3, common school, t. Stockholm, n. Ellis family.

Ellithorpe School: no. 1, common school, t. Lawrence, n. Danforth and William Ellithorpe.

Ells Road: misprint for **Eells Road**.

Ellsworth: h., t. Pierrepont, p. o. changed from **East Pierpont** to **Ellsworth**, July 3, 1861, Alexander Bradley, first pm, changed to **Hannawa Falls**, Dec. 29, 1875.

Elm: n. presence of the American elm tree, **Ulmus americana**, popular for shade and stateliness: **Elm Circle**: s., v. Massena; **Elm Circle**: s., v. Norfolk. / **Elm Creek**: t. Edwards, Hermon, DeKalb, Canton, flows out of Cedar Lake. *Quarterly*, 11 (1966), no. 2, p. 20. / t. Hermon, flows into Grass(e) River. *Quarterly* 16 (1971), no. 1, p. 9. / t. Canton, trib. Harrison Creek. 1964 Canton Quad. / t. Edwards. / **Elm Creek District**: t. Russell. Clarke, 4. / **Elm Flat**: flatland, t. Clare. 1915 Russell Quad. / **Elm Street**: s., v. Canton; s., h. Madrid; s., v. Massena; s., v. Morristown; s., h. Newton Falls; s., v. Norwood; s., v. Potsdam, called "Turkey Hill" by older residents. / **Elm Tree Island**: in St. Lawrence River, t. Hammond. 1958 USGS Chippewa Quad.

Elmdale: h., t. Gouverneur, n. tree + **dale** (vale or valley) and "bucolic interests." *Quarterly*, 7 (1962), no. 3, p. 4; p. o. est. Apr. 5, 1890, Philemon Olds, pm, closed Dec. 31, 1903, reopened, Mar. 29, 1904, James Russell, pm, closed Jan. 15, 1907. / **Elmdale School**: no. 12, common school, t. Gouverneur.

Elsa Gunnison Appleton Riding Hall: on St. Lawrence University campus, stabling and riding complex, n. granddaughter of President Almon Gunnison.

Elvy Clearing: t. Clare.

Elwood Point: on Black Lake, t. Morristown, n. Elwood family. 1961 USGS Hammond Quad.

Emerson Road: r., t. Potsdam, n. Emerson family.

Emery Island: in Black Lake, t. Morristown. 1961 USGS Hammond Quad.

Emeryville: h., t. Fowler, n. metal mines; p. o. est. Mar. 29, 1894, Arlington D. Balmat, pm, closed Dec. 31, 1920. Derived n., **Emeryville Road**: r., t. Fowler.

Emilyville: a survey township, t. Fine.

n. Emily, daughter of William Constable. Durant, 446.

Emporium Forestry Company: Lumber company. *Quarterly*, 3 (1958), 4, p. [6].

Empress Isle: in St. Lawrence River. Also, **Macks**.

Endersbee Corners: t. Russell, n. Endersbee family. 1915 USGS Russell Quad.

English Settlement: t. Morristown. Settled by English emigrants in 1817-1818, primarily from Roxburghshire (Scotland), Northumberland, Yorkshire, and Lincolnshire. / **English Settlement Road**: r., t. Morristown, Hammond, Heuvelton. / **English Settlement School**: no. 6, common school, t. Morristown. Bogardus, 60.

Erin Street: v. Waddington, n. Ireland (Erin). Now, **Franklin Street**.

Erwin: surname used as a specific: **Erwin Road**: r., t. Madrid, n. George Erwin, attorney and son of Joseph Erwin from NH. / **Erwin Street**: s., v. Massena, n. Erwin family.

Eskar Pond: t. Fine, n. generic used as a specific to denote a geological narrow ridge or mound of gravelly, sandy drift, deposited by a subglacial stream; on state land near New York State Ranger School, Wanakena. Also **Esker**. 1919 USGS Cranberry Lake Quad.

Ethel Street: s., v. Gouverneur, n. daughter of Frank Babcock.

Ethridge School: no. 17, common school, t. DeKalb, n. Ethridge family, settled 1835 from Norfolk County, England. Also **Ethredge**. 1915 USGS Gouverneur Quad.

Euphemia Street: s., c. Ogdensburg, n. a daughter of Nathan Ford. Changed to **State Street**, May 27, 1824.

Evans Road: r., t. Hermon, n. Evans family.

Evergreen Cemetery: t. Canton, on U. S. 11. 1964 USGS Canton Quad.

Eyensawye: a form of Akwesasne; see **St. Regis River**.

F

Factory: n. place where a factory is located, or a road which leads to one: **Factory**: settlement, t. Hammond, n. the only glass factory in the county. The unusually fine texture and light aquamarine color of the glass was attributed to the quality of sand-stone in the area. / **Factory Road**: r., t. Brasher; r., t. DePeyster; r., t. Hammond; r., t. Lawrence; r., v. Gouverneur, n. for a cheese factory. / **Factory Street**: s., h. Brasher Falls; s., h. North Lawrence.

Fairbanks: surname used as a specific: **Fairbanks Corners**: t. Russell, n. Fairbanks family. 1915 USGS Russell Quad. / **Fairbanks Road**: r., t. Hermon, n. Luther and Daniel Fairbanks.

Fairburn Road: r., t. Lisbon, n. Fairburn family.

Fairlane Drive: s., v. Canton.

Fairlawn Avenue: s., h. Raymondville.

Fairview Cemetery: popular name for cemetery, symbol- izing pastoral view and peacefulness: t. Brasher, near Brasher Falls. 1964 USGS Brasher Falls Quad. / t. Canton. 1964 USGS Canton Quad / t. Edwards, near v. Edwards. 1956 USGS Edwards Quad. / t. Parishville, on Southville Road, edge of v., north view.

Fallon Brook: t. Colton, trib. Racquette River, n. Fallon family. 1920 USGS Childwold Quad.

Fanner Meadows: 1964 USGS Sylvan Falls Quad (error for **Fenner Meadows**)

Fanning School: no. 3, common school, t. Russell, n. John Fanning, pioneer.

Farden Road: r., t. Lisbon, n. Farden family.

Farley School: no. 15, common school, t. Macomb, west of Pleasant Lake, n. Farley family. 1949 USGS Hammond Quad.

Farm to Market Road: r., t. Fowler. Also **Spragueville- Fowler Road.**

Farmer Street: s., v. Canton, n. Farmer family. Beers Atlas, p. 13, shows W. Farmer and A. Farmer lived near present street.

Farmer's Woods: t. Canton, above St. Lawrence University's sandbanks. *Quarterly*, 13 (1968), no. 3, p. 8.

Farnes Road: r., t. Canton, Pierrepont, n. Oda B. Farns, with spelling change. Also **Plains Road.**

Farnsworth School: no. 11, common school, t. Norfolk, n. Joel Farnsworth from NH.

Farrisee Hall: on Clarkson University campus, n. William James Farrisee (1898-1958), a member of the faculty for 31 years, teaching civil engineering and serving as dean of the college and of students.

Farrs: possessive of **Farr**; also **Farr's**: **Farr's Creek**: t. DeKalb. n. James Farr, early settler. His son, Elijah Farr, built a dam in the stream and erected a carding machine before 1814. Durant, 353. Also, **Farrs Creek, Farr Creek.** / **Farr's Crossing**: t. DeKalb, n. Miles Farr, who owned a farm and lived at the crossing. Mark Hemenway, "Forgotten Mines," *Quarterly*, 11 (1966), no. 2, p. 19.

Fay School: no. 9, common school, t. Potsdam, n. Seth Fay family.

Fayette: During the debate in the 1810s to remove the county seat from Ogdensburg to a more central location, a plan was also proposed "for dividing the county, by a line running between Lisbon and Canton on the west, and Madrid and Potsdam on the east, to extend in a direct line to the southern bounds of the county. The new county was to have been named **Fayette**." Hough, 210-211. **Fayette** is an Americanized shortened version of **LaFayette**, the name of The Marquis de Lafayette (1757-1834), French statesman and soldier who aided the Americans during the Revolutionary War and who was tremendously popular in the United States, with many places named in his honor. Two places in the county carry the name: **Fayette Road**: r., t. Norfolk. / **Fayette Street**: s., c. Ogdensburg; now **LaFayette Street**.

Featherbed Road: r., t. Colton. A near-mythical, rocky road about which many stories are told.

Fearlbridge Road: r., t. Stockholm, n. John Fearl.

Felton: surname used as a specific: **Felton Street**: s., v. Norwood. / **Felton's Island**: n. Lloyd Felton.

Fenner: family: **Fenner Meadow Brook**: t. Parishville and Hopkinton, n. Fenner family. 1964 USGS Sylvan Falls Quad. / **Fenner Meadows**: t. Hopkinton. 1964 USGS Sylvan Falls Quad.

Fenton Street: s., v. Waddington, n. Fenton family.

Ferguson: surname used as a specific: **Ferguson Point**: on St. Lawrence River, t. Hammond. Prob. n. James Ferguson. / **Ferguson Road**: r., t.

Rossie, n. Ferguson family. / **Ferguson School**: no. 13, common school, later abandoned, t. Oswegatchie, n. Ferguson family.

Ferris Road: r., t. Lawrence, n. either John or James Ferris.

Ferry's: a community in the Childwold area, n. John Ferry, one of the first settlers.

Fifth Street: s., h. Wanakena.

Fine: southern border with Lewis and Herkimer Counties, t. formed Mar. 27, 1844 (Durant, 447), from t. of Russell and Pierrepont and n. that day for John Fine (1794-1850). Fine was born in New York City, earned an M. A. in 1812 from Columbia University and came to St. Lawrence County in 1815, settling in Ogdensburg, where he was a partner in the purchase of the t. of Scriba. He was a lawyer, jurist, and state senator. Durant, 446-447; Hough, 298. Formerly, **Scriba**, n. George Scriba who surveyed the land prior to the sale in 1787. / **Fine**: h., in t. Fine. First n. **Scriba**, in 1854 renamed **Smithville**, for William P. Smith, first pm; later, renamed **Andersonville**, for Joseph Anderson, who built the oar factory. Because of its having the same name as the infamous Southern prison of Andersonville, the name was changed to **Fine**; p. o. est. Sept. 9, 1954, Smith, pm; p. o. existing, ZIP 13639. 1916 USGS Oswegatchie Quad. Other n. include **Fine Road**: r., t. Pitcairn. / **Fine School**: no. 1, common school, t. Fine, **Village of Fine School.** Reynolds, 199 / **Fine Street**: s., c. Ogdensburg.

Fineview Cemetery: v., t. Hammond. 1961 USGS Hammond Quad.

Finley Road: r., t. Fine, prob. n. Hugh Finley from Scotland; the old homestead still there.

Finnegan: family n. used as a specific: **Finnegan Road**: r., t. Potsdam, Canton, n. family; r., t. Lawrence, n. Thomas Finnigan (or Finnegan). Also, **South Brasher Road.**

Fire-Fall State Forest: #27, t. Hermon and Edwards; n. land devastated by fire about 1903, but timber and vegetation was fully grown and developed fifty years later. Also, **Firefall.**

First: cardinal number n., the beginning one: **First Pond**: t. Colton; see **Lows Lake.** / **First Street**: s., h. Cranberry Lake (**1st Street**); s., v. Edwards; s., h. Wanakena.

Fish: usually indicates a place for good

fishing when it was n.: **Fish Creek**: t. DePeyster. / **Fish Creek**: t. Fine (St. Lawrence Co.) and t. Diana (Lewis Co.). 1916 USGS Oswegatchie Quad. / **Fish Creek**: t. Macomb and Morristown, trib. Hickory Lake and Black Lake. *Quarterly*, 2 (1957), no. 4, npn. 1961 USGS Pope Mills Quad. / **Fish Creek Road**: r., t. De Peyster. / **Fish Creek Wildlife Management Area**, t. DePeyster, Macomb. / **Fish Hawk Rapid**: in Racquette River, t. Piercefield, n. bird

Fisher: surname used as a specific: **Fisher Road**: r., t. Lisbon, n. Thomas Fisher; r., t. Louisville, n. Fisher family. / **Fisher School**: no. 6, common school, t. Madrid, n. George, William, and James Fisher from Scotland. / **Fisher Street**: s., v. Canton, n. Professor (Rev. Dr.) Eben Fisher (Beers, p. 13), first head of the theological school that became St. Lawrence University, 1858. Durant, p. 125, col. 2.

Fishpole Pond: t. Clifton, alt. 1,719. 1883 **Oral Pond** Ely-Wallace; 1898 EGB, p. 27; 1902 **Fishpate Pond** (misprint) Blankman; 1908 Adm; 1912 Stoddard; 1919 USGS Cranberry lake Quad. Reason for n. unknown.

Fisk Road: r., t. Lawrence, n. Charles A. Fisk family.

Fitzwilliam: a survey township, now **Hermon**. Also **Fitz William.**

Five: a number n., usually desc. of a place with five items: **Five Corners School**: no. 32, common school, t. Potsdam. / **Five Falls Reservoir**: in Racquette River, Colton. 1964 USGS Rainbow Falls Quad. / **Five Mile Road**: r., t. Lisbon, divides the town which is a ten-mile square. / **Five Mile Line Road**: r., t. Lisbon. / **Five Pond Outlet**: t. Fine, trib. Oswegatchie River. 1896 New.

Flack Road: r., t. Lisbon, n. Flack family.

Flackville: h,, t. Lisbon, n. John P. Flack, founder, who erected many buildings; p. o. est. July 8, 1847, Lauren Sage, pm (Hough, 574), closed Dec. 31, 1903 (New York Postal History). Durant gives date of p. o. as 1830, Flack as first pm (Durant, 274). 1963 USGS Lisbon Quad. The cluster of n. includes **Flackville Cemetery**: t. Lisbon. 1963 USGS Lisbon Quad. See **Campbell Cemetery**. / **Flackville Road**: r., t. Lisbon. / **Flackville School**: no. 6, common school, t. Lisbon.

Flagg Hall: on SUC, Potsdam campus, n. Edward W. Flagg, a professor of history.

Flat: n. level area, or for incident: **Flat Island**: see **Manzanita Island.** / **Flat Iron Street**: see **Flatiron Street.** / **Flat Rock**: a distinctive geological feature, desc.: **Flat Rock**: t. DeKalb. Nina W. Smithers, "The Railroad Made DeKalb Junction," *Quarterly*, 7 (1962), no. 4, p. 7. / **Flat Rock**: t. Fine, the place where the New York Public Utilities (now Niagara Mohawk) built a dam (1924) in the Oswegatchie River. Reynolds, 77. / **Flat Rock Hill**: t. Fine. / **Flat Rock Point**: on Cranberry Lake, t. Clifton. 1896 New. / **Flat Rock Road**: r., t. Potsdam. / **Flat Rock School**: no. 9, common school, t. DePeyster. / **Flat Rock School**: no. 8, common school, t. Morristown. Bogardus, 60, lists two: one near Irelan Road and one on De Mot [De Mott] Road.

Flatiron Street: r., t. Russell, reportedly n. because of a family disturbance in which the wife threw a flatiron at the husband. *Quarterly*, 10 (1965), no. 4, p. 9. Also **Flat Iron Street**.

Flats School: no. 11, common school, t. Massena, n. geological feature, a flat area.

Flemming Road: r., t. Rossie, n. Flemming family.

Fletcher Road: r., t. Hopkinton, n. Fletcher family.

Flight Road: see **Hermon-DeKalb Road**, n. Flight family.

Flint: surname used as a specific: **Flint Hall**: on St. Lawrence University campus, n. Benjamin Flint, benefactor. / **Flint School**: no. 20, common school, t. Brasher, n. Flint family. / **Flint-Chaffee Cemetery**: t. Brasher, near junction of Murray and Youmell Roads, n. two families. 1964 USGS North Lawrence Quad.

Flower: surname used as a specific: **Flower Group**: buildings at St. Lawrence State Hospital, n. Gov. Roswell P. Flower, who recommended that funds be appropriated after a disastrous fire in 1893. *Quarterly*, 11 (1966), no. 4, p. 19. / **Flower Hill**: t. Hopkinton, alt. 1,520 ft., n. George A. Flower. 1964 USGS Sylvan Falls Quad.

Foot of the Sault School: no. 15, common school, t. Massena, n. placement and feature.

Foote-Legge-Stocking Tavern: on Canton to Ogdensburg Road, operated by Stillman Foote, whose father, Stillman Foote (1763-1834) was the first settler in Canton, and a man named Legge whose daughter married a Stocking. Also **Halfway House**. *Quarterly*, 16 (1971), no. 4, p. 6.

Footes Falls: t. Canton, n. Stillman Foote, first settler in Canton.

4-H Forest: county forest, t. Parishville.

Forbes: n. family: **Forbes Road**: r., t. Massena, n. George Forbes from Nova Scotia; r., t. Russell, connects Backus and Boyd Roads, n. Forbes family.

Ford Avenue: s., c. Ogdensburg, n. Nathan Ford (1763- 1829), served in the Revolutionary War, sent by land speculators to explore the northern part of the state, settled at Oswegatchie, appointed first judge at Ogdensburg, and prominent citizen. Six streets of Ogdensburg were n. for his daughters: Catherine, Isabella, Euphemia, Gertrude, Caroline, and Elizabeth. Durant, 188; Hough, 589. Also n. for him: **Ford Cemetery**: c. Ogdensburg. 1963 USGS Odgensburg East Quad. / **Ford Street**: s., c. Ogdensburg; s., v. Brasher Falls (possibly not for Nathan Ford).

Fordham: surname used as a specific: **Fordham Hill Road**: r., t. Russell, n. Wiers C. Fordham (1794-1862), farmer. Durant, 433. / **Fordham's Corners**: crossroads, t. Russell, n. Robert Fordham, landowner, born in England. *Quarterly*, 19 (1974), no. 2, p. 19. 1915 USGS Russell Quad.

Fordsburgh: n. Nathan Ford, about 1805. Later, **East Branch**; now **Heuvelton**. *Quarterly*, 8 (1963), no. 2, p. 10.

Forest: prob. n. family: **Forest Place**: s., v. Massena. / **Forest Road**: r., t. Louisville. / **Forest View Drive**: s., h. Star Lake, n. promotional and the wooded area.

Forsythe Road: r., t. Lisbon, n. John Forsythe from Ireland.

Fort Covington-Massena Springs Railroad: serviced Massena. Dumas, 61.

Fort Jackson: h., t. Hopkinton, n. Andrew Jackson, 7th president of the United States, by his admirers in the area, who claimed that the rock formation looked like a fort; n. in 1824; p. o. est. Apr. 3, 1873, Franklin Kellogg, first pm, ZIP 12938, now rural branch of **North Lawrence**. See also Durant, 322. 1919 USGS Nicholville Quad; 1964 USGS Nicholville Quad. A cluster of n. include **Fort Jackson Cemetery**: t.

Hopkinton. 1964 USGS Nicholville Quad. / **Fort Jackson-Hopkinton Road**: r., t. Hopkinton. / **Fort Jackson-Laverys Corners Road**: r., t. Lawrence, n. Fort Jackson and the Lavery family. / **Fort Jackson-Winthrop Road**; r., t. Stockholm, Hopkinton. / **Fort Jackson School: no. 10, common school, t. Hopkinton.** / **Fort Jackson State Forest**, #22, t. Stockholm.

Fort La Presentation: Founded by Abbe Francois Picquet, a Sulpician missionary from Lyons, France; n. changed by British to **Fort Oswegatchie**. Now, **Ogdensburg**.

Fort Levis: t. Lisbon, on **Oraconenton Island**, also known as **Isle-Royal**, now **Chimney Island**. n. Monsieur the Chevalier de Levis, who superintended its building. The English changed the n. to **Fort William Augustus**, August, 1760. The last French stronghold in North America, it became a part of the United States through Jay's Treaty, June 1, 1796. The n. **Chimney** derives from chimneys remaining from the ruins of the French fort. Hough, 108-109. *Quarterly*, 1 (1956), no. 3, npn; 11 (1966), no. 4, p. 3. The site was inundated when the Seaway was completed.

Fort Oswegatchie: See **Fort La Presentation.**

Fort William Augustus: formerly **Fort Levis**. On **Chimney Island**. *Quarterly*, 11 (1966), no. 4, p. 3.

Foster Road: r., t. Lawrence, n. Hiram D. Foster.

Foster S. Brown Hall: on St. Lawrence University campus, n. president from 1963 to 1969.

Fountain Road: r., t. Hopkinton, poss. n. Luke Fountain.

Four Rod Road: from Black Lake to St. Lawrence River, n. for its width (4 rods).

Fourth: number n. usually in a series: **Fourth Pond**: t. Colton; see **Lows Lake**. / **Fourth Street**: s., h. Wanakena

Fowler: t. southwestern border with Jefferson County, n. Theodosius Fowler, of New York, on Apr. 15, 1816, when formed. Fowler purchased the land in 1810; t. formed from Rossie and Russell. Fowler had served in the Revolutionary War and was at the surrender at Yorktown. He conveyed the tract to his son Theodosius O. Fowler, who developed it. Durant, 377. 1956 USGS Gouverneur Quad. Derived n.: **Fowler Cemetery**:

1956 USGS Gouverneur Quad. / **Fowler Road**: r., t. Edwards.

Fowler: h,. t. **Fowler**, which see; p. o. est. Nov. 19, 1821, Theodosius Fowler, pm, closed Jan. 15, 1915. 1956 USGS Gouverneur Quad. Formerly **Little York**, to celebrate the capture of the town of Little York (now Toronto) during the war of 1812. *Quarterly*, 5 (1960), no. 4, p. 9.

Fox: usually n. animal: **Fox Farm Road**: r., t. Gouverneur, n. early experiment in raising foxes. / **Fox Marsh**: swamp, t. Colton. 1921 USGS Stark Quad.

Frances Sheard Banford Elementary and Junior High School: v. Canton, n. teacher and principal of many years.

Francis: usually surname: **Francis Hill/Mountain**: t. Fine, alt. 1,840 ft., in the Streeter Lake area, near Star Lake on State land, n. Francois, believed to have been a woodsman or lumberjack. 1916 USGS Oswegatchie Quad. / **Francis Street**: s., v. Massena, Potsdam.

Frank Foy Road: r., t. Brasher, from Factory Road into Franklin County, n. Frank Foy, farmer in northeast corner of Brasher. 1964 USGS Hogansburg Quad.

Frank P. Piskor Hall: on St. Lawrence University campus, n. former President, 1969-1981. Formerly **Cook Hall.**

Frank School: no. 6, common school, t. Colton.

Franklin: surname: **Franklin Street**: s., v. Hammond, n. Benjamin and Festus Franklin, local residents. Durant, 384, 386. / **Franklin Street**: A popular name was that of Benjamin Franklin (1706-1790), statesman, patriot, inventor. Streets named for him include s., v. Massena; s., c. Ogdensburg, formerly **Gertrude Street**; s., v. Waddington, also known as **Franklin Road. Franklin and St. Lawrence Turnpike**: A company was formed on Apr. 21, 1828, by Benjamin Holmes, Ebenezer Hubbard, Azel Shepard, Robert Watts, and Clark Lawrence, stock $5,000.00, to construct a turnpike from Moira through Brasher to Stockholm. The tolls were as follows: "for every cart, or wagon drawn by one ox, mule or horse, six and a quarter cents; for every cart or wagon drawn by two horses, mules, or oxen, twelve and an half cents, for every additional horse, mule or ox, four cents; for every stage, wagon, coach, curricle, or other pleasure carriage drawn by two horses, twenty-five cents; for every additional horse, three cents; for every chair, sulkey or chaise, twelve and a half cents; for every horse ridden, six and a quarter cents; for every horse or mule driven, three cents; for every sleigh or sled drawn by one horse, mule or ox, four cents; for every sleigh or sled drawn by two horses, mules or oxen, six and a quarter cents; for every additional horse, mule or ox, three cents; for every score of neat cattle, eighteen and three quarter cents; for every score of hogs or sheep, six and a quarter cents, and so in like proportion for a greater or less number." Chap. 330, Fifty-First Session, p. 453-4, "An Act to incorporate the Franklin and St. Lawrence Turnpike Road Company."

Fraser Road: r., t. Rossie, n. Fraser family.

Fray Road: r., t. Stockholm.

Fred's Islands: in Cranberry lake, t. Clifton. 1896 New.

Freeman: surname used as a specific: **Freeman Road**: r., t. Waddington. / **Freeman School**: no. 6, common school, t. Edwards, n. William Freeman. / **Freeman Street**: s., v. Gouverneur. Now appears to be **Trinity Avenue**. Shown as **Freman**, Beers, 33. / **Freemansburgh**: t. Edwards, n. for Freeman family. *Quarterly*, 7 (1962), no. 2, p. 15. See **Talcville.**

Frego Street: s., v. Massena, n. Thomas Frego family (wife and ten children) from Canada.

French: usually n. a French-Canadian who lived in the vicinity, but sometimes for a personal n.: **French Cemetery**, t. Potsdam, same as **Grants Cemetery**, Rte. 11. / **French Hall**: on SUNY Canton College of Technology campus, n. Albert French, former president, 1948-1972. / **French Hill**: t. Parishville. 1964 USGS Rainbow Falls Quad. / **French Hill Road**: r., t. Colton, Parishville. / **French Hill School**: no. 14, common school, t. Hopkinton. / **French Lake**: pond, t. Colton. 1883 **Trout Pond** Ely-Wallace; 1896 **French Pond** New; 1902 **French Pond** Blankman; 1908 **French Pond** Adm; 1912 **French Pond** Stoddard; 1921 USGS Stark Quad. / **French Pond**: *Quarterly*, 9 (1964), no. 4, p. 17. See **French Lake.** / **French Pond Road**: r., t. Colton. / **French Road**: r., t. Potsdam, n. French family.

Frier Settlement: t. Russell. *Quarterly*, 20 (1975), no. 3, p. 11

Froman Ridge School: a misprint for **Vroman Ridge School**.

Front Street: s., h. Newton Falls; s., v. Rensselaer Falls. n. fronts on Oswegatchie River; s., h. Wanakena.

Frost Brook: small tributary of Grass(e) River. *Quarterly*, 16 (1971), no. 1, p. 11.

Fuhr Road: r., t. Colton, off Gulf Road in Higley Flow area.

Fullerville: h., t. Fowler. Founded by the Fuller brothers from VT: Sheldon, Stillman (or Stilman), Heman, and Ashbel. The ironworks and blast furnace, completed in 1833, operated until 1882, was n. S. Fuller & Co.; p. o. est. Dec. 31, 1833, Stillman Fuller as the first pm, changed to **Fullersville Iron Works**, Apr. 6, 1848, Charles G. Edgerton, pm, changed Dec. 1895 to **Fullerville Ironworks**, Abbie E. Spicer, pm, changed Dec. 1907, Albert J. Monier, first pm, to **Fullerville Iron Works**, closed Oct. 31, 1918 (New York Postal History). See also Durant, 380. 1956 USGS Edwards Quad. Also **Fullersville**. Other derived n.: **Fullerville Cemetery**. / **Fullerville-Edwards Road**: r., t. Fowler. / **Fullerville Iron Works**: t. Fowler; see **Fullerville** for p. o. information. / **Fullerville Iron Works School**: no. 3, common school, t. Fowler. / **Fullerville-Jefferson Road**: r., t. Fowler, also Route 37 and Russell Turnpike Road. / **Fullerville Road**: r., t. Fowler. / **Fullerville Road**: r., t. Pitcairn. / **Fullerville Sands**: flatlands, t. Edwards. 1956 USGS Edwards Quad. / **Fullerville School**: t., Edwards.

Fulsom Road: r., t. Fine, n. Fulsom family.

Fulton: surname used as a specific: **Fulton Road**: r., t. Lisbon, n. Fulton family. / **Fultons Ferry**: t. Massena, n. John Fulton, operated a ferry across the St. Lawrence River, 1805.

Furnace Street: s., h. Norfolk, n. presence of a furnace.

Furniss Flouring-Mills: in Ogdensburg, n. William E. Furniss (1806-1872).

Fyfe Road: r., t. Clare, east off Route 115, west-central of t., n. Fyfe family.

G

Gaddis Road: r., t. Edwards, n. James Gaddis.

Gain Twist Falls: in Racquette River, t. Parishville. 1896 **Gaintwist Falls** New; 1912 **Gaintwaist Falls** Stoddard (misprint); 1908 USGS Potsdam Quad.

Gale: southeast of Childwold, h., t. Piercefield, n. E. P. Gale, store owner and pm; p. o. est. Dec. 30, 1887, Emery P. Gale, pm, closed July 31, 1895, reopened Feb. 22, 1896, Mary A. Gale, pm, closed Jan. 15, 1923. See **Windfall.** *Quarterly*, 7 (1962), no. 1, p. 9. 1880 Ely; 1883 Ely-Wallace; 1896 New; 1902 Blankman; 1908 Adm; 1912 Stoddard; 1920 USGS Childwold Quad. / **Gale Cemetery**: t. Piercefield, n. Gale family.

Galilee; on Black Lake, h., t. Oswegatchie, n. Biblical, known as the "land of milk and honey," and because the shape of the area is similar to Galilee. *Quarterly*, 10 (1965), no. 4, p. 14; p. o. est. May 24, 1895, Charles W. Nolan, pm, closed Nov. 30, 1901. [Charles W. Nonal listed as pm in New York Postal History]. 1963 USGS Edwardsville Quad. / **Galilee School**: no. 7, common school, t. Oswegatchie.

Gallagher Road: r., t. Gouverneur, n. Gallagher family.

Gallooville / Gallopville / Galloupville: see **Red Mills.**

Gallup Rapids: rapid flow of water around Gallup Island, t. Lisbon. Amerindian n.: **Tsiiakotennitserronttietha,** "where the canoe must be pushed up stream with poles." See Beauchamp, 73. 1906 USGS Red Mills Quad.

Gallups, The: in St. Lawrence River. French name: **L'isle au Galop,** n. rapids in the river. Also **The Galloups.** See **Galop Island.**

Galop Island: in St. Lawrence River, t. Lisbon. 1963 USGS Sparrow Quad. Also **Gallop Island, Gallou Island.**

Ganataragoin: see **Indian Point.**

Garden: usually commendatory or for presence of garden: **Garden Cottage**: at St. Lawrence State Hospital, now the administration building. *Quarterly*, 11 (1966), no. 4, p. 19. / **Garden Island**: in St. Lawrence River, t. Hammond. 1958 Chippewa Quad. / **Garden Street**: s., v. Potsdam, n. by extension from the garden alongside LeRoy Street.

Gardner: surname used as a specific: **Gardner Pond**: in Tanner Creek, t. Hermon, n. John Gardner, sawmill owner. Now **Goose Pond. / Gardner Mill Road**: t. DeKalb, but Gardner has long been lost in history. See

Bryan Thompson, "The Coming and Going of a Road and its Residents," *Quarterly*, 25 (1990), no. 3, pp. 3-7.

Garfield: usually James Abram Garfield (1831-1881), 20th United States' president, but in St. Lawrence County, with the exception of **Garfield Avenue**: s. v. Massena, all n. Horace Garfield: **Garfield Brook**: t. Potsdam, trib. Racquette River. 1964 USGS Potsdam Quad. / **Garfield Cemetery**: t. Potsdam. 1943 USGS Potsdam Quad. / **Garfield Road**: r., t. Potsdam, between Old Potsdam-Parishville r. and Rte. 72.

Garlough Road: r., t. Parishville and Colton, southeast off Jo Indian Road into t. Colton, n. Stephen Garlough (1819-1896) and son James, first settlers in Stark Region.

Garond Road: r., t. Lawrence, connects Hallahad and Morgan Roads.

Garonoquoy: see **Long Sault Island.**

Garrison Cemetery: on land owned by Charles Garrison, t. Pitcairn, but no Garrisons are buried there. Eugene Hatch, "A Grand Old Name: The Garrison Letters," *Quarterly*, 20 (1975), no. 2, p. 5. 1951 USGS Harrisville Quad. / **Garrison Road**: r., t. Pitcairn.

Garvin Avenue: s., v. Massena, n. John Garvin, early settler from Stockbridge, VT. Also claimed for Capt. W. S. P. Garvin, Civil War officer of 142nd Infantry.

Gates: surname used as a specific: **Gates Cemetery**: t. Edwards. / **Gates Road**: r., t. Hermon, n. Isaac R. Gates. / **Gates School**: no. 6, common school, t. Rossie. / **Gates Street**: s., c. Ogdensburg, n. Horatio Gates (1728?-1806), general in the Revolutionary War.

Geer: n. family: **Geer School**: no. 6, common school, t. Pitcairn. / **Geers Corners**: hamlet, t. Pitcairn. 1951 USGS Harrisville Quad.

Geneva Street: s., v. Waddington.

George: either a given n. or surname: **George Street**: s., v. Brasher Falls; r., t. Lawrence; s., v. Massena; s., v. Parishville.

Gerald Hunter Road: r., t. Waddington.

German Street: see **Germain Street**.

Germain Street: s., v. Hermon, n. Germain Sutherland, early settler.

Listed erroneously on some maps as **German Street**.

Gertrude Street: s., c. Ogdensburg, n. a daughter of Nathan Ford. Now **Franklin Street**.

Gibbs School: no. 2, common school, t. Russell, n. Thomas and Joseph Gibbs families. 1915 USGS Russell Quad. Also **Beech Grove School**.

Gibbons Brook: t. Russell, trib. Grass(e) River, n. Gibbons family, early settlers. 1915 USGS Russell Quad.

Gibson Road: r., t. Stockholm, n. Gibson family.

Giffin: n. Nathan Ford Giffin, who in 1868 built a grist mill at the northwest corner of State and Union Streets, owned Giffin's Store, and other businesses in Heuvelton: **Giffin's Hill**: v. Heuvelton, where St. Lawrence National Bank is now. / **Giffin School**: no. 2, common school, t. Potsdam, n. Giffin family.

Gilbert: n. family: **Gilbert Road**: r., t. Gouverneur. / **Gilbert Street**: s., c. Ogdensburg, n. Silvester Gilbert (1787-1865), who arrived in 1810, became a merchant and banker, and served as president of Ogdensburgh Village in 1835-36 and 1856-57.

Gilmore Street: s., v. Potsdam. n. Jeremiah Gilmore.

Gilmour Road: r., t. Morristown, n. Gilmour family.

Gilson School: no. 11, common school, t. DeKalb, n. James and Israel Gilson from VT.

Gimlet Street: r., t. DeKalb. Residents once petitioned to change Gimlet to Jefferson Street (some maps show it.). Change did not win approval.

Ginn Road: r., t. Canton; r., v. Rensselaer Falls, n. Ginn family who owned all the farms on that part of the road. The extension of Ginn Road is **Congress Street**.

Gladding Road: r., t. Norfolk, from Brouse Road to Route 420, n. the many Gladding families. 1964 USGS Massena Quad.

Glasby: surname used as a specific: **Glasby Creek**: t. Fine, trib. Oswegatchie River, n. Glasby family. 1919 USGS Cranberry Lake Quad. / **Glasby Mountain**: t. Clifton, alt. 2,050 ft. 1902 Blankman. / **Glasby Pond**. t. Clifton, south of Cranberry, alt. 1,743. *Quarterly*, 17 (1972), no. 2, p. 12. 1896 New; 1898 EGB, p. 27; 1902 Blankman; 1908 Adm; 1912 Stoddard; 1919 USGS Cranberry Lake Quad.

Gleason: surname used as a specific: **Gleason Street**: s., v. Gouverneur, n. George M. Gleason, Civil War veteran, New York State legislator for six terms beginning in 1866, member of County Board of Supervisors, and v. justice of the peace. Cent. Souv., 66-67. Webster, 51. / **Gleasons Mill**: t. Clare, n. Lansing "Lant" Gleason, operator of the mill built in 1860 by a man named Morgan. Gleason bought it in 1892. The mill operated until 1928. Formerly, **Morgan's Mill.** *Quarterly*, 13 (1969), no. 4, p. 6. 1921 **Gleasons Mill** Stark Quad. Also **Gleason's Mill.**

Glenmeal State Forest: #19, t. Pierrepont.

Glenn Street: s., v. Massena, n. Daniel Glenn. Formerly, **Lovers Lane.**

Goat Town Road: r., t. Canton, dead end and unpaved, southeast off Rice Road.

Goblet: n. shape: **Goblet Spring**: t. Colton. 1921 USGS Stark Quad. / **Goblet Spring**: t. Clare.

Gokey Avenue: s., h. Star Lake, n. Arthur Gokey, a Jones & Laughlin Steel Corporation employee, who with his family built a home on this new road off Route # 3 near Star Lake, t. Clifton.

Golden Street: s., v. Morristown.

Golf Course Road: s., h. Star Lake.

Goodrich Street: s., v. Canton, n. prob. William B. Goodrich, who lived in the area. Beers, p. 13. He was a captain in the Union Army during the Civil War, 60th Regiment, Company A, promoted to Lt. Col. and was killed at the battle of Antietam, 1862. He may have owned *The St. Lawrence Plaindealer* at one time. A claim is also made for Chauncy, Allen, and Thomas Goodrich, tanners and shoemakers. Durant, pp. 477-478.

Goodridge Lane: s., v. Massena, n. Ira Goodridge.

Goose: usually n. bird or relating to the bird: **Goose Neck Island**: see **Gooseneck Island. / Goose Pond**: n. because migrating geese stopped on the pond; wide and deep spot in Tanner Creek, t. Hermon. According to a newspaper report, two Bevins children drowned Aug. 2, 1884, in 20-foot deep water there

(Scrapbook from **Hermon Courier** of 1871-1889, p. 95). Also **Gardner Pond.** / **Goose Pond**: t. Pitcairn, n. fowl. 1865 Beers, p. 72; 1951 Harrisville Quad.

Gooseberry Mountain: t. Clare, alt. 1,425 ft., n. the shrub (genus *Ribes*) that bears an acid, prickly fruit. 1921 Stark Quad.

Gooseneck Island: in St. Lawrence River, t. Louisville, n. shape. 1942 USGS **Gooseneck Island** Murphy Island Quad; 1964 USGS Louisville Quad. / **Gooseneck Island Shoals**: shallow area around the island.

Gordon Street: s., v. Gouverneur, n. W. A. Gordon in the 1850s.

Gore Street: s., h. Star Lake, located near the Clifton-Fine School off Route # 3 in Star Lake, n. William Gore, a farmer, who sold the land for the purpose of the building of the school.

Gorge, The: narrow channel in the St. Regis River, t. Parishville.

Gouverneur: southwestern interior of the county, one of the original 10 townships, n. **Cambray** in 1787, but changed to its present n. when formed on Apr. 5, 1810, to honor Gouverneur Morris (1751-1816), born in Morrisania, Westchester Co., of a famous family. He was a member of the provincial congress, a delegate to the first state constitutional convention, a minister to France during the French Revolution, where he befriended Chaumont and helped him and his family come to America. Morris also gave the funeral oration at the death of George Washington. Durant, 153; Hough, 306-307). Nathan Ford said of Morris, "He travels in the style of an Eastern Prince." Morris built a summer home in Gouverneur at Natural Dam, now a historic site. 1956 USGS Richville Quad. Other n. derived from the t. n. and Morris's n.: **Gouverneur**: v. in t. **Gouverneur**, which see; p. o. est. Oct. 28, 1818, changed from **Cambray**, Richard Townsend, pm; p. o. existing, ZIP 13642; baseball team in 1892 nicknamed **Rockets**. 1956 USGS Gouverneur Quad. / **Gouverneur Airport**: t. Gouverneur. 1956 USGS Gouverneur Quad. / **Gouverneur Central School**, v. Gouverneur./ **Gouverneur Drive**: s., v. Potsdam, on State University College campus. / **Gouverneur High School**: no. 1, common school, t. Gouverneur, now Gouverneur Central School. 1956 USGS Gouverneur Quad. / **Gouverneur Street**: s., v.

Canton, n. village of Gouverneur. / **Gouverneur Street**: s., v. Morristown, n. Gouverneur Morris. / **Gouverneur-DePeyster Road**: r., t. DeKalb, DePeyster.

Graham: surname used as specific: **Graham Hall**: n. Dr. John Graham, a former president of Clarkson University, Potsdam. / **Graham Pond**: t. Pitcairn. 1865 Beers, p. 72, notes a J. Graham living in the area; 1951 USGS Harrisville Quad. / **Graham Island**: t. Hermon, in Trout Lake. Earlier n.: **J. S. Brown Island, Jordan Island**. *Quarterly*, 16 (1971), no. 1, p. 10. / **Graham Road**: r., t. Pitcairn. See **Graham Pond**.

Grand: impressive, imposing, magnificent: **Grand Eddy Island**: n. river feature, water current. See **Croils Island**. / **Grand Island**: formerly **Hog Island**, translated from French, **Isle de Porcs**. / **Grand Street**: s., v. Massena. / **Grand Trunk Railroad**: serviced Massena. Dumas, 61.

Grandy: surname: **Grandy Road**: noted in 1925 Census for Judson C. Grandy. Now **White Road**, a dead end r. south from Woods Bridge Road. / **Grandy Road**: r., t. Russell, dead end r. north from Woods Bridge Road, n. Samuel Grandy, Jr., who settled in 1844; was briefly **Terry Road**, n. Florice Grandy Terry; homestead now owned by Lloyd G. Grandy; private cemetery on property. Listed on 1988 Highway Map (St. Lawrence County) as **Terry Road**.

Grange: t. Brasher, survey township n., origin unknown, but possibilities include the meaning of "farm," derived from French **grange**, or commemorating **La Grange**, n. of the home of Marquis de La Fayette.

Grannis Brook: n. Cyrus Grannis, first supervisor t. Pierrepont. *Quarterly*, 16 (1971), no. 1, p. 11. Also **Granis Creek, Granis Brook**. 1898 Blankman; 1964 **Grannis Brook** Canton Quad.

Granshue: also, **Granshuck** (misprint on map), one of the survey townships. in the eastern part of St. Lawrence County, south of the original ten. Hough, 255. Now a part of t. Colton. / **Granshue Club**: Private forest and game preserve, Great Tract Two, Macomb's Purchase. The preserve was incorporated June 27, 1890, and within it were Long, Amsberg, and Little Blue Ponds, and also a stretch of the Grass(e) River, over three miles. Origin, Irish place name, home of Daniel McCormick.

Grant: surname used as specific: **Grant Island**: see **Grants Island**. / **Grant Road**: r., t. Norfolk, n. Grant family. Julius Grant and Andrew Grant and their families came from Canada in 1836, although Julius Grant, Sr., was born in 1785 in MA. Maude Wing, "Norfolk Was a Wilderness in 1809," *Quarterly*, 6 (1961), no. 1, p. 13. / **Grant School**: no. 6, common school, t. Norfolk, on Grant Road. / **Grant Settlement**: t. Norfolk. "At one time six large families of Grants lived within about a mile radius and the neighborhood was known as Grant Settlement." See also **Grant Road**. / **Grant Street**: s., v. Colton; s., v. Edwards, n. William Grant (1833-1918), local builder. Freeman, 31. / Ulysses Simpson Grant (1822-1885) Civil War general and 18th president of the United States: s., v. Massena ; s., c. Ogdensburg ; s., v. Potsdam. / **Grant's Cemetery**: t. Potsdam, same as **French Cemetery**. See **French**. / **Grant's Crossing**: n. Tom Grant (?), farm owner. *Quarterly*, 14 (1969), no. 3, p. 14. / **Grants Island**: in St. Lawrence River, t. Hammond. 1958 USGS Chippewa Quad. / **Grantville**: corners, t. Norfolk. See **Grant Road**. 1964 USGS Norfolk Quad. / **Grantville School**: see **Grant Road**.

Grantville State Forest: #15, t. Norfolk; n. Grant Family.

Grasmere Avenue: s., v. Massena.

Grass: descriptive n. for any open area that is covered with grass, the area extending to the whole of the feature: **Grass Creek**: rises in Grass Lake, t. Rossie, trib. Black Lake. 1961 USGS Hammond Quad. / **Grass Hill**: t. Colton. 1921 USGS Cranberry Lake Quad. / **Grass Lake**: see **Massawepie Lake**, t. Piercefield / **Grass Lake**: t. Rossie (St. Lawrence Co.) and t. Theresa (Jefferson Co.) translation from Amer-indian n.: **Osakentake**, "grass lake." See Beauchamp, 73; Hough, 180. 1961 USGS Muskellunge Quad. / **Grass Pond**: t. Colton. 1921 USGS Stark Quad. / **Grass Pond**: t. Clifton, alt. 1,736. 1880 Ely; 1883 Ely-Wallace; 1896 Grass Pond (also, **Echo Lake**) New; 1898 EGB, p. 27; 1902 **Echo Lake** Blankman; 1908 Adm; 1912 Stoddard; 1919 USGS Cranberry Lake Quad. / **Grass Pond**: t. Pitcairn. 1916 USGS Oswegatchie Quad. / **Grass Pond Mountain**: t. Clifton, alt. 2,300. 1896 New; 1902 Blankman; 1919 USGS Cranberry Lake Quad. / **Grass River**: t. Madrid, p. o. est. Jan. 12, 1858, George W. Bragdon, pm, changed to **Madrid Springs**, July 15, 1869. / **Grass River Falls**: See **Madrid**. / **Grass Road**:

r., t. Hermon.

Grass(e) River: enters St. Lawrence River at St. Regis, t. Massena. Formerly **Black River**. Durant, 277, writes: "The name of this stream is written in the old records of 1803 and 1804 'La Grasse,' showing clearly that it is of French origin. It may mean 'Greasy river,' or it may be a corruption of the name 'Riviere a la Grace,' River of Grace. It certainly does not mean 'grass,' the French word of which is 'herbe.' Nevertheless, custom has made the name 'Grasse River,' which we shall use in this sketch." Amerindian name: **Nikentsiake**, "place of fishes." Hough, 179-180; *Quarterly*, 6 (1961), no. 4, p. 13; 8 (1963), no. 2, p. 8. The river has three branches: North, Middle, and South. The South Branch rises in Jocks Pond, t. Piercefield, with all branches touching or flowing through t. Piercefield, Colton, Clifton, Clare, Pierrepont, Fine, Russell, Hermon, DeKalb, Potsdam, Canton, Lisbon, Madrid, Waddington, Louisville, and Massena. 1964 USGS **Grass River** Raquette River Quad. / **Grasse River Club**: private forest and game preserve. See **Forest Commission Report**, 1893, p. 143. / **Grass(e) River Flow**: t. Colton. 1896 reservoir New; 1908 **Grass River Flow** Adm; 1912 **Grass River Flow** Stoddard; 1920 **Grass River Flow** USGS Childwold Quad. / **Grasse River Railroad**: from Childwold Station, 11 m. to Brandy Brook Junction. *Quarterly*, 3 (1958), no. 4, p. [6]. [The editors have consistently here used **Grass(e)**, since both **Grass** and **Grasse** indicate divided usage in spelling, which, of course, has no bearing on pronunciation.]

Grasshopper Hill: t. Stockholm, n. for an invasion of the insects. 1964 USGS Brasher Falls Quad.

Grassy Pond: see **Chain Ponds**. t. Clifton. 1919 USGS Cranberry Lake Quad.

Gravel: small stones and pebbles, sometimes mixed with sand: / **Gravel Pit Road**: r., t. Piercefield, n. feature. / **Gravel Road**: r., t. Gouverneur, n. type of road bed. / **Gravel Road Cemetery**: t. Gouverneur, on Gravel Road near Little Bow. 1961 USGS Natural Bridge Quad. / **Gravel Pit Road**: r., t. Piercefield, n. feature.

Graves: surname used as a specific: **Graves Mountain**: t. Colton, alt. 2,300 ft. 1896 New; 1902 Blankman; 1919 USGS Cranberry Lake Quad. / **Graves Pond**: t. Colton, alt. 1,768 ft. 1880 Ely; 1883 Ely-Wallace; 1896 New; 1902

Blankman; 1908 Adm; 1919 USGS Cranberry Lake Quad. / **Graves School**: no. 7, common school, t. Macomb. / **Graves Street**: s., v. Gouverneur, n. Graves family. The street runs perpendicular to Riverside Cemetery.

Gray: surname used as a specific: **Gray School**: no. 20, common school, t. Oswegatchie, n. Walter R. Gray. / **Grays School**: t. DeKalb, on Bigelow River Road. 1915 USGS Gouverneur Quad; 1956 USGS Richville Quad. Not noted in 1896 listing. / **Gray's Island**: formerly, **Long Island**.

Graysville: settlement, t. Lisbon, p. o. est. Feb. 17, 1831, n. Isaac H. Gray, pm, closed Apr. 22, 1836.

Great: large, impressive, sometimes a contrast with "small": **Great Swamp**: t. Clifton, on Oswegatchie River south of Cranberry Lake. 1858 Rogerson. / **Great Falls**: on Grass(e) River. *Quarterly*, 14 (1969), no. 2, p. 11. / **Great Windfall**: see **Slash, The**, and **Windfall**. / **Great River Road**: Laid out in 1802 by Amos Lay, n. reference to St. Lawrence River.

Green: color-n., sometimes derogatory, for green scum on surface of water, but usually commendatory for freshness and depth of color; very common personal and place n. in the United States: **Green Bay**: in Cranberry lake, t. Clifton. 1896 New. / **Green Meadow Road**: r., t. Stockholm. / **Green Point Road**: r., t. Colton, off Gulf Road. /**Green Pond**: see **Johns Pond**, t. Colton. / **Green Road**: r., t. Hopkinton; r., t. Pierrepont. / **Green Settlement**: v. Heuvelton, t. Oswegatchie, on West Road, n. Green family. See Smithers, **History of Heuvelton.** / **Green School**: t. Fine, Dist. 7, held in home of Francis Green. Reynolds, 199. Also **Guiles School**, Dist. 7. / **Green Street**: r., t. DeKalb, n. Orange Green; s., v. Waddington. / **Green Valley School**: t. Russell. 1915 USGS Russell Quad. Identified only on USGS map.

Greene Street: s., c. Ogdensburg, n. Nathanael Greene (1742-1786), commander of the Continental Army of the South, which he used to great effect against the British in Georgia and the Carolinas. Also, **Green Street**, the **e** occasionally omitted.

Greenfield Pond: t. Fine, small pond north of Scott's Bridge, n. Alonzo L. Greenfield. But see Catherine Brownell, "The Albany Road," *Quarterly*, 11 (1966), no. 4, p. 15;

Catherine Brownell, "Lakes and Ponds in the Town of Fine," *Quarterly*, 5 (1960), no. 1, npn.

Greenwood: desc., commendatory, romantic, but sometimes n. person + **wood**, sometimes also personal n. **Greenwood: Greenwood Cemetery**: Main Street, v. Morristown. Bogardus, 233. 1963 USGS Morristown Quad. / **Greenwood Creek**: t. Fine, Pitcairn, trib. Jenne Creek; poss. n. F. Green. 1898 Blankman. / **Greenwood Creek State Forest**, #4, Pitcairn. / **Greenwood Falls**: in Greenwood Creek. / **Greenwood Lake**: pond, t. Fine, off Route 3 near Oswegatchie and Jayville, on Carthage and Adirondack Railroad, near the summit of the Jayville grade. *Quarterly*, 11 (1966), no. 1, p. 16. 1916 USGS Oswegatchie Quad. Also, **Greenswood Lake**. / **Greenwood Road**: r., t. Pitcairn.

Gregory: surname used as a specific: **Gregory Corners**: crossroads, t. Lisbon, n. Ira W. Gregory. 1963 USGS Lisbon Quad. / **Gregory School**: no. 21, common school, t. Lisbon, n. Gregory family.

Grems Street: s., v. Hermon, n. William Grems. Now **Howard Street**.

Griffin: surname used as a specific, usually n. family: **Griffin Avenue**: s., h. Star Lake. / **Griffin Island**: t. Hermon, in Trout Lake. *Quarterly*, 16 (1971), no. 1, p. 10. / **Griffin Road**: r., t. Canton, Potsdam; t., Fine, n. Michael Griffin, settled in 1842. Reynolds, 16. / **Griffin School**: t. Potsdam. Not identified. / **Griffin Rapids**: in Oswegatchie River, t. Fine, near Jones & Laughlin site, also near High Falls on the Oswegatchie River, n. Michael Griffin. 1919 USGS Cranberry Lake Quad.

Griffith: n. family: **Griffith School**: no. 9, common school, t. Gouverneur; t. Macomb. 1949 USGS Hammond Quad. Listed on USGS map but not identified locally.

Griffiths Arts Center: on St. Lawrence University campus, n. Eben Griffiths, trustee, and Bessie Green Griffiths.

Grindstone: a generic n., poss. for the location of stones for mill: **Grindstone Bay**: in Black Lake, t. Macomb. 1961 USGS Hammond Quad. / **Grindstone Bay**: in Tupper Lake, t. Piercefield. 1860 Merrit; 1860 Street, p. 188; 1880 Ely; 1883 Ely-Wallace; 1912 [**Grind**(stone Bay)] Stoddard; 1954 USGS Tupper Lake Quad. / **Grindstone Brook**: trib. Tupper Lake, t. Piercefield. 1860 Street, pp 157, 188; 1896 New; 1954 USGS Tupper Lake Quad. /

Grindstone Falls, t. Fine.

Grinnel Street: s., v. Massena, prob. n. Grinnell College.

Grove: n. usually associated with a stand of trees; popular place n., and generic, although used here as a specific: **Grove School**: t. Morristown, at corner of Atwood and Chippewa Roads. Bogardus, 60. / **Grove School**: no. 9, common school, t. Hammond, no. 14/Morristown, no. 9 (joint district), n. located in a grove of shade trees. / **Grove Street**: s., v. Canton; s., v. Gouverneur, n. Dodge Grove; s., h. Hannawa Falls; s., v. Massena; r., and s., h. North Lawrence; s., v. Norwood; s., c. Ogdensburg; s., v. Potsdam.

Guiles: n. family: **Guiles Road**: r., t. Pitcairn. / **Guiles School**: no. 7, common school, t. Fine. Reynolds, 199, claims District no. 6.

Gulf: a generic, here used to n. a stream that disappears and then appears again at a distance: **Gulf, The**: see **The Gulf**. / **Gulf Cemetery**: t. Fowler, south end of Gulf Road. 1956 USGS Edwards Quad. / **Gulf Brook**: trib. Racquette River, t. Colton. / **Gulf Creek**: t. Clare, stream, trib. Cook Creek. 1963 Rensselaer Falls Quad. Also noted as a trib. North Branch Grass(e) River. 1921 USGS Stark Quad; 1912 **Gulf Brook** Stoddard; 1902 **Gulf Brook** Blankman. / **Gulf Creek**, trib. Racquette River, t. Piercefield. / **Gulf Road**: r., t. Colton; r., t. DeKalb. Now **Lobdell Road**; r., t. Fowler. / **Gulf Stream**: t. Pitcairn, trib. Jenne Creek. 1916 USGS Oswegatchie Quad.

Gull: n. of the long-winged bird, numerous near large bodies of water; often used as a specific for ponds and lakes: **Gull Brook**: trib. Racquette River, t. Piercefield. 1860 **Gull Pond Brook** Street, p. 267; 1883 Ely-Wallace; 1902 Blankman. / **Gull Island**: see **Eagle Island**. / **Gull Pond**: t. Piercefield (St. Lawrence Co.), Altamont (Franklin Co.), alt. 1,561. 1860 Merritt; 1865 **Bull Pond** (misprint?) Beers, p. 86; 1880 Ely; 1883 Ely-Wallace; 1896 New; 1902 Blankman; 1908 Adm; 1912 Stoddard; 1954 USGS Tupper Lake Quad. / **Gull Pond Bay**: in Tupper Lake, unidentified, t. Piercefield. 1860 Street, p. 188, "so called by Harvey [Moody]." / **Gull Pond Brook**: see **Gull Brook**. / **Gull Pond Mountain**: t. Piercefield, unidentified. 1860, Street, p. 178, "The north and west shores [of Tupper Lake] are hilly, Gull Pond Mountain extending along a portion of the course." / **Gull Rock**: on

Cranberry Lake, t. Clifton. 1898 **Gull Rocks** New; 1902 Blankman (see **Eagle Island**); 1919 USGS Cranberry lake Quad.

Gunnison Memorial Chapel: on St. Lawrence University campus, n. Dr. Almon Gunnison, a former president.

Gynn Road: r., t. Parishville, n. Mathew Gynn. Now **Morgan Road**.

Gypsy Lane: r., t. Canton, prob. n. for place where gypsy caravans were allowed to park.

H

Hadlock Road: r., t. Hammond, n. Edwin Hadlock family.

Hadley: surname: **Hadley Road**: r., t. Pierrepont, n. Hiram and Joshua Hadley; r., t. Potsdam, n. Hadley family.

Haggart Road: r., t. Oswegatchie, n. Daniel Haggart.

Haggerty: n. Patrick Haggerty: **Haggerty Road**: s., v. Potsdam. / **Haggerty School**: no. 25, common school, t. Potsdam, n. Haggerty family.

Hague: one of the original ten townships; a survey t.; n. The Hague, Holland. Now, **Morristown**. Derived n. include **Hague Crossing**: railroad crossing, t. Lisbon. 1964 USGS Morley Quad. / **Hague Point**: on Black Lake, t. Morristown. 1963 USGS Pope Mills Quad.

Haig: n. family: **Haig Road**: r., t. Norfolk; r., t. Potsdam, Madrid, n. John Haig family of Madrid.

Hailes Hopyard: island, in Oswegatchie River, t. Fowler, n. James Haile family. 1956 USGS Gouverneur Quad.

Hailes Mills: t. Fine, later **Browns Mills**.

Hailesboro: h. in t. Fowler, n. James Haile, Revolutionary War brigadier general, who came to explore in June, 1807, and purchased the land in 1807 which is the present site of the h. Durant, 377. *Quarterly*, 7 (1962), no. 2, p. 15; p. o. est. Sept. 30, 1858, as **Hailesborough**, Seymour M. Farmer, pm, closed Jan. 13, 1870, reopened Jan. 21, 1870, George D. Morrison, pm, changed to **Hailesboro** Oct. 27, 1893, Edwin Noble, pm; p. o. existing, ZIP 13654. Also, **Hailesborough**. 1956 USGS Gouverneur Quad. Other names derived from the h. n.: **Hailesborough Cemetery**. /

Hailesboro School: no. 4, common school. / **Hailesborough Street**: s., v. Gouverneur.

Hale: surname used as specific: **Hale Cemetery**: t. Norfolk. / **Hale Road**: r., t. Canton, n. Hale family. / **Hale School**: no. 12, common school, t. Norfolk. n. Ira and Moses Hale, brothers. *Quarterly*, 26 (1981), no. 2, p. 19.

Haleville Cemetery: t. Lawrence, south of U.S. 11C on McEwen Road. 1964 USGS North Lawrence Quad. Mapped in error as **Hailville** by USGS.

Haley Drive: s., v. Canton, poss. n. Ledyard Haley.

Half: partial, usually a distance or number n., assuming two equal parts, as in **Halfway**: **Half Mile Hill**: t. Fowler, 1/2 mile from Balmat. / **Half Way**: see **Halfway House Corners** and **Halfway School House**. / **Halfmoon Pond**: t. Clifton, n. shape. 1919 USGS Cranberry lake Quad. / **Halfway Island**: in St. Lawrence River, t. Hammond. 1958 USGS Chippewa Bay Quad. / **Halfway House Corners**: t. Waddington, approximately midway between the villages of Madrid and Waddington, "where Rookey Road and the Half Way House Road intersect with Route 345." Tedford, 43. 1964 USGS Waddington Quad. Also, **Half Way House Courners** (a misprint). / **Halfway House Corners**: between t. Canton and Lisbon. / **Halfway House Road**: r., t. Waddington. / **Halfway School House**: no. 6, common school, t. Waddington, now used as a home. Also, **Half Way School House**, **Halfway House School**. "The school house was built in 1855 by George B. Oliver for $117.63," Tedford, 47.

Hall: surname used as a specific: **Hall Avenue**: s., h. Star Lake, located off Rte. 3 near Clifton-Fine School, n. Addison Hall, Gouverneur native, former state trooper and guard at Jones & Laughlin Steel Corporation. / **Hall Creek**: t. Norfolk, trib. Racquette River, n. Erastus Hall, receiver of the first contract for land at Raymondville in 1809. 1964 USGS Norfolk Quad. / **Hall Lake**: pond, t. Fine, n. Hall family. 1915 USGS Russell Quad. / **Hall Road**: all are named for local families: r., v. Edwards; r., t. Lisbon; r., t. Macomb; r., t. Massena; r., t. Rossie.

Hallahan Road: r., t. Lawrence, n. Timothy Hallihan, with spelling change.

Hallock School: no. 8, common

school, t. Madrid, n. Philander Hallock family.

Halls: possessive of **Hall**: **Halls Corners**: crossroads, t. Gouverneur, intersection of Peabody and Stevens Roads, n. Addison G. Hall (1915 Census). Beers, 31, shows J. D. Hall and E. Hall living near the intersections. **Cent. Souv.**, 58-59. 1956 USGS Richville Quad. / **Halls Rapids**: in Racquette River, t. Colton. 1920 USGS Childwold Quad.

Hamele Street: in Wanakena, n. Otto B. Hamele, supervisor of t. Fine for many years and first St. Lawrence County Historian (1944).

Hamill Road: r., t. Morristown, n. Michael Hamill family.

Hamilton: popular surname used as a specific, occasion- ally appears as a first n.: **Hamilton**: See **Waddington**. / **Hamilton Hill**: t. Russell, off Russell- Hermon Road, n. Isaac Hamilton, who came to Russell in 1837. *Quarterly*, 16 (1971), no. 4, p. 7; 11 (1966), no. 2, p. 20. 1915 USGS Russell Quad. / **Hamilton Mountain**: t. Hopkinton, alt. 1,720. 1896 New; 1902 Blankman; 1908 Adm; 1912 Stoddard; 1919 USGS **Ton Mountain** Nicholville Quad; 1964 USGS Sylvan Falls Quad. / **Hamilton Smith Road**: r., t. Hammond, n. Hamilton Smith, early settler. / **Hamilton Street**: s., v. Massena, n. Alexander Hamilton (1757-1804), American statesman, secretary of treasury in George Washington's cabinet, died in a duel with Aaron Burr at Weehawken Heights, NJ. He was associated in business with the Ogden brothers. The v. Waddington was originally n. **Hamilton.** A claim is also made for Hamilton College, since Massena has several streets n. for colleges. Other **Hamilton Streets** n. Alexander Hamilton: s., c. Ogdensburg; s., v. Potsdam; s., v. Waddington. / **Hamiltons Corners**: corners, t. Pierrepont, n. Charles Hamilton family. 1915 USGS Russell Quad.

Hamlin: surname used as specific: **Hamlin Hall**: on Clarkson University campus, n. Truman L. Hamlin (1874-1966), a member of the faculty of Mathematics for 35 years. / **Hamlin Bay**: in Tupper Lake, t. Piercefield, origin n. unknown. 1954 USGS Tupper Lake Quad.

Hammill Road: r., t. Massena, n. Arthur Hammill family.

Hammond: western corner, bordering on St. Lawrence River , and Jefferson County, t. formed from Rossie and Morristown, Mar. 30, 1827, n. Abijah Hammond, of New

York, who owned the t. previous to the purchase of David Parish. He was a brother-in-law of David A. Ogden (nephew of Samuel Ogden), and a merchant and speculator who had a scheme for purchasing vacant lands. During the Revolutionary War, he was captain of artillery. He "never visited his northern purchases and took no further interest in them than as a subject of speculation." Durant, 383. *Quarterly*, 5 (1960), no. 4, p. 9. The v. **Hammond** took its n. from the t. and was known as **Hammond Corners**. In the 1870s v. was moved about 1/2 m. to be near the railway; p. o. est. Apr. 29, 1822, Hiram Blackmon, first pm; p. o. existing, ZIP 13646 (New York Postal History lists Hiram Blackman). Hough, 574, gives date as Oct. 16, 1824, Arnold Smith, pm. 1961 USGS Hammond Quad; 1963 USGS Morristown Quad. / **Hammond Airport**: t. Hammond. 1949 USGS Hammond Quad. Mapped by USGS but does not exist as a n. locally. / **Hammond Cemetery**: v. Hammond. 1961 USGS Hammond Quad. / **Hammond-Chippewa Bay Road**: r., t. Hammond. / **Hammond Corners**: see **Hammond**. / **Hammond Drive**: s., v. Canton, n. former town clerk. / **Hammond Four Corners**, same as **Hammond Corners**. / **Hammond Road**: r., t. Hammond. / **Hammond, Rossie and Antwerp Plank-Road**: see **Plank Roads**. / **Hammond School**: no. 1, common school, t. Hammond. Also, **Hammond Village School**. / **Hammond Village School**: see **Hammond School**.

Hamtown: nickname of Hopkinton. **Moira SB**, p. 146.

Hand Hill: t. Fowler, alt. 580 ft., n. Hand family. 1956 USGS Gouverneur Quad.

Hanger Road: r., t. Massena, n. hangar at airport. Listed on highway map as **Hanger**, error in spelling.

Hanks Road: s., h. Star Lake, a private road off Lake Road in back of Star Lake, n. Paul B. Hanks, a summer resident from Brockport, NY. Also, **Hanks Street**.

Hanlon: n. family: **Hanlon Road**: r., t. Lisbon; r., t. Waddington.

Hannawa Falls: h., t. Pierrepont, formerly **Cox's Mills** (n. the Cox brothers, Gardner and Benjamin, early settlers and mill owners), p. o. est. Dec. 29, 1875, Jacob H. Miles, pm, changed from **Ellsworth**; p. o. existing, ZIP 13647. Earlier names, **East Pierrepont**, **Ellsworth**. *Quarterly*, 7 (1962), no. 3, p. 13; 9 (1964), no. 2, p. 22. Also, **Hannaway Falls**. Amerindian name: **Nihanawate**, "noisy water." 1964 USGS Colton Quad. / **Hannawa Falls Schools**: nos. 4 (west side) and 11 (east side), common schools, t. Pierrepont.

Hanson Road: r., t. Hammond, near Chippewa Bay, n. Henry "Hank" Hanson, said to have been a bootlegger during Prohibition times. Two other roads carry a family n. of **Hanson**: r., t. Parishville. / r., t. Pierrepont, Colton.

Hard Pine Island: in Black Lake, owned by Special County Judge Gerrit S. Conger, who was also Commander of the County's first (Barnes) GAR Post. His sentenced criminals taken to county jail were "vulgarly called Hard Piners," according to item in **Commercial Advertiser** (Canton), July 26, 1890. On 1896 lake map, **Conger Island**.

Hardscrabble: n. a difficult place to make a living, usually derogatory but humorous: **Hardscrabble**: settlement, t. Fine. / **Hardscrabble Road**: r., t. Lisbon; r., t. Waddington, Madrid, apparently once a nickname for Route. 345, connecting Waddington and Madrid.

Hardwood: n. presence of tough timber growth of broad-leaved trees (**angiosperm**): **Hardwood Island**: hill, surrounded by swamp, t. Clifton, alt. 1,575 ft. 1919 USGS Stark Quad. Alt. 1,625 ft. on 1954 USGS Tupper Lake Quad. / **Hardwood Ridge**: hill, t. Colton, alt. 1,800 ft. 1921 USGS Stark Quad.

Harewood: a survey township, now in t. Clifton; p. o. est. May 11, 1893, changed from **Cranberry Lake**, Adolphus E. Caul, pm, changed to **Cranberry Lake**, Aug. 26, 1902. See **Star Lake**. Also, see **Cranberry**. Mapmakers are confused as to whether Star Lake or Cranberry was called **Harewood**. Origin of n. unknown, but prob. for a place in England, either in Hampshire, Derbyshire, or West Riding of Yorkshire; ety., OE **har** "grey" + **wood** (grey wood), but also poss. the first element is OE **haer** "stony," or OE **hares** "high." / **Harewood School**: no. 2, common school, t. Clifton.

Hargus Brook: t. Colton, trib. Racquette River. 1908 USGS Potsdam Quad. Mapped by USGS but unknown locally.

Hariman Road: r., t. Hopkinton.

Harison: Thomas Harison, owner of many fine estates: **Harison Creek**: t. Canton, trib. Grass(e) River. It is

Tanner Creek in t. Hermon. 1898 Blankman; 1963 USGS Canton Quad. / **Harison Drive**: s., v. Canton. Same as **Harison Street**. The street signs with the spelling **Harrison** are incorrect.

Harmon Cemetery: t. Edwards, n. James Harmon family and his many offspring. / **Harmon Road**: r., t. Edwards. / **Harmon School**: no. 5, common school, t. Edwards. Freeman, 22. 1915 USGS Russell Quad.

Harper: surname used as a specific: **Harper**: settlement, t. Parishville, p. o. est. May 10, 1904, John P. Harper, pm, closed June 15, 1905. / **Harper Island**: t. Hopkinton, in West Branch St. Regis River, n. owner. 1896 New. / **Harper Road**: r., t. Waddington, n. Robert Harper family. / **Harper School**: no. 3, common school, t. Hopkinton. 1919 USGS Nicholville Quad.

Harriet: s., v. Parishville, n. daughter of David Parish.

Harrigate School: see **Harrowgate School**.

Harrington Court: s., v. Potsdam.

Harris Point: on Cranberry lake, t. Clifton. 1896 New.

Harrison: surname used as a specific n.: **Harrison Avenue**: see **Harrison Street**. / **Harrison Brook**: see **Harrison Creek**, t. Piercefield. / **Harrison Avenue**: s., c. Ogdens- burg. / **Harrison Creek**: see **Harison Creek**, t. Canton / **Harrison Creek**: t. Piercefield, trib. Racquette River. n. W. H. Harrison, owner of tract of land near mouth of stream (1896). 1896 **Harrison Brook** New; 1902 Blankman; 1908 **Harrison Brook** Adm; 1912 **Harrison Brook** Stoddard. / **Harrison Drive**: see **Harison Creek**. **Harrison Street** [misprint for **Harison**]: see **Harison Creek**; s., v. Norwood.

Harrisville Road: r., t. Fowler, also as a s., h. Balmat, n. Charles Harris. / **Harrisville-Fullerville Road**: r., t. Pitcairn.

Harrowgate School: v. Massena, n. Harrowgate, England, the street being named first. Mapped as **Harrigate** in error by 1964 USGS Massena Quad. / **Harrowgate Street**: see **Main Street North**, Massena.

Hartford School: no. 15, common school, t. Norfolk, n. Hartford family.

Hartley School: t. Gouverneur, n. Sylvester F. and Edward Hartley. 1915 USGS Gouverneur Quad.

Harts Falls: on Grass(e) River, down river from Jackson Falls, t. Russell, n. Albert Hart family.

Harvey Brook: stream, trib. Racquette River, t. Colton. 1921 USGS Rainbow Falls Quad.

Hasbrouck: Louis Hasbrouck (1777-1834), Princeton graduate, settler in 1801, attorney, first St. Lawrence County Clerk (1802-1817) when Ogdensburg was the county seat, senator (1832-1834). His mansion was erected in 1804. Hough, 594; Durant, 189: **Hasbrouck Street**: s., c. Ogdensburg. / **Hasbrouck Island**: opposite Chippewa Bay in St. Lawrence River. Also called **Huguenot Island** (for Hasbrouck's native affiliation).

Haskell Ridge: t. Madrid, n. Israel P. and David Haskell. 1964 USGS Chase Mills Quad. / **Haskell School**: no. 4, common school, t. Madrid.

Hastings Falls: falls in St. Regis River, t. Brasher, between Brasher Falls and Helena, personal n.

Hatch Road: r., t. Potsdam, n. Daniel R. Hatch; r. t. Stockholm, n. Sylvester Hatch; r. t. Russell, n. Timothy B. Hatch. / **Hatch School**: t. Russell, n. Hatch family. 1915 USGS Russell Quad.

Hatfield: settlement, t. Massena, p. o. est. Jan. 11, 1881, George H. Dutton, pm, changed to **Massena Springs**, May 21, 1902.

Haverstock Road: r., t. Massena, n. Edmund G. Haverstock family.

Hayden Road: r., t. DeKalb, Hermon, n. Elias Hayden family.

Hayes School: no. 25, common school, t. Stockholm.

Hays School: t. DeKalb. 1915 USGS Gouverneur Quad. Not listed among 1896 common schools.

Haystack Rock: on Route 56, a rock shaped like a haystack, very popular among college students for outside graffiti.

Haystack Mountain: t. Piercefield, alt. 2,185. 1954 USGS Tupper Lake Quad.

Hayward Street: s., c. Ogdensburg.

Hazen Road: r., t. Potsdam, n. Herman L. Hazen family.

Head of the Sault School: no. 10, common school, t. Massena, n. position and feature. See **Foot of the Sault School.**

Head's Creek: see **Roulston's Creek.**

Heath: surname used as a specific: **Heath Pond**: t. Clifton, alt. 1,448. 1883 Ely-Wallace; 1896 New; 1898 EGB, p. 27; 1902 Blankman; 1908 Adm; 1912 Stoddard; 1919 USGS Cranberry Lake Quad. / **Heath Road**: r., t. Potsdam, Stockholm.

Heck Street: s. in Terrace Park, t. Morristown, n. a Methodist bishop.

Hedding Street: s. in Terrace Park, t. Morristown, n. a Methodist bishop.

Hedgehog: an animal (*Erethizon dorsatum*) with hard sharp spines, known in the U. S. as the porcupine. The places n. animal are variously spelled: **Hedge Hog Mountain**: See **Hedgehog Mountain.** / **Hedge Hog Pond**: see **Clear Pond**, t. Colton. / **Hedge Hog Rapids**: see **Hedgehog Rapids.** / **Hedgehog Falls**: see **Hedgehog Rapids.** / **Hedgehog Mountain**: t. Colton, alt. 2,075. 1896 **Hedge Hog Mountain** New; 1902 **Hedge Hog Mountain** Blankman; 1912 **Bear Mountain** (error) Stoddard; 1919 USGS Cranberry Lake Quad. /**Hedgehog Rapids**: in Racquette River, t. Piercefield. 1880 **Hedgehog Falls** Ely; 1883 Ely-Wallace; 1896 **Hedge Hog Rapids** New; 1920 USGS Childwold Quad.

Helena: h. in t. Brasher, located at mouth of Deer River; n. Helen, only daughter of Joseph Pitcairn, proprietor. A claim is made for Helen, daughter of Benjamin Nevin, land agent for Daniel McCormick (*Quarterly*, 24 (1969), no. 4, p. 6). Inc. as v., Mar. 17, 1817; p. o. est. Feb. 13, 1827, David McMurphy, pm (Hough, 268, 574); p. o. existing, ZIP 13649. Amerindian name: **Oiekarontne**, "trout river," Hamilton Child, p. 63; Durant, 414; Hough, 269. 1964 Hogansburg Quad. Other derived n.: **Helena-Bombay Road**: r., t. Brasher. / **Helena Cemetery**: t. Brasher / **Helena School**: no. 1, common school, t. Brasher. / **Helena Street**: s., v. Gouverneur, n. origin unknown.

Hemlock Island: in St. Lawrence River, t. Hammond, n. tree. 1958 USGS Chippewa Quad.

Hen Island: Trout Lake, t. Hermon, in front of Pliny Gardner's Front Lake Hotel where Pliny got his morning eggs for his patrons.

Henry: n. family: **Henry Road**: r., t. Waddington. / **Henry Street**: s., c. Ogdensburg. / **Henrys Corners**: t.

Waddington. 1964 USGS Waddington Quad.

Hepburn: surname. **Hepburn Hall**: on St. Lawrence University campus, dedicated by Mme. Marie Curie, Oct. 26, 1929, n. Emily Eaton Hepburn and A. Barton Hepburn, benefactors. / **Hepburn House**: on Clarkson University campus, n. Mabelle Hepburn Matthews and her parents, Hawley S. Hepburn and Amelia P. Hepburn, by her husband Archibald J. Matthews, who donated the money to establish a home for the president. / **Hepburn Street**: s., v. Norfolk, n. local Hepburn family.

Hermit's Camp: *Quarterly*, 13 (1968), no. 4, p. 20.

Herm Towne Road: t. Gouverneur, n. **Hermon Towne**, a resident.

Hermon: west of center of the county, t. formed on Apr. 17, 1830 from DeKalb and Edwards, originally the Fitzwilliam survey township, under the n. **Depau**, n. Francis DePau, who also owned land in Jefferson Co. Changed to **Hermon**, Feb. 28, 1834, because of similarity to **Depeauville**, Jefferson County. **Hermon** is Biblical, derived from Hebrew, "cursed," prob. n. Mt. Hermon, Palestine, in derision as first settlement was on the only high spot, now **West Hermon**. Durant writes, "[B]ut the bounties of Providence have been bestowed on the town, regardless of the significance of its name." Hough, 574; Durant, 435; *Quarterly*, 8 (1963), no. 4, p. 16. / **Hermon**: p. o. named first, est. Dec. 20, 1828, Benjamin Healey, first pm; v. n. **Hermon**, after the p. o., on Feb. 28, 1834, p. o. existing, ZIP 13652. Baseball team in 1882 was nicknamed **The Tormentors**. 1915 USGS **Hermon** Russell Quad. Other derived names: **Hermon Cemetery**, v. Hermon. / **Hermon Crossroad**: r., t. Gouverneur, n. t. **Hermon**, since it runs into the t. Hermon on Gouverneur's eastern boundary. / **Hermon-DeKalb Central School**, 1952, located in East DeKalb. / **Hermon-DeKalb Road**: also, **Flight Road**. / **Hermon-Edwards Road**: r., t. Edwards. / **Hermon Hill Cemetery**: t. Hermon. Also **Porter Hill Cemetery**. / **Hermon Plank-Road**: see **Plank Roads**. / **Hermon-Pyrites Road**: r., t. Hermon, Canton. / **Hermon-Richville Road**: r., t. Hermon. Route 23. / **Hermon-Richville Road**: r., t. Hermon, De Kalb. Route 27. / **Hermon Road**: r., t. Gouverneur, n. t. **Hermon**, since it is near t. Hermon on Gouverneur's eastern boundary. / **Hermon School**:

TYPICAL HEPBURN LIBRARY

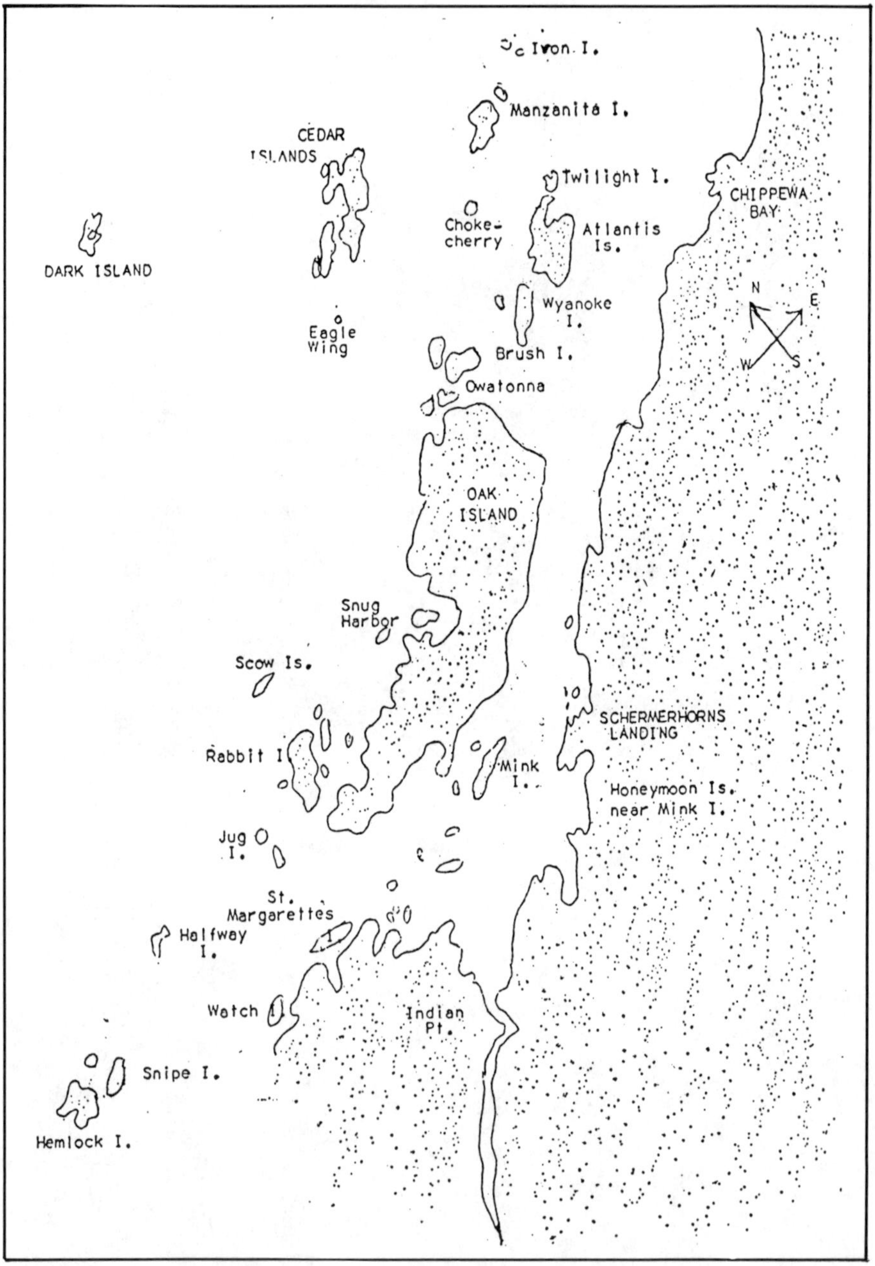

Islands in Chippewa Bay, town of Hammond.
(Map by Mary H. Biondi, 1968)

no. 1, common school, t. Hermon. / **Hermon Street**: s., h. Dekalb Junction. / **Hermon Village**: v. in t. Hermon; situated on Elm Creek. First settled, 1815; incorporated, 1877. Durant, 437. / **Hermon Village School**: see **Hermon School.**

Heron Road: r., t. Hammond, located along Chippewa Bay, St. Lawrence River, and n. Robert Heron, landowner and developer.

Herring-Cole Hall: on St. Lawrence University campus; origin n. not available.

Heuvel: n. Jacob Van den Heuvel, of New York City, mill owner and land developer. *Quarterly*, 8 (1963), no. 2, p. 10; p. o. est. Feb. 5, 1828, George Seaman, pm, changed to **Heuvelton**, Dec. 20, 1831. See **Heuvelton**.

Heuvelton: v. in southern part of t. Oswegatchie, n. Jacob Van den Heuvel. Formerly, **Fordsburgh**, n. Nathan Ford (1763-1829), early settler, jurist. Also, **East Branch** because the road crossed the East Branch, or Oswegatchie River. Durant, 198. First called Heuvel in honor of Van den Heuvel, the v. became **Heuvelton**, Jan., 1832; p. o. changed from **Heuvel** to **Heuvelton**, Dec. 20, 1831, Thomas Bacon, pm; p. o. existing, ZIP 13654. New York Postal History; Hough, 574; Durant, 188, 199. Jacob A. Van den Heuvel (1789-1874) changed his name to Jacob Van Heuvel by Act of Legislature, Feb. 8, 1832. He came from Holland in 1792 to New York City, attended Yale College, practiced law, and purchased land in St. Lawrence County through the influence of Thomas L. Ogden. 1963 USGS Heuvelton Quad. Other derived n.: **Heuvelton and Canton Falls Plank-Road**: see **Plank Roads.** / **Heuvelton and De Kalb Plank-Road**: see **Plank Roads.** / **Heuvelton Cemetery**: v. Heuvelton. See **Hillcrest Cemetery**. / **Heuvelton-Flackville Road**: r., t. Oswegatchie, Lisbon. / **Heuvelton Road**: r., t. Lisbon. / **Heuvelton Road**: r., t. Oswegatchie / **Heuvelton School**: no. 5, common school, t. Oswegatchie. / **Heuvelton Street**: s., v. Rensselaer Falls, n. v. Heuvelton, although n. derives from the road, Rensselaer Falls-Heuvelton Road; also called **The Plank Road**. The street runs from where the railroad tracks meet Front Street to v. incorporation sign. From there, it is the Rensselaer Falls-Heuvelton Road.

Hewittville: h., t. Potsdam, n. Henry Hewitt, credited with improving the channel of the Racquette River so that large quantities of logs could be floated down; p. o. est. Apr. 4, 1881, Elliot Fay, pm, closed May 30, 1888, reopened Mar. 27, 1901, William J. Tucker, pm, closed June 30, 1903. Also see Durant, 246. 1964 USGS West Potsdam Quad. / **Hewittville Road**: r., t. Potsdam. / **Hewittville School**: no. 31, common school, t. Potsdam.

Hewlett Road: r., t. Russell, Pierrepont, n. George Hewlett.

Hickory: n. tree: **Hickory**: h., t. Macomb; p. o. est. Dec. 20, 1887, Vilas Ingram, pm, closed July 30, 1910. *Quarterly*, 7 (1962), no. 4, p. 14; 6 (1961), npn. / **Hickory Lake**: t. Macomb, alt. 317. 1961 USGS Pope Mills Quad. / **Hickory Lake State Forest**, #38, t. Macomb. / **Hickory School**: no. 5, common school, t. Macomb. 1915 USGS Gouverneur Quad.

Hicks Pond: t. Fine.

Hida Road: r., t. Norfolk, connects Cook and Hough Roads in extreme northeast of t. Reason n. unknown.

High: denotes tallness or height in areas, such as falls or mountains; sometimes upper in contrast with lower in north and south directions, and sometimes for importance or respect, as for n. streets: **High Falls**: n. falls on the Racquette River, now **Colton**. *Quarterly*, 5 (1960), no. 2, p. 5. / **High Falls**: on Oswegatchie River, t. Fine. *Quarterly*, 11 (1966), no. 4, p. 15. 1919 USGS Cranberry Lake Quad. / **High Falls**: on Grass(e) River, now **Pyrites**. *Quarterly*, 10 (1965), no. 3, p. 12. / **High Flats**: h. and land area, n. elevation, t. Parishville; p. o. as **Highflats** est. Apr. 8, 1892, Delmar H. Christy, pm, closed Aug. 31, 1911. 1896 New; 1898 EGB map; 1908 Adm; 1908 USGS Potsdam Quad; 1912 Stoddard; 1964 USGS Colton Quad. / **High Flats Forest**: county forest, t. Parishville. / **High Flats School**: no. 14, common school, t. Parishville. See High Flats. / **High Flats State Forest**, #20, t. Parishville. / **High Pond**: t. Clifton, alt. about 2,000 ft., 250 ft. above nearest pond. 1919 USGS Cranberry Lake Quad. / **High Rock**: ledge, t. Fine, alt. 1,900 ft. 1919 USGS Cranberry Lake Quad. / **High Street**: s., v. Morristown; s., h. Norfolk, both **East High** and **West High**; s., v. Norwood. / **High Street Cemetery**, h. Norfolk.

Highland: n. desc. feature. **Highland Avenue**: s., v. Massena. / **Highland Park**: s., v. Massena. / **Highland Road**: r., t. Massena.

Highway: see **State Highway** and

United States Highway.

Higley: n. Jesse Colton Higley (See **Colton**): **Higley Falls**: in Racquette River, t. Colton. Also **Higley's Falls.** 1896 New; 1964 USGS Colton Quad. / **Higley Flow**: desc. of water. / **Higley Flow State Park.** / **Higley Road**: r., t. Colton, Higley Flow area.

Hill: elevated terrain, but also surname: **Hill Campus**: on Clarkson University campus, n. terrain. / **Hill Road**: r., t. Russell, Hill family. / **Hill School**: no. 16, common school, t., Parishville, n. Reuben Hill family.

Hillcrest: n. top of rise (or hill), but often a promotional n. in real estate: **Hillcrest Avenue**: s., v. Massena; s., v. Potsdam, sometimes appears as **Hillcrest Boulevard.** / **Hillcrest Cemetery**: v. Heuvelton, t. Oswegatchie. 1963 USGS Heuvelton Quad; t. Lawrence, near Nicholville. 1964 USGS Nicholville Quad; 1964 USGS North Lawrence Quad. / **Hillcrest Drive**: s., v. Potsdam; s., h. Star Lake. Also, **Hill Crest**: h. Parishville, top of Dugway Hill. 1964 USGS Nicholville Quad.

Hillside Circle: desc., but also promotional: **Hillside Circle**: s., v. Canton / **Hillside Drive**: s., v. Canton.

Hinman Cemetery: t. Potsdam.

Hitchins: a cluster of names (**Hitchins/Hitchings**): **Hitchins Park**: t. Colton, n. by Marion Low, with n. taken from **Hitchins Pond**. *Quarterly*, 19 (1974), no. 1, p. 9. / **Hitchins Pond**: see **Hitchins Park.** t. Colton, alt. 1,720 ft. 1880 **Hitchins Pond, Middle Pond, North Pond** Ely; 1883 Ely-Wallace, same as Ely; 1896 New, same as Ely; 1902 Blankman lists **Hitchings Pond**, divided into **Middle Pond** and **North Pond**; 1908 Adm; 1912 Stoddard; 1954 USGS Tupper Lake Quad. / **Hitchings Pond**: same as **Hitchins Pond.** / **Hitchings Pond Mountain**: t. Colton, alt. 2,175 ft. 1902 Blankman.

Hobbs School: no. 1, common school, t. Lisbon, n. Hobbs family.

Hobkirk School: no. 12, common school, in Chipman, t. Waddington, n. Hobkirk family.

Hochelaga: also known as **The River Hochelaga, Riviere de Hochelaga, Cataroqui**, and now **The St. Lawrence River**, which see. Jacques Cartier, French explorer, n. the area Saint Laurent, in honor of the saint's day, August 10, 1535. The site of Montreal was called Hochelage.

Quarterly, 17 (1972), no. 4, p. 3.

Hockens School: no. 21, common school, t. DeKalb, n. Hockens family.

Hodskin: surname used as a specific: **Hodskin Island**: in Grass(e) River, t. Canton, n. Hodskin family. *Quarterly*, 25 (1980), no. 4, p. 4. / **Hodskin Street**: s., v. Canton, n. either for Nathaniel Hodskin or his son Barzillai. Nathaniel was an early settler (1827)and furnace builder, while Barzillai was a prominent merchant, hotel owner, and politician. Durant, p. 218b.

Hogback Brook: t. Parishville, trib. West Branch St. Regis River, n. shape. / **Hogback Island**: in Black Lake, t. Morristown, n. shape. 1961 USGS Hammond Quad.

Hogle Road: r., t. Potsdam, n. Hogle family.

Ho-Jack: n. St. Lawrence division of Northern Railroad, from French greeting by workers. *Quarterly*, 7 (1962), no. 4, p. 7.

Holcomb Mills: t. Gouverneur, six m. above Gouverneur on Oswegatchie River, n. owner.

Holcroft House: on Clarkson University Campus, originally built in 1821-1822 as the home of John C. Clarkson, n. Elizabeth Holcroft, of royal descent, wife of Rev. David Clarkson (1622-1686), whose son Matthew came to New York City in 1691 and was commissioned as Secretary of the Province of New York by William and Mary. Annie Clarkson deeded Holcroft House to the then college in 1927.

Holland Road: r., t. Stockholm, n. Holland family.

Hollow School: no. 6, common school, t., Parishville, n. geological feature.

Hollywood: originally a survey township; formerly **The Bog**, on Jordan River, settlement, t. Colton, Clifton, Hopkinton, n. holly tree of the genus *Ilex*. *Quarterly*, 5 (1960), no. 1, p. 1; p. o. est. May 28, 1890, Jeremiah Reynolds, pm, closed Feb. 28, 1905, reopened Apr. 5, 1905, Carrie A. Day, pm, closed July 30, 1932. A favorite camping and courting site for young persons in the 1920s and 1930s. 1896 New; 1908 Adm; 1912 Stoddard; 1920 USGS Childwold Quad. Other derived names: **Hollywood Club**: private forest and game preserve, inc. Dec. 9, 1898, situated in the t. Clifton and Colton. / **Hollywood Road**: r., t. Colton. /

Hollywood School: no. 11, common school, t. Colton. / **Hollywood Stillwater**: t. Colton.

Holmes: surname used as a specific: **Holmes Cemetery**: t. Stockholm, near Stockholm Center. at Holmes Hill, n. Holmes families. 1964 USGS Brasher Falls Quad. Also **Holmes Hill Cemetery**. / **Holmes Hill**: t., Stockholm. *Quarterly*, 11 (1966), no. 2, p. 13. / **Holmes Point**: on St. Lawrence River, t. Morristown, n. Marion Holmes. 1963 USGS Morristown Quad.

Holts Ferry: t. Massena, later Brewer Ferry, near mouth of the Grass(e) River. Dumas, 3.

Holy Family School: v. Massena. 1964 USGS Massena Quad.

Homecroft Court: s., v. Massena.

Homer A. Vilas Hall: on St. Lawrence University campus, n. Chairman of the Board of Trustees, 1954-1968; a Trustee, 1929-1984.

Homer's Mills: h. two m. northeast of Hailesborough, n. William Homer, operator of a group of mills. Durant, 380.

Homestead: h., t. Gouverneur, n. large dairy operation; p. o. est. Feb. 11, 1892, Eli C. Mosher, pm, closed Sept. 30, 1903. / **Homestead School**: no. 14, common school, t. Gouverneur. / **Homestead**: s. v., Gouverneur.

Hooker Street: s., v. Morristown, n. Henry Hooker, merchant, steamboat owner, and collector of customs. Bogardus, 55-56.

Hopkins Bay: in St. Lawrence River, t. Massena, n. Hopkins family. 1964 USGS Massena Quad.

Hopkinton: eastern border with Franklin Co., n. Roswell Hopkins, who settled in the area in 1802; t. formed Mar. 21, 1805, from Massena. Hopkins had been Secretary of State in Vermont for 14 years. He had also fought in the Revolutionary War and had been captured. Formerly, **Islington**. survey township. *Quarterly*, 14 (1969), no. 2, p. 20. Pronounced locally, **Hopkitten**. 1964 USGS Nicholville Quad. / **Hopkinton**: h., t. **Hopkinton**, p. o. est. Nov. 5, 1806, Thaddeus Laughlin, first pm, changed to rural station from **North Lawrence**, Apr. 8, 1966, p. o. existing, ZIP 12940 (New York Postal History). Hough, 574, gives the date of opening as Nov. 3, 1807, with Theophilus Laughlin, pm. 1919 USGS Nicholville Quad. / **Hopkinton Brook**: t. Hopkinton. 1865 **Lyd**

Brook Beers; 1873 **Lyd Brook** Hamilton Child; 1896 **Lyd** New; 1896 New; 1896 **Lyd** EGB map; 1908 Adm; 1908 USGS Nicholville Quad; 1908 Adm; 1964 USGS Nicholville Quad. See **Lyd Brook.** / **Hopkinton Pond**: t. Hopkinton. 1919 USGS Nicholville Quad; 1964 USGS Sylvan Falls Quad. / **Hopkinton Road**: known also as **Old Military Road**, and the **Northwest Bay Road**, built in the 1810s, to connect Northwest Bay, now Westport, Essex County, to Hopkinton. / **Hopkinton School**: no. 2, common school, t. Hopkinton; also called **Hopkinton Village School.** / **Hopkinton Village School**: see **Hopkinton School.**

Hopson: n. family: **Hopson Road**: r., t. Brasher, r. on Massena town line, then south to Maple Ridge. / **Hopson School**: no. 4, common school, t. Massena.

Hornet Ponds: three ponds, t. Colton, alt. 1,786 ft., n. presence of hornets, stinging insects. 1883 **Hornet Pond, 3 Pound Pond** Ely-Wallace; 1896 **Big Hornet Pond, Little Hornet Pond, Three Pond** New; 1902 **Hornet Pond, Little Hornet Pond, Three Pound Pond** Blankman; 1908 **Hornet Pond** Adm; 1912 Stoddard; 1954 USGS Tupper Lake Quad. Also known waggishly as **Horny Ponds**.

Horse: n. animal, usually the result of an incident: **Horse Brook**: trib. Racquette River, t. Piercefield. 1896 New. / **Horse Heaven**, also **Horseheaven**, district of Canton, about 2-1/2 m. from v., n. because horses were buried in the sandbanks which were easy to dig into for graves (now site of Canton landfill). / **Horse Heaven School**: see **Jingleville School**.

Horse Shoe: a common shape-n. in an area where many ponds and lakes exist, the n. having been given during the days when horses were prominent in the lives of the settlers. Usually, **Horseshoe.** / **Horse Shoe Lake**: t. Piercefield, also appears as **Horseshoe Lake, Horse Shoe Pond,** and **Horse-shoe Pond.** / **Horse Shoe Pond**: t. Clare; t. Hopkinton. / **Horseshoe**: h., t. Hopkinton; p. o. est. Oct. 29, 1896, George A. Dukelow, pm, first pm, closed Nov. 20, 1942, reopened June 1, 1947, Albert J. Tremblay, pm, closed Sept. 30, 1953, reopened rural route, June 16, 1954, closed Sept. 30, 1954. / **Horseshoe**: t. Piercefield, n. from **Horseshoe Pond** (now, **Horseshoe Lake**). A. A. Low obtained a p. o. here. *Quarterly*, 19 (1974), no. 1, p. 9. 1896 New; 1902 **Horse Shoe** Blankman; 1903 Mathews; 1908 **Horse Shoe** Adm; 1912 Stoddard;

1954 USGS Tupper Lake Quad. / **Horseshoe Lake**: t. Piercefield, alt. 1,717 ft. 1896 **Horse Shoe Pond** New; 1858 **Horse Shoe Pond** Rogerson; 1860 **Horse Shoe Pond** Merrit; 1865 **Horseshoe Pond**; 1873 **Horseshoe Pond** Hamilton Child; 1880 **Horseshoe Pond** Ely; 1883 **Horseshoe Pond** Ely-Wallace; 1896 **Horse Shoe Pond**; 1902 **Horse Shoe Pond**; 1908 **Horse Shoe Lake**; 1912 Stoddard; 1954 USGS Tupper Lake Quad. / **Horseshoe Pond**: see **Horseshoe Lake**, t. Piercefield. 1858 Rogerson; 1860 **Horse-shoe Pond** Merrit; 1865 Beers, p. 86; 1873 Hamilton Child; 1880 Ely; 1883 Ely-Wallace; 1896 **Horse Shoe Pond** New; 1902 Blankman; 1908 Adm; 1912 Stoddard; 1954 USGS Tupper Lake Quad. / **Horseshoe Pond**: t. Piercefield, alt. 1,528. / **Horseshoe Pond**: alt. 1,009, t. Clare. 1915 Russell Quad. Same as **Horseshoe Lake**. / **Horseshoe Road**: r., t. Oswegatchie, along the Oswegatchie River.

Horton: surname used as a specific: **Horton Ponds**: two ponds, t. Colton, n. Horton family. 1908 USGS Potsdam Quad; 1964 USGS Rainbow Falls Quad. / **Horton Road**: s., v. Massena, and r., t. Massena, n. Hezekiah Horton. Dumas, 57.

Hosley Road: r., t. Russell, n. Hosley family.

Hosmer Hall: n. Helen Hosmer, music teacher and music administrator at SUC, Potsdam campus. *Quarterly*, 11 (1966), no. 3, p. 12.

Hospital Drive: s., v. Massena, n. presence of the hospital.

Hotel Sternberg: see **Inlet** and **Sternberg**.

Hough Road: r., t. Norfolk, n. Hough family.

Houghton School: no. 15, common school, t., Potsdam, n. Houghton family.

House School: t. Fine, Dist. 4, prob. for the Van House family. Also, **Clintsman**. Reynolds, 199.

Howard: n. family: **Howard Cemetery**: t. Rossie. / **Howard School**: t. Pierrepont, Dist. 6, attended by Irving Addison Bacheller, novelist. *Quarterly*, 17 (1972), no. 1, p. 7. / **Howard Street**: s., v. Gouverneur; s., v. Hermon. Formerly, **Grems Street**; s., v. Massena. / **Howard School**: no. 6, common school, t. Pierrepont. / **Howard's Mill**: See **Rossie**. Also **Howard's Mills, Howards**

Mills. / **Howardville**: t. Pierrepont, formerly **Crandallville.** *Quarterly*, 2 (1957), no. 4, npn. / **Howardville Hill**: t. Pierrepont. n. Orrin Howard and Howard family. *Quarterly*, 2 (1957), no. 4, npn. / **Howardville Road**: r., t. Canton, Pierrepont. See **Howardville Hill.**

Howe Boulevard: s., v. Canton, n. Dr. Harry Howe.

Howland Road: r., t. Clifton and s., h. Cranberry Lake, n. Howland family.

Hub of the North: nickname of Russell, for its geographical position in the North Country and through which travelers had to go to the Russell Turnpike from west to east.

Hubbard Road: s., v. Massena, n. Calvin Hubbard. Dumas, 57.

Huckleberry: n. presence of the plant and berry of the genus *Gaylussacia*: **Huckleberry Mountain Hills**: t. Gouverneur, alt. 539 ft. 1956 USGS Richville Quad. / **Huckleberry Lake**: t. Fowler and Edwards. 1956 USGS Edwards Quad. / **Huckleberry Rocks**: feature on Carthage and Adirondack Railroad, near the summit of the Jayville grade, a berrying place. Cecil H. Graham, "The C & A Railroad," *Quarterly*, 11 (1966), no. 1, p. 16.

Huest Road: r., t. Macomb, n. Huested family. Spelling changed.

Huftle Hill: t. Clare, n. Frank N. Huftle family and farm. / **Huftle Hill Road**: super highway in the 1870's, n. hill. *Quarterly*, 14 (1969), no. 2, p. 11; 14 (1969), no. 3, p. 11.

Hughes School: no. 4, common school, t. Russell, n. Edward Hughes, oldest resident, b. 1833. 1915 USGS Russell Quad.

Hulett: Edwin Lee Hulett, Dean of the College, St. Lawrence University, 1915-1941. **Hulett Hall**: on St. Lawrence University campus. / **Hulett Lodge**: on St. Lawrence University land along the Grass(e) River.

Hull: n. family: **Hull Road**: r., t. Colton; **Hull Road**: r., t. Fowler and s., h. Hailesboro, prob. n. Royal Hull family.

Hungry: usually for a place where food is difficult to obtain: **Hungry Bay**: on Lake Ozonia. / **Hungry Bay**: on St. Lawrence River, trans. from French **La Famine**. Doc. Hist. NY, Vol. III, map 1791. / **Hungry Hollow**: t. Edwards. *Quarterly*, 7 (1962), no.

2, p. 15.

Hunter Road: r., t. Waddington.

Hurlbut School: no. 3, common school, t. DePeyster, possibly n. Philo Hurlbut family; no. 8, common school, t. Pitcairn, n. Hurlbut family.

Hurley: n. family: **Hurley Road**: r., t. Stockholm; r., t. Brasher.

Hutchins: surname used as a specific, and sometimes misspelled (hypercorrection) as **Hutchings**: **Hutchins Creek**: t. Massena, trib. Racquette River, n. Jacob Hutchins. 1964 USGS Massena Quad. / **Hutchins Street**: s., v. Norfolk, n. Hutchins family. / **Hutchings Falls**: three miles below Ray-mondville. *Quarterly*, 6 (1961), no. 1, p. 12. Also, **Hutchin's Falls**.

Hutchinson Road: r., t. Oswegatchie, n. Hutchinson family. / **Hutchinson School**: no. 19, common school, t. Oswegatchie.

Hutton: n. family. **Hutton Road**: r., t. Macomb; r., t. Rossie.

Hyde: n. family: **Hyde Road**: r., t. Hammond; r., t. Macomb, n. Hyde family. Also **Macomb-Pope Mills Road.** / **Hyde School**: no. 12, common school, t. Macomb.

I

Ike Noble Drive: s., v. Canton, n. Robert "Ike" Noble, shoe merchant. St. Lawrence University graduate (1919), athlete, leader in sports for youth, established scholarship at SLU.

Ideauma (pronunciation, eye-doó-mee): origin n. unknown: **Ideauma Road**: r., t. De Kalb. Also, **Ideuma, Ideumea.** / **Ideauma School**: no. 18, common school, t. DeKalb. Also, **Idumea School.**

Ile au Chamailles: see **Croil's Island.**

Independent Hill: t. Hopkinton. 1964 USGS Nicholville Quad. Reason n. unknown.

Indian: n. usually vague and suggestive of presence of Amerindians, either one or many. See Stewart, p. 219-220. **Indian Chief Islands**: two islands, **Big** and **Little**, in St. Lawrence River, t. Hammond. 1958 USGS Chippewa Quad. / **Indian Creek**: t. Canton and DeKalb, natural canal between Grass(e) and

Oswegatchie Rivers, between Canton and Rensselaer Falls. **Upper Indian Lake** on Oswegatchie River side, and **Lower Indian Lake** on Grass(e) River side. *Quarterly*, 17 (1972), no. 4, p. 7. 1963 Rensselaer Falls Quad; 1956 USGS Richville Quad. / **Indian Fishing Ground**: old-time resort of Oswegatchie Indians. *Quarterly*, 14 (1969), no. 1, p. 17. / **Indian Kettle**: geographic feature, just off Route 37, v. Morristown, at Rock Cut, in imagined shape of a kettle, said to have been used as a cooking place by Indians. Bogardus, 156. / **Indian Hut Island**: in Chippewa Bay, t. Hammond. "Supposed to derive its name from the fact that an Indian called 'The Quaker' lived there." Durant, 385. / **Indian Meadows**: t. Massena, along the Grasse(e) River. Dumas, vii. / **Indian Mountain**: t. Clifton, alt. 2,275. 1896 New; 1902 Blankman; 1919 USGS Cranberry Lake Quad. / **Indian Mountain Pond**: t. Clifton, alt. 1,750. 1896 New; 1902 Blankman; 1919 USGS Cranberry Lake Quad. / **Indian Point**: below Ogdensburg, on St. Lawrence River, where Psychiatric Center now is. See **Point Airy**. *Quarterly*, 11 (1966), no. 4, p. 3. French n.and spelling: **Point de Ganataregoin**, "big lake." Durant, 33. 1958 USGS Chippewa Quad. / **Indian Point**: t. Hammond, on Black Lake, contains Amerindian "writings"; Amerindian n.: **Ganataragoin**. "big lake." See Beauchamp, 72. / **Indian River**: t. Macomb, trib. Black Lake. 1961 USGS Hammond Quad. / **Indian Road**: r., t. Massena, to Mohawk Reservation.

Industrial Park: v. Massena, n. industry area.

Ingham Cemetery: at Brier Hill, t. Morristown. See **Chippewa Street Burying Ground.**

Inlet: a stream entrance or indentation, usually generic term: **Inlet**: h., t. Fine. 1896 **Sternberg's Hotel** New; 1902 **Sternberg** Blankman; 1908 **Hotel Sternberg** Adm; 1912 **Sternberg** Stoddard; 1919 USGS Cranberry Lake Quad. / **Inlet Club**: private forest and game preserve; see **Forest Commission Report**, 1893. **Inlet Flow**: into Cranberry Lake, t. Clifton. 1896 New; 1908 Adm; 1912 Stoddard. / **Inlet House**: Formerly, **Sternberg's Hotel**, t. Fine. *Quarterly*, 17 (1972), no. 2, p. 12. / **Inlet Road**: r., t. Fine.

Inwood: building at St. Lawrence State Hospital (now Psychiatric Center), for tuberculosis patients, finished 1906. *Quarterly*, 11 (1966), no. 4, p. 19. / **In-**

wood Club: private forest and game preserve. See **Forest Commission Report**, 1893, p. 154.

Irelan Road: r., t. Hammond, Morristown, n. Irelan family.

Ireland Road: r., t. Potsdam, poss. n. Ireland family.

Irish: n. applied to the presence of one or several persons from Ireland, usually first generation immigrants. The Irish in the 19th century were subjected to ethnic discrimination and generally forced into separate living areas: **Irish Brook**: stream, trib. South Branch Grass(e) River, t. Clifton. n. family surname. 1921 USGS Stark Quad. / **Irish School**: t. Fine. n. family surname. Error for **Irish Hill School**. 1915 USGS Russell Quad. / **Irish Hill**: t. Fine. 1921 USGS Stark Quad. / **Irish Hill Road**: r., t. Fine. / **Irish Hill School**: t. Fine, Dist. 6. Also, **Kirk School**. Reynolds, 199. / **Irish Settlement**: t. Colton. 1921 USGS Stark Quad. / **Irish Settlement**: t. Waddington, along Route 37, three miles west of Waddington, existed prior to 1819, when Mrs. Charlotte Seton Ogden mentioned that workmen came from the "Irish Settlement" to work on Ellerslie, her house. Tedford, 48. / **Irish Settlement Road**: r., t. Canton; r., t. Oswegatchie; r., t. Pierrepont; r. t. Waddington; s. v. Heuvelton / **Irish Settlement School**: no. 20, common school, t. Canton; no. 25, common school, t. Canton; no. 12, common school, t. Pierrepont

Irocoisia: lands of the Iroquois in northern New York and northern Vermont. Noted on Delisle's map of 1785. Durant, 70.

Iron: n. indicating the presence of iron deposits or of the iron industry: **Iron Islands**: two islands, in St. Lawrence River, t. Hammond. Iron was scowed (1812) from Rossie to the islands to be picked up by larger river ships. 1958 USGS Chippewa Quad. / **Iron Mountain**: t. Colton, alt. 2,437 ft. 1858 **Iron Ore Mt.** Rogerson; 1865 **Iron Ore Mt.** Beers, p. 86; 1896 **Iron Mt.** New; 1902 **Iron Mt.** Blankman; 1903 **Iron Ore Mountain**, J. N. Mathews, **New York**, Buffalo, 1903; 1954 USGS Tupper Lake Quad. / **Iron Mountain Pond**: see **Iron Pond**. / **Iron Ore Mountain**: see **Iron Mountain**. / **Iron Pond**: t. Colton. 1896 New; 1902 **Iron Mt. Pond** Blankman; 1912 Stoddard; 1954 USGS Tupper lake Quad. / **Iron Works Cemetery**: t. Brasher. See **Brasher Iron Works**. / **Iron Works Road**: r., t. Brasher, near Brasher Falls. / **Iron Works School**: t. Brasher, near Brasher Falls. *Quarterly*, 14 (1969), no. 4, p. 5.

Ironsides Island: now a national natural landmark, in St. Lawrence River, t. Hammond and t. Alexandria (Jefferson Co.). 1958 USGS Chippewa Quad. The 20-acre island is owned by the Nature Conservancy. A glacier-scoured granite knoll, the island has steep, rust-stained cliffs 30 to 40 feet high, which accounts for the n. Source: newspaper clipping, 1966.

Ironton: h., t. Brasher, n. "iron town." 1964 Hogansburg Quad.

Iroquois Dam: n. Amerindians, built as a part of the Seaway project, it is a 2,741 foot structure located between Massena and Ogdensburg and regulates the waters of Lake Ontario. CB, 35.

Irvins Island: in Oswegatchie River, t. Fine. Recorded as **Irving's Island** in Reynolds, 77. Mohawk Power Corporation., formerly New York Public Utilities, constructed a power house and dam here. Also **Irvin's Island**.

Irwin: n. family: **Irwin Road**: r., t. Lisbon; s., c. Ogdensburg.

Isabella: feminine given n.: **Isabella Street**: also called **Isabel Street**, s., v. Massena; s., c. Ogdensburg, n. a daughter of Nathan Ford.

Island: functions as both a specific and generic n.: **Island Branch [Oswegatchie River]**: t. Fowler, a part of the Oswegatchie River that flows around an island. 1956 USGS Gouverneur Quad. / **Island Branch Road** or **Street**: r., t. Fowler and s., h. Hailesboro. / **Island Branch School**: no. 12, common school, t. Fowler. 1915 USGS Gouverneur Quad. / **Island House**: on Ogden Island, built by David A. Ogden, begun in 1811 and completed in 1816. The house, a landmark, is the subject of much folklore and is supposed to have a ghost. See Tedford, 23 ff., for stories. / **Island Street**: s., v. Edwards; s., h. Norfolk; s., v. Potsdam.

Isle au Long Saut: see **Long Saut Island.**

Isle au Rapid: See **Ogden Island.** *Quarterly*, 3 (1958), no. 1, npn.

Islington: a survey township, now in t., Hopkinton, n. Islington ("the town of Elesa's people"), Norfolk, England. Now, **Hopkinton.**

Italian Road: r., t. Potsdam, n. families of Italian descent.

Ives Park: v. Potsdam, along Racquette River south of Fall Island

Bridge, n. H. L. Ives, prominent Potsdam businessman and politician.

J

J. S. Brown Island: in Trout Lake, t. Hermon, now **Graham Island**. *Quarterly*, 16 (1971), no. 1, p. 10.

Jacobs School: no. 18, common school, t. Pierrepont, n. Jacobs family.

Jackson: surname: **Jackson Falls**: in Grass(e) River, t. Russell, n. Rollin C. Jackson. 1915 USGS Russell Quad. / **Jackson Street**: s., c. Ogdensburg, n. Andrew Jackson, 7th president of the United States.

Jacques Cartier State Park: t. Morristown, on the St. Lawrence River, n. Jacques Cartier, who discovered and explored the St. Lawrence River and Gulf. *Quarterly*, 6 (1961), no. 4, p. 4.

James: here, surname: **James Street**: s., v. Massena; s., c. Ogdensburg, n. Amaziah Bailey James, attorney, publisher of **Northern Light**, later n. **Times and Advertiser**, and supreme court justice; s., v. Waddington, see s., c. Ogdensburg.

Jamestown: a survey township, now in t. Colton.

Jamestown Falls: in Racquette River, t. Colton. 1860 Merrit; 1880 Ely; 1883 Ely-Wallace; 1902 Blankman; 1920 USGS Childwold Quad.

Jamieson Road: r., t. Canton, off Rte. 11 near Eddy, n. Jamieson family.

Janacks Landing: on Cranberry Lake, t. Fine, n. John Janack, one of first Forest Rangers on Cat Mountain near Wanakena. Reynolds, 179.

Janes Road: s., t. Canton, n. Janes family.

Janestown: t. Hopkinton, n. daughter of William Constable. Durant, 77.

Jay Street: s., v. Canton, n. Jay family, perhaps for Samuel Jay, from Vermont. / s., c. Ogdensburg, n. John Jay (1775-1892), statesman, chief justice of the U. S. Supreme Court, governor of New York, negotiated treaty with Great Britain, known as Jay's Treaty, 1794.

Jayville: railroad station, t. Fine, on the Carthage and Adirondack Railroad. Jayville was the scene of "tarring and feathering of an errant couple, contrary to the wishes of their legally wedded spouses."

Quarterly, 11 (1966), no. 1, p. 16; p. o. est. Feb. 11, 1889, Harvey E. Esler, pm, closed Mar. 31, 1890, reopened July 8, 1890, Thomas Richardson, pm, closed Dec. 15, 1905. 1915 USGS Oswegatchie Quad. Other **Jayville** n. include **Jayville Mines**: t. Pitcairn. / **Jayville Road**: r., t. Pitcairn. / **Jayville School**: no. 1, common school, t. Pitcairn. The origin of the n. has not been determined.

Jeffers Road: r., t. DeKalb, n. George Jeffers. Now **Rundell Road**.

Jefferson: Thomas Jefferson, 3rd president of the U. S., is commemorated in many n., but occasionally a local n. occurs: **Jefferson Avenue**: s., v. Massena; s., c. Ogdensburg. / **Jefferson School**: t. Massena. 1964 USGS Raquette River Quad. Not in 1896 list of common schools. / **Jefferson Street**: s., v. Hermon, n. Jefferson family. / **Jefferson Street**: s., v. Gouverneur, n. Thomas Jefferson. / **Jefferson Street School**: no. 5, common school, t. DeKalb.

Jencks Hall: on St. Lawrence University campus, n. Millard H. Jencks, Chair of the Board of Trustees, 1934-1941.

Jenkins Bay: in Tupper Lake, t. Piercefield, n. Jenkins family. 1896 New. / **Jenkins Corners Road**: r., t. DeKalb, n. David Jenkins. / **Jenkins Road**: r., t. DeKalb, n. David Jenkins. / **Jenkins School**: no. 16, common school, t. Stockholm, n. Jenkins family.

Jenne Creek (pronounced jenny): t. Pitcairn, Fine, trib. Big Creek, n. Major Prince Jenne, Pitcairn, builder of first sawmill (1828) there. 1885 Beers, p. 72; 1951 USGS Harrisville Quad shows **Jenny Creek**. See **Jenny Creek**. / **Jenne School**: no. 14, common school, t. Fowler, n. Jenne family.

Jenner: n. family: **Jenner Road**: r., t. Waddington. / **Jenner School**: no. 1, common school, t. Pierrepont. Also **Sand Hill School**, Dist. 1.

Jennies Island: in Black Lake, t. Morristown, n. Jennie Apple. 1961 USGS Hammond Quad; 1963 USGS Edwardsville Quad.

Jenny Creek: 1865 Beers, p. 72; 1951 USGS Harrisville Quad. Spelling reflects the local pronunciation for **Jenne**, which see. / **Jenny Lake**: pond, t. Pitcairn. 1916 USGS Oswegatchie Quad.

Jersey Avenue: s., c. Ogdensburg, origin n. unknown.

Jerusalem: a section or neighborhood near Morristown, n. the capital of ancient Israel, considered a holy city by Christians, Jews, and Moslems; the n. is often found in Christian communities for places. / **Jerusalem Corners**: t. Canton / **Jerusalem Corners Cemetery**: at Eddy on Canton-DeKalb (Route 11) Road / **Jerusalem Corners School**: no. 8, common school, t. Canton, near Eddy. 1964 USGS Potsdam Quad.

Jewett Creek: t. Hammond, trib. Black Lake, n. Jewett family. 1958 USGS Redwood Quad.

Jingleville Road: r., t. Canton, connects Miner St. and Rich Road, origin n. unknown. / **Jingleville School**: no. 3, common school, t. Canton. Also known as **Horse Heaven School.**

Jo Indian: see **Joe Indian.**

Jo Point: See *Quarterly*, 9 (1964), no. 2, p. 12.

Jock: an English spelling of French **Jacques**: **Jock Pond**: t. Fine, n. Jock family. / **Jock Pond**: t. Hopkinton. *Quarterly*, 6 (1961), no. 4, p. 11. See, also, **Jocks Pond.** / **Jock Pond Road**: r., t. Fine. / **Jocks Pond**: t. Piercefield, alt. 1,532. 1858 **Jock Pond** Rogerson; 1860 **Jock Pond** Merrit; 1865 **Jock Pond** Beers; 1873 **Jock Pond** Hamilton Child; 1880 **Jock Pond** Ely; 1896 **Jock Pond** New; 1902 **Jock Pond** Blankman; 1908 **Jock's Pond** Adm; 1912 **Jock's Pond**; 1920 USGS Childwold Quad. / **Jocks Pond Outlet**: stream, trib. Grass(e) River Flow, t. Colton. 1920 USGS Childwold Quad.

Joe Indian: n. Amerindian who lived in the area. According to one version, he arrived with his young wife after he had been exiled from his tribe. For story, see *Quarterly*, 21 (1976), no. 1, p. 16: **Joe Indian**: settlement by the lake, p. o. changed from **Sterlingwick** to **Joeindian**, Apr. 10, 1920, Edith B. Chase, pm, closed Sept. 14, 1935. / **Jo(e) Indian Inlet**: same as **Joe Indian Inlet.** / **Joe Indian Inlet**: t. Parishville, trib. Joe Indian Pond. 1896 **To Indian Inlet** New (misprint); 1898 **Jo Indian Inlet** EGB map; 1902 **Jo Indian Inlet** Blankman; 1908 Adm; 1912 **Jo Indian Inlet** Stoddard; 1920 USGS Childwold Quad. / **Joe Indian Island**: island in Cranberry Lake, t. Clifton. *Quarterly*, 9 (1964), no. 2, p. 12. The island is indicated as **Joe Point** on earlier maps. / **Joe Indian Lake Road**: r., t. Parishville. / **Joe Indian Pond**: t. Parishville, pond n. first. Also, **Jo Indian Lake.** / **Jo(e) Indian School**: t. Parishville, n. pond; locally, **Jo Injun School.**

See *Sketches of Parishville*. / **Joe Indian Road**: r., t. Parishville. / **Joe's Point**: point on Joe Indian Island, Cranberry Lake, t. Clifton. 1896 New. Also, see **Jo Point.**

John Pond: t. Colton, alt. 1,780. 1896 **Cherry Patch Pond** New; 1902 **Cherry Patch Pond** Blankman; 1919 USGS Cranberry Lake Quad.

John Street: s., v. Gouverneur; s., v. Heuvelton; s., c. Ogdensburg.

Johns Pond: t. Colton. 1908 USGS Potsdam Quad; 1964 **Green Pond** USGS Colton Quad. Now, **Green Pond.**

Johnson: second to **Smith** as the most common surname in the U. S.: **Johnson Drive**: r., t. Louisville. / **Johnson Road**: r., t. Canton; r., t. Pierrepont. / **Johnson School**: no. 6, common school, t. Canton.

Johnstown Road School: no. 7, common school, t. Gouverneur. See **Johnstown Street**. / **Johnstown Street**: s., v. Gouverneur, n. by settlers who came from Johnstown, Montgomery Co., NY, ca 1817-1820. Cent. Souv., 26, 51. Also, **Johnston Road.**

Joint Schools: common schools listed in 1896 as joining with others: Districts nos. 7 and 8, t. Brasher; no. 7, t. Rossie, joined with Jefferson Co. school; and no. 14, t. Hammond.

Jones: noted as the 5th most popular surname in the U. S.: **Jones Pond**: t. Edwards, alt. 715 ft., n. Elijah Jones. Freeman, 4. 1915 USGS Edwards Quad. / **Jones Pond Road**: r., t. Edwards, Pitcairn. / **Jones Road**: r., t. Gouverneur; r., t. Hopkinton; r., t. Lisbon; r., t. Madrid.

Jonesville Road: r., t. Hermon, n. Joshua Jones. / **Jonesville School**: no. 4, common school, t. Hermon. n. Joshua Jones family. 1915 USGS Gouverneur Quad.

Jordan: usually n. biblical Jordan River: **Jordan**: see **Little Jordan Lake**. / **Jordan Island**: in Trout Lake, t. Hermon, also known as **J. S. Brown Island**. Now, **Graham Island.** *Quarterly*, 16 (1971), no. 1, p. 10. / **Jordan Lake**: t. Hopkinton, alt. 1,503. 1853 HMC; 1858 Rogerson; 1860 Merrit; 1873 Hamilton Child; 1878 Durant & Pierce; 1880 Ely; 1896 New; 1902 Blankman; 1908 Adm; 1912 Stoddard; 1920 USGS Childwold Quad. / **Jordan Outlet**: t. Hopkinton, trib. Jordan River. 1920 USGS Childwold Quad. / **Jordan River**: t. Hopkinton, flows out of Jordan Lake, trib. Racquette River. 1853 HMC; 1853 **East Brook** HMC; 1858 **River Jordan** Rogerson; 1880 Ely; 1882 Ely-Wallace; 1896 New; 1902 Blankman; 1912 Stoddard; 1920 USGS Childwold Quad.

Jorstadt Island: see **Dark Island**.

Josephine Street: s., h. DaKalb Junction.

Joy Road: r., t. Norfolk, n. Joy family.

Judd School: no. 7, common school, t. Massena, n. Judd family.

Judith Street: s., v. Massena.

Judson: a popular name in St. Lawrence County: **Judson Road**: r., t. Canton, Potsdam, n. David C. Judson (1808-1875). Durant, 192-193. / **Judson School**: no. 5, common school, t. Norfolk, n. Judson family. Eben Judson, from Williston, VT, homesteaded in Norfolk in 1809. / **Judson School**: no. 8, common school, t. Oswegatchie, n. Judson family. / **Judson Street**: s., v. Canton, n. David C. Judson; s., c. Ogdensburg, n. Roscius. W. Judson.

Jug Island: in St. Lawrence River, t. Hammond, n. surviving from prohibition days. 1958 USGS Chippewa Quad.

Jumbo Rock: at Lake Ozonia, t. Hopkinton, n. size. *Quarterly*, 19 (1974), no. 1, p. 6.

Justina Street: s., v. Heuvelton, n. Van den Heuvel's daughter.

K

Kalurah: h. and railroad station on Carthage and Adirondack Railroad, t. Pitcairn. *Quarterly*, 9 (1964), no. 2, p. 13; 11 (1966), no. 1, p. 16; p. o. est. Mar. 1, 1904, Avery H. Swift, pm, closed Sept. 30, 1910, reopened May 3, 1916, Andrew Collins, pm, closed July 15, 1918. 1916 USGS Oswegatchie Quad. Also **Kulurah**.

Kanaswastakeras: see **Massena Springs**.

Kanataseke: see **Norfolk**.

Kanawaga: Iroquois, "rapid river," **St. Lawrence River**, because of the numerous rapids along what is now the St. Lawrence County section of the river.

Kansas Road: r., t. Pitcairn, n. state, reason not known.

Karonkwi: see **Long Sault Island.**

Katherine Street: s., h. Star Lake, n. Katherine Bickers, by her husband Clarence Bickers who gave the land in the village for the street.

Kathleen Street: s., v. Massena.

Katsenekwar: see **Yellow Lake.**

Kearney Bridge/Mine/Falls: t. Hammond and Macomb. n. Philip Kearney. See Eugene Hatch, "Storybook Soldier," *Quarterly*, 7 (1962), no. 3, p. 4. Hatch spells the name **Kearny.** / **Kearney Road**: r., t. Gouverneur, n. Philip Kearney, who bought land extending from the St. Lawrence River to the southern boundary of Gouverneur, known as the Kearney Tract. Cent. Souv., 54. It was settled by land agent James Browne in 1814 who lived near Kearney Bridge. The tract was 3/4-mile (64 chains 71 links) wide and covered 10,000 acres. Durant, 74, writes that it was purchased by Kearney from Nicholas Low, John Delafield, and Benjamin Sexias in the 1790s. Also, **Kearny.**

Keaton's Rift: see **Caty's Rift.**

Keenan Road: r., t. Brasher, n. Keenan family.

Keene Iron Mines: t. Rossie, n. Hiram Keene, owner.

Keener Road: r., t. Parishville. Also **Punkin Hill Road** and **Pumpkin Hill Road.**

Keenes Station: railroad station, t. Rossie, n. Hiram Keene. 1961 USGS Natural Dam Quad. Also **Keene's Station**, **Keens Station**, **Keen's Station.**

Keenesville: n. Hiram Keene; p. o. changed from **Shingle Creek** Dec. 16, 1878, Lucius G. Draper, pm, changed to **Spragueville** Jan. 3, 1883. See **Spragueville.**

Kellas Hall: houses lecture halls on SUC, Potsdam campus, n. Katherine and Eliza Kellas, graduates of the normal school and teachers and administrators in colleges and private schools in New York.

Kellog: t. Stockholm. Mapped on 1964 USGS Nicholville Quad, but not known locally.

Kellogg's Corners: at Sylvia Lake, t. Fowler, n. Kellogg family.

Kelly Road: r. t., Canton, Lisbon; r. t.,

Colton; r., t. DeKalb. All n. Kelly families.

Kendall Road: s., h. Hannawa Falls.

Kenny Road: s., h. Star Lake.

Kendrew Cemetery: t. DeKalb. 1963 USGS Rensselaer Falls Quad. See **Kendrew Corners**. / **Kendrew Corners**: crossroads, t. DeKalb, n. Charles and Thomas Kendrew, emigrants from England. 1963 USGS Rensselaer Falls Quad. / **Kendrew School**: no. 8, common school, t. DeKalb.

Kennedy Court: s., v. Massena.

Kent: surname used as a specific: **Kents**, possessive: **Kent Street**: s., v. Massena. / **Kent Mill Cemetery**: t. Norfolk. Mapped on 1964 USGS Massena Quad but not identified. /**Kents Corners**: crossroads, t. Hermon, n. Nathaniel Kent. It was the site of the first t. meeting. 1956 USGS Bigelow Quad. Also **Kent's Corners**. Now **West Hermon**. / **Kent Corners Cemetery**: t. Hermon. Also known as **Tom Bean Cemetery**. / **Kents Corners- Red Rock Road**: r., t. Hermon, DeKalb. *Quarterly*, 11 (1966), no. 2, p. 19. / **Kents Corners School**: no. 5, common school, t. Hermon. Also, **Kent's Corners School**. / **Kents Mills**: t. Norfolk, n. Kent family. Also, **Kent's Mills**. / **Kents Mills School**: no. 8, common school, t. Norfolk. Also, **Kent's Mills School**.

Kerr Street: s., h. Star Lake, part of a new housing development, n. Ralph Kerr, supervisor.

Keys Road: r., t. Lisbon, n. Keys family.

Keystone Road: r., t. Lisbon.

Kiah Street: s., c. Ogdensburg, n. John Kiah family.

Kildare: a survey township, n. Kildare, Ireland. t. in eastern St. Lawrence Co., south of the ten t., later a subdivision of t. Hopkinton, but no longer existing; p. o. est. 1911, Jules S. Ehrich, pm, closed May 16, 1917. / **Kildare Creek**: t. Hopkinton. / **Kildare Outlet**: t. Hopkinton, trib. Joe Indian Outlet. 1896 New; 1908 Adm; 1912 Stoddard; 1920 USGS Childwold Quad. / **Kildare Pond**: t. Hopkinton. 1896 New; 1902 Blankman; 1908 Adm; 1912 Stoddard; 1920 USGS Childwold Quad.

Kilkenny: p. o. est. as **Kilkenny**, Apr. 28, 1815, Theodosius Fowler, pm, closed Nov. 19, 1821, t. Fowler. Variant of **Killarney**.

Killarney: a survey-township, n. county in Ireland. Now, t. **Fowler**. / **Killarney Lake**: t. Fowler. Now, **Sylvia Lake**. See **Kilkenny**.

Kimball Hill: t. Russell, off Russell-Hermon Road, n. Kimball family. *Quarterly*, 16 (1971), no. 4, p. 7. 1915 USGS Russell Quad. Also misspelled **Kimble**. / **Kimball Island**: in Cranberry Lake, t. Clifton. 1896 New. Also misspelled **Skimball**. / **Kimball Street**: s., h., Lawrence, t. Lawrence, n. James Kimball. / **Kimball Street School**: no. 8, common school, t. Lawrence, n. street.

King: a popular surname in St. Lawrence County, seldom if ever refers to royalty: **King Bridge**: see **Spile Bridge**. / **King Cemetery**: t. Canton, on Route 62 between Pink School Road and Townline Road. 1964 USGS Canton Quad. / **King House**: t. Canton. /**King Street**: s., v. Massena, n. Charles King. / **King Street**: s., c. Ogdensburg, n. John King (1772-1816), who came to the Ogdensburg area as an associate of Nathan Ford, who was working for Samuel Ogden. King was the speaker at the first local observance of independence, July 4, 1802. His son, Preston King (1806-1865), who is claimed by some to be the one for whom the street is n., was publisher of the **St. Lawrence Republican**, attorney, pm Ogdensburg (1831-34), U. S. Represent- ative (1843-47), U. S. Senator (1857-63), collector of the Port of New York (1865), drowned in New York Harbor. Durant, 190. / **King Street**: s., v. Rensselaer Falls, n. the maiden name of Mrs. Henry Van Rensselaer (Elizabeth King). / **King's Corners**: t. Depeyster; a hamlet on Fish Creek. n. prob. for a member of the King family, Moses King being an assessor of the town of DePeyster; p. o. est. as **Kokomo**, Feb. 19, 1891, George W. Petrie, pm, closed Dec. 31, 1907. Also **Kings Corners**. Now, **Kokomo**. *Quarterly*, 10 (1965), no. 3, p. 9. See **Kokomo Corners**. / **Kings Corner(s)**: See **King's Corners**.

Kingsley: surname used as specific: **Kingsley Falls**: t. Hopkinton, in West Branch St. Regis River. 1964 USGS Sylvan Falls Quad. / **Kingsley Road**: r., t. Hopkinton. / **Kingsley Road**: r., t. Louisville.

Kingston Brook: t. Lawrence, trib. Deer River, n. Kingston family. 1964 USGS North Lawrence Quad.

Kinney: prominent surname in the county: **Kinney Road**: s., h. Star Lake, n. John Kinney, farmer near Star Lake who sold part of his farm near the Kerr Brothers Airport. / **Kinney School**: no. 14, common school, t. Oswegatchie, n. Kinney family. Also, **Kennys School**.

Kinnie Road: r., t. Massena, n. Kinnie family.

Kinsman School: no. 12, common school, t. Potsdam, n. John Kinsman.

Kirk: n. family: **Kirk School**: no. 6, common school, t. Fine, n. Kirk family. Reynolds, 199; no. 11, common school, t. Stockholm, n. Olivet Kirk family.

Klock Street: s., t. Morristown, n. Abram Klock, settler and soldier in War of 1812. Also same as **Klock Road** and **Black Lake Road**. Sometimes noted as **Clock Street**.

Knap Island: t. Hammond. See **Manzanita Island.**

Knapps Station. t. Stockholm, n. Moses Knapp who settled the site in 1828. Durant, 392. Also **Knapp's Station, Knapp Station** / **Knapp Station State Forest**, #11, t. Stockholm. / **Knapps Station Road**: r., t. Norfolk, Stockholm. / **Knapps Station-Stockholm Center Road**: r., t. Stockholm. / **Knapps Station-Norfolk Road**: r., t. Norfolk.

Knott School: in some references, error for **Mott School**.

Knowles: Liberty Knowles (1784-1859), Potsdam's first lawyer, served as Treasurer of the St. Lawrence Academy Board of Trustees for 32 years beginning at the first meeting, Sept. 17, 1816, and was Head of the Academy for 40 years, Knowles also operated a tannery, built a sandstone house (experimented building with Potsdam sandstone), farmed, and promoted education. *Quarterly*, 11 (1966), no. 3, p. 18. Also see Durant, 111. **Knowles Burying Ground**: first cemetery in v. Potsdam, located at the end, "foot," of Willow Street. The first person who died in the v. Potsdam was buried here. / **Knowles Hall**: student residence hall on SUC, Potsdam, campus. / **Knowles Hill**: s., v. Potsdam. North Street became known as Knowles Hill for Liberty Knowles who built the first two-story home in Potsdam, now the Helen Hosmer House on Elm Street.

Knox: prominent surname in the county: **Knox School**: no. 11, common school, t. Canton, n. Knox family. / **Knox Settlement**: t. Russell, "in the vicinity of the crossroad that connects the East Road with the West Road." Clarke, 7. n. the families of Nathan, Loren, and David Knox, among the earliest settlers. / **Knox Street**: s., c. Ogdensburg, n. Henry Knox (1750-1806), general in the Revolutionary War, commander-in-chief (1783-84), first U. S. Secretary of War (1785-1795). Many counties and places in the United States n. for him, including Knoxville, TN, and Fort Knox, KY. / **Knox Memorial High School**: t. Russell, n. Seymour Horace Knox, who, with his cousins, began the Frank W. Woolworth mercantile empire. Frank and Seymour were also cousins. He gave the money to t. Russell for the school. *Quarterly*, 21 (1976), no. 2, p. 13. The school was dedicated on July 30, 1913. In 1989 it was combined with Edwards as Edwards-Knox Central School. The original Tiffany windows were moved to the new building.

Kokomo: t., DePeyster. See **Kokomo Corners**. See **King** for p. o. information: **Kokomo Corners**: n. Kokomo, Amerindian tribe, but here n. Kokomo, Indiana, n. recommended by members of the King family. Formerly, **King's (Kings) Corner**, for the King family, t. De Peyster. *Quarterly*, 10 (1965), no. 3, p. 7. 1963 USGS Heuvelton Quad. / **Kokomo School**: no. 4, common school, t. DePeyster.

Krake School: t. Macomb, n. Krake family, among the earliest settlers in the Black Lake area. Bogardus, 122. John and S. M. Krake are mentioned in Durant, 374, 382. Not in 1896 listing of common schools; no. 16, common school, t. Morristown, n. Krake family. Bogardus, 60.

Kulurah: see **Kalurah**.

Kyle: family n.: **Kyle Cemetery**: t. Norfolk. / **Kyle Road**: r., t. Norfolk.

L

L Pond: t. Clare, n. shape. 1896 New; 1908 Adm; 1921 Stark Quad.

La Gallette: French, "cake." n. for either an event or for shape of bay, located where Oswegatchie River flows into St. Lawrence River. *Quarterly*, 10 (1965), no. 4, p. 8.

La Presentation: In 1784, a French Sulpician, Father Francois Picquet, built the Indian Mission at the site." *Quarterly*, 9 (1964), no. 4, p. 15. Now,

Ogdensburg. / **La Presentation Riviere**: now, **Oswegatchie River**.

Lacomb Road: r., t. Norfolk, n. Lacomb family.

Laduke Road: r., t. Fine, n. Laduke family.

Lafaver Road: r., t. Russell, n. Lafaver family.

Lafayette Street: s., c. Ogdensburg, n. Marquis de Lafayette (1757-1834), French statesman and soldier who volunteered to serve with the Revolutionary army and as George Washington's aide. Given the command of a division of Virginia light troops, he fought in the battle of Yorktown and was present at the surrender of General Cornwallis. He made three visits to the U. S, 1780, 1784, and 1824, the last visit when he was received with great admiration. Many names in the United States honor him, most of them dating from his last visit. See **Fayette**.

LaGrasse Street: v. Waddington, n. LaGrasse River, now **Grass(e) River**.

Laidlaw Road: r., t. Macomb, n. Andrew Laidlaw from Scotland, 1832; his son Alexander became permanent resident after parents moved to Canada. / **Laidlaw School**: no. 10, common school, t. Macomb, n. Alexander Laidlaw family. Also, **Laidlow.** 1949 USGS Hammond Quad **Laudlow School**, an error.

Lake: a generic sometimes used as a specific as in **Lake Road**. The n. often occurs as promotional: **Lake and Kokomo Road**: r., t. DePeyster. / **Lake Ann**: Irving Bacheller claimed that **Clear Pond** is now **Lake Ann**. *Quarterly*, 13 (1969), no. 1, p. 22. / **Lake Colvin**: see **Colvin Pond.** / **Lake Ely**: see **Little Fish Pond.** / **Lake George Road**: r., t. Clare and others. The route was surveyed to go to Lake George but not completed. / **Lake Hills**: t. Piercefield. 1896 New. / **Lake Marian**: t. Colton, n. Marian Low; el. 1990 ft. 1956 Tupper Lake Quad. / **Lake Ozonia**: t. Hopkinton, n. clear, fresh, invigorating air. Since the n. did not occur until the 1890s, it prob. is n. Hotel Ozonia, a health spa owned by Mr. Heath, ca 1893. Formerly, **Trout Lake.** 1853 **Trout Lake** HMC; 1858 **Trout Lake** Rogerson; 1865 **Trout Lake** Beers; 1873 **Trout Lake** Hamilton Field; 1878 **Trout Lake** Durant & Pierce; 1896 New; 1902 Blankman; 1908 Adm; 1919 USGS Nicholville Quad;

1964 USGS Lake Ozonia Quad. The folk myth of the sea monster surfaced when someone claimed in June 3, 1896 that a large serpent was seen swimming around in the lake. The incident was graphically reported in the July 1, 1896 issue of the *Courier-Freeman*, causing many citizens to visit the lake on July 4 in hope of seeing the monster, but apparently no one ever saw it again (note by W. A. McLoughlin, "The Insoluble Mystery of the Water Monster of Lake Ozonia," unpublished). / **Lake Ozonia Outlet**: t. Hopkinton, trib. St. Regis River in Dickinson (Franklin Co.). 1858 **East Brook** Rogerson;1896 **East Brook** New; 1898 **East Brook Creek** EGB map; 1912 **East Brook** Stoddard; 1919 USGS Nicholville Quad; 1964 USGS St. Regis Falls Quad. See **East Brook**. / **Lake Ozonia School**: t., Hopkinton. / **Lake Placid Drive**: s., v. Potsdam, on State University College campus. / **Lake Road**: See **Black Lake Road**, Hammond to Morristown. / **Lake Road**: r., t. Fowler; r., t. Fine, around Star Lake. / **Lake St. Lawrence**: expansion of St. Lawrence River, t. Massena. 1964 USGS Raquette River Quad. / **Lake Street**: r., t. Fine; s., v. Hammond, from v. to Black Lake; s., c. Ogdensburg, from c. to Black Lake; s., h. Piercefield.

Lakeshore Drive: s., v. Norwood, and r., t. Potsdam. Also **Cemetery Road.**

Lalone Island: in St. Lawrence River, t. Lisbon, n. Lalone family. 1966 USG Red Mills Quad.

Lamb Road: r., t. Fowler, n. Lamb family.

Lampsons Falls: falls in Grass(e) River, t. Russell, n. either John or Stephen Lampson, early residents. 1915 Russell Quad. Variant, **Lamson.**

Landing School: no. 17. common school, t. Brasher.

Lang Street: s., v. Norwood, n. Lang family.

Langdon: n. Frank Langdon, from Dorset, VT, who opened first store in South Canton in 1807. Durant, 208: **Langdon Corners**: crossroads, t. Canton. 1964 Pierrepont Quad; 1873 **South Canton** Hamilton Child, p. 97. / **Langdon Corners-Crary Mills Road**: r., t. Canton. / **Langdon School**: no. 18, common school, t. Canton, n. Langdon family.

Lantry School: no. 8, common school, t. Massena, n. Lantry family.

Laplante Road: r., t. Clifton, n.

Laplante family.

Larnard Street: s., v. Potsdam, n. Larnard family. Also, **Larned**, but **Larnard** is accepted spelling.

LaRoux Avenue: r., h. Cook Corners, t. Clifton.

Larue: n. family: **Larue Road**: r., t. Massena; r., t. Potsdam.

Lashure Road: r., t. Macomb, n. Joseph Lashure family.

Laurel Avenue: s., v. Massena, n. the tree of the genus *Laurus*.

Laurentia: west of Ogdensburg, home of J. A. Van den Heuvel, built for "a young lady." When the romance ended, Heuvel moved back to Blue Mansion. See **Blue Mansion Road**.

Laverys Corners: crossroads, t. Lawrence. 1964 USGS North Lawrence Quad.

Lawrence: t. on eastern border with Franklin Co., n. William Lawrence, New York City merchant, who purchased lands in the survey township of Chesterfield, with title taken by Lawrence on Feb. 17, 1820; t. formed Apr. 21, 1828. Lawrence died in 1824, never having visited his lands. The first settler in the area came in 1801. The area was organized Mar. 2, 1805. Lawrence was formed from Brasher and Hopkinton. Durant, 419. 1964 USGS North Lawrence Quad. Derived n. include **Lawrence Avenue**: s., v. Potsdam, which leads from Potsdam toward Lawrence, US 11. / **Lawrence Avenue Elementary School**: t. Potsdam, on Lawrence Avenue. / **Lawrence Brook**: stream in t. Lawrence and Brasher, trib. Deer River. 1964 Lawrence Brook, North Lawrence Quad; 1873 Lawrence, Hamilton Child map. / **Lawrence Street**: s., v. Massena, leads to Lawrence. / The following are named for Lawrence families: **Lawrence Cemetery**: t. Lisbon; **Lawrence Road**: r., t. Fine; r., t. Lisbon; **Lawrence School**: no. 22, common school, t. Lisbon.

Lawrenceville: h., t. Lawrence, near center of t, both sides of Deer River; p. o. est. Apr. 7, 1829, Josiah Sanders, pm (Hough, 574); p. o. existing, ZIP 12949. Durant, 421-422. 1865 **Deer River** Beers; 1964 USGS North Lawrence Quad. / **Lawrenceville School**: no. 6, common school, t. Lawrence.

Lays: Proposed n. for Massena, in honor of Amos Lay, one of the first mapmakers in the United States. He "was the first surveyor in the Massena area, hired by Jeremiah Van Rensselaer in 1798 to lay out lots and roadways." Also, **Lay's**. Dumas, 54. See **Massena**.

Lazy River: t. Russell, tranquil section of the Grass(e) River above Woods Bridge, n. by John B. Grandy family. / **Lazy River Bridge**: formerly, **Woods Bridge**. / **Lazy River Playground**: t. Russell, recreation park started by John B. Grandy in the 1930s; still operated by members of the family. / **Lazy River Road**: t. Russell. Locally used for **Woods Bridge** and **Smith Roads**. Roads changed 1992.

Leach Avenue: also **Leach Street**, s., v. Massena, n. Leach family.

Lead Mine Road: r., t. Macomb; r., t. Gouverneur. Both n. mine. Also, **Leadmine Road**.

Lead Mines: mines, t. Rossie.

Leary Road: r., t. Colton; r., t. Potsdam. Both n. Leary families.

Leary's Mills School: no. 16, common school, t. Hop- kinton. Also **Learys Mills School**.

Lee: surname. **Lee Hall**: on St. Lawrence University campus, n. the first President of the College of Letters, the Rev. John Stebbins Lee. / **Lee Road**: r., t. Oswegatchie, n. Thomas Lee, carpenter and pioneer settler from NJ, Durant, 199. / **Lee School**: no. 6, common school, t. Oswegatchie, n. Lee family.

Leete Cemetery: t. Potsdam, n. Leete family.

Lehman Hall: on SUC, Potsdam campus, n. Clarence O. Lehman, who taught in the School of Education.

Leigh: surname: **Leigh Street**: s., v. Canton, n. Leigh family. / **Leigh's Falls**: in Grass(e) River, t. Canton. / **Leigh's Falls Bridge**: in Canton. *Quarterly*, 13 (1968), no. 3, p. 8.

Leishman Point: on St. Lawrence River, t. Waddington, n. Leishman family. 1964 USGS Waddington Quad.

Lem Pond: t. Colton, poss. n. Lem Merrill, famous guide. 1896 **Lem's Pond** New; 1921 USGS Stark Quad. Also **Lem's Pond**.

Lenney School: no. 26, common school, t. Stockholm, n. Lenney family.

Lenny Road: r., t. Parishville, n. John and Henry Lenny.

Leonard: surname used as a specific: **Leonard Brook**: trib. Grannis Brook, t. Pierrepont, n. Leonard family. 1964 USGS Pierrepont Quad. / **Leonard Drive**: s., h. Star Lake, n. James B. Leonard, former supervisor, t. Fine. / **Leonard Falls**: in Racquette River, t. Parishville. 1896 New. / **Leonard Pond**: t. Colton, alt. 1,465. 1860 Merrit; 1896 New; 1902 Blankman; 1908 Adm; 1912 Stoddard; 1920 USGS Childwold Quad.

Lewis House: the student union on Clarkson University campus, n. Harry Slocum Lewis, trustee from 1945 to 1950, the building dedicated Oct. 10, 1953.

Leroy Street: in Potsdam, n. Herman Le Roy, member of a land company in 1803. His house, which he bought from Benjamin Raymond, is now Merritt Apartments. The garden later provided the n. **Garden Street**. Durant, 236.

Liberty: commendatory and patriotic n., but sometimes personal n.: **Liberty Avenue**: s., v. Massena. / **Liberty Street**: s., v. Potsdam, claimed for Liberty **Knowles**.

Lightning Point: on Cranberry Lake, t. Colton. 1896 New.

Lilypad: the large floating leaf of the lily, a common n. for bodies of water in which the lily leaves float: **Lilypad Brook**: trib. Racquette River, t. Piercefield. 1896 **Lily Pad Brook** New; 1920 USGS Childwold Quad. / **Lilypad Pond**: t. Colton. 1896 New; 1902 Blankman; 1912 Stoddard; 1954 USGS Tupper Lake Quad. / **Lilypad Pond**: t. Parishville. 1865 **Strawford Pond** Beers; 1898 **Stamford Pond** EGB map; 1902 **Stamford Pond** Blankman; 1908 **Stamford Pond** Adm; 1908 USGS Potsdam Quad; 1912 Stoddard; 1964 USGS Rainbow Falls Quad.

Lime Hollow Road: r., t. Potsdam, Madrid, Norfolk.

Limekiln Road: s., v. Richville, for the kiln. Also **Davis Road**.

Limestone Island: in Black Lake, t. Morristown. 1961 USGS Pope Mills Quad

Lincoln: some of the n. honor Abraham Lincoln, 16th president of the United States, and others reflect a local surname: **Lincoln Avenue**: s., v. Massena: s., c. Ogdensburg, known also as **Lincoln Lane**, poss. for a family / **Lincoln**

Bridge: over St. Regis River in Stockholm, n. Lyman Lincoln. *Quarterly*, 2 (1957), no. 1, npn / **Lincoln Drive**: s., v. Massena; s., h. Louisville. / **Lincoln Place**: s., v. Massena. / **Lincoln Road**: r., t. Canton, n. J. Lincoln. Also **Eddy-Pyrites Road**; r., t. Louisville. / **Lincoln School**: v. Massena. 1964 USGS Massena Quad; c. Ogdensburg. / **Lincoln Street**: s., v. Canton, n. Sylvester Lincoln; s., v. Waddington, poss. n. a Lincoln family.

Linden: n. the North American forest tree (**Tilia americana**), also called basswood. All the following specifics, **Linden**, derive from the tree: **Linden Lane**: s., c. Ogdensburg. / **Linden Street**: r., t. Oswegatchie; s., v. Massena; s., c. Ogdensburg; s., v. Waddington.

Line Creek: runs in a straight line for much of its course, t. Madrid, trib. Grass(e) River. 1964 USGS Morley Quad.

Lintz Road: between Chippewa Street and Oak Point Road, r., t. Morristown, n. Solomon Lintz, early settler from Mohawk Valley; he settled at the southern end of Black Lake; r. is now abandoned. Bogardus, 142, claims n. Sidney Lintz, farmer and hotel owner.

Lisbon: t. northern border on St. Lawrence River. One of the original ten t. and first to be recognized by the state. n. Lisbon, Portugal. Nickname, **Square Township**, because it contains 100 square miles; formed Mar. 6, 1801. 1963 USGS Ogden East Quad. Other derived n. include: **Lisbon**: h., t. **Lisbon**, built in 1804 and called **Red Mills**, for color of the mills built by D. W. Church, a millwright; p. o. est. Oct. 1, 1808, George C. Conant, pm, closed Dec. 31, 1901, reopened Mar. 17, 1903, Charles G. Wallace, pm, existing, ZIP 13658 (New York Postal History). Hough, 574, erroneously gives est. date July 1, 1810, with James Thompson, pm. 1963 USGS Lisbon Quad. / **Lisbon Cemetery**: t. Lisbon, between Five Mile Road and Heuvelton Road. 1963 USGS Lisbon Quad. / **Lisbon Center**: t. Lisbon, p. o. est. as **Lisbon Centre** Dec. 19, 1850, John McBride, pm, changed to **Lisbon Center**, Peter R. Mullen, pm, Mar. 17, 1903, when changed to **Lisbon**, Also, **Lisbon Centre**. / **Lisbon Center School**: no. 5, common school, t. Lisbon. / **Lisbon Center State Road**: r., t. Lisbon. / **Lisbon Central School**. h. Lisbon. 1963 USGS Lisbon Quad. / **Lisbon Creek**: t. Lisbon, trib. Oswegatchie River. 1963 USGS Heuvelton Quad. / **Lisbon-Flackville Road**: r., t. Lisbon.

/ **Lisbon-Madrid Road**: r., t. Lisbon, Madrid / **Lisbon-Morley Road**: r., t. Lisbon. / **Lisbon Street**: s., v. Heuvelton; s., c. Ogdensburg. / **Lisbon School**: no. 2, common school, t. Lisbon.

Liston Road: r., t. Brasher, n. Liston family.

Literature Lots: By act passed on May 5, 1786, the State could market unappropriated lands, among them the lands of what are now St. Lawrence and Franklin counties. In every township one lot would be set aside for "gospel and schools," and another "for promoting literature"; hence such lots became n. Literature Lots. Durant, 69-71.

Little: a size-n. usually contrasted in the United States with **Big**, which see. Sometimes used for features smaller than the expected, and occasionally a personal n.: **Little Bear Mountain**: see **Little Mountain**, t. Colton. / **Little Black River**: an early n. of the **Racquette River**. / **Little Blue Mountain**: t. Colton, alt. 1,822. 1896 **Blue Mt.** New; 1902 **Blue Mountain** Blankman; 1921 USGS Stark Quad. See **Blue Mountain**. / **Little Blue Pond**: in Hollywood area, t. Colton. 1896 New; 1921 USGS Stark Quad. / **Little Bog**: on Racquette River, t. Colton, near McEwen's. 1860 Merrit. See **Bog Falls**. / **Little Bow**: crossroads, t. Gouverneur. 1961 USGS Natural Dam Quad. / **Little Bow Cemetery**: t. Gouverneur. 1949 USGS Hammond Quad. / **Little Bow Corners**: n. land within the bow or bend in the Oswegatchie River, t. Gouverneur. *Quarterly*, 12 (1967), no. 3, p. 5. / **Little Bow Corners School**: no. 2, common school, t. Gouverneur. / **Little Bow Road**: s. and r, v. Gouverneur. / **Little Brant**: see **Littlebrant**. / **Little Chippewa Point**: on St. Lawrence River, t. Hammond. 1958 USGS Chippewa Quad. / **Little Cold Brook**: stream, trib. Racquette River, t. Colton. 1853 HMC; 1858 Rogerson; 1865 Beers, p. 17; 1896 New; 1902 Blankman; 1921 USGS Stark Quad. / **Little Falls**: in Racquette River, t. Parishville. 1908 USGS Potsdam Quad. / **Little Fish Pond**: t. Clifton, Colton. 1880 **Lake Ely** (identification uncertain) Ely; 1896 New; 1902 Blankman; 1912 Adm (1908); 1919 USGS Cranberry lake Quad. / **Little France**: settlement, t. Brasher, n. French-Canadian residents. / **Little France School**: no. 21, common school, t. Brasher. / **Little Hammond Point**: on St. Lawrence River, t. Hammond. 1958 USGS Chippewa Quad. / **Little Hornet Pond**: southernmost of the **Hornet Ponds** (which see). /

Little Ironsides Islands: in St. Lawrence River, only one of which is in St. Lawrence Co., t. Hammond. 1958 USGS Chippewa Quad. See **Ironsides Islands**. / **Little John**. See **Littlejohn**. / **Little Jordan Lake**: t. Hopkinton, alt. 1,526. 1896 New; 1902 **Jordan** Blankman; 1908 Adm; 1912 Stoddard; 1920 USGS Childwold Quad. / **Little Lake**: pond, t. Russell. 1915 USGS Russell Quad. / **Little Long Lake**: t. Pitcairn. / **Little Moosehead Pond**: t. Clifton. 1919 USGS Cranberry Lake Quad. / **Little Mountain**: t. Clifton, alt. 1,675 ft. 1921 USGS Stark Quad. / **Little Mountain**: t. Colton, alt. 1,115 ft. 1896 **Little Bear Mt**. New; 1902 **Little Bear Mt.** Blankman; 1954 USGS Tupper Lake Quad. / **Little Mud Pond**: t. Fowler. 1956 USGS Edwards Quad. / **Little Oak Island**: in Chippewa Bay, St. Lawrence River, n. desc. / **Little Oswe- gatchie**: t. Fine, on south bank, 9 mi. from Edwards. / **Little Otter Pond**: t. Fine. *Quarterly*, 5 (1960), no. 1, npn. 1916 USGS Oswegatchie Quad. / **Little Pine Pond**: t. Colton. 1896 New; 1902 Blankman; 1954 USGS Tupper Lake Quad. / **Little Red School**: now, **Brasher Center**. *Quarterly*, 14 (1969), no. 4, p. 5. / **Little Red School**: no. 1, Rensselaer Falls [Canton Falls]. / **Little River**: h., t. Canton, p. o. est. Jan. 2, 1892, Margaret Stevenson, pm, closed Nov. 15, 1901. / **Little River**: t. Canton, river, trib. Grass(e) River. 1964 Canton Quad; 1908 Adm; **Butterfields Mills** Hamilton Child, p. 97. / **Little River**: t. Fine, flows into Oswegatchie River near Benson Mines. *Quarterly*, 11 (1966), no. 4, p. 15. 1916 USGS Oswegatchie Quad. / **Little River**: t. Waddington, two-mile stretch of St. Lawrence River between Waddington and Ogden or Crapser Island. *Quarterly*, 3 (1958), no. 1, npn; p. o. existed in 1896. 1964 USGS Waddington Quad. / **Little River Creek**: t. Clifton. / **Little River Nature- Recreational Area**: belongs to St. Lawrence University, borders on Little River just south of the campus. / **Little River Road**, r., t. Canton. / **Little River School**: no. 22, common school, t. Canton. / **Little Rock Pond**: t. Clare. 1921 Stark Quad. / **Little Rock Pond**: t. Parishville. 1908 USGS Potsdam Quad; 1912 Stoddard; 1964 USGS Rainbow Falls Quad. / **Little Saut Island**: t. Massena. Elijah Bayley had an early inn there. / **Little Sucker Brook**: trib. St. Lawrence River, t. Waddington. 1964 USGS Waddington Quad. / **Little Trout Pond**: t. Colton, Piercefield, alt. 1,756. 1880 Ely; 1908 Adm; 1912 Stoddard; 1954 USGS 1954 Tupper Lake Quad. / **Little York**: settlement, t. Fowler, n. Little

York, then Toronto, Canada, in honor of the capture of Little York by the Americans in 1813. It was the seat of the Fowler p. o. for years. Durant, 379-380. See **Fowler.** / **Little York School**: no. 1, common school, t. Fowler.

Littlebrant Road: r., t. Gouverneur, n. Littlebrant family. Also **Little Brant**, error.

Littlejohn Road: r., t. Colton. / **Littlejohn School**: no. 5, common school, t. Colton. 1921 Stark Quad. Both n. Littlejohn family. Also **Little John**, error.

Livingston: n. family: **Livingston Cemetery**: t. Lisbon, n. Robert Livingston; a small family cemetery on Rte. 37, n. Livingston family. 1963 Sparrowhawk Point Quad. / **Livingston Road**: r., t. Stockholm, n. William Livingston family from Washington County.

Lobdell Road: r., t. DeKalb, n. Seymour Lobdell family. Formerly, **Gulf Road**.

Lockie: n. George Lockie who settled near the present road in 1818. His father, who brought him to the area, settled to the west in Rossie and a "trail between his father's house and his land, about six miles in length, was covered by a dense woods, there being but two small clearings in the whole distance." Cent. Souv., 62. George Lockie was an officer of the town of Gouverneur, a director in the Gouverneur Agricultural and Mechanical Society, and a founder of the Presbyterian Society. Durant, 337, 348; Cent. Souv., 103. Beers, p. 31, shows his house near the present site of Lockie Road, near Elmdale: **Lockie Road**: r., t. Gouverneur; r., t. Rossie.

Lockwood School: no. 26, common school, t. Lisbon, n. Lockwood family; no. 2, common school, t. Madrid, n. Levi Lockwood family.

Lone: usually for something solitary or apart: **Lone Brother Island**: in St. Lawrence River, t. Hammond. 1958 USGS Chippewa Quad. / **Lone Pine Point**: see **Bullhead Point.** / **Lone Pine Road**: r., h. Cranberry Lake. / **Lone Pond**: t. Colton, in Hollywood area, middle of township, near Route 56. / **Lone Star Club**: private forest and game preserve. See **Forest Commission Report**, 1893, p. 154. / **Lone Tree Island**: in St. Lawrence River, t. Hammond. 1958 USGS Chippewa Quad.

Lonesome: appearing to be alone,

separate: **Lonesome Bay**: in Black Lake, t. Morristown and Hammond. 1961 USGS Hammond Quad. / **Lonesome Bay State Forest**, #36, t. Hammond. / **Lonesome Pond**: t. Clifton, Fine. See **Sunny Pond**.

Long: a length-n. very common in the United States, although its contrast **Short** is quite rare: **Long Bog**: six m. long, in Racquette River, t. Colton. 1858 Rogerson; 1860 Merrit; 1883 Ely-Wallace. / **Long Bow**: h., t. Parishville, p. o. est. as **Longbow** Aug. 21, 1903, William Murphy, pm, closed Dec. 31, 1914, reopened July 25, 1916, closed Aug. 15, 1919. 1908 USGS Potsdam Quad; 1908 Adm; 1912 Stoddard. / **Long Bow**: island and river channel, t. Parishville. 1908 USGS Potsdam; 1912 Stoddard. / **Long Causeway/Long Crossway**: t. Hammond, Rossie, a wide swamp and road requiring constant rebuilding from days of corduroy crossing, "an eternal problem for road builders." / **Long Island**: see **County Line Island**, t. Piercefield. / **Long Island**: now **Gray's Island**. / **Long Lake**: pond, t. Fine, alt. 1,359 ft. 1916 USGS Oswegatchie Quad. / **Long Lake**: pond, t. Pitcairn. 1916 USGS Oswegatchie Quad. / **Long Mountain**: see **Berkley Mountain**. / **Long Point**: on Joe Indian Island, Cranberry lake, t. Clifton. 1896 New. / **Long Pond**, t. Colton, alt. 1,475 ft. 1858 Rogerson, identity uncertain; 1860 Merrit, identity uncertain; 1883 Ely-Wallace, identity uncertain; 1896 New; 1902 Blankman; 1908 Adm; 1921 USGS Stark Quad. / **Long Pond**: t. Colton, alt. 1,777 ft. 1880 Ely; 1883 Ely-Wallace; 1896 New; 1912 Stoddard; 1954 USGS Tupper Lake Quad. / **Long Pond**: see **Eagle Crag Lake**, t. Piercefield. / **Long Pond**: t. Hopkinton, in Granshue area. / **Long Pond**: t. Fine, alt. 1,336 ft. *Quarterly*, 5 (1960), no. 1, npn. 1915 USGS Russell Quad. / **Long Pond**: t. Piercefield. 1858 Rogerson; 1860 Merrit; 1865 Beers, p. 86; 1880 Ely; 1883 Ely-Wallace; 1896 New; 1902 Blankman; 1908 Adm. / **Long Pond Outlet**: t. Hopkinton. 1896 New; 1902 Blankman; 1908 Adm; 1912 Stoddard; 1919 USGS Nicholville Quad. / **Long Rapids**: in Racquette River, t. Colton / **Long Rapids**: h., t. Canton, p. o. est. Apr. 3, 1839, Lorenzo Fenton, pm, changed to **Morley** May 20, 1839. 1880 Ely; 1883 Ely-Wallace; 1920 USGS Childwold Quad. See **Morley**. / **Long Sault Dam**: 2,350 feet long, channels water into the Moses-Saunders Power Dam. Water through it flows into the **South Channel of the St. Lawrence River**. / **Long Sault Islands**: fifteen islands, in St.

Lawrence River, t. Massena. 1964 USGS Raquette River Quad. / **Long Sault Overlook**: vantage point overlooking the Seaway area in t. Massena. / **Long Sault Rapids**: in St. Lawrence River, t. Massena. 1942 USGS Barnhart Quad. / **Long Saut Island**: in St. Lawrence River, t. Massena. Measures 5 m. by 1/2 to 2 m. French name: **Isle au Long Saut**. Also **Long Sault Island. Garonquoy** and **Karonkwi** (same n., different spellings) are Amerindian, "The place where one speaks with a loud voice," or "with a confused voice," and applies specifically to lower Long Sault Island. See Beauchamp, 72. / **Long Swamp**: t. Rossie. / **Long Tom Mountain**: t. Colton, alt. 2,600 ft. 1902 Blankman; 1908 Adm; 1912 Stoddard; 1954 USGS Tupper Lake Quad.

Longs Corners: crossroads, t. Morristown, n. Long family. 1963 USGS Edwardsville quad. / **Longs Corners School**: no. 11, common school, t. Morristown. Also **Long's Corners School**. Bogardus, 60.

Longshore Road: r., t. Canton.

Lookout Island: in Black Lake, t. Morristown. 1961 USGS Hammond Quad.

Loon Island: in Hamlin Bay, Tupper Lake, t. Piercefield, n. the bird of the genus *Gavia*. 1896 New. / **Loon Mountain**: t. Hopkinton, alt. 1,580 ft. 1919 USGS Nicholville Quad; 1964 USGS Sylvan Falls Quad.

Lord Cottage: boat stop on Black Lake, n. the Lord family. *Quarterly*, 10 (1965), no. 1, p. 8.

Losee Creek: trib. St. Lawrence River, t. Morristown, n. Losee family. Bogardus, 174.

Lost: n. something missing, as **Lost Nation**, or disappeared underground, as **Lost River**. The n. is widespread but somewhat complicated. See Stewart, p. 265. The n. can be applied to any generic or specific: **Lost Nation**: t. Louisville. Origin uncertain. *Quarterly*, 10 (1965), no. 4, p. 9. / **Lost Nation-Brasher Center Road**: r., t. Brasher. / **Lost Nation Road**: now **Canton Road**. *Quarterly*, 11 (1966), no. 1, p. 3. / **Lost Nation School**: no. 9, common school, t. Louisville. / **Lost Nation State Forest**, #9, t. Norfolk. / **Lost Pond** (1): t. Clifton, alt. 1,500. 1883 Ely-Wallace; 1919 USGS Cranberry Lake Quad. See Blankman, p. 28. / **Lost Pond** (2): t. Clifton, alt. 1,475. 1919 USGS Cranberry Lake Quad. / **Lost Pond**: t. Pitcairn. 1951 USGS Harrisville

Quad. / **Lost Village**: crossroads, t. Oswegatchie, along Black Lake. Two versions exist: (1) area lost for weeks because of heavy snow; (2) lost Indian tribe lived there. *Quarterly*, 10 (1965), no. 4, p. 9. 1963 USGS Heuvelton Quad. / **Lost Village Road**: r., t. Oswegatchie. / **Lost Village School**: no. 15, common school, t. Oswegatchie.

Lotus Island: in St. Lawrence River, t. Lisbon. 1906 USGS Red Mills Quad. 1964 USGS Massena Quad.

Louisville: t., northeastern part of county, bordering on St. Lawrence River, containing 33,424 acres, one of the ten original t., n. King Louis XVI of France for aid during the Revolutionary War; formed Apr. 5, 1810, from Massena. Durant, 397; *Quarterly*, 6 (1961), no. 1, npn. / **Louisville**: h., first known as **Millerville**, n. Reverend Levi Miller, "a licensed preacher of the Methodist Episcopal denomination, who came from Massachusetts, but immediately from Turin, Lewis County, N.Y., as agent for James McVickar, the purchaser from Macomb of the tract, including the site of the village." Quoted from Durant, 399; p. o. est. Sept. 9, 1811, Benjamin Willard, pm, closed May 22, 1823, reopened Nov. 11, 1824, Levi Miller, pm, closed Nov. 23, 1929. 1965 USGS Louisville Quad. Other derived n. include **Louisville Bay**: *Quarterly*, 7 (1962), no. 1, p. 17. / **Louisville Cemetery**. / **Louisville School**: no. 6, common school. 1964 USGS Louisville Quad. / **Louisville Landing**: h. and landing on St. Lawrence River and served as a port of entry; p. o. est. Apr. 9, 1850, Ralph D. Marsh, pm (Hough, 574), closed June 30, 1917. No longer used as landing. Also see Durant, 400. / **Louisville Landing Cemetery**. Bodies removed to other cemeteries at time of the building of the Seaway. / **Louisville Landing School**: no. 3, common school. / **Louisville Road**: r. / **Louisville-Raymondville Road**: r. / **Louisville-Wilson Hill Road**: r.

Loux Island: in St. Lawrence River, t. Massena. Now **Aults.**

Lovers Lane: see **Glenn Street.**

Lovejoy Road: r., t. Oswegatchie, n. Henry Lovejoy family.

Lower: n. denotes place below, further down, or in southern direction; usually in contrast with **Upper**. See Stewart, p. 266. St. Lawrence County n. include **Lower Big Bay**: in Black Lake, t. DePeyster. 1963 USGS Heuvelton Quad. / **Lower Deep Bay**: in Black

Lake, t. Morristown. 1961 USGS Pope Mills Quad. / **Lower District School**: t. Clare. 1915 USGS Russell Quad. / **Lower Indian Creek Lake**: pond, part of **Indian Creek**, t. Canton. See **Indian Creek**. / **Lower Lake**: 1963 Rensselaer Falls Quad. See **Lower Indian Creek Lake**. / **Lower Oswegatchie**: h. t. Fine. 1916 USGS Oswegatchie Quad. / **Lower Pine Street**: s., v. Potsdam. / **Lower Pond**: see **Lows Lake**. / **Lower School**: h., Clare, t. Clare. No longer exists. Clarke, 26. / **Lower Wick**: t. Parishville, section extending from Stark Corner to Hopkinton line.

Lows Lake: lake of ponds in Bog River, t. Colton, n. A. A. Low, who claimed the ponds as his private preserve: 1860 **Lower Pond** for first pond, Street, p. 238; 1880 **Chain Ponds, 4th Pond** Ely; 1882 Ely-Wallace, same as Ely; 1896 **Fourth Pond, Third Pond, Second Pond, First Pond** New; 1902 **4th Pond, 3rd Pond, 2nd Pond, 1st Pond** Blankman; 1908 Adm, same as Blankman; 1912 **First Pond, Second Pond, Third Pond**; 1954 USGS Tupper Lake Quad. See **First Pond**, etc.

Luke Brown Road: t. Parishville, n. Luke Brown, early settler who arrived in 1809; his son, Luke Parish Brown, born 1812, was the first white child recorded in the v. Parishville. Also, **Mud Street**.

Luther School: no. 7, common school, t. Pitcairn, n. Luther family.

Lyd Brook: t. Hopkinton, trib. Hopkinton Brook, n. **Lyd** in honor of Lydia Hopkins. 1964 USGS Nicholville Quad. Also **Lyde Brook**.

Lynch Road: r., t. Stockholm, n. Dennis Lynch family.

M

Mackay Road: r., t. Potsdam, n. Mackay family.

Mackin Road: r., t. Russell, terminates at South Russell, n. Frank Mackin. .

Macks: island in St. Lawrence River, t. Massena. Formerly, **Empress Isle**.

Macomb: western interior of county, t. formed on Apr. 30, 1841 (Durant, 363), n. for Alexander Macomb, patentee of Macomb's Purchase, formed from t. of Morristown and Gouverneur. Durant, 363; Hough, 339. Macomb, for whom Macomb, Illinois, also was named, began his career as a fur trader and was nicknamed "The Speculator" for his land dealings in the late 1780s and early 1790's. At one time he held almost all the unpatented portions of what are now the counties of Jefferson, St. Lawrence, and Franklin. (see **Macomb's Purchase**). His claims on much of the land in St. Lawrence County were not honored, and this is the only place that bears his n. See "Million Bank," *Watertown Daily Times*, July 3, 1976, p. B-9, cols. 4-5. Also, *Quarterly*, 4 (1959), no. 1, p. 1. 1963 USGS Edwardsville Quad. Also see Brown and Walton, **John Brown's Tract**. / **Macomb**: h. and p. o., May 13, 1842. Formerly, **Washburnville**, p. o. est. May 13, 1842 as **Washburnville**, David Day II, first pm (Hough, 574), closed Feb. 15, 1907, changed to **Macomb** Jan 25, 1908, Vilas Ingram, pm, closed July 15, 1935. Also see *Quarterly*, 7 (1962), no. 4, p. 14. Also **Pierces Corners** before Washburnville. / **Macomb-DePeyster Road**: r., t. Macomb, DePeyster. / **Macomb-Pope Mills Road**: r., t. Macomb. / **Macomb School**: no. 3, common school, t. Macomb.

Macomb's Purchase: On July 10, 1787, bidders were awarded lands at the land sale in New York City for Herkimer, Jefferson, Lewis, Oswego, Franklin, and St. Lawrence Counties. Alexander Macomb bought the land, an estimated 3,934,899 acres for about eight cents an acre, the area known as Macomb's Purchase, bought mostly in 1787. The land included all the ten towns along the St. Lawrence River. The St. Lawrence County tract is listed as 640,000 acres. In this area, the bidders turned their purchases over to Alexander Macomb. For further information on the Purchase, see Hough, **History of St. Lawrence and Franklin Counties**, pp. 238 ff. Also, Atwood Manley, "The Little-Known Alexander Macomb," *Quarterly*, 4 (1959), no. 1, [1-8]. Later, Macomb was involved in a bank failure, causing him to lose his holdings and also to be lodged in debtor's prison. See Hough, 242, for details. Daniel McCormick and William Constable were also involved in the purchase but did not suffer the land loss that Macomb did. See "Macomb's Purchase," in **State of New York Annual Report of the Forest Commission For the Year 1893**, Vol. 1, pp. 79-94, which includes a copy of "The Macomb Patent."

MacVicar Hall: on SUC, Potsdam, campus, n. Malcolm MacVicar, principal and teacher of intellectual and moral philosophy and school economy at the State Normal and Training School, now **State University College at Potsdam.** Durant, 122.

Madill: surname used as a specific: **Madill School**: c. Ogdensburg. / **Madill Hall**: on St. Lawrence University campus, now the military studies office, n. an academic officer form Canton Agriculture and Technical College, with the name retained after St. Lawrence University acquired the building; n. Dr. Madill, a faculty member. / **Madill Road**: r., t. Lisbon, n. Madill family.

Madison: n. James Madison, 4th president of the United States: **Madison Avenue**: r., c. Ogdensburg. / **Madison Street**: s., v. Massena.

Madonna Court: s., v. Massena, n. Virgin Mary, in a cluster of such n. given by the land developer for a housing project. See **Urban**.

Madrid: n. Madrid, Spain; [pronounced **mad rid**, with stress on first syllable], one of the ten original t. formed on March 3, 1802 from Lisbon, the same time St. Lawrence County was inc. In 1837, an attempt was made to unify Madrid, Lisbon, Canton, and Potsdam under the name of **Madrid**, but it failed. / **Madrid**: inc. 1803, the h. was n. **Robert's Mill.** Previous to the War of 1812, the n. was changed to **Columbia Village (Columbiaville).** Later, h. was n. **Madrid** for the t.; p. o. est. Oct. 28, 1807, from **Waddington**, closed as **Columbia** April 15, 1819, reopened Mar. 1, 1826 as **Madrid**, Alexander Richards, first pm, existing, ZIP 13660 (New York Postal History). Hough, 574, erroneously gives date as Apr. 5, 1826, with John Horton, pm. 1964 USGS Morley Quad. Other derived n. include **Madrid Avenue**: s., v. Potsdam. / **Madrid Cemetery**: h. Madrid. 1964 USGS Waddington Quad. / **Madrid-Chase Mills Road**: r., t. Madrid. / **Madrid Depot**: t. Madrid, p. o. est. Mar. 3, 1855, Alonzo H. Hall, pm, closed May 6, 1857 ; **Madrid Road**: r., t. Madrid, Norfolk. / **Madrid School**: no. 1, common school, t. Madrid. Also, **Madrid Village School.** / **Madrid Springs**: spa, t. Madrid, n. for the two springs that furnished water for the h. The health spa operated on the site for many years; p. o. est. July 15, 1869, changed from **Grass River**, Charles A. Chandler, first pm, closed May 15, 1920. / **Madrid Springs School**: no. 10, common school, t. Madrid. / **Madrid Village School**: see **Madrid School.** / **Madrid-Waddington High School**: t. Madrid. 1964 USGS Waddington Quad.

Mahoney Road: r., t. Brasher, Stockholm, n. James Mahoney family.

Maiden Lane: s., v. Massena. *Quarterly*, 10 (1965), no. 4, p. 14. Also **Maldon Lane**, result of a misprint; s., h. Russell; s., v. Waddington.

Main Street: The most popular street name in the United States, occurring in almost every place of habitation (town, village, city); usually represents the most important thoroughfare for business: s., v. Brasher Falls; s., v. Canton; s., v. Colton; s., v. Edwards; r., t. Fine; r., t. Fowler; s., v. Hammond; s., h. Hannawa Falls; s., v. Hermon; s., h. Lisbon; s., h. Madrid; s., v. Massena; s., v. Morristown; s., h. Norfolk; s., v. Norwood; s., v. Parishville; s., c. Ogdensburg; s., h. Piercefield; s., v. Potsdam, formerly **South Street**; s., h. Pyrites, along the Grass(e) River, t. Canton. See **Bridge Street**, Pyrites; s., v. Waddington; s., v. Richville; s., h. Star Lake. / **Main Street North**: s., v. Massena. Main Street was formerly **Bridge Street**, then **Harrowgate Street**. / **Main Street South**: s., v. Massena.

Mainliner: New York to Buffalo line of Northern Railroad. *Quarterly*, 7 (1962), no. 4, p. 7.

Malby Avenue: s., v. Massena, n. Malby family. Also, **Molby**, a misprint.

Malterna Creek: t. Gouverneur, trib. Oswegatchie River, n. Malterner family (spelling changed). Albert Malterner settled in nearby Somerville around 1813 where he owned a farm and lived until 1863. The creek runs from Gouverneur through Somerville in the town of Rossie and then into Jefferson Co. 1961 USGS Natural Dam Quad.

Manchester School: no. 5, common school, t. Pitcairn, n. Manchester family.

Mansion Avenue: s., c. Ogdensburg, n. the Nathan Ford Mansion.

Manzanita Island: in Chippewa Bay, St. Lawrence River, t. Hammond, n. by James G. Knap, after he spent a winter in California. Spanish, "little apple." *Quarterly*, 16 (1971), no. 3, p. 11. Formerly, **Cleared Island, Flat Island**. 1958 USGS Chippewa Quad.

Maple: a tree of the genus *Acer*; one of the more popular specific n., especially for streets, in the United States, honoring the tree for its beauty, shade, and sap for making syrup: **Maple Avenue**: s., v. Edwards. / **Maple City**: nickname for **Ogdensburg**. / **Maple Grove Cemetery**: t. DeKalb, in Richville. 1956 USGS Richville Quad; t. Lawrence, slightly south of North Lawrence. 1964 USGS North Lawrence Quad. / **Maple Mountain**: t. Fine, alt. 1,840 ft. 1916 USGS Osweegatchie Quad. / **Maple Ridge**: t. Brasher. 1964 Raquette River Quad. / **Maple Ridge**: t. DeKalb / **Maple Ridge Road**: r., t. Gouverneur; r., t. Lisbon. / **Maple Ridge School**: no. 10, common school, t. Brasher; no. 12, common school, t. DeKalb. 1915 USGS Gouverneur Quad. / **Maple Street**: s., v. Canton; s., v. Colton; s., v. Edwards; s., v. Hermon; s., v. Massena, first street laid out in the v., 1803; s., h. Norfolk; s., v. Norwood; s., v. Potsdam, formerly. **Nicholville Turnpike**; s., v. Waddington.

Marble: n. presence of the mineral: **Marble City**: t. Gouverneur, a nickname for the leading marble-producing community. / **Marble Hill**: t. Norfolk. 1964 USGS Norfolk Quad. / **Marble Hill School**: no. 7, common school, t. Norfolk. / **Marble Mountain**: t. Clifton, alt. 1,800. 1919 USGS Cranberry Lake Quad.

Marie Street: s., v. Massena.

Marine Street: s., c. Ogdensburg, n. Marine Railway connection with railcar ferry to Canada.

Market Street: a popular street n., connoting a place of commerce, although in reality just another street: s., c. Ogdensburg; s., v. Potsdam. / **Market Street School**: no. 17, common school, t. Potsdam.

Marsh: a generic often used as a specific, as **Marsh Pond**, to denote a land periodically covered with water. Occurs as a personal n., too. **Marsh Pond**: t. Colton. 1921 USGS Stark Quad; t. Colton. 1908 USGS Potsdam Quad; t. Fine, possibly n. J. Marsh (1896 map); see **Buck Pond**, t. Hopkinton. / **Marsh Hunting**: t. Colton, a hunting ground. / **Marsh Ponds**: two ponds, t. Piercefield, alt. 1,548. 1896 New; 1908 Adm; 1920 USGS Childwold. / **Marsh Road**: r., t. Norfolk, n. Morgan Marsh family. / **Marsh School**: no. 7, common school, t. Fowler, n. marsh.

Marshall: n. family: **Marshall Avenue**: s., h. Star Lake, n. H. and G. Marshall, early settlers. / **Marshall Road**: r., t. Lisbon, n. William Marshall family. / **Marshall School**: no. 28, common school, t. Lisbon, n. Marshall family. / **Marshall Street**: s., h. Star Lake.

Marshville: h., t. Hermon, n. Amos Marsh, gristmill owner. Now a ghost town. *Quarterly*, 8 (1963), no. 1, p. 4. 1915 USGS Russell Quad. Derived n. are **Marshville Cemetery**, t. Hermon. / **Marshville Road**: t. Hermon, Russell. / **Marshville School**: no. 2, common school, made famous by book **Deacon Babbitt**, by Edgar Blankman.

Martin: a popular surname: **Martin Athletic Fields**: on campus of Canton College of Technology, n. Edson A. Martin (1901-1991), a former St. Lawrence County sheriff and father of U. S. Rep. David O'Brien Martin. He donated the land on which the Canton Tech campus now sits. / **Martin Brook**: t. Pierrepont, n. William C. Martin family. / **Martin Cemetery**: t. Lisbon, near Chapel Road. 1935 USGS Sparrowhawk Point Quad. / **Martin Road**: r., t. Louisville, n. Robert Martin family. / **Martin School**: no. 10, common school, t. Waddington, n. Martin family. / **Martin Street**: s., v. Massena, n. Martin family.

Martyn School: no. 9, common school, t., Canton, n. Tyler Martyn.

Marvin Hill: located in North Hammond, n. Ebenezer Marvin, a resident of Hammond and a t. supervisor in 1819. The Oak Point Road was built up this large hill, its steepness a test for early cars. See **Battle Hill**.

Mary-George Inn: see **Chase Mills Inn**.

Marysburgh: t. Morristown; origin n. unknown. Now, **Edwardsville**. Also, **Marysborough**.

Massawepie: Amerindian name, meaning not known: **Massawepie**: settlement, t. Piercefield; p. o. est. June 29, 1903, Cornelius R. Eldridge, pm, closed June 30, 1913, reopened as rural branch from Tupper Lake, June 16, 1954, ZIP 12986, Tupper Lake. 1896 New; 1908 Adm; 1912 Stoddard. / **Massawepie Lake**: t. Pierce- field, alt. 1,512. See, also, *Quarterly*, 6 (1961), no. 4, p. 11. 1858 Rogerson; 1865 Beers; 1873 Hamilton Child; 1880 Ely; 1883 notes **Grass Lake** and **Massawepie Lake** Ely-Wallace; 1902 Blankman; 1908 Adm; 1912 Stoddard; 1920 USGS Childwold Quad. / **Massawepie Road**: t. Piercefield.

Massena: t. northern border with St. Lawrence River and Franklin Co., and includes the islands of Long Saut and Barnhart, n. Andre Massena, Marshal of France, who distinguished himself at the Battle of

Rivoli against the Austrian Army on Jan. 14, 1797. In 1802, at height of Massena's popularity, a petition was made to name the t. for him, and was approved. The t. was formed on Mar. 3, 1802, when St. Lawrence County was formed. Others later tried to n. it **Jefferson**, **Liberty**, **Americus**, or **Lays (Lay's) Falls**, but were not successful. Dumas, 2; *Quarterly*, 10 (1965), no. 4, p. 8. / **Massena**: v., n. t. Amerindian name: **Nikentsiake**, "where the fish live." Nicknames of the v. include **Aluminum City** (for the presence of the Massena Operations of the Aluminum Company of America), **Settlement of the Pines**, and **Orphan City** ("left alone after six other townships were taken from it"); p. o. est. Sept. 19, 1811, Calvin Hubbard, pm (Hough, 574), existing, ZIP 13662. 1964 USGS Massena Quad. / **Massena Cemetery**: t. Massena. 1964 USGS Massena Quad. / **Massena Center**: h., t. Massena, p. o. est. as **Massena Centre** July 13, 1851, Augustus Wheeler, first pm (Hough, 574), changed to Massena Center July 24, 1893, Chloe Atwood, pm, closed May 15, 1919. 1964 USGS Raquette River Quad. Also **Massena Centre** (Hough, 574). / **Massena Center Cemetery**: t. Massena. / **Massena Center Road**: r., t. Massena. / **Massena Center School**: no. 5, common school, t. Massena. / **Massena-Cornwall International Bridge**: over the St. Lawrence River, between t. Massena and Canada. 1964 USGS Hogansburg Quad. / **Massena Country Club**: formerly, the Talcott Farm. Dumas, 51. / **Massena- Helena Road**: r., t. Massena, Brasher. / **Massena High School**: no. 1, common school, v., t. Massena. / **Massena Intake**: "a 700-foot long concrete structure, provides water to the village of Massena and the Massena Operations of Alcoa." CB, 35. / **Massena Junior High School**: v. Massena. 1964 USGS Massena Quad. / **Massena Mile Square**: t. Massena, a square of land that the Mohawks did not deed to New York state in 1796; "covered part of the mill site of the Aluminum Company of America and the section of East Orvis Street lying east of Water Street." Dumas, vii. / **Massena Point**: on Barnhart Island, t. Massena. Dumas, 30; 1942 USGS Barnhart Quad. / **Massena Point Road**: r., t. Massena. / **Massena Point School**: no. 6, common school, t. Massena. / **Massena-Raquette River Road**: r., t. Massena. / **Massena Springs**: t. Massena, a health spa in the late 1800's, waters used for curative purposes. *Quarterly*, 9 (1964), no. 3, p. 4; p. o. est. Mar. 19, 1867 from **Crocker**, Thomas Crocker, pm, closed Nov. 6, 1868, reopened May 21, 1892, George H. Dulton, pm, closed June 30,1928. Amerindian name: **Kanaswas-takeras**, or **Kangawasta- karas**, "where the mud smells bad." 1964 USGS Massena Quad. / **Massena Town Line Road**: r., t. Massena.

Mater Dei College: Catholic college, c. Ogdensburg, t. Oswegatchie. 1963 USGS Ogdendsburg West Quad.

Matilda Bay: in Cranberry Lake, t. Clifton. 1896 New. / **Matilda Island**: in Cranberry Lake, t. Clifton. 1896 New; 1902 Blankman; 1908 Adm; 1912 Stoddard; 1919 USGS Cranberry Lake Quad. Origin of n. unknown.

Matildaville: a survey township, now in t. Colton, said to be n. daughter of Alexander Macomb. *Quarterly*, 5 (1960), no. 2, p. 5; also 9 (1964), p. 16. One of the 18 t. in eastern St. Lawrence County formed on Jan. 10, 1792. / **Matildaville**: settlement, p. o. est. June 17, 1837, William P. Stark, pm, closed June 19, 1851. Also, **Matildavale.**

Mattoon: n. family: **Matoon Bridge**: see **Matoon Creek.** / **Matoon Creek**: t. Fowler, trib. Sawyer Creek. *Quarterly*, 23 (1978), no. 1, p. 12. 1956 USGS Gouverneur Quad.

Matumbla Mountain: see **Mount Matumbla.**

Maxcy Hall: physical education and athletic complex on SUC, Potsdam campus, n. John Wesley Maxcy, a professor of Physical Education.

May Road: s., r., v. Potsdam, n. John May from VT. / **May School**: no. 19, common school, t. Potsdam, n. May family.

Mayhew Road: r., t. DePeyster, n. Mayhew family

Maynard Street: s., v. Potsdam, n. Levi Maynard.

Mayne: n. family: **Mayne School**: no. 30, common school, t. Lisbon, n. William Mayne family; no. 21, common school, t. Oswegatchie.

McAdoo Road: r., t. DeKalb, Canton, n. Samuel and William McAdoo family. / **McAdoo School**: no. 21, common school, t. Canton, n. McAdoo family.

McAllister Road: r., t. Gouverneur, n. McAllister family.

McBrier Cemetery: t. Hermon, new

section of Hermon Cemetery, donated with mausoleum, ornamental fences, Cedars of Lebanon, and other contributions by Mr. E. Merton McBrier, a t. and v. benefactor.

McCabe School: t. Pierrepont, Dist. 12, common school. Also, **Irish Settlement School**.

McCarthy Road: r., t. Brasher, n. Jeremiah McCarthy family; r., t. Russell, n. McCarthy family; r., t. Stockholm, n. Dennis McCarthy family.

McCauslin: family n.: **McCauslin Road**: r., t. Lawrence, n. John McCauslin family. / **McCauslin School**: no. 7, common school, t. Lawrence, n. McCauslin family. Also, **McCaslin**.

McClear Road: r., t. Fine, n. James McClear family.

McCluskey Avenue: s., v. Massena, n. Timothy McCluskey family.

McConnell Creek: t. Louisville, trib. Grass(e) River, n. McConnell family. 1964 USGS Louisville Quad.

McCormick Road: r., t. Oswegatchie, from Black Lake to St. Lawrence River, n. McCormick family. / **McCormick School**: no. 20, common school, t. Lisbon, n. Robert McCormick family. 1904 USGS Ogdensburg Quad.

McCoy Road: r., t. Oswegatchie, n. Arthur or Francis McCoy; r., t. Parishville, n. McCoy family.

McCuen: family n.: **McCuen Pond**: t. Brasher. Also **McCuin**. / **McCuen Pond**: t. Hopkinton. 1896 New; 1902 Blankman; 1908 Adm; 1912 Stoddard; 1920 USGS Childwold Quad. / **McCuen School**: no. 14, common school, t. Brasher. Also **McCuin School**. All n. McCuen families.

McEwen: a popular surname: **McEwen Road**: t. Lawrence, n. Carlton McEwen, first supervisor of Lawrence. / **McEwen School**: n. 5, common school, t. Lawrence. / **McEwens Corner**: crossroads, t. Lawrence, n. Carlton McEwen. 1964 USGS North Lawrence Quad.

McFadden Road: r., t. Lisbon, n. Sharp McFadden family.

McGinnis Road: r., t. Potsdam, n. McGinnis family; r., t. Waddington. n. John, William, James, and Thomas McGinnis families.

McGovern Road: r., t. Stockholm,

n. John and Thomas McGovern families.

McGowan Road: r., t. Oswegatchie, n. F. McGowan family.

McIlwee Road: r., t. Oswegatchie, n. Johnson McIlwee family.

McIntyre Road: r., t. Brasher, n. Neil McIntyre family; r., t. Oswegatchie, n. Archibald McIntyre family. Also **Mummery Road** r., t. Stockholm. n. Parker McIntyre family.

McKabe Road: r., t. Colton, Pierrepont, n. McKabe family.

McKean Street: s., v. Gouverneur. Beers, 33, shows a W. McKean owning two houses near the present McKean Street on the road to Somerville. Poss. n. Wallace McKean (**Centennial Souvenir**, 14). A claim is made for William McKean who sold land to Whitney Marble Co., 1881, but this obviously is late.

McKinley: n. William McKinley, 25th president of the United States: **McKinley Avenue**: s., v. Massena. / **McKinley Court**: s., v. Massena. / **McKinley Street**: s., v. Norwood.

McKnight Road: r., t. Waddington, n. Orange McKnight family.

McMartin Road: r., t. Dekalb, n. Fred McMartin.

McMaster Drive: s., h. Hannawa Falls, n. McMaster family.

McNaughton School: no. 10, common school, t. DePeyster, n. Joseph McNaughton family.

McNeil Road: connects Stowe and River Roads, t. Morristown.

McRostie School: no. 13, common school, t. Waddington, n. the James McRostie family of many offspring; related to the Ogdens.

Meacham Road: r., t. Hopkinton, n. Meacham family.

Mead Road: r., t. Canton, n. Orville A. and Luman Mead. Also **Meade Road**.

Meadow: n. open, grassy space or field: **Meadow Brook**: trib. West Branch Oswegatchie River, t. Pitcairn. 1951 USGS Harrisville Quad. / **Meadow Drive**: r., t. Louisville. / **Meadow Lane**: s., v. Gouverneur. n. presence of an open space. / **Meadows, The**: see **The Meadows**.

Mechanic Street: an older street n., connoting a place for the making and repairing of tools and equipment, or the place where such skilled workers lived. The surviving names indicate an earlier age and also the importance of the individual artisan or craftsperson: **Mechanic Street**: s., v. Canton; s., v. Norwood; s., c. Ogdensburg; s., v. Potsdam.

Medbury Pond: t. Pierrepont, n Medbury family. Also **Medberry**.

Mehaffy Road: r., t. Lisbon, n. Mehaffy family.

Meigs School: no. 8, common school, t. Waddington, n. Meigs family.

Mein Road: r., t. Louisville. / **Mein School**: no. 8, common school, t. Lousiville. n. Mein family. Also, **Mien** (error).

Melhinch School: no. 32, common school, t. Lisbon, n. William Melhinch family.

Memorial: an area or building memorializing someone or something. **Memorial Hall**: on St. Lawrence University campus. / **Memorial Forest**: county forest, t. Pitcairn.

Mercer Street: s., v. Morristown, poss. n. Hugh Mercer, Revolutionary War general, killed at Princeton in 1877. See Stewart, 290.

Merchant: n. family: **Merchant Street**: v. Nicholville, n. Edward Merchant and son Silas, from Connecticut. / **Merchant Street School**: no. 3, common school, t. Lawrence. 1919 USGS Nicholville Quad.

Merrill Creek: t. DeKalb, trib. Oswegatchie River. 1956 USGS Richville Quad.

Merritt: surname used as a specific: **Merritt Avenue**: s., v. Massena. / **Merritt Hall**: on SUC, Potsdam, campus, n. Edwin Adkins Merritt, who supported the normal school and was president of its Board. He was a charter member and trustee of Clarkson College of Technology. *Quarterly*, 11 (1966), no. 3, p. 12.

Meyers Road: r., t. Brasher, n. Meyers Road.

Middle: Very popular specific that can be joined with any generic to connote between places that are similar. See Stewart, p. 294: **Middle Branch Grass(e) River**. t. Russell. See **Grass(e) River**. 1915 USGS **Middle Branch** Russell Quad. / **Middle Branch Oswegatchie River**:

t. Fine, trib. Oswegatchie River. 1916 USGS Oswegatchie Quad. / **Middle Branch Road**: r., t. Clare. Also **Dean Road.** / **Middle Brother Pond**: t. Clifton. See **Brothers Ponds.** / **Middle Island**: in St. Lawrence River, at the center of those surrounding it on the United States side of the boundary, t. Hammond. 1958 USGS Chippewa Bay Quad. / **Middle Point Bay**: in Black Lake, t. Morristown. 1961 USGS Pope Mills Quad. / **Middle Pond**: see **Hutchins Pond.** / **Middle Pond**: t. Colton. / **Middle Road**: r., t. Morristown, Oswegatchie, between and parallel to Black Lake and St. Lawrence River. / **Middle Road**: r., t. Parishville, Hopkinton. Also, **Allen Falls Road.**

Middlebury Avenue: s., v. Massena, n. Middlebury College.

Midget Pond: t. Colton, facetious n. size. 1920 USGS Childwold Quad.

Mien: see **Mein.**

Mildon Street/Road: s., v. Canton.

Mile: a distance-n.: **Mile Arm Bay**: in Black Lake, t. Hammond. 1961 USGS Hammond Quad. / **Mile Pond**: t. Clare. 1896 New; 1902 Blankman; 1908 Adm; 1912 Stoddard; 1921 Stark Quad. / **Mile Rapids**: t. Hopkinton, rapids in West Branch St. Regis River. 1896 New.

Milepost 60: t. Pitcairn, on Carthage & Adirondack Railroad, near summit of the Jayville grade. *Quarterly*, 11 (1966), no. 2, p. 16.

Miles Road: s., v. Hermon, n. Ansel (also spelled Asel) Miles family.

Militia Road: See **Webster Road.**

Mill: During the 18th and 19th centuries, some kind of mill was built on nearly every stream that had continuous flowing water or along any road or street; and, hence, the feature was given a **Mill** name; occurs occasionally as a personal n.: **Mill Brook**: t. Edwards, trib. Elm Creek. 1915 USGS Russell Quad. / **Mill Road**: r., t. Lawrence, Hopkinton; r., t. Lisbon, n. Mill family; r., t. Norfolk; s., v. Morristown. / **Mill Street**: s., v. Brasher Falls; r., t. Clifton; s., v. Colton; s., h. Cranberry Lake; r., t. Fowler; s., v. Gouverneur; s., h. Hailesboro; s., v. Hammond, where the Soper family est. a sawmill and grist mill on the street, formerly **Soper Street**; s., h. Hannawa Falls; s., h. Lisbon; s., v. Massena, n. millsites along the Grass(e) River. Now, **Water Street**; s., c. Ogdensburg; s., v. Parishville; s., h. Russell.

Mille Isles: French, "thousand islands." "I believe there are about five hundred," translated from an account of Father Charlevoix, May 14, 1721. Durant, 28.

Miller: a popular surname; here does not reflect occupa- tion: **Miller Brook**: t. Hopkinton, trib. St. Regis River. 1964 USGS Nicholville Quad. / **Miller Road**: r., t. Lawrence; r., t. Potsdam; r., t. Waddington.

Millerville: n. Rev. Levi Miller, licensed preacher of Methodist Episcopal denomination, originally from MA, agent of James McVickar, Durant, 399, col. 1. See **Louisville**, v. Also **Millersville**.

Mills Road: r., t. Fowler, n. William Mills, whose descendants have become prominent medical persons and educators.

Mine Road: r., t. Edwards, n. talc mine; r., t. Rossie, to lead mine.

Miner Street: s., and r., v. and t. Canton, n. Ebenezer Miner, settled permanently in 1829, merchant, president of Board of Trustees of the v., 1859, 1865-1867. Durant, pp. 215, 227, 232.

Mineral: n. presence of some type of mineral: **Mineral Point**: on Black Lake, t. Macomb, n. after lead was discovered in 1836; mine closed in 1869. See **Army**. *Quarterly*, 2 (1957), no. 4, npn; 9 (1964), no. 1, p. 7. Also called **Mineral Point Lead Mine Village**. / **Mineral Mountain**: near Lake Ozonia.

Miners Hill: t. Hopkinton, alt. 1,880. 1919 USGS Nicholville Quad; 1964 USGS Lake Ozonia Quad.

Mink: n. of the semiaquatic animal of the genus *Mustela vison* found around streams; n. occurs from sightings or incidents: **Mink Brook**: stream, trib. Grass(e) River Flow, t. Colton. 1920 Childwold Quad. / **Mink Creek**: t. Fine (St. Lawrence Co.) and t. Diana (Lewis Co.). trib. Fish Creek. 1916 USGS Oswegatchie Quad. / **Mink Island**: in St. Lawrence River, t. Hammond. 1865 Beers, p. 37; 1958 USGS Chippewa Quad.

Minklers Corners: t. Massena, n. Christopher Minkler family.

Missouri Avenue: s., v. Potsdam, n. state.

Mitchell: a surname used as a specific: **Mitchell Bay**: in Black Lake, t. Morristown. 1963 USGS Edwardsville Quad. / **Mitchell Road**: r., t. Macomb, n. Mitchell family. / **Mitchell School**: no. 9, common school, t. Macomb, poss. n. Moses B. Mitchell; no. 7, common school, t. Morristown, n. John R. Mitchell family.

Mohawk Reservation: the **St. Regis Reservation**, but is now generally known by the n. for the Mohawk Amerindians. The reservation (known also as the **Akwesasne**) is in the northeast corner of St. Lawrence County and straddles the U.S.-Canadian border.

Monkey Hill: t. Oswegatchie, reason n. unknown. Formerly **Tierney**. / **Monkey Hill Road**: r., t. Oswegatchie.

Monroe: n. James Monroe, 5th president of the U. S.: **Monroe Avenue**: s., c. Ogdensburg. / **Monroe Parkway**: s., v. Massena.

Monterey: h., t. Russell, reason n. unknown; p. o. est. June 12, 1882, A. H. Armstrong pm. Became **Degrasse** in 1893. *Quarterly*, 15 (1969), no. 2, p. 3. 1915 USGS **De Grasse** Russell Quad. 1915 USGS **Monterey** Russell Quad. / **Monterey School**: no. 5, common school, t. Russell.

Montgomery: surname: **Montgomery Street**: s., v. Morristown, n. county in Wales. / s., c. Ogdensburg, n. Richard Montgomery (1736-1775), American Revolutionary general.

Moody: n. family: **Moody Falls**: rapids, in Racquette River, t. Colton. 1880 Ely; 1883 Ely-Wallace; 1902 Blankman; 1920 USGS Childwold Quad. / **Moody Road**: r., t. Parishville.

Moon Lake: pond, t. Edwards, n. shape. 1956 USGS Edwards Quad.

Moore: surname used as a specific: **Moore Field**: near h. Clare, t. Clare, airport, n. Lloyd Moore, legislator, and John Moore. / **Moore House**: on Clarkson University campus, n. Emilie Clarkson Moore (1863-1946), who contributed substantially to the university. / **Moore School**: no. 4, common school, t. Potsdam, n. Moore family. / **Moores Corners**: crossroads, t. Pierrepont; also noted in t. Russell, n. Samuel Moore. 1915 USGS Russell Quad. / **Moores Corners-Burnhams Corners Road**: r., t. Potsdam.

Moose Head: Also **Moosehead**: n. usually for the shape: **Moose Head Mountain**: see **Moosehead Mountain**. / **Moose Head Mountain Road**: r., t. Fine, n. mountain. / **Moosehead Mountain**: in Jamestown area, t.

Colton, alt. 2,075 ft., n. shape. 1853 HMC; 1858 Rogerson; 1860 Merrit; 1865 **Moose Head Mt.** Beers, p. 86; 1880 Ely; 1883 Ely-Wallace; 1896 New; 1903 **Moose Head Mt.** J. N. Mathews, **New York**, Buffalo; 1908 Adm; 1912 Stoddard; 1920 USGS Childwold Quad. / **Moosehead Pond**: t. Clifton, alt. 1,417 ft. n. shape. 1858 Rogerson; 1883 Ely-Wallace; 1896 New; 1898 EGB, p. 28; 1902 Blankman; 1908 Adm; 1912 Stoddard; 1919 USGS Cranberry Lake Quad. / **Moosehead Pond Outlet**: stream, trib. South Branch Grass(e) River, t. Clare. 1921 Stark Quad. / **Moosehead Rapids**: in Racquette River, t. Colton. 1920 USGS Childwold Quad. / **Moosehead Still Water**: see **Stillwater**, t. Piercefield.

Moran Road: r., t. Lisbon, n. John Moran family.

Moreland Road: r., t. Oswegatchie, n. William Moreland, Irishman, and family. The son, Forrest K. Moreland, attorney, prepared important bills for national legislators, and admitted to the bar in 1878. His clients "ranged from Mexico to Sweden," and apparently places in between.

Morey: surname used as a specific: **Morey Hall**: on SUC, Potsdam campus, faculty offices and classrooms, n. Amelia Morey, teacher at the Normal School.

Morgan: a popular surname, with places being n. different families: **Morgan Rapids**: in Racquette River, t. Colton, n. Morgan family. 1964 USGS Rainbow Falls Quad. / **Morgan Road**: r., t. Colton; r., t. Lawrence; r., t. Parishville, n. Cornelius Morgan, one of the first settlers. Formerly **Gynn Road**; r., t. Potsdam. / **Morgan School**: no. 21, common school, t. Stockholm. / **Morgan Street**: s., v. Norwood. / **Morgan's Mill**: t. Clare, built about 1860; became **Gleason's Mill**. *Quarterly*, 14 (1969), no. 1, p. 6.

Morley: h., t. Canton, n. a surname in the family of W. H. Harison, first permanent settler and proprietor; n. 1835. Formerly, **Long Rapids**. Stillman Foote was the first settler and in the spring of 1810 built a sawmill on the site; p. o. est. from **Long Rapids** May 20, 1839, Lorenzo Fenton, pm, closed Aug. 3, 1962, reopened as rural station Aug 4, 1962, closed June 30, 1968, reopened as rural branch 1973, closed 1977. Ety., OE **mor** "moor" + **leah** "meadow." 1964 Morley Quad. Derived names are **Morley Cemetery**. / **Morley-Lisbon Road**: r., t. Lisbon. / **Morley-Potsdam**

Road: r., t. Canton, Potsdam. / **Morley Ridge**: t. Lisbon. 1964 USGS Morley Quad. / **Morley Ridge School**: t. Lisbon. / **Morley School**: no. 16, common school, built 1857, t. Canton. / **Morley-Woodbridge Road**: r., t. Canton.

Morningside Drive: s., v. Potsdam, n. commendatory and promotional.

Morrow Road: r., t. Hermon, n. Morrow family.

Morrill: n. family: **Morrill Drive**: s., v. Massena. / **Morrill Road**: r., t. Pierrepont.

Morris: n. Gouverneur Morris. See **Morristown**. **Morris Mills**: t. Gouverneur. See **Natural Dam**. / **Morris Street**: s., v. Morristown; s., h. Norfolk, not n. Gouverneur Morris; s., c. Ogdensburg.

Morrison Road: r., t. Gouverneur, n. Morrison family.

Morristown: northern border on St. Lawrence River, one of the ten original t., n. **The Hague**. Surveyed in 1799 by Jacob Brown and given the name of **Morrisville**, but remained **Hague** on maps and in legal documents for many years. When Gouveneur Morris died on Nov. 6, 1816, a proposal was made to change the name formally and legally to **Morristown**, which was granted on Mar. 11, 1821. On Mar. 27, 1821, the t. was formed from t. Oswegatchie. Durant, 370-371. Hough, 359. 1963 USGS Edwardsville Quad. / **Morristown**: v. in t. **Morristown**, p. o. est. July 18, 1816, David Ford, pm (Hough, 575), p. o. existing, ZIP 13664. Inc. Apr. 3, 1884. 1963 USGS Morristown Quad. / **Morristown and Hammond Plank-Road**: see **Plank Roads**. / **Morristown Bay**: in St. Lawrence River, t. Morristown. The bay is within the v. 1963 USGS Morristown Quad. / **Morristown Center**: crossroads, once a thriving community, t. Morristown. 1963 USGS Edwardsville Quad. Bogardus, 135-137. / **Morristown Central School**: centralized 1945, v. Morristown. / **Morristown Park**: t. Morristown, p. o. est. June 11, 1883, Samuel H. Wadsworth, pm, closed Oct. 20, 1885. / **Morristown Point**: on St. Lawrence River, t. Morristown. 1963 USGS Morristown Quad. / **Morristown School**: no. 1, common school, in v., t. Morristown. Bogardus, 60. / **Morristown Union Free School**: est. 1876.

Mortlake: a survey township, t. Piercefield, n. Mortlake, Surrey, England; ety., OE **mort** "young salmon" + OE **lacu** "stream," but personal n. **Morta** + **lacu**, "Morta's Brook," is possible; it can also be interpreted as **mort**, "dead" + **lake**, Dead Lake, an early name for Tupper Lake. Durant, p. 2.

Morton Street: s., v. Norwood, n. Morton family.

Mosher Road: r., t. Hopkinton, n. Mosher family.

Moses-Saunders Power Dam: in St. Lawrence River, its main power structure, 3,230 ft. long. The International Boundary between Canada and the United States runs through the center of it; n. Robert Moses, developer and politician, and Robert Sanders (see **Sanders Dam**).

Moss Ridge: t. DeKalb. 1956 USGS Bigelow Quad.

Mott Creek: t. Edwards, trib. Bonner Lake. Poss. n. Theodore C. Mott, early resident. 1956 USGS Edwards Quad. / **Mott Road**: r., t. Macomb, in Pleasant Lake area. / **Mott School**: t. Russell, on Sweet Road, no. 12, common school, also n. Theodore C. Mott. 1915 Russell Quad. Some references mistakenly record **Knott School**.

Mound Hill Cemetery: h. Nicholville, t. Lawrence.

Mount Alone: t. Heuvelton, alt. 450 ft., only hill in area not in the Adirondack chain. The romantic story is that a mean man married a woman and left her after two weeks; thereafter, she lived on the mountain – alone. *Quarterly*, 20 (1975), no. 3, p. 19. See **Mount Lona**. Derived names include **Mount Alone Cemetery**: t. Oswegatchie. / **Mount Alone Road**: r., t. DePeyster, Oswegatchie.

Mount Arab: h., t. Piercefield, p. o. est. from **Pleasant Lake** Feb. 21, 1922, William A. Andrews, pm, closed May 15, 1947. 1954 USGS Tupper Lake Quad. Also **Arab Mountain**. / **Mount Arab Lake**: t. Piercefield, alt. 1,659. All maps and sources list **Pleasant Lake**: 1858 Rogerson; 1873 Hamilton Child; 1880 Ely; 1883 Ely-Wallace; 1896 New; 1902 Blankman; 1908 Adm; 1912 Stoddard. 1954 USGS Tupper Lake Quad indicates change to present name. See **Arab Mountain**. / **Mount Arab Road**: t. Piercefield.

Mount Lona: same as **Mount Alone**. 1963 USGS Heuvelton Quad. / **Mount Lona Cemetery**: t. Oswegatchie. 1963 USGS Heuvelton Quad.

Mount Matumbla: t. Piercefield, alt. 2,700, origin n. unknown. 1860 **Blue Mt** Merrit; 1880 **Blue Mt.** Ely; 1883 **Matumbla Mt.** Ely-Wallace; 1896 **Blue Mt.**, but also **Mt. Matumbla** New; 1902 Blankman; 1912 **Matumbla Mtn** Stoddard; 1920 USGS Childwold Quad.

Mount Pisgah: t. Colton. n. biblical, the place from which Moses saw the Promised Land. 1896 New; 1902 Blankman; not recorded on USGS maps.

Mountain Brook: flows from Mount Matumbla, trib. Racquette River, t. Piercefield. 1880 Ely; 1883 Ely-Wallace; 1896 New; 1908 Adm; 1912 Stoddard; 1920 USGS Childwold Quad.

Mountain Camp: t. Piercefield, n. for camp for veterans, known also as **Veterans Mountain Camp**. 1954 USGS Tupper Lake Quad. Now privately owned.

Moyer School: no. 23, common school, t. Canton, n. Moyer family.

Mud: a common n. for bodies of water, referring to murky condition of the water or the type of soil at the bottom. Only the time of the n. may the place have been muddy, while all the rest of the water was clear: **Mud Brook**: see **Deerskin Creek**. / **Mud Brook**: t. Colton. / **Mud Creek**: see **Deerskin Creek**. / **Mud Creek**: see **Blue Mountain Stream**. / **Mud Creek**: t. Fine, trib. Aldrich Pond. 1916 USGS Oswegatchie Quad. / **Mud Lake**: t. Clifton, and Long Lake, Hamilton Co., alt. 1,735. 1858 Rogerson; 1860 Street, p. 74; 1880 Ely; 1883 Ely-Wallace; 1896 New; 1898 EGB, p. 26; 1902 Blankman; 1903 J. N. Mathews, **New York**, Buffalo; 1908 Adm; 1919 USGS Cranberry Lake Quad. "It's a dreary, skeery, dark hole of a place, that Mud Lake." Harvey Moody, **Street, Woods & Waters**, 1860, p. 76. / **Mud Lake**: t. DePeyster, n. because not fit to swim in and is in a swampy area. *Quarterly*, 7 (1962), no. 3, p. 10. 1873 Hamilton Child; 1956 USGS Richville Quad; 1963 USGS Heuvelton Quad. / **Mud Lake**: t. Edwards. / **Mud Lake**: t. Macomb, alt. 411. 1961 USGS Natural Dam Quad. / **Mud Lake Road**: r., t. DePeyster, Macomb. / **Mud Lake School**: no. 2, common school, t. DePeyster. / **Mud Pond**: t. Clare. 1915 Russell Quad. / **Mud Pond**: t. Fine, alt. 1,031 ft. *Quarterly*, 5 (1960), no. 1, npn. 1915 USGS Russell Quad. / **Mud Pond**: t. Fine. 1916 USGS Oswegatchie Quad. / **Mud Pond**: t. Fowler. 1956 USGS Gouverneur Quad. / **Mud**

Pond: t. Colton. 1883 Ely-Wallace. / **Mud Pond**: t. Colton. 1921 USGS Stark Quad. / **Mud Pond**: t. Colton. 1858 Rogerson; 1908 Adm; 1908 USGS Potsdam Quad. / **Mud Pond**: t. Hopkinton. 1896 New; 1902 Blankman; 1908 Adm; 1919 USGS Nicholville Quad; 1964 USGS Sylvan Falls Quad. / **Mud Pond**: t. Piercefield, near Jocks Pond. 1880 Ely; 1883 Ely-Wallace; 1896 New. / **Mud Pond**: t. Pitcairn. 1951 USGS Harrisville Quad. / **Mud Pond Outlet**: t. Hopkinton, trib. West Branch St. Regis River. 1919 USGS Nicholville Quad; 1964 USGS Sylvan Falls Quad. / **Mud Pond Road**: r., t. Piercefield. / **Mud Street**: see **Luke Brown Road**.

Mulholland School: no. 5, common school, t. Louisville, n. Mulholland family.

Mullen Road: r., t. Lisbon, n. Mullen family.

Mullins Marsh/Creek: t. Fine, near Jock Works, a lumber camp, trib. Middle Branch Oswegatchie River. 1916 USGS Oswegatchie Quad. Origin of n. unknown.

Mulleta: Oswego line of Northern Railroad. *Quarterly*, 7 (1962), no. 4, p. 7.

Mummery Road: r., t. Oswegatchie, n. Mummery family. Also **McIntyre Road.**

Munson: a surname; several places n. different families.: **Munson Road**: r., t. Brasher; r., t. Stockholm. / **Munson School**: no. 10. common school, t. Stockholm. / **Munson Street**: s., v. Potsdam, n. Myron C. Munson.

Murdock Street: s., v. Gouverneur, n. Murdock family.

Murphy: very popular surname and family name: **Murphy Flat**: t. Parishville, n. Dan Murphy, first settler. Early horse races were held on the flat. / **Murphy Island**: in St. Lawrence River, t. Waddington, n. Murphy family. 1942 USGS Murphy Island Quad. Also, **Allison Island**. / **Murphy Point**: on St. Lawrence River, t. Waddington, n. Murphy family. 1942 USGS Murphy Island Quad. / **Murphy Road**: r., t. Brasher; r., t. Lisbon; r., t. Stockholm, Norfolk. / **Murphy School**: no. 33, common school, t. Lisbon; no. 5, common school, t. Madrid.

Murray: family n.: **Murray Hill**: t. Stockholm. / **Murray Hill School**: no. 24, common school, t. Stockholm.

Muskrat Pond: t. Clifton, alt. 1,499 ft., n. aquatic rodent, **Ondatra zibethica**. 1896 New; 1898 EGB, p. 28; 1902 Blankman; 1908 Adm; 1912 Stoddard; 1919 USGS Cranberry Lake Quad.

Myers Swamp: t. Fowler. 1956 USGS Gouverneur Quad.

N

Narrow Alley: s., c. Ogdensburg.

Narrows, The: at **Edwardsville**; p. o est., but records lost. *Quarterly*, 3 (1958), no. 3, back p. The narrowest place on Black Lake, with first a ferry and then a bridge. Treacherous swirls of water have caused several drownings here. See **Edwardsville** for additional information.

Nation Road: r., t. Louisville, Norfolk, n. **Lost Nation**.

Natural Dam: t., Gouverneur, n. land feature, a solid, natural rock formation crossing the Oswegatchie River, giving a fall of 17 feet. The site was the country home of Gouverneur Morris, built in 1806 into the hillside, with 1/2 of the walls buried and the rear portion facing north. The building had no windows. The site was formerly called **Morris Mills**, for the sawmill and grist mill that Gouverneur Morris had built. *Quarterly*, 7 (1962), no. 4, p. 5. Historical marker now on the home. / **Natural Dam**: h., t. Gouverneur, p. o. est. Mar. 29, 1890, Edward J. Loveless, first pm, closed Sept. 30, 1949. 1961 USGS Natural Dam Quad. See **Natural Dam**, feature. / **Natural Dam Road**: listed on some maps as r., t. Gourverneur, now, **Smith Road**. / **Natural Dam School**: no. 15, common school, t. Gouverneur.

Needham: n. family: **Needham Road**: r., t. Stockholm. / **Needham School**: no. 20, common school, t. Stockholm.

Nelmanor Drive: s., v. Waddington. Origin n. undeter- mined.

Nelson: n. family: **Nelson Corners**: t. Rossie. 1961 USGS Muskellunge Lake Quad. / **Nelson Road**: r., t. Lisbon. / **Nelson School**: no. 13, common school, t. Rossie.

Nettle Creek: trib. Grass(e) River, t. Potsdam, n. plant. 1964 USGS Morley Quad.

Nevaldine Hall: on SUNY Canton College of Technology campus, n. Pete Nevaldine, Professor of Engineering Technology, 1937-1973.

Nevin: surname used as a specific: **Nevin House, The**: t. Brasher, in 1828, John Nevin and his son Benjamin built a house in the h. Helena for Joseph Pitcairn. Because his daughter soon died, Pitcairn never lived in it; the house, still standing, retains the n. / **Nevin Memorial Church Cemetery**: t. Massena. 1963 USGS Sparrowhawk Point Quad. / **Nevins Point**: on St. Lawrence River, t. Oswegatchie, n. Benjamin Nevin (1797-1866), born in Ireland, came to New York City and then to Helena, t. Brasher, as land-agent for Daniel McCormick, served as pm of Brasher, moved to Oswegatchie and bought a farm which he named Rockingham Place. Durant, 202-3. 1963 USGS Ogden East Quad. / **Nevins School**: no. 2, common school, t. Massena, n. Nevins family. / **Nevin Street**: s., c. Ogdensburg, n. Benjamin Nevin.

New: n. of several meanings, but usually prefixed to a specific as a time-n. for something just built, first seen, or recently happened: **New Bridge**: t. Clare, p. o. est. Aug 10, 1906, Joseph E. Bickens, pm, closed Dec. 31, 1919. 1912 Stoddard. See **Newbridge**. / **New Cairo**: p. o., Apr. 1, 1804. Became **Canton**, July 1, 1807. *Quarterly*, 11 (1966), no. 3, p. 16. / **New Cemetery**: t. Madrid. / **New Connecticut Road**: r., t. Rossie. / **New Germany**: See **Matildaville.** *Quarterly*, 5 (1960), no. 2, p. 9. / **New Pine Grove Cemetery**: v. Massena, on Cook Street, which received the remains of the bodies from Pine Grove Cemetery on Barnhart Island when the Seaway Project was finished. / **New Road**: r. t. Hammond. / **New Street**: s., v. Edwards; s., v. Norwood. / **New York Avenue**: s., c. Ogdensburg. / **New York Central and Hudson Valley**: Railroad with a terminal in Massena. / **New York State Fish Hatchery**: on St. Lawrence River, t. Lisbon. 1963 USGS Ogdensburg Quad. Now abandoned.

Newbridge: h., t. Clare, ghost town. Clarke, 26. 1921 Stark Quad. See **New Bridge**, variant.

Newcomb Road: r., t. DePeyster, n. Newcomb family.

Newell Hall: on Clarkson University campus, n. William Allan Newell, industrialist and public servant from Ogdensburg, a trustee for 41 years.

Newton: surname used as a specific: **Newton Falls**: h. in t. Clifton, n. James L. Newton, who built a sawmill on the site in 1894. Home now of the Newton Falls Paper Company, currently owned by the Macmillan Book Company; p. o. est. as **Newtonfalls**, Mar. 13, 1896, John R. Coburn, first, pm, changed to **Newton Falls** July 1930, Wilfred D. Cheney, pm, p. o. existing, ZIP 13666. 1902 Blankman; 1908 Adm; 1912 Stoddard; 1919 USGS Cranberry Lake Quad. / **Newton Falls School**: no. 1, common school, t. Clifton. / **Newton Road**: r., t. Parishville, n. Daniel Newton family.

Newtonfalls: see **Newton Falls**.

Nichols: surname used as a specific: **Nichols Cemetery**: t. Louisville, n. Nichols family. / **Nichols Hill Island**: in St. Lawrence River, t. Louisville, Harold Nichols. 1964 USGS Louisville Quad. / **Nichols Road**: r., t. Gouverneur, probably n. G. W. Nichols who owned two places on the present road. Beers, 31. He was a farmer who settled in Gouverneur in 1811. Durant, 513; r., t. Stockholm, n. Nichols family.

Nicholville: h. in southern part of t. Lawrence, n. E. S. Nichols, "the executor of the estate of William Lawrence." Sawmill built in 1817 on east branch of St. Regis River. p. o., est. Jan. 9, 1831, Clemens C. Palmer, pm, existing, ZIP 12965. Hough, 575, claims that p. o. est. Jan. 7, 1831. Formerly, **Sodom** (1817). Durant, 424. 1964 USGS Nicholville Quad. / **Nicholville Hill**: t. Parishville. / **Nicholville-Lavery's Corners Road**: begins in h. Nichol- ville. / **Nicholville River**: *Quarterly*, 20 (1975), n. 1, p. 11; not official, usually River at Nicholville. / **Nicholville School**: no. 11, common school, t. Lawrence. / **Nicholville Turnpike**: in v. Potsdam, now **Maple Street**.

Nickerson: surname used as a specific: **Nickerson Road**: r., t. Canton, probably n. Anson Nickerson, shown as A. Nickerson in Beers Atlas as living at intersection of present Nickerson Road and Route 1 (county road) D. Nickerson also shown as living at the other end of the road, Beers, p. 11. / **Nickerson's Bend**: near Canton, n. Nickerson family. *Quarterly*, 13 (1968), no. 3, p. 8. / **Nickerson Street**: s., v. Canton.

Nicks Pond: t. Fine. 1883 Ely-Wallace; 1896 New; 1902 Blankman; 1908 **Nick's Pond** Adm; 1912 **Nick's Pond** Stoddard; 1919 USGS Cranberry lake Quad.

Nightengale Avenue: s., v. Massena, n. William H. Nightengale, tavern owner, arrived with family in 1821 from

Chester, VT. Also, **Nightingale.** / **Nightengale School:** v., Massena, n. avenue. 1964 USGS Massena Quad.

Nihanawate: see **Hannawa Falls.**

Niionenhiasekowane: see **Barnhart Island.**

Nikahionhakowa: see **Black River.**

Nikentsiake: see **Grass River.**

Niourne Bay: in St. Lawrence River, origin n. unknown. Noted in **Documentary History of New York,** Vol. IV, map 1771.

Noble: surname used as a feature: **Noble Drive:** see **Ike Noble Drive.** / **Noble Athletic Field:** on St. Lawrence University campus. See **Ike Noble Drive.** / **Noble Hospital:** n. Edward John Noble, who made a fortune manufacturing a candy called Life Savers, supposed to make the breath smell better. The hospitals were located in Canton, Gouverneur, and Alexandria Bay.

Noblett Road: r., t. Stockholm, n. Noblett family.

Nolan Road: r., t. Russell, n. Nolan family.

Noreen Drive: r., t. Norwood, n. Noreen Hopsicker, wife of Joseph Hopsicker, real estate developer.

Norfolk: northwestern interior of county, t. formed Apr. 9, 1823, by dividing t. Lousiville in half; in 1834 and 1844 portions of Stockholm were added. Origin of n. uncertain, probably transfer from Norfolk, England, but some claim that its a local blend and pronunciation of **North Fork.** Locally pronounced, **Norfork.** Amerindian name: **Kanataseke,** "new village." See "Norfolk History," *Quarterly*, 22 (1977), no. 4, p. 15; Durant, 299. / **Norfolk:** h. in t. **Norfolk**; p. o. est. May 22, 1823, Phineas Atwater, first pm, existing, ZIP 13667. 1964 USGS Norfolk Quad. / **Norfolk-Chamberlain Corners Road:** r., t. Madrid. / **Norfolk, Raymondville and Massena Plank-Road:** see **Plank Roads.** / **Norfolk School:** no. 1, common school, t. Norfolk. Also **Norfolk Village School.**

North: a direction-n. often used in contrast with **South,** but may exist independently, as in **North Corners** without a **South Corners;** sometimes a surname: **North Branch Grass(e) River:** t. Clare and t. Russell, trib. Grass(e) River. 1915 USGS Russell Quad. / **North**

Branch Mountain Brook: trib. Mountain Brook, t. Piercefield. 1896 New; 1920 **North Branch** [Mountain Brook] USGS Childwold Quad. / **North Brother Pond:** t. Clifton. See **Brothers Ponds.** / **North Canton:** t. Canton, p. o. est. Jan. 27, 1834, Thomas D. Olin, pm, closed July 16, 1841. / **North Corners:** crossroads, t. Lisbon. 1963 USGS Lisbon Quad. / **North Country:** coined or named by Irving Addison Bacheller (1859-1950), novelist, born in Pierrepont. Bacheller claimed that it was the territory between the Black River and the St. Lawrence River. It now roughly coincides with the area north of an imaginary line between Albany and Syracuse. *Quarterly*, 15 (1970), no. 1, p. 16. / **North Gouverneur:** t. Gouverneur, p. o. est. Apr. 22, 1862, Albert M. Spink, pm, closed Oct. 23, 1862. 1956 USGS Richville Quad. / **North Gouverneur Cemetery:** t. Gouverneur, east of Peabody Road. 1956 USGS Richville Quad. / **North Hammond Corners:** t. of **Hammond;** p. o. est. as **North Hammond** Feb. 6, 1862, Asa T. Barber, first pm, closed Oct. 1, 1900. 1964 USGS Hammond Quad. / **North Hammond School:** no. 10, common school, t. Hammond. / **North Lawrence:** h. in t. Lawrence, p. o. est. Dec. 12, 1850, John H. Conant, pm (Hough, 575), p. o. existing, ZIP 12967. See **Lawrence.** Durant, 420. 1964 USGS North Lawrence Quad. / **North Lawrence-Moira Road:** r., t. Lawrence, Brasher. / **North Lawrence School:** no. 4, common school, t. Lawrence. / **North Lawrence Toomey Bridge Road:** r., t. Brasher. / **North Pond:** see **Hitchins Pond.** / **North Pond:** t. Colton. / **North Potsdam:** t. Potsdam, p. o. est. Dec. 30, 1850, Rollin Ashley, pm (Hough, 575), closed Oct. 30, 1867. Other names: **Racquetteville, Potsdam Depot** (for the railroad station). Now, **Norwood,** which see. / **North Racket Street:** s., v. Massena. / **North Raquette Road:** r., t. Norfolk, Louisville: r., t. Massena. / **North Road: r., t. Brasher; r., t. Lisbon.** / **North Road:** see **Parishville Turnpike.** / **North Rosseel Street:** s., c. Ogdensburg;see **Rosseel Street,** / **North Russell:** h., t. Russell; settled 1805; p. o. est. Feb. 17, 1848, Linus A. Clark, first pm, closed Jan. 31, 1911 (New York Postal History; Hough, 575; Clarke, 19; Durant, 430). 1964 USGS Pierrepont Quad. Originally, **DeWitt** as a survey township n. Simeon De Witt. Clarke, 18. / **North Russell Cemetery:** on Route 62, h. North Russell. 1964 USGS Canton Quad. / **North Russell School:** no. 6, common school, t. Russell. / **North State**

Street: s., v. Rensselaer Falls, n. direction. / **North Stockholm**: h., t. Stockholm, p. o. est. Mar. 8, 1851, Stephen House, pm (Hough, 575), closed Aug. 31, 1958. 1964 USGS Norfolk Quad. / **North Stockholm School**: no. 13, common school, t. Stockholm. / **North Street**: s., v. Brasher Falls; r., t. Madrid and s., h. Madrid; r., t. Piercefield; s., v. Potsdam, now Elm Street. / **North Water Street**: s., c. Ogdensburg. / **North Woods**: t. Canton. See **North Woods Road**. / **North Woods Road**: r., t. Canton, goes from Pyrites to Woods Bridge Road. / **North Woods Road**; r., t. Fowler; r., t. Russell, ran north to Pyrites from Woods Bridge Road; now dead end.

Northern Railroad: first railroad, 1850, through St. Lawrence County.

Northrup Corners: t. Oswegatchie, n. Lewis Northrup, who owned a hotel there. He was a farmer, lumberman, boater, and rafter. *Quarterly*, 16 (1971), no. 4, p. 6. 1963 USGS Ogden East Quad. Also **Northrup's Corners**. / **Northrup Corners Cemetery**: now abandoned cemetery, t. Oswegatchie. 1963 USGS Ogdensburg East Quad. / **Northrup School**: t. Oswegatchie, Dist. 12. n. Lewis Northrup. / **Northrup School**: no. 14, common school, t. Pierrepont, n. Northrup family.

Northumberland Street: s., v. Morristown, n. county in northeast England ("land north of the River Humber"), from which the residents on the street came.

Northmoor Park: s., h. Raymondville, n. promotional.

Northview Drive: s., v. Massena, n. directional and promotional.

Northwest Bay Road: see **Hopkinton Road**.

Norton Cemetery: on Rte. 68 next to Grass(e) River, t. Canton, n. Norton families. 1964 USGS Canton Quad.

Norway: n. family, but sometimes for the nation: **Norway Island**: see **Pine Island**. / **Norway Pond**: see **Silver Lake**. / **Norway Road**: r., t. Lisbon, n. James Norway family. / **Norway School**: no. 17, common school, t. Lisbon, n. James Norway family.

Norwood: v. north of Potsdam, in t. Potsdam; founded by Benjamin G. Baldwin; n. title of book written by Henry Ward Beecher, a famous preacher and brother of Harriet Beecher Stowe, author of **Uncle Tom's Cabin**. The n. was suggested by Reverend Chase, pastor of the local Methodist Church because it was a simple name, one that did not need dotted i's or crossed t's. The name was selected by a vote taken on Apr. 15, 1875; Norwood was first, with Potsdam Junction, Onowa, Oakley, and Duck Pond in descending order of number of votes. Petitioned to Washington May 11, 1875, to change the name to Norwood. On Sept. 13, 1943, the St. Lawrence County Clerk's office advised the village board that their records showed the village as Potsdam Junction. The matter was soon straightened out. *Quarterly*, 20 (1975), no. 1, p. 8; p. o. est. Nov. 24, 1875, William T. Leonard, first pm, existing, ZIP 13668. Formerly, **Racquetteville** (1856), for the river that flows through it; also formerly, **North Potsdam, Potsdam Junction** (1872), **Potsdam Station.** Renamed **Norwood** (1875). 1964 USGS Norfolk Quad. / **Norwood-Knapps Station Road**: r., t. Stockholm. / **Norwood Union School**: no. 1, common school, t. Potsdam.

Notre Dame Cemetery: t. Oswegatchie. 1964 USGS Ogdensburg East Quad.

Noyes Road: r., t. Pierrepont, n. W. H. Noyes family.

Number Eight School: no. 8, common school, t. Potsdam.

Number 9 Road: r., t. Clifton, in Higley Flow area.

Number 10 Road: r., t. Colton, in Higley Flow area.

Number 19 Mountain: t. Colton, alt. 2,275 (?). 1920 USGS Childwold Quad. Located in section 19, Kildare Survey Township, Buck Pond Preserve. See **Thirty-five Pond**.

Nunns: settlement, t. Fine, p. o. est. Sept. 7, 1910, George M. Preston, pm, closed Aug 31, 1911.

Nyando: h., t. Massena, railroad point between New York and Ottawa, Canada, n. blend of **New York** and **Ottawa**. Later, **Rooseveltown**; p. o. est. Mar. 28, 1901, Martin R. Young, first pm, changed to **Rooseveltown** Nov. 1, 1933.

O

Oak: a popular n. from the tree of the genus *Quercus*, found plentifully in temperate climates in the United States. The n. may derive from a lone sentinel tree or from a grove: / **Oak Island**: in Chippewa Bay. St. Lawrence River, t. Hammond.

Quarterly, 16 (1971), no. 3, p. 11. 1865 Beers, p. 37; 1958 USGS Chippewa Quad. / **Oak Point**: on Black Lake, t. DePeyster. 1963 USGS Edwardsville Quad. / **Oak Point**: h., on St. Lawrence River, t. Hammond, p. o. est. Mar. 31, 1841, James H. Consall, pm (Hough, 575), closed Jan. 14, 1867, reopened Mar. 28, 1892, William C. Brooks, pm, changed to **Oakpoint** Dec. 1895, closed Sept. 29, 1900, opened as rural branch July 16, 1915, closed Sept. 15, 1919. *Quarterly*, 23 (1978), no. 3, p. 10; 7 (1962), no. 7, p. 4. "Small village and landing at the point where the original line of Hammond and Hague (now Morristown) touched the river" (Hough, 315). n. for the numerous oak trees. George Elliot was the first settler. 1858 Beers, p. 37; 1963 USGS Morristown Quad. / **Oak Point Cemetery**: t. Hammond. / **Oak Point Road**: r., t. Hammond, from v. Hammond to Oak Point; r., t. and v. Morristown, from v. to Oak Point. / **Oak Point School**: no. 4, common school, t. Hammond. / **Oak Street**: s., c. Ogdensburg; s., v. Waddington.

Oakham: a survey township, now t. Colton. / **Oakham Tract Survey**: The surveyor wrote, "The Oakham Tract is neither fit for man nor beast and agriculture or other enterprises should not be undertaken." Kerr notes, "The Tract lies easterly of Cranberry Lake in the town of Colton." *Quarterly*, 9 (1964), no. 2, p. 12. Origin of n. unknown, but is English, n. occurring in Rutland and Derbyshire; ety., personal n. in OE, **Oc(c)a**'s + **ham** "home."

Oakvale: t. Hammond; railroad stop on RW&O, near South Hammond; n. **oak** + **vale**, "oak valley," romantic and commendatory.

Ober Street: s., v. Massena, n. Ober family.

O'Brien Road: r., t. Norfolk; r. t. Pierrepont; r., t. Potsdam. All n. O'Brien family.

Office Road: s., h. Balmat, way to the offices of the mines.

Ogden: Father Charles Lalement, a Jesuit from France, is said to have landed here in the spring of 1626 and named the place **La Galette** ("cake" or "muffin") and the River **La Presentation** (now Oswegatchie River). Later **La Galette** was changed to **Fort La Presentation** (see accounts in Hough and Durant). The Iroquois called the place **Soegasti**, "black water," the term later becoming **Oswegatchie**.

The French Jesuit priest and missionary, Joseph Antoine Poncet, came in 1653 to the French and Amerindian settlement at the present site of Ogdensburg. In 1749, a missionary station and fort were established at the mouth of the river **La Presentation**, by Francois Picquet (1708-1781), a "Sulpician." Later, historians called the place **Picquet's Folly**. In 1760, the English assumed control of the area, which at the end of the Revolutionary War became a part of the United States. The settlement was inc. as v. Apr. 5, 1817, after the p. o. was est. as **Ogdensburg**, Mar. 24, 1807 (Hough, 575, claims erroneously, Apr. 1, 1807), Lewis Hasbrouck, pm, changed to **Ogdensburgh** 1827, changed to **Ogdensburg** Mar. 25, 1891, Alonzo A. Smith, pm, p. o. existing, ZIP 13669; chartered as a c. Apr. 27 1868, as **Ogdensburg**, amended May 2, 1873, as a city. It was n. Samuel Ogden, son of David Ogden. Samuel Ogden was in the iron business in New Jersey and served as a colonel in the Revolutionary War but was never in battle. He married a sister of Gouverneur Morris. Formerly, **Ogdenburg Village**, but an **h** was added and then dropped, as was **Village**. The **s** was inserted at the suggestion of Judge Nathan Ford, as noted in a letter from Joseph Rosseel to David Parish, Jan. 16, 1809. *Quarterly*, 17 (1972), no. 1, p. 4. The v. was the first county seat of St. Lawrence County. *Quarterly*, 13 (1968), no. 2, p. 3. Nickname, **Maple City.** 1963 USGS Ogden East Quad. A cluster of n. derive from **Ogden**: **Ogden Island**: in St. Lawrence River, t. Waddington, n. Samuel Ogden, original proprietor. French n.: **Isle au Rapide Plat**, "island at flat rapid." Indian n.: **Tiehonwinatha**, "where the canoe is towed with a rope." Also **Ogden's Island.** Tedford, 1. 1964 **USGS Waddington Quad.** / **Ogden Street**: s., c. Ogdensburg; s., v. Waddington. / **Ogdensburg and Lake Champlain Railroad**: serviced Massena. Dumas 61. / **Ogdensburg Cemetery**: outside c. Ogdensburg, on Oswegatchie River, t. Oswegatchie. 1963 Ogdensburg East Quad. / **Ogdensburg International Airport**: t. Oswegatchie. 1963 Ogdensburg East Quad. / **Ogdensburg-Prescott Bridge**: across the St. Lawrence near Ogdensburg, connecting the United States and Canada. / **Ogdensburg to Heuvelton Plank Road**: see **Plank Roads.**

O'Horo Road: t. Canton, between Old Dekalb-Canton Road and Route 11; n. family.

Ojibway: variant spelling of **Chippewa.**

Old: age-n., widely used to contrast with **New**, but may occur without the presence of **New**, as in **Old Forge Road**, but not **New Forge Road.** Sometimes age is not involved, since Old Forge Road may be a new road, with the specific as **Old Forge: Old Bear Mountain**: t. Clifton, behind Cranberry Lake. Not identified, but may be **Bear Mountain**, Cranberry Lake area. 1858 Rogerson. Listed as **Old Rear Mountain [misprint]**. / **Old Canton Road**: r., t. DeKalb. / **Old Cemetery**: t. Ogdensburg. / **Old DeKalb**: n. first settlement of DeKalb, distinct from **DeKalb Junction.** / **Old DeKalb-Canton Road**: r., t. Canton. / **Old DeKalb Cemetery**: t. DeKalb. / **Old Forest House Road**: r., t. Canton, has been called **Cunningham Road**, n. Isadore Cunningham. / **Old Forge Dam**: on Oswegatchie R. between Cook's Corners and Cranberry Lake. / **Old Forge Road**: r., t. Stockholm. / **Old Forge School**: no. 15, common school, t. Stockholm. / **Old Hammond Cemetery**: t. Hammond. / **Old Lake George Road**: *Quarterly*, 13 (1968), no. 1, p. 6. See **Lake George Road** / **Old Log School House**: t. Waddington. No longer exists. / **Old Madrid Cemetery**: t. Madrid. / **Old Main**: on Clarkson University campus, building of Potsdam red sandstone from the Clarkson quarries, comprised the whole college down through World War II, now housing the Mechanical Engineering Department. / **Old Mans Island**: in St. Lawrence River, t. Morristown. In 1848, 4-acre island deeded for $50.00 to Col. Elisha Buell of Brockville, Ont., Canada, "late in possession of W. B. H. Johnson and previously occupied by Geo. Grayham and known as Ogden Island, by William E. Parsons and Azariah Walton." (No n. 1855. Beers, 1896, shows J. Bann). 1925 Soil Survey shows "Old Mans Island" upriver between Morristown v. and Holmes Point opposite Eager Bay. 1963 USGS Morristown Quad. Also **Old Man's Island.** / **Old Market Road**: r., t. Norfolk, Stockholm. / **Old Military Road**: see **Hopkinton Road.** Two other roads are called Old Military Roads, both terminating in Russell. / **Old Military Turnpike**: See **St. Lawrence Turnpike.** *Quarterly*, 6 (1961), no. 1, p. 8. / **Old Mill Road**: r., t. Morristown, n. Leonards Mill. / **Old Mormon Hole**: t. Pierrepont, in brook on Howardville Hill where Mormons were baptized. *Quarterly*, 2 (1957), no. 4, npn. / **Old Northerner Road**: r., t. DeKalb, n. Old Northerner Inn, hostelry between Richville and Old DeKalb. now razed. / **Old Notre Dame Cemetery**: t. Oswegatchie.

1963 Ogdensburg East Quad. / **Old Potsdam-Parishville Road**: r., t. Potsdam, Parishville. / **Old Richardson Cemetery**: t. Brasher. / **Old River Road**: r., t. Massena. / **Old Road**: r., t. Hopkinton. / **Old St. Marys Cemetery**: t. Canton. / **Old St. Marys Cemetery**: t. Potsdam. 1943 USGS Potsdam Quad. / **Old Route 58**: r., t. Edwards. / **Old Side Cemetery**: t. Hermon. / **Old Slab Bridge**: see **Slab City.** / **Old State Hospital Cemetery**: t. Lisbon. 1963 Ogdensburg East Quad. /**Old State Road**: r., t. Canton, off Route 11; r., t. Gouverneur, also called **Governeur-Johnstown Road.** Beers, 31; r., t. Hammond; r., t. Lisbon; r., t. Macomb; r., t. Massena, off Route 131; r., t. Massena, from Route 37C to Franklin County Line; r., t. Piercefield; r., t. Pierrepont; r., t. Potsdam. / **Old Vermont Road**: *Quarterly*, 13 (1968), no. 1, p. 6.

Olds Mill Road: from River Road to Route 37, crossing Oak Point Road, t. Morristown, n. mill owned by James Olds. Since it ran directly south from the river, it was "a paradise for smugglers," who moved horses, tobacco, dry goods, and, occasionally, Chinese from the river to the interior. Bogardus, 142-144. The road is now abandoned.

Oldsville: in t. Macomb, n. Benjamin Olds, who built dam and mill on Birch Creek, opened grinding mill in Morristown. See Carlton B. Olds, "A Ghost Town," *Quarterly*, 11 (1966), no. 4, p. 7. Also claimed for Benjamin Olds' son James Olds, miller and farmer. *Quarterly*, 6 (1961), npn. / **Oldsville Cemetery**: on Route 184, t. Macomb. 1949 Hammond Quad; 1961 Pope Mills Quad.

Olin Cemetery: t. Canton. in Olin District. / **Olin District**: t. Canton; probably n. Thomas D. Olin. *Quarterly*, 25 (1980), no. 4, p. 21. / **Olin School**: no. 2, common school, t. Canton, n. Olin family.

Oliver: personal n. or family n.: **Oliver Island**: in St. Lawrence River, t. Hammond, origin n. unknown. 1958 USGS Chippewa Quad. / **Oliver Road**: r., t. Louisville, n. Oliver family.

Olson Hall: on Clarkson University campus, n. Luther Emanuel Olson, a graduate of Clarkson, served on the Board of Trustees for 23 years (1945-1968).

Olmstead Pond: t. Clifton, n. Olmstead family. 1896 New; 1898 EGB, p. 28; 1902 Blankman; 1908

Adm; 1912 Stoddard; 1919 USGS Cranberry Lake Quad. Also **Olmsted**.

O'Malley: surname used as a specific: **O'Malley Brook**: trib. Racquette River, t. Colton. 1908 USGS Potsdam Quad; 1912 Stoddard; 1964 USGS Colton Quad. / **O'-Malley Forest**: county forest, t. Colton.

O'Neil Road: r., t. Lisbon, n. Andrew O'Neil family; r., t. Madrid, n. Bryant O'Neil family; r., t. Massena, n. Jeremiah O'Neil family; r., t. Norfolk, Brasher, n. Cornelius O'Neil family. / **O'Neil School**: no. 14, common school, t. Massena, n. O'Neil family. Also, **O'Niel** (error).

Onontehen: see **Oxbow**.

Oral Pond: see **Fishpole Pond**.

Oracotenton: Amerindian n., meaning unknown. Now **Chimney Island**.

Orchard: n. place where fruit trees are present: **Orchard Bay**: in Black Lake, t. Morristown. 1961 USGS Pope Mills Quad. / **Orchard Road**: s., v. Massena. / **Orchard Street**: s., v. Norwood.

Ore: n. mining and mineral deposits, formerly a major industry in St. Lawrence County: **Ore Bed**: see **Ore Bed Road**. / **Ore Bed Mine**: t. De-Kalb, "near the Ore Bed road which runs from Route 11 south of East DeKalb to the Bigelow-Hermon Road." Mark Hemenway, "Forgotten Mines," *Quarterly*, 11 (1966), no. 2, p. 19. / **Ore Bed Road**: Formerly, **Parish's Ore Bed**; see *Quarterly*, 10 (1965), no. 4, p. 14. / **Ore Bed Pond**: t. Clare. / **Ore Bed Road**: see *Quarterly*, 13 (1969), no. 4, p. 6. Also, **Old Ore Bed Road**. Floyd Hanson, "The Old Ore Bed Road," wrote that "the Ore Bed Road wended its way from Claflin's Corners in the Town of Pierrepont to the north branch of the Grass River in what is now the Town of Clare" and then across the Middle Branch of the Grass(e) River and to the ore beds. / **Ore Bed School**: t. DeKalb. 1915 Gouverneur Quad. It is the same as **Ore Bed School**: no. 12, common school, t. Hermon. / **Ore Road**: Road which at one time connected the Rossie Road to the Chippewa Bay Road. Miners drew iron ore from Rossie via the road to Chippewa Bay Road to be loaded on scows. Today this road is referred to as the Toland Road, because James Toland operates a dairy farm on the property. The road no longer connects the two previously mentioned roads. / **Orebed Creek**: t. Clare. / **Orebed Creek**: trib. Plumb Brook, t. Russell. 1915 USGS Russell Quad. / **Orebed Creek State Forest**, #14, t. Russell. / **Orebed Ponds**: two ponds, t. Clifton, alt. 1,195 and 1,209. 1915 Russell Quad. / **Orebed Road**: r., t. DeKalb, Hermon; r., t. Pierrepont; / r., t. Pitcairn.

Ormsbee Pond: in Granshue area, t. Parishville, n. Lyman Ormsbee. 1858 **Berkley Pond** Rogerson; 1873 **Berkley Pond** Hamilton Child; 1883 **Berkeley Pond** Ely-Wallace; 1896 New; 1898 EGB map; 1902 Blankman; 1908 **Berkley Pond** Adm; 1921 USGS Stark Quad. Also known locally as **Round Pond**.

Ormsby Hall: on Clarkson University campus, n. Andrew Stuart Ormsby (1895-1965), chair of the Department of Business Administration from 1948 to 1959.

Orvis Street East: s., v. Massena, n. Uriel. H. Orvis, from Vergennes, VT, mill owner in the 1820's.

Orvis Street West: s., v. Massena, n. Uriel H. Orvis.

Osakentake: see **Grass Lake**.

Osborn: n. family: **Osborn Pond**: t. DeKalb. See **Osborn Lake**. / **Osborn Lake**: pond, t. DeKalb, n. Osborn family. 1956 USGS Richville Quad.

Osborne: n. family: **Osborne Drive**: s., h. Newton Falls. / **Osborne Road**: r., t. Pitcairn.

Osborneville: t. Fowler, n. Timothy W. Osborn (change in spelling) from Georgia, VT, who in 1810 built first sawmill on Trout Brook. *Quarterly*, 18 (1973), no. 2, p. 4; p. o. est. Mar. 5, 1891, Martin V. McIntyre, pm, closed Dec. 31, 1903. The h. no longer exists. Also **Osborn**. / **Osborneville**: h., t. DeKalb; p. o. existed in 1896. / **Osborneville Cemetery**: t. DePeyster. / **Osbornville School**: no. 16, common school, t. DeKalb.

Oswegatchie: northern border with St. Lawrence River. Translation from Iroquois **Seogasti**, Huron **swekatsi**, Mohawk **oswagahonsti**, "black river." It was first described by Monsieur Chaussegros de Lery in 1749 as an Iroquois word meaning "mouth of the Black River," **oswa**, "river" + **gahonsti**, Mohawk, "black." The t. was n. Amerindian tribe, the Oswegatchie. A misinformed account appears in the *Quarterly*, 9 (1964), no. 3, p. 11, "Did you know that Oswegatchie river was known in Indian language as 'Swagatchie' meaning 'River that runs around and through the hills'?" Beauchamp, 72, points out that this was **Onontohen**, a local n. for the "oxbow" on Oxbow River in Jefferson County. Many variant spellings appear, a few being the following: **Soegatzy**, **Swegatchie, Wegatchie**. The French called it **Riviere de la Presentation**. See Hough, 367 ff. for early history. Different interpretations of the n. have appeared, but the meaning is "black." The t. inc. Mar. 3, 1802, from Lisbon, and is one of the original ten t. / **Oswegatchie**: h. in t. Fine. For years known as **the Crossing** because the upper end of the h. was built around the railroad crossing. The lower end was called **Little River**, for the river that flowed through the settlement. The h. is one and one-half miles from the Oswegatchie River, and no one knows now why it was so named; p. o. est. Feb. 24, 1885, Webster Partlow, first pm, existing, ZIP 13670 (New York Postal History). Also see Reynolds, 5. 1916 USGS Oswegatchie Quad. / **Oswegatchie-Newton Falls Road**: r., t. Clifton. **Oswegatchie Second Presbyterian Church Cemetery**, t. Oswegatchie. Also, **Stone Church**. / **Oswegatchie School**: no. 2, common school, h., t. Fine, n. **Village of Oswegatchie School**, Dist. 2. Reynolds, 199. / **Oswegatchie River**: flows into the St. Lawrence River at Ogdensburg. Rises in Cranberry Lake and flows west and north through t. Clifton, Fine, Edwards, Fowler, Rossie, into Jefferson County (Oxbow), Gouverneur, DeKalb, DePeyster, and Oswegatchie. French name: **Riviere de La Presentation.** 1963 USGS Ogden East Quad. / **Oswegatchie Road**: r., c. Ogdensburg. / **Oswegatchie School**: Formerly, **Alger School**, then **Volans**, but also sometimes spelled **Vollens** (which see). Harriet Doren Smith, "We Walked to District School #9 Town of Oswegatchie," *Quarterly*, 15 (1970), no. 3, p. 10. / **Oswegatchie Trail Road**: r., t. Fine.

Otsikwake: see **Black Lake**.

Otter: aquatic fur-bearing animal of the genus *Lutra*, inhabiting water bodies; occasionally sighted in St. Lawrence County. / **Otter Pond**: t. Colton. 1880 Ely; 1883 Ely-Wallace; 1896 New; 1902 Blankman; 1908 Adm; 1912 Stoddard; 1954 USGS Tupper Lake Quad. / **Otter Pond**, t. Fine, alt. 1,600 ft. 1883 Ely-Wallace; 1902 Blankman; 1908 Adm; 1912 Stoddard; 1919 USGS Cranberry Lake Quad. / **Otter Pond**: t. Hopkinton. 1858 Rogerson; 1860 Merrit; 1873 Hamilton Child; 1896 New; 1902 Blankman; 1920 USGS Childwold Quad.

Outer Elm Street: s., h. Madrid.

Oven Lake: *Quarterly*, 14 (1969), no. 1, p. 18; origin unknown.

Overlook Avenue: s., h. Newton Falls, n. view.

Owatonna Island: in St. Lawrence River (Chippewa Bay), t. Hammond; n. romantically claimed to be Amerindian, "garden of the gods." 1958 USGS Chippewa Quad.

Owen D. Young Library: on St Lawrence University campus, n. long-time trustee and chair of the University corporation.

Owens Corners: t. Russell. 1915 USGS Russell Quad.

Owl: common n. for natural features, especially hills and mountains; n. usually arises from the bird being heard. / **Owl Mountain**: t. Fine. / **Owl Mountain Road**: r., t. Fine. / **Owl Road**: r., t. Gouverneur.

Oxbow: The Oswegatchie River crosses t. Rossie twice, forming the "ox-bow." Indian name: **O-non-to-heh**, "A hill with a river on each side," and "oxbow." The h. is in Jefferson County. / **Oxbow-Gouverneur Road**: t., Rossie, Gouverneur. / **Oxbow Road**: r., t. Rossie. / **Oxbow School**: no. 12, common school, t. Rossie.

Ozonia: see **Lake Ozonia.**

P

Pace Avenue: s., h. Piercefield.

Paddock Street: s., v. Massena, n. William S. Paddock, first physician in the area.

Paddy Brown Brook: t. Edwards, trib. Stammer Creek, n. Paddy Brown, farmer. 1915 USGS Russell Quad.

Page School: no. 12, common school, t. Stockholm, n. Page family.

Palmer Hill: t. Russell, alt. 920 ft., n. Julius M. Palmer. He was a surveyor, early merchant, town officer, and pm (appointed, 1861), state assemblyman. 1915 USGS Russell Quad. Durant, 432. Also claimed for father, Ichabod Palmer.

Palmerville: h., t. Russell; see **Palmer Hill** for origin; p. o. est. June 5, 1897,

James O. Wigglesworth, first pm, closed June 15, 1911. 1915 USGS Russell Quad. / **Palmerville Cemetery**: t. Russell. / **Palmerville Road**: r., t. Russell. Also **Blanchard Hill Road**. / **Palmerville School**: no. 9, common school, t. Russell.

Palmeter: see **Parmeter Cemetery.**

Pansy: poss. n. plant or flower, but uncertain: **Pansy Pond**: t. Fine, an old trail through the woods between Star and Streeter Lake. 1916 USGS Oswegatchie Quad. / **Pansy Road**: t. Fine. *Quarterly*, 5 (1960), no. 1, npn.

Panther Pond: t. Colton, east of Cranberry Lake, alt. 2,095 ft., n. wild cat. *Quarterly*, 16 (1971), no. 1, p. 11. 1880 Ely; 1883 Ely-Wallace; 1896 Nwq; 1902 Blankman; 1912 Stoddard; 1954 USGS Tupper Lake Quad.

Paradise Point: on Tupper Lake, t. Piercefield, n. commendatory. 1954 USGS Tupper Lake Quad.

Parish's Ore Bed: see **Ore Bed Road**.

Parishville: t., eastern interior of the county, originally the territory between Lake Champlain and the St. Lawrence River. In 1804, J. D. Le Ray de Chaumont purchased the land from the heirs of William Constable. The t. was originally called **Chaumont**, in his honor. David Parish purchased 844,000 acres of land from Chaumont on Dec. 2, 1808. On Mar. 18, 1814, the t. and h. took the name of **Parishville**, being formed from Hopkinton. Parish was a banker from Hamburg, Germany, but was of Scottish descent, being among those Scotsmen who made their fortunes, if any, in places other than Scotland. Parish came here to live, however, and spent a fortune trying to develop and improve the lands he purchased. After failing, he returned to Europe and became a partner in a firm which he believed to be lucrative but proved to be bankrupt. Hough, 422 ff. and 600-604. 1964 USGS Parishville Quad. / **Parishville**: h. in t. **Parishville**, p. o. est. Aug. 2, 1813, Daniel Hoard, first pm (Hough, 575), existing, ZIP 13672. 1908 USGS Potsdam Quad; 1964 USGS Parishville Quad. / **Parishville Center**: h., t. Parishville, p. o. est. as **Parishville Centre** Oct. 7, 1861, Lincoln Brown, first pm, changed to **Parishville Center** Dec. 1893 (day unknown), George W. Boody, pm, closed July 30, 1904. 1858 Rogerson; 1865 Beers; 1873 Hamilton Child; 1903 **Parishville Centre** Mathews; 1908 USGS Potsdam Quad; 1964 USGS

Potsdam Quad. See *Sketches of Parishville*. Also, **Parishville Centre.** / **Parishville Center Cemetery**: n. h. / **Parishville Center School**: no. 4, common school, t. Parishville. / **Parishville-Colton Road**: r., t. Parishville. / **Parishville-Hopkinton Central School**: t. Parishville. 1964 USGS Parishville Quad. / **Parishville River**: n. not official. *Quarterly*, 20 (1975), no. 1, p. 11. / **Parishville School**: no. 1, common school, t. Parishville. / **Parishville-Smithville Road**: r., t. Parishville. / **Parishville Turnpike**: built in the early 1800s, between Parishville and Potsdam. Also, **The Turnpike**, **The Straight Road**, **North Road**. See, *Sketches of Parishville*.

Park: generally the n. occurs when a park is nearby; in recent years the name has also become promotional since the n. connotes wealth and stateliness reflecting Park Avenue, New York City. / **Park, The**: v. Gouverneur. "The Park" is 450 feet long and about 100 feet wide and serves as the village green. The idea of the park came about when the Wesleyan Seminary burned, January 1, 1839. See Julius Bartlett, "Gouverneur's Village Park," *Quarterly*, 7 (1962), no. 1, p. 5. / **Park Avenue**: s., v. Massena; s., v. Norwood. / **Park Island**: in Oswegatchie River at Newton Falls, t. Clifton. 1896 New. / **Park Place**: s., v. Canton. / **Park Street**: s., v. Canton; s., v. Gouverneur; s., h. Norfolk; s., v. Norwood; s., v. Ogdensburg; s., v. Potsdam.

Parker: the surname often occurs; the places n. different families: **Parker Avenue**: s., v. Massena, n. Salmon Parker. / **Parker Road**: r., t. Macomb, n. Noahdiah Parker; r., t. Parishville, n. Francis Parker, a doctor; s., v. Gouverneur, could be n. any one of the numerous Parkers in Gouverneur's history. Early settlers, John and James Parker came in April, 1808. James Parker built the 2nd bridge across the Oswegatchie, 1819. Cent. Souv, 9, 348. Cent. Souv., 348. A claim is also made for Capt. George Parker, son of Alexander Parker who settled in 1808. George Parker organized the first company to leave Gouverneur for the Civil War. Cent. Souv., 349.

Parkers Corners: t. Fowler, probably n. Ebenezer Parker who settled ca 1811. Durant, 109.

Parkhurst Brook: trib. Racquette River, t. Potsdam, n. Porter Parkhurst, Parishville Center. 1964 USGS Potsdam Quad.

Parkhurst Road: r., t. Potsdam, n.

Parkhurst family, especially Porter Parkhurst.

Parmeter: a cluster of places carry the n., which is sometimes misspelled **Palmeter**: **Parmeter Cemetery**: t. Potsdam. 1943 Potsdam Quad. / **Parmeter Pond**: t. Clare, n. Parmeter family. 1896 New; 1902 Blankman; 1908 Adm; 1912 Stoddard; 1921 Stark Quad. / **Parmeter Road**: r., t. Potsdam, n. Nathan Parmeter. / **Parmeter School**: no. 28, common school, t. Potsdam, n. Parmeter family. Also appears as **Parmenter Road**.

Partlow Pond: t. Fine, n. David Partlow in the 1840's. *Quarterly*, 5 (1960), no. 1, npn. 1915 USGS Russell Quad.

Paskuugemah: see **Tupper Lake**.

Patch Creek: t. Hammond. May have been originally **Pat's Creek**.

Paterson Street: see **Patterson Street**, Ogdensburgh.

Patterson: a common surname: **Patterson Road**: r., t. Louisville, n. Joseph Patterson family. / **Patterson School**: no. 15, common school, t. DeKalb, n. William, James, and John Patterson families. / **Patterson Street**: s., c. Ogdensburg, n. John Paterson (1744-1808), Revolutionary War general, member of the court-martial that tried Major John Andre, took part in the capture of General John Burgoyne at Saratoga, land owner, and Congressman (1803-1805). Somehow the spelling was changed, although **Paterson Street** was one of the original 15 streets after inc. of **Ogdensburgh** (note the **h**) in 1817 and appears again on the 1835-1836 map.

Patton Road: r., t. Lawrence, n. David Patton.

Paul Road: r., t. Lisbon, n. Anthony Paul family.

Payne Road: v. Massena, n. Barnabas Payne.

Payson: surname. **Payson Hall**: on St. Lawrence University campus, n. Canton Agriculture and Technical College president, the n. being retained after St. Lawrence University acquired the building. / **Payson Hall**: on SUNY Canton College of Technology campus, n. Dr. James M. Payson, teacher and administrator from 1907 to 1929.

Pea Vine Creek: see **Peavine Creek**.

Peabody Road: r., t. Gouverneur, n.

Peabody family. Beers, 31, shows S. Peabody, with two houses, living near site of present road.

Peach Island: in St. Lawrence River, t. Hammond, n. tree and fruit. 1958 USGS Chippewa Quad.

Pearl: a family name: **Pearl Street**: s., v. Canton; **Pearl Street**: s., v. Gouverneur; **Pearl Street**: s., c. Ogdensburg.

Pearson Road: r., t. DePeyster, n. John Pearson (1794-1871) from Lyme NH; r., t. Madrid, n. John Pearson family.

Peavine Creek: stream, trib. Oswegatchie River, t. Clifton, n. presence of the vines. 1896 **Pea Vine Creek** New; 1902 **Pea Vine Creek** Blankman; 1919 USGS Cranberry Lake Quad.

Peck: surname used as a specific: **Peck Road**: r., t. Hopkinton. / **Peck School**: no. 13, common school, t. Hopkinton. Both for the Peck family. / **Peck Street**: s. in Terrace Park, t. Morristown, n. a Methodist bishop.

Pelkys Falls: in North Branch Grass(e) River, t. Clare, n. Pelky family. 1915 Russell Quad.

Pennsylvania Avenue: s., h. Cranberry Lake, n. state with a mischievous glance at the famous ave. in Washington, DC.

Perch Bay: in St. Lawrence River, t. Morristown. 1963 USGS Morristown Quad. / **Perch Island**: in St. Lawrence River, near Oak Point, t. Hammond. Both n. fish.

Perkins: family n.: **Perkins Road**: r., t. Parishville. / s., v. Massena, n. Matthew and John Perkins. Dumas, 57. / **Perkins School**: no. 17, common school, t. Parishville.

Pero Lane: s., c. Ogdensburg, n. Charles Pero.

Perrin Road: r., t. Potsdam, from 11B to Parkhurst, and from Sayles Road to Route 72 t. Parishville, n. Asa Perrin, early settler; r., t. Potsdam, from Route 72 to Sayles Road.

Perry Road: r., t. Canton, in Morley area, n. William Perry, from VT, farmer.

Peru: poss. for country, but reason n. unknown: **Peru Road**: r., t. Lawrence, road to Peru, Clinton County. / **Peru Street School**: no. 9, common school, t. Lawrence, n. road.

Pest House Road: r., t. Potsdam. In the 19th century, each town had a pest

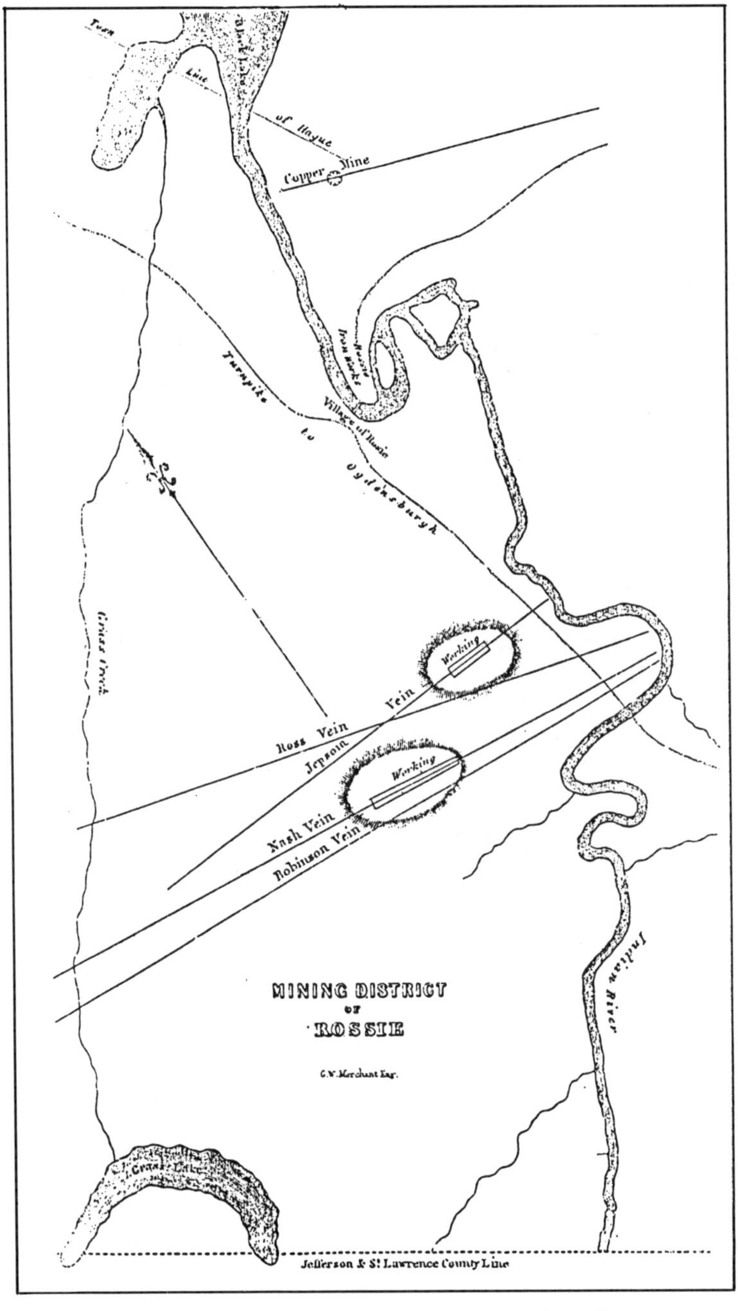

Map of ore veins in Rossie 1839, including Turnpike route.

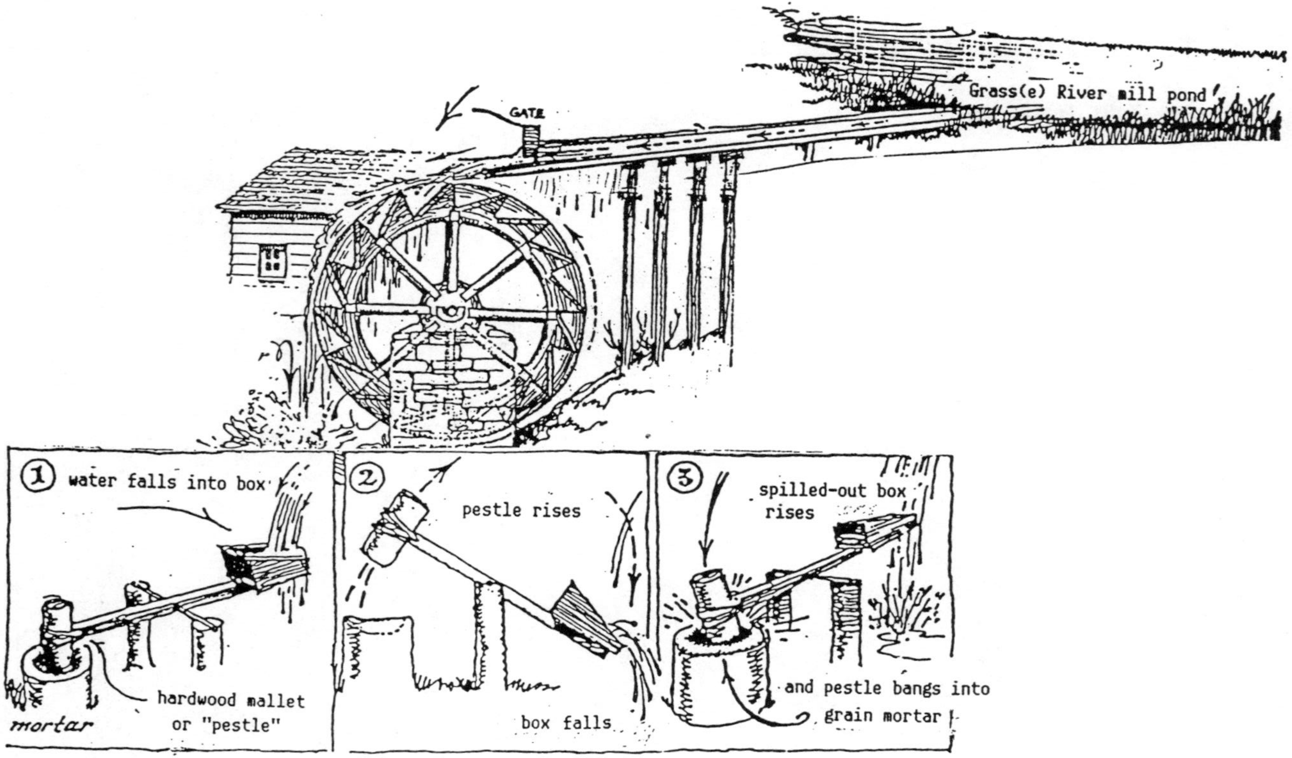

Could there have been a plumping mill on Pestle Street in Russell?

house where people went with communicable diseases or when they were quarantined.

Pestle: n. the instrument, made of hardwood, used for grinding or pounding a substance, such as grain, into a powder. **Pestle Street**: r., t. Russell and s., h. Russell, from Woods Bridge Road south along the Grass(e) River to h. Russell. / **Pestle Street School**: no. 12, common school, t. Russell; only school to have a suspension bridge across the river. 1915 USGS Russell Quad.

Peyton House: on Clarkson University campus, n. William Charles Peyton on Oct. 15, 1955, by his son Bernard Peyton, chairman of the board of the New York Air Brake Company.

Phelix Road: r., t. Stockholm, prob. n. Nelson Phelix family.

Phillips: n. family: **Phillips School**: no. 9, common school, in South Hammond, t. Hammond, n. Samuel and Christopher Phillips. / **Phillips Street**: s., v. Massena, n. John and Benjamin Phillips.

Pickering Street: s., c. Ogdensburg, n. Timothy Pickering (1745-1829), U. S. adjutant general, congressman, postmaster general, and secretary of war.

Picketville: variant of **Pickettville**: **Picketville Road**: r., t. Parishville. / **Picketville Forest**: county forest, t. Parishville.

Pickettville: h., t. Parishville, n. Ephraim Picket, land speculator. 1896 New; 1898 EGB map; 1908 USGS Potsdam Quad; 1908 Adm; 1912 Stoddard; 1964 USGS Rainbow Falls Quad. Also **Picketville.** See *Sketches of Parishville.* Also spelled **Picketville.** / **Pickettville Cemetery**: Cleared of bodies and now a meadow, t. Parishville. See *Sketches of Parishville.* / **Pickettville School**: no. 11, common school, t. Parishville. *Quarterly*, 13 (1968), no. 1, p. 10.

Pickle Road/Street: r., t. Stockholm and Brasher (s., v. Brasher Falls), n. John Pickle family. The name has led to some wild assumptions and apocryphal stories, one as follows: The residents bought vinegar at a local store to make pickles; one day a salesman came through and asked for a resident, and the store clerk said that the resident lived on Pickle Street. Another version is that so many cucumbers were grown that the excess was thrown into the road where the horses trampled them into "pickles."

Picquet Monument: commemorates Fort La Presentation, which was built by Father Picquet in 1749. See **Ogdensburg.**

Picquet's Folly: Fort La Presentation, built by Father Picquet. See **Ogdensburg.**

Pierce: a surname: **Pierce Road**: t. Macomb; **Pierce School**: t. Canton; t. Macomb.

Piercefield: formed from the survey townships of Piercefield and Atherton in eastern St. Lawrence County, now t. Piercefield, origin n. unknown. Hough, 255. Until 1900 Piercefield was a part of Hopkinton, but was separated by a vote of the Board of Supervisors 30-4. The first t. meeting was Feb. 12, 1901; t. formed 1901. / **Piercefield**: h. in t. Piercefield; p. o. est. Nov. 8, 1895, Clora E. Adams, first pm, existing, ZIP 12973. Township No. 11 in t. Parishville, known as **Wick** but became **Piercefield**, Oct. 5, 1882. Charles I. Ruderman purchased "ghost village" of Conifer in 1921; he expected to sell it to a toy manufacturer (Transogram) and rename it "Toytown." **Tupper Lake News**, May 1946. Origin of n. unknown, but possibly from England; ety., personal n. **Piers + field.** 1902 **Piercefield Falls** Blankman; 1908 Adm; 1912 Stoddard; 1954 USGS Tupper Lake Quad. / **Piercefield Falls**: falls, Racquette River, t. Piercefield. 1860 **Perciefield Falls** (possibly a misprint, but may have been thought of as the n.) Street, p. 177; 1860 **Piercefield High Falls** Merrit; 1868 Merrit; 1883 Ely-Wallace. / **Piercefield Falls School**: no. 17, common school, t. Hopkinton. Later the area became a part of t. Piercefield. / **Piercefield Flow**: inlet, Racquette River, t. Piercefield. 1908 Adm; 1912 Stoddard; 1954 USGS Tupper Lake Quad. / **Piercefield High Falls**: see **Piercefield Falls.**

Pierces Corners: t. Macomb. See *Quarterly*, 6 (1961), npn. 1961 USGS Pope Mills Quad. Also **Pierce's Corners**. Formerly **Washburnville.** / **Pierces Corners Cemetery**: t. Macomb.

Pierrepont: t. east of center of county, n. Hezekiah Beers Pierrepont (1768-1838), landowner, at one time of about 1-1/2 million acres. Born in New Haven, CT, of a family that came to the colonies in 1640, he became a businessman in Philadelphia and achieved wealth. He went to France on business during that country's revolution (he saw Robespierre beheaded). Because of the Revolution, he could not enter into any business transaction. He voyaged to India and China and returned with a ship of valuable cargo, which was immediately seized by the French. He never received compensation. He returned to New York and married Anna Maria, daughter of William Constable, and settled in Brooklyn Heights as a distiller of gin, which made him rich. Attracted to the lands that his father-in-law speculated in, he purchased in 1806 the t. of Pierrepont and later Louisville and Stockholm. He oversaw his lands but retained his permanent residence in Brooklyn Heights. Hough, 712-714. The t. of **Pierrepont** was formed on Apr. 15, 1818. Benjamin Raymond surveyed the t. Pierrepont. *Quarterly*, 5 (1960), no. 4, p. 8; 18 (1973), no. 2, p. 5. / **Pierrepont**: h., t. Pierrepont; p. o. est. as **Pierpont** July 24 1819, Cyrus Grannis, first pm, changed to **Pierrepont** in 1870 (day and month unknown), Austin C. Leonard, pm, closed June 29, 1935. Hough, 575, erroneously gives date of est. June 5, 1820, with Peter Post, pm. Also, **Pierpont**. 1964 USGS Pierrepont Quad. / **Pierrepont Avenue**: s., v. Potsdam. / **Pierrepont-Brown's Bridge Road**: r., t. Pierrepont. / **Pierrepont-Canton Road**: r., t. Canton, Pierrepont. / **Pierrepont Center School**: no. 2, common school, t. Pierrepont. Also **Pierrepont School.** / **Pierrepont Hill Cemetery**: t. Pierrepont.

Pig: n. domesticated animal: **Pig Island**: in Trout Lake in front of Old Trout Lake Hotel. Pliny Gardner kept his pork meals on the hoof there. / **Pig Road**: r., t. Potsdam, between Route 345 and River Road, n. because a family living on the road raised pigs.

Pike: numerous Pike families live in St. Lawrence County. The places with specific **Pike** are named for them. **Pike** may also be a short form of **turnpike**: **Pike Road**: r., t. Brasher; r., t. Canton; r., t. Fowler. / **Pike School**: no. 16, common school, t. Brasher. / **Pikes Corner**: crossroads, t. Rossie. 1961 USGS Natural Dam Quad. Also **Pike's Corners, Pikes Corners.** / **Pikes Corners School**: no. 8, common school, t., Rossie. Also **Pike's Corners School.** / **Pikes Road**: r., t. Fowler.

Pile Bridge: See **Spile Bridge**. *Quarterly*, 10 (1965), no. 4, p. 14.

Pin Island: in Black Lake, t. Morristown. 1961 USGS Pope Mills Quad. [Prob. misprint for **Pine Island**].

Pinchgut Road: t. Macomb. n. for difficult living in the area. *Quarterly*, 10 (1965), no. 4, p. 9.

Pine: n. any evergreen, coniferous tree of the genus *Pinus*, either for a lone pine or for a grove. The name is common but extremely popular where pines grow in the United States. **Pine Hill** occurs often: **Pine**: h., t. Pitcairn, on Carthage and Adirondack Railroad. No longer exists. / **Pine Grove**: h. t. Pitcairn. 1963 USGS Sparrow Quad. / **Pine Grove Cemetery**: on Barnhart Island, t. Massena, now removed to **New Pine Grove Cemetery**, outside v. Massena, in t. Norfolk, on bank of Racquette River. 1964 USGS Massena Quad. / **Pine Hill**: t. Oswegatchie; t. Macomb, 1961 USGS Pope Mills Quad. / **Pine Hill Cemetery**: Columbia and High Streets, v., t. Morristown. 1963 USGS Morristown Quad. Bogardus, 233; t. Oswegatchie, near Lost Village. 1963 USGS Heuvelton Quad. Also **Eel Weir Cemetery**. / **Pine Hill Pond**: t. Edwards and Pitcairn. 1915 USGS Russell Quad. / **Pine Hill Road**: r., t. Macomb; r. t. Rossie. / **Pine Hill School**: no. 11, common school, t. Macomb. 1949 USGS Hammond Quad. / **Pine Island**: in Cranberry Lake, t. Clifton. 1896 **Norway Island** New; 1919 USGS Cranberry Lake Quad, / **Pine Island**: in Hamlin Bay, Tupper Lake, t. Piercefield. 1896 New. / **Pine Mountain**: t. Colton. 1896 New. / **Pine Plains**: t. Piercefield. 1853 HMC. / **Pine Pond**: t. Colton. 1896 **Big Pine Pond** New; 1902 **Big Pine Pond** Blankman; 1954 USGS Tupper Lake Quad; t. Fine. *Quarterly*, 5 (1960), no. 1, npn. 1916 USGS Oswegatchie Quad; t. Piercefield. 1858 **Egg Pond** Rogerson; 1860 **Egg Pond** Merrit; 1873 **Egg Pond** Hamilton Child; 1880 Ely; 1883 Ely-Wallace; 1896 New; 1908 Adm; 1912 Stoddard; 1920 USGS Childwold Quad; **Pine Pond**: t. Colton. See **Big Pine Pond**. / **Pine Road**: r., t. Colton, Higley Flow area. / **Pine Street**: s., v. Canton; s., v. Massena; s., v. Norwood; s., c. Ogdensburg; s., v. Potsdam; s., v. Rensselaer Falls, runs perpendicular to Front Street; s., h. Star Lake; s., v. Waddington. / **Pine Street Beach**: v. Potsdam. / **Pine Street School**: no. 30, common school, t. Potsdam. / **Pine Tree Island**: in St. Lawrence River. 1958 USGS Chippewa Quad.

Pink School: t. Canton. The school number was painted the color. The building is now a private home. / **Pink Schoolhouse Road**: t. Canton to Pyrites.

Pinkerton Road: r., t. Oswegatchie, n.

THE AVERAGE PLANK ROAD

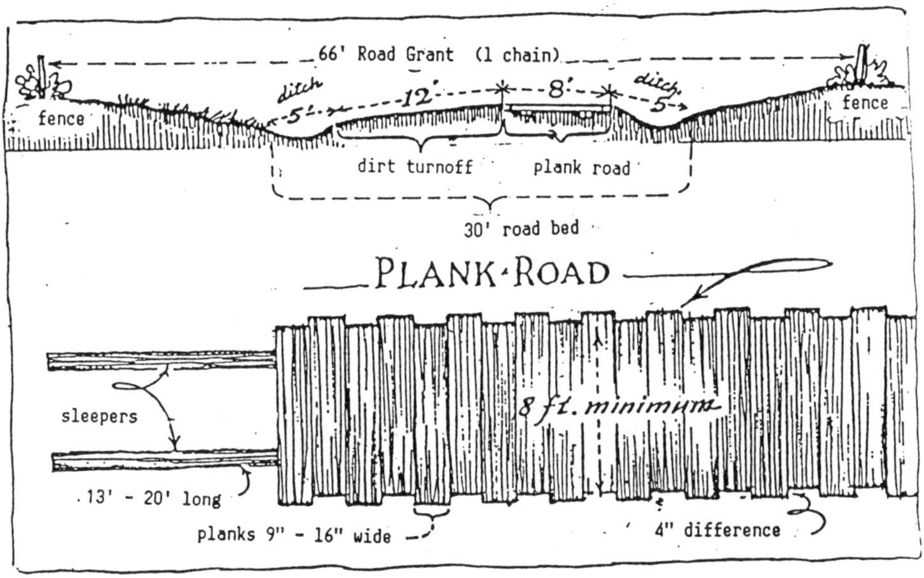

The planks themselves were laid on top of "sleepers" or rails.
Sleepers varied in size from four by six inches to four by twelve, the maximum, laid flat. Long stone rollers were used to flatten out the road and push the sleepers into the dirt before laying the planks on top. American custom was to lay planks loose and let gravel and their own weight keep them in place. Even when the planks went across a bridge, they were laid loose.

THE MANSION FROM AN OLD SKETCH

Fowler Mansion at Sylvia Lake, Fowler, 1818.

James, Simon, and William Pinkerton families.

Pinner Road: r., t. Pitcairn, runs southwest from Harrisville-Fullerville Road, n. Pinner family.

Pinney Cemetery: t. Edwards, n. Pinney family.

Pins Creek: t. Fine, trib. Middle Branch Oswegatchie River. 1916 USGS Oswegatchie Quad. Origin n. unknown. [Poss. misprint for **Pine**].

Piquet Drive: s., c. Ogdensburg. See **Ogdensburg**.

Pitcairn: t. southwestern border with Lewis County; n. Joseph Pitcairn and formed Mar. 29, 1836, landowner, born in Scotland, served as U. S. Consul in Paris. He purchased the land from Daniel McCormick, a distant relative, in 1817. / **East Pitcairn**, p. o. est., Jan. 15, 1850. / **Pitcairn Forks** is the name of a portion of Pitcairn. Durant, 448. 1865 Beers, p. 72; 1916 USGS Oswegatchie Quad; 1951 USGS Harrisville Quad. Other derived names: **Pitcairn**: h., t. Pitcairn; p. o. est. June 3, 1840 from **Harrisville**, John Sloper, first pm, closed in 1868 (day and month unknown), reopened Mar. 16, 1870, George Miller, first pm, closed June 14, 1902. / **Pitcairn Cemetery**. / **Pitcairn-Fowler Road**: r., t. Pitcairn. / **Pitcairn Mines**, on Carthage & Adirondack Railroad. / **Pitcairn School**: no. 2, common school.

Plains: a common feature generic for flat areas, sometimes used as a specific: **Plains, The**. see **The Plains**, t. Parishville. / **Plains, The**: area between Parishville and Potsdam. / **Plains Mountain**: see **Roundtop Mountain**. / **Plains Road**: r., t. Canton, Pierrepont. Also **Farnes Road**. / **Plains School**: no. 9, common school, at Beech Plains, t. Pierrepont.

Plank Roads: The need to find road material that would allay dust and eliminate miring in mud led to the use of wood in the form of rough thick planks for roads. Although proven unsuccessful, several such roads were contracted in the mid-nineteenth century. Some of the main companies were **Ogdensburg to Heuvelton**, **Canton Plank-Road**, **Canton, Morley and Madrid Plank-Road Co.**, **Potsdam Plank-Road Co.**, **Hammond, Rossie and Antwerp Plank-Road Co.**, **Morristown and Hammond Plank-Road Co.**, **Heuvelton and Canton Falls Plank-Road Co.**, **Hermon Plank-Road**

Co., and **Norfolk, Raymondville and Massena Plank-Road Co.** For details of length, cost, and dates of these roads, see Hough, 569-571; Durant, 130-131. / **Plank Road:** t. Hammond. / **Plank Road, The:** Formerly n. of the Heuvelton Road. See **Heuvelton Street**, Rensselaer Falls.

Plant Road: s., v. Waddington.

Planty Road: r., t. Madrid, n. Planty family.

Pleasant: a commendatory specific for pleasant land or community, sometimes imagined or wished for: **Pleasant Avenue**: s., c. Ogdensburg. / **Pleasant Creek**: trib. Grass(e) River, t. Russell. 1915 USGS Russell Quad. / **Pleasant Lake**: t. Colton. *Quarterly*, 10 (1974), no. 3, p. 12; p. o. est. Mar. 22, 1911, William A. Andrews, pm, changed to **Mount Arab** Feb. 21, 1922. 1896 New; 1902 Blankman; 1909 Adm; 1912 Stoddard; 1921 USGS Stark Quad; t. Fowler. *Quarterly*, 19 (1974), no. 3, p. 12; t. Hopkinton. *Quarterly*, 19 (1974), no. 3, p. 12; t. Macomb. *Quarterly*, 19 (1974), no. 3, p. 12; t. Macomb, alt. 335 ft. 1961 USGS Pope Mills Quad; t. Piercefield. See **Mount Arab Lake**. / **Pleasant Lake Cemetery**: t. Macomb. 1961 Pope Mills Quad. / **Pleasant Lake Road**: r., t. Macomb, off Brasie Corners; r., t. Macomb, off Pleasant Lake. / **Pleasant Lake State Forest**, #39, t. Macomb. / **Pleasant Lake Stream**: t. Clifton. 1896 New; 1902 Blankman; 1908 Adm; 1912 Stoddard; 1921 USGS Stark Quad. See **South Brook**. / **Pleasant Mound Cemetery**: t. Colton. / **Pleasant Street**: r., t. Stockholm; s., v. Canton; s., v. Edwards; s., v. Hermon; s., v. Massena; s., v. Norwood; s., h. Parishville; s., v. Potsdam. / **Pleasant Valley**: t. Hammond. "This peaceful valley is nestled between Marvin Hill of North Hammond and Chippewa Creek. The area is green and plush" / **Pleasant Valley Cemetery**: t. Hammond, on Pleasant Valley Road. 1961 USGS Hammond Quad / **Pleasant Valley Road**: r., t. Hammond; r., t. Potsdam / **Pleasant Valley School**: no. 8, common school, t. Hammond; t. Edwards, Dist. 10. Freeman, 16. 1915 USGS Gouverneur Quad. / **Pleasant View Cemetery**: t. Clare.

Plover: Henry Plover, a Revolutionary War soldier. See George Liebler, "Ogdensburg Flashback," *Quarterly*, 12 (1967), no. 1, p. 16, for the story of Plover's love for the lovely Alice Pritchard. Some claim the hill was n. the bird of the genus *Charadriidae*:

Plover Hill: c. Ogdensburg. / **Plover Hill Avenue**: s., c. Ogdensburg. See **Plover Hill**.

Plum: n. tree of the genus *Prunus*, a very popular flora n. in the United States because of the delicacy of the fruit and for the rural connotation: **Plum Brook**: t. Clifton; t. Fine; t. Hopkinton; t. Norfolk, trib. Racquette River. 1964 USGS Massena Quad. / **Plum Brook**: h., t. Potsdam, p. o. est. June 2, 1876, Rinaldo Barrett, pm, closed Apr. 5, 1880. / **Plum Brook Road**: r., t. Norfolk. / **Plum Brook School**. see **Branch School**. / **Plum Creek**: t. Russell. Clarke, 4. / **Plumb Creek Valley**: t. Russell. Clarke, 29. Prob. **Plum Creek Valley**. / **Plum Street**: s., v. Massena.

Plumb Brook: t. Russell, trib. Grass(e) River, source of early pearl business in freshwater clams, rises near Branch School with two branches. 1915 USGS Russell Quad. Also **Plum Brook**.

Plumbrook: h., t. Norfolk; p. o. est July 1, 1895, Dellia Van Kennen, first pm, closed Apr. 30, 1932. 1964 USGS Norfolk Quad. / **Plumbrook School**: no. 3, common school, t. Norfolk.

Podunk: an area within the t. Hermon; n. Amerindian tribe, but in recent years the n. has become synonymous with insignificance. Nina W. Smithers and Mary H. Biondi, "From Podunk to Zip Code 13652," *Quarterly*, 10 (1965), no. 4, p. 8. / **Podunk Road**: t. Hermon, from Grove Road to Edwards. 1956 USGS Bigelow Quad. / **Podunk School**: no. 6, common school, t. Hermon. 1915 USGS Gouverneur Quad.

Point: a generic indicating a strip of land extending into a body of water: **Point Airy**: t. Oswegatchie, known also as **Indian Point**, where battle of Fort Levis took place in Aug., 1790. Now the site of the Psychiatric Center, Ogdensburg. *Quarterly*, 11 (1966), no. 4, p. 3. / **Point Comfort**: on St. Lawrence River, t. Morristown. 1963 USGS Morristown Quad. / **Point de Ganataregoin**: See **Indian Point**. / **Point Iroquois**: on St. Lawrence River, t. Waddington. See Durant, 55, for **Point aux Iroquois**. See Beauchamp, 73. / **Point Lake**: see **Pointed Lake**. / **Point Rockaway**: public beach on St. Lawrence River, t. Waddington. Tedford, 55.

Pointed Lake: now **Star Lake**. Also, **Point Lake**. t. Fine. *Quarterly*, 5 (1960), no. 1, npn.

Pollock: a family name: **Pollock Road**: r., t. Canton; r., t. Madrid.

Polly: n. John Polley, first settler at Massena Springs: **Polly Lane**: v. Massena. Dumas, 57. Spelling changed. / **Pollys Bay**: in St. Lawrence River, t. Massena. 1964 USGS Raquette River Quad. / **Pollys Creek**: t. Massena, trib. St. Lawrence River. 1964 USGS Raquette River Quad. / **Pollys Gut**: water passage between St. Lawrence State Park and Cornwall Island, t. Massena and Stormont Co., Ontario. 1941 USGS Barnhart Quad; 1964 USGS Raquette River Quad.

Pond: both a generic and specific, relating to usually a small body of water: **Pond Road**: r., t. Hermon to Trout Lake; r., t. Russell to Trout Lake. / **Pond School**: no. 3, common school, t. Edwards, Freeman, 22. / **Pond Settlement**: t. Edwards. Durant, 444. Constant Wells was the first settler, 1820's. *Quarterly*, 7 (1962), no. 2, p. 15. 1915 USGS Russell Quad.

Pontoon Bridge Road: r., t. Massena, n. type of bridge.

Pooler Road: r., t. DeKalb, prob. n. Charles T. Pooler. Durant, 43; s., v., also r., t. Gouverneur, n. Pooler family.

Poor House: see **Alms House** and **County Home**.

Poor Road: r., t. DeKalb, n. Poor family.

Pope: surname used as a specific: **Pope's Creek**: t. Macomb, n. Pope family. / **Pope Mills**: h. in t. Macomb, on Fish Creek, two miles from Black Lake, p. o. est. as **Pope's Mills** July 14, 1849, Russell Covell, pm (Hough, 575), changed to **Pope Mills** Nov. 14, 1893, James R. Covell, pm, closed May 15, 1936; n. Timothy Pope (? - 1835), who moved from Oswegatchie to the site in 1818 and built a sawmill, grist mill, distillery, dam, and tannery. He was killed on Nov. 7, 1835 when a defective millstone burst. Durant, 363. *Quarterly*, 6 (1961), npn.Also, **Pope's Mills**. 1961 USGS Pope Mills Quad. Historical marker. / **Pope Mills School**: no. 8, common school, t. Macomb. Also, **Pope's Mills School**. / **Pope's Pond**: t. Macomb, n. Pope family. Also **Popes Pond**.

Poplar: n. the tree of the genus of *Populus*, often used in place n., especially for streets: **Poplar Street**:

s., v. Massena; s., v. Potsdam. / **Poplar Hill**: t. Fowler, alt. 660. 1956 USGS Gouverneur Quad.

Pork Creek: t. Edwards, trib. Oswegatchie River. 1956 USGS Edwards Quad.

Port: usually a place next to a body of water where goods are loaded and unloaded: **Port Street**: r., t. Waddington, to the port on St. Lawrence River. / **Port Ferry Lake**: folk-etymologized form of **Portaferry** (which see). / **Port Kent-Hopkinton Road**: r., t. Lawrence, through Hopkinton and Nicholville to Port Kent, Essex County; surveyed 1827, constructed in 1829 at cost of $38,000; tollgates at first but removed as towns took over repairs. Stages were inaugurated in 1833.

Portaferry: a survey township, now h., t. Pitcairn, n. town in Ireland. / **Portaferry Lake**: pond, t. Pitcairn. 1865 **Port Ferry Lake** Beers, p. 72; 1916 USGS Oswegatchie Quad.

Porteous Bay: on north side of Ogden Island, n. John S. Porteous who bought the Ogden farm from Sarah M. Ogden in 1869. Five generations of the Porteous family owned the land until it was acquired by the St. Lawrence Seaway and Power Project. Tetford, 17.

Porter: a surname used as specific: **Porter Hill**: *Quarterly*, 16 (1971), no. 1, p. 9; t Hermon. / **Porter Hill Cemetery**: t. Hermon. Also **Hermon Hill Cemetery**. / **Porter Hill Road**: r., t. Edwards; r., t. Hermon; / **Porter Hill School**: no. 3, common school, t. Hermon. 1915 USGS Russell Quad.

Post: Here, personal n.: **Post Henderson Road**: r., t. Clifton, south of Route 3, southwest corner of t. Origin n. unknown. / **Post Road**: r., t. Pierrepont, n. Peter Post family.

Postwood: desc. n., place where posts are cut from the woods: **Postwood Park**: t. Potsdam, on Racquette River near Hannawa Falls. / **Postwood Road**: t. Potsdam, from Hannawa Falls to Postwood Park.

Potato Street: r., t. Morristown, in Brier Hill, named either for a giant crop of potatoes or for the potato starch mill. *Quarterly*, 10 (1965), no. 4, p. 14. Also **Brier Hill-Longs Corner Road**.

Potsdam: t. northern interior of the county. One of the ten original t., formed as 7th in the county on Feb. 21, 1806. Sold to William Constable when the Macomb Purchase was divided. Constable sold his land to

David, Matthew, and Levinus Clarkson and their associates. Benjamin Raymond was the land agent for the Clarkson family; n. Potsdam, Germany, from a Slavic word meaning "under the oak." 1964 USGS Morley Quad. / **Potsdam**: v. inc. Mar. 3, 1831, in t. Potsdam. Amerindian n.: **Tewatenetarenies**, "place where the gravel rolls (settles) under the feet in dragging up the canoe." In 1803, the settlement began when Raymond built a sawmill and the dam; p. o. est. Mar. 6, 1807, Pierce Shepherd, first pm (Josiah Fuller, pm appointed in 1806, but the p. o. never opened), p. o. existing, ZIP 13676. 1964 USGS Potsdam Quad. See **Potsdam** t. / **Potsdam Drive**: s., v. Potsdam, on SUC campus. / **Potsdam Junction**: p. o. est. Oct. 30, 1867, John Raymond, pm, changed to **Norwood**, Nov. 24, 1875; now, **Norwood**. / **Potsdam, Morley and Madrid Plank-Road**: see **Plank Roads**. / **Potsdam Station**: now **Norwood**.

Potter: surname used as a specific: **Potter Brook**: t. Hopkinton, trib. Jordan River, n. Potter family. 1920 USGS Childwold Quad. / **Potter Mountain**: t. Colton, alt. 1,775, personal n. 1921 USGS Stark Quad.

Powell Road: r., t. Pitcairn, n. Powell family.

Power: n. related to a source of energy: **Power City**: nickname for **Massena**, for the power generated by the dams. Also **Power Village**. / **Power Road**: s., h. Hailesboro.

Powerhouse Hill Road: s., v. Norwood. Also **River Road**. Also **Power House Road**.

Powers: surname used as specific, but sometimes possessive: **Powers Hall**: on Clarkson University campus, n. Alfred Raymond Powers (1885-1968), a faculty member in the Electrical Engineering Department for 41 years, / **Powers Road**: r., t. Pierrepont, n. Simon Powers family. / **Powers Street**: s., v. Canton, n. J. C. Power. Beers, p. 13, shows Power living in the general area, but shows no street.

Prairie Street: s., v. Norwood.

Pratt Place: s., v. Massena, n. Solomon Pratt family.

Pray: family n.: **Pray Road**: r., t. Lisbon, n. Hiram, Jack, and Aaron Pray families. / **Pray School**: no. 29, common school, t. Lisbon.

President's House: a house designated as the president's house is located on or near each of the campuses of SUNY Canton College of Technology, St. Lawrence University, Clarkson University, and SUC at Potsdam.

Preston: surname used as a specific: Preston Isle: in St. Lawrence River, t. Hammond. 1958 USGS Chippewa Quad. Origin of name undetermined. / **Preston Street**: s., v. Gouverneur, n. John Bower Preston (1837-1898), attorney, Civil War officer, "good citizen." Cent. Souv., 63-64.

Prince Island: in Black Lake, t. Morristown. 1961 USGS Pope Mills Quad. Origin n. unknown.

Pritchard Pavilion: at St. Lawrence State hospital, n. John A. Pritchard, a physician and director. *Quarterly*, 11 (1966), no. 4, p. 19.

Proctor: surname used as a specific: **Proctor Avenue**: s., c. Ogdensburg, n. Walter L. Proctor from NH, president of the successful Skillings, Whitney and Barnes Lumber Company, trustee, city alderman, and mayor from 1871-1875. / **Proctor Lane**: s., c. Ogdens- burg, n. Proctor family.

Proctors Point: on St. Lawrence River, t. Morristown. Also, **Proctor's Point**. Bogardus, 81.

Prospect: commendatory n., usually hoping for a good future, especially in commerce; sometimes for the view. **Prospect Avenue**: s., v. Massena. / **Prospect Court**: s., v. Massena. / **Prospect Street**: s., v. Canton; s., v. Gouverneur; s., v. Norwood; s., v. Potsdam.

Public Campsite Road; r. around part of the shore of Cranberry Lake, t. Clifton.

Pudding Hill: t. Potsdam. Also, **Puddin' Hill**. See **West Potsdam** for folk legend.

Pulp Mill School: no. 10, common school, t. Fine, n. mill.

Pulpit Rock: t. Rossie, near Brasie Corners, a natural rock formation used as a pulpit by early settlers who held services at the rock. It is 70 feet high, with a cavity at its base measuring 18 feet deep by 12 feet wide. *Quarterly*, 11 (1966), no. 2, p. 18.

Pump House Road: s., h. Piercefield, n. desc.

Pumpkin Hill Road: r., t. Parishville. Also **Keener Road**.

Punchlock: see **Punch Lock**.

Punch Lock: An affectionate nickname for **Depeyster**: "In 1862 Punchlock was the center of social life as well as being the trading center." The Punchlock or Pill-lock gun was made here in the early 1840s. Nina Smithers, "Depeyster in 1862," *Quarterly*, 10 (1965), no. 3, p. 7. Also, see *Quarterly*, 9 (1964), no. 3, p. 11.

Purmort Cemetery: t. DePeyster, on West Road between Factory Road and Kokomo Road, n. Richard Purmort family. 1963 USGS Heuvelton Quad.

Putney School: no. 10, common school, t. Lisbon, n. Obadiah Putney family.

Putnam Corners: t. Russell, n. Bainbridge Putnam from Sutton, MA; came with parents through Jefferson Co. 1915 USGS Russell Quad. Also, **Putnams Corners.**

Pyrites: h., n. iron pyrite deposits, t. Canton. *Quarterly*, 10 (1965), no. 3, p. 12.; p. o. est. Feb. 12, 1894, Frank L. Pelton, pm, existing, ZIP 13677. In 1903 the DeGrasse Paper Co developed property here and built a $700,000 paper mill. *Watertown Daily Times*, Sept. 26, 1902, p. 16, cols. 2-6, illus. 1964 **Pyrites (Station)** Canton Quad. 1963 Canton Quad. / **Pyrites-Russell Road**: r., t. Russell, Canton. / **Pyrites School**: no. 28, common school, t. Canton.

Q

Quaker Settlement: t. Brasher; begun in 1824 by a group of Quakers. *Quarterly*, 14 (1969), no. 4, p. 5. / **Quaker Settlement School**: no. 2, common school, t. Brasher.

Quarry: place where stone is excavated: **Quarry Road**: s., v., and r., t. Gouverneur. / **Quarry School**: no. 21, common school, t. Potsdam.

Quenell Road: r., t. Massena, n. Quenell family.

R

Rabbit: for presence of the animal: **Rabbit Island**: in St. Lawrence River, t. Hammond. 1958 USGS Chippewa Quad. / **Rabbit Island Group**: four islands (includes **Rabbit Island**), in St. Lawrence River, t. Hammond. 1958 USGS Chippewa Quad.

Rackerton: See **Raymondville**. This n., which may be claimed as a misprint, appears in Durant, 301:

"The village of Raymondville was originally called Racker- ton, but is generally known as the lower village."

Racket: The n. of the river has been a subject of debate and scholarly papers. A good case can be made for **Racket River** as an early n., one which appears on very early maps. The r. known now as **Racquette** or **Raquette** (depending on the way one wishes to spell it) was described as a "noisy river" because the many rapids sounded noisy. In fact, the Amerindians recognized this quality and in one instance named a place **Nihanawate**, "noisy water," from which the spelling of **Hannawa Falls** developed. Whether this **Racket** was written by the French as **Racquette** or that **Raquette** was anglicized as **Racket** has not been determined and may never be unless historical records are found to substantiate either theory. Some of the **Racket** n. include **Racket Lake**: see **Racquette River**. *Quarterly*, 8 (1963), no. 2, pp. 7-8. / **Racket River**: see **Racquette River**. / **Racket River School**: no. 3, common school, t. Massena.

Racketon: t. Norfolk, n. compound of **Racket** + **town**.

Rackett River: h., t., Massena, p. o. est. Sept. 4, 1830, Amos Ransom, first pm, closed Nov. 6, 1865, reopened Feb. 1, 1866, Smith T. Barnes, pm, closed Feb. 5, 1870, reopened Mar. 6, 1870, Mary D. Forbes, pm, closed May 31, 1919. Hough, 575, erroneously claims est. Feb. 28, 1842, with Peter Vilas, pm. This spelling prob. represents a confusion of **Ra(c)quette** and **Racket**. Also, **Racket River**. The h. no longer exists.

Racketville: see **Norwood**, n. compound of **Racket** + **ville**.

Racquette River: Origin of n. uncertain. In its French form it means "snow shoe," perhaps for the shape of the meadow where it flows into the St. Lawrence River at Massena. Another theory is that it was first n. for the lake (**Racquette Lake**, Franklin County) that is the source of the river. The n. occurred when "Sir John Johnson's party of Tories and Indians, fleeing from Johnstown to Montreal in 1776, abandoned their snowshoes in a huge pile there with the onset of spring weather." (Clipping, ca 1974). A compelling theory is that it is a translation from the Amerindian name, **Nihanawate**, "noisy river." On very early maps it appears as **Racket River** (see **Racket**). The spelling has not become stabilized. The USGS uses **Ra-**

quette. 1964 USGS Hogansburg Quad. Also, **Little Black River**, to distinguish it from **Black River**. See **Raquette** for other entries. / **Racquette Road**: s., v. Massena; r., t. Potsdam.

Racquetteville: see **Norwood.**

Radch Road: r., t. Stockholm, north off Pleasant Valley Road, western part of t. Origin of n. undetermined; may be a misspelling. See 1988 Highway Map, St. Lawrence County, 13F.

Ragnarock: t. Canton, the Cowen Mansion on the Canton-Madrid Road. Claimed to be of German origin, but also seems to be a play on words: **Rag-on-a-Rock.**

Ragnavok Island: in Chippewa Bay. *Quarterly*, 16 (1971), n. 3, p. 11. Also **Ragney Island**.

Ragney Island: see **Ragnavok Island.**

Railroad: trains and railroads being of utmost importance in the 19th and early 20th centuries, each community usually had a road, street, or avenue of the n. leading to the station or depot: **Railroad Avenue**: s., v. Canton; s., v. Gouverneur; s., v. Norwood; r., t. Potsdam. / **Railroad Street**: r., t. Gouverneur; r., t. Lawrence; s., v. Massena; s., c. Ogdensburg.

Rainbow: desc. of many-colored vegetation or rock, or of rainbows seen in the spray of falls, or for reflection from a body of water: **Rainbow Brook**: t. Parishville, trib. Racquette River. 1908 USGS Potsdam Quad; 1964 USGS Rainbow Falls Quad. / **Rainbow Falls**: in South Branch Grass(e) River, t. Clare. 1865 Beers, p. 86; 1902 Blankman; 1921 Stark Quad. / in Racquette River, t. Parishville. 1896 New; 1908 USGS Potsdam Quad; 1912 Stoddard; 1964 USGS Rainbow Falls Quad. / **Rainbow Falls Reservoir**: in Racquette River, t. Parishville. 1964 USGS Rainbow Falls Quad.

Rampart Mountain: t. Colton, alt. 2,411 ft., n. massive rocks that look like a fortification. 1896 **Rampart Mts.** New; 1908 Adm; 1954 USGS Tupper Lake Quad.

Randall: many families in the county have the n.: **Randall Road**: r., t. Lisbon. / **Randall Brook**: stream, trib. South Branch Grass(e) River, t. Clare. 1915 Russell Quad. / **Randall Court**: s., v. Massena. / **Randall Drive**: s., v. Massena. / **Randall Hill**: t. Clare. 1915 Russell Quad. / **Ran-**

dall Road: r., t. Waddington.

Randle Meadow Brook: t. Hopkinton, trib. West Branch St. Regis River, Hopkinton Brook, and Stony Brook, n. Randle family. 1964 USGS Sylvan Falls Quad.

Ranger School: state school for forest rangers, t. Fine.

Ranger School Road: r. t. Fine, n. forest rangers and the school; r., h. Wanakena, n. ranger school.

Ransom Avenue: s., v. Massena, n. Amos Ransom.

Rapid Isle Road: s., t. Hailesboro.

Rapid Plat: see **Rapide Plat**.

Rapide Plat: in channel of St. Lawrence River, t. Waddington. *Quarterly*, 3 (1958), no. 1, npn. See **Ogden Island**. 1942 USGS Murphy Island Quad.

Rapids School: no. 10, common school, t., Rossie, on bank of Indian River. 1949 USGS Hammond Quad.

Raquette: an alternate spelling of **Racquette**: **Raquette Club**: private forest and game preserve, 1,750 acres, t. Clifton. See **Forest Commission Report**, 1893. / **Raquette River**: t. Massena; see **Racquette River**. 1964 USGS Raquette River Quad. / **Raquette River Post Office**: h., t. Massena, on both banks of river, six miles below Massena Springs, settled about 1804. Durant, 405, writes, "It contains a few stores, shops, and a post-office, which was established about 1830, with A. Ransom, postmaster." Hough, 575, gives the date of Feb. 28, 1842, for **Rackett River**, with Peter Vilas, first pm. / **Raquette River Road**: r., t. Massena; r., t. Parishville. / **Raquette Road**: s., v. Potsdam, along Racquette River.

Raquetteville: near Norfolk, founded by Benjamin G. Baldwin; also, **Racketville**. Durant, 22. In 1852, a dam eight feet tall was built; p. o.,est. Dec. 30, 1850, as **North Potsdam**, with Rollin Ashley as first pm., disc. Oct. 30, 1867. Also, **Potsdam Junction/Station**. Now, **Norwood**. *Quarterly*, 9 (1964), no. 3, p. 4.

Rarick Cemetery: t. Hammond, n. Rarick family, on Route 37, north of South Hammond. 1961 USGS Hammond Quad.

Raspberry Island: in Black Lake, t. Morristown, n. shrub of the genus *Rubus*. 1961 USGS Hammond Quad.

Ratman Road: see **Rutman Road.**

Rayburn School: no. 25, common school, t. Lisbon, n. Rayburn family.

Raymond: several places in the county are named for Benjamin Raymond, a surveyor of the Macomb Purchase, the founder of Potsdam, and land agent for the Clarkson family. In 1816, he moved to **Rackerton** (Durant, 301) and immediately the place became known as **Raymondville** in his honor. Durant, 237, described "Land-agent Raymond standing in the door of his log office, with a bottle of rum ready to welcome newcomers, . . ." He built a school on what is now Union Street, Potsdam, in 1816, which is claimed as the beginning of SUC, Potsdam. *Quarterly*, 6 (1961), no. 1, p. 12. Places n. for him: **Raymond Hall**: the administration building on the SUC, Potsdam, campus. / **Raymond School**: no. 10, common school, t. Norfolk. / **Raymond Street**: s., v. Potsdam. / **Raymondville State Forest**, #33, t. Norfolk. / **Raymondville**: h. in northern part of t. Norfolk, p. o. est. Sept. 2, 1840, John Woodard, pm (Hough, 575), existing, ZIP 13678; Amerindian name: **Tssilakoontieta**, "where they leave their canoes." 1964 USGS Norfolk Quad. / **Raymondville Cemetery** / **Raymondville School**: no. 2, common school, t. Norfolk.

Readway Ponds: four ponds, t. Fine. 1916 USGS Oswegatchie Quad. Poss. **Red Way** or **Redway Ponds**. n. Redaway family.

Reagan: family n.: **Reagan Road**: r., t. Stockholm. Also **Reagon Road**. / **Reagan School**: no. 9, common school, t. Norfolk.

Rebert Hall: on St. Lawrence University campus, n. Professor Charles M. Rebert.

Red: a popular color-n., sometimes desc. of a feature that has a russet color from a mineral deposit or of a place or building that has been painted red: **Red Brook**: t. Lawrence. / **Red Mills**: h., t. Lisbon, formerly **Gallooville**, **Gallopville**, or **Galloupville** after the Gallop Rapids in the St. Lawrence River. In 1804, Daniel W. Church built the first of two mills and painted them red. *Quarterly*, 18 (1973), no. 3, p. 13. 1963 USGS Red Mills Quad. Derived name: **Red Mills Cemetery**, near site of old Episcopal Church. / **Red Point Island**: in Black Lake, t. Morristown. 1961 USGS Pope Mills Quad. / **Red Rock to Kents Corners Road**: t. DeKalb, near marble quarry. Red Rock was n. of cheese factory and terminus of Clifton Railroad. Ruins still there. *Quarterly*, 11 (1966), no. 2, p. 19. / **Red School**: t. Fine. 1916 Oswegatchie Quad; t. Russell, no. 16, common school, n. color. 1915 USGS Russell Quad.

Redington School: no. 22, common school, t. Stockholm, n. Redington family. Also **Reddington School** [a misprint].

Redfield Road: r., t. Gouverneur; now, **Smith Road**.

Redwater Brook: t. Brasher, stream, trib. Deer River, n. color from bog iron ore in area. 1964 North lawrence Quad.

Reed Road: r., t. Stockholm, n. Reed family; s., v. Massena, n. Stephen Reed.

Reese Road: r., t. DeKalb, prob. n. Rev. Thomas D. Rees. Welsh pastor, but with spelling change.

Regan: a common surname in the county: **Regan Road**: r., t. Colton, Higley Flow area; r., t. Potsdam; r., t. Stockholm.

Regis Boulevard: s., v. Massena, n. for St. Regis.

Reid Street: s., v. Gouverneur, n. Reid family.

Reimer Road: s., h. Star Lake, private s., n. C. C. Reimer, a summer resident.

Remington: a famous surname in the county: **Remington Avenue**: s., h. Norfolk, n. Remington family. / **Remington Circle**: s., c. Ogdensburg, n. Frederic Remington. / **Remington Museum**: The man- sion built by David Parish was converted into a museum to honor Frederic Remington (1861-1909), b. in Canton, NY, became a noted artist of the American West, known for his illustrations and sculptures of cowboys and Amerindians. / **Remington Road**: r., t. Hopkinton, n. Remington family.

Rensselaer: a famous surname in the county: **Rensselaer Falls**: v. in t. Canton, p. o. est. Dec. 19, 1851, Archibald Shull, pm (Hough, 575), existing, ZIP 13680; n. Stephen and Henry Van Rensselaer, who owned land and built a sawmill in 1839. Stephen became lieutenant governor, state senator, supporter of the Erie Canal, and a founder of Rensselaer [Polytechnic] Institute. Formerly, **Canton Falls**. Also, formerly, **Tateville**, n. Robert Tate, surveyor, first sawmill owner, forge builder, and original member of firm of Tate, Chafee, & Co. He donated the land for the village. 1963 Rensselaer Falls Quad; Hamilton Child, p. 96. **Tateville** is sometimes spelled **Taitville**. The 1892 baseball team was nicknamed **Red Stockings**. Derived names: **Rensselaer Avenue**: s., c. Ogdensburg, n. Henry Van Rensselaer. / **Rensselaer Falls Cemetery** / **Rensselaer Falls-Heuvelton Road**: r., t. Oswegatchie. See **Heuvelton Street**, v. Rensselaer Falls. / **Rensselaer Falls School**: no. 24, common school, t. Canton. / **Rensselaer Street**: s., v. Heuvelton, n. Henry Van Rensselaer but more immediately for the v. and the Rensselaer Falls-Heuvelton Road. / **Rensselaer Street**: s., v. Rensselaer Falls, n. Henry Van Rensselaer. The street goes from West Front Street to the Aldrich home, crossing the bridge over the Oswegatchie River and also State Street.

Reservoir Hill: t. Gouverneur, alt. 636. 1956 USGS Gouverneur Quad.

Reuben: personal n.: **Reuben Hill**: t. Parishville, n. Reuben Hill family. / **Reuben Hill School**: no. 16, common school, t. Parishville. Listed as **Hill School**.

Reves Road: r., t. DeKalb, east off Old Northerner Road, poss. n. Henry Reve. Durant, 83.

Reynolds: surname used as a specific: **Reynolds Corners**: t. Russell, n. Reynolds family. 1915 USGS Russell Quad. / **Reynolds Hall**: on Clarkson University campus, n. Blythe M. Reynolds (1894-1961), a graduate in 1916, served 17 years as trustee. / **Reynolds Road**: r., t. Potsdam, n. Reynolds family.

Rice: a surname used as a specific: **Rice Road**: r., t. Canton; r., t. Edwards. / **Rice School**: no. 5, common school, t., Fowler. / **Rice Corners Cemetery**: t. Fowler. 1951 Lake Bonaparte Quad. / **Rices Corners**: t. Fowler, n. Rice family. 1951 USGS Lake Bonaparte Quad. Also, **Rice Corner**.

Rich Road: r., t. Canton, n. Rich family; r., t. Macomb, Pleasant Lake area.

Richard Eddy Sykes Residence: see **Sykes**.

Richard Street: s., h. Parishville, n. son of David Parish.

Richards: surname used as a specific: **Richards Field**: airport, t. Massena. 1964 Raquette River Quad. / **Richards Point**: on St. Lawrence

River, t. Louisville. 1964 USGS Massena Quad. / **Richards Street**: s., v. Massena.

Richardson: surname. **Richardson Hall**: on St. Lawrence University campus, the first building, 1856, then **College Hall**, n. Gary Richardson, benefactor and friend of President Almon Gunnison. / **Richardson School**: no. 3. common school, t., Brasher, n. Richardson family; no. 27, common school, t. Colton. / **Richardson Street**: s. in Terrace Park, t. Morristown, n. a Methodist bishop.

Richville: v., t. DeKalb, p. o. est. Mar. 5, 1828, John C. Rich, pm (Hough, 575), existing, ZIP 13681; n. for one of its founders, Salmon (also known as Solomon) Rich, who migrated from Westertown, MA, in 1803. The other founder was Jonathan Haskins, who had been a member of Cooper's party. The v. was first known as **Riches Settlement**. The v. was then named **Richville**. Information by letter, May 17, 1976, from Pauline H. Maas, 21 Sweden Hill Rd., Brockport, NY, daughter of Edward C. Rich, a grandson of Salmon. Also, **Rich's Settlement**. Hamilton Child, p. 107; 1956 USGS Richville Quad. / **Richville-Bigelow Road**; r., t. DeKalb. / **Richville Bridge Road**: r., v. Richville, t. DeKalb, extension of River Street. / **Richville School**: no. 3, common school, t. DeKalb. / **Richville Station**: On Rome, Watertown & Ogdensburg Railroad, 1-1/2 m. from Richville. See also, **Bigelow.**

Rickard Road: s., v. Massena, n. Leonard and Weston Rickard.

Rickards Creek: t. Massena, n. Israel Rickard, early settler and blacksmith shop owner. Noted as **Rickard's Creek** in Dumas, 15. A descendant, Alpheus Rickard, operated a scow ferry across the Grass(e) River in the 1890s. Dumas, 17.

Rickey Rapids: t. Colton, Hollywood, on Jordan River. 1860 Merrit; 1880 Ely; 1883 Ely-Wallace. Also **Rickey's Rapids** and **Hawes Rapids**.

Ridge: elevated land areas were naturally attractive passages for horse-drawn vehicles; hence, the desc. specific n.: **Ridge Road**: r., t. Brasher; r., t. Fine; r., t. Louisville; r., t. Pierrepont; r., t. Waddington. / **Ridge Road School**: no. 4, common school, t. Oswegatchie. / **Ridge School**: no. 4, common school, in Chipman, t. Waddington. / **Ridge Street**: s., h. DeKalb Junction; s., v. Norwood.

Ridgewood Avenue: s., v. Massena, desc. and promotional.

Riehl Road: r., t. Colton. A fatal accident occurred in the 1960s near the home of William Riehl. Troopers suggested the n. for identification in an emergency.

Riggs: n. David Riggs, early settler in Parishville Center: **Riggs Corner**: t. Parishville. / **Riggs School**: no. 8, common school, t. Parishville. / **Riggs Drive**: s., h. Hannawa Falls.

Ripley Street: s., v. Massena.

Risley: family n.: **Risley Cemetery**: on **Risley Road**. / **Risley Road**: r., t. DeKalb, n. Nelson Ariel Risley, settled with wife Orpha Stiles, ca 1830. / **Risley School**: no. 19, common school, t. DeKalb.

Ritchie Road: r., t. DeKalb, n. Thomas Ritchie, early settler.

Rite Road: see **Wright Road**.

River: serves as both a specific and generic n., widely used in many ways, to indicate a view of a stream, to designate a road leading to or alongside a stream, or to promote real estate: **River Jordan**: see **Jordan River**. / **River Road**: r., t. Clifton; r., t. DeKalb; r., t. Edwards; r., t. Fowler; s., h. Hailesboro; r., t. Hammond, Morristown; r., t. Lisbon; r., t. Madrid; s., h. Newton Falls; r., t. Norfolk; r., t. Oswegatchie; r., t. Pierrepont; r., t. Potsdam, in Hannawa Falls; r., t. Rossie; r., t. Waddington; s., v. Norwood. Also **Powerhouse Hill Road**. / **River Road School**: no. 14, common school, t. DeKalb. / **River School**: no. 7, common school, t. Waddington. / **River Street**: s., v. Brasher Falls; s., t. Colton; r., t. Hopkinton; s., v. Gouverneur; s., v. Massena; s., h. Morley, along Grass(e) River; s., h. Nicholville, along St. Regis River; s., v. Norfolk, along Racquette River; s., h. Norwood, along Racquette River; s., v. Richville; s., h. Russell. / **River Street East**: s., c. Ogdensburg. / **River Street West**: s., c. Ogdensburg. / **River View Drive**: r., t. Louisville, of the St. Lawrence River; r., t. Norfolk, of the Racquette River. / **River View Road**: s., v. Morristown, n. view of St. Lawrence River.

Riverdale: a survey township, now t. Hopkinton. *Quarterly*, 5 (1960), no. 2, p. 9. Although desc., the n. is also has ameliorative and “romantic” connotations. / **Riverdale Mountain**: t. Hopkinton, alt. 1,975 ft. 1908

Adm; 1912 Stoddard; 1912 USGS Nicholville Quad; 1964 USGS Sylvan Falls Quad.

Riverhill Forest: county forest, t. Stockholm.

Riverside: a desc. placement, commendatory or promotional: **Riverside Avenue**: s., c. Ogdensburg, along St. Lawrence River. / **Riverside Cemetery**: v., t. Gouverneur, on bank of Oswegatchie River; v., t. Edwards. 1956 USGS Edwards Quad; t. Oswegatchie. 1963 USGS Ogdensburg East Quad; t. Pierrepont, at Hannawa Falls; t. Potsdam, on bank of Racquette River, near Norwood. 1943 USGS Potsdam Quad; t. Rossie, on Indian River. 1961 USGS Muskellunge Lake Quad. / **Riverside Drive**: r., t. Colton, along the Racquette River (Route 56); r., t. Oswegatchie, along the St. Lawrence River (Route 37); s., v. Canton, along Grass(e) River, formerly Water Street; s., h. Cranberry Lake, along Oswegatchie River; s., v. Norwood, along Racquette River; s., h. Raymondville, along Racquette River. / **Riverside Forest**: county forest on north side of St. Regis River, t. Hopkinton. / **Riverside Parkway**: s., v. Massena, along St. Lawrence River. / **Riverside School**: no. 26, common school, t. Canton.

Riverview: both desc. and commendatory: **Riverview Cemetery**: t. Parishville, formerly **Willisville Cemetery**. / **Riverview Drive**: s., v. Potsdam, along Racquette River. Formerly, **Water Street**. / **Riverview Street**: s., v. Massena, along St. Lawrence River

Roaring Brook, three brooks noted; desc. of sound: t. Piercefield, trib. Hamlin Bay, Tupper Lake 1896 New; t. Colton, flows into Racquette River near Hollywood. 1896 New; t. Colton, trib. South Branch Grass(e) River. 1954 USGS Tupper Lake Quad.

Rob Roy Island: in St. Lawrence River, t. Hammond, perhaps n. novel by Sir Walter Scott. 1958 USGS Chippewa Quad. Also **Robroy Island**. Also see *Quarterly*, 16 (1971), no. 3, p. 11.

Robb: early Scots family in the area: **Robb Road**: r., t. Rossie. / **Robb School**: no. 9, common school, t. Rossie, n. Robb family. 1949 USGS Hammond Quad.

Robbin Lake: see **Big Lake**.

Robert Moses State Park: t. Massena, park n. for the Port Authority commissioner who directed the construction of the Seaway.

Robert's Mill: See **Madrid**.

Robin Lake: Irving Batcheller claimed that **Bog Lake** is now **Robin Lake**. *Quarterly*, 14 (1969), no. 1, p. 22.

Robinson: a rather common surname used as a specific for several places: **Robinson Bay**: in St. Lawrence River, t. Massena, n. Daniel Robinson, first permanent settler in Massena. He came from Shrewsbury, VT, and was said to have been a slave owner. Dumas, 3; 1964 USGS Raquette River Quad. / **Robinson Creek**: t. Fowler, trib. Oswegatchie River, n. Robinson family. 1956 USGS Gouverneur Quad; t. Massena, trib. Wiley-Dondero Canal, but flowed into Robinson Bay before construction of St. Lawrence Seaway. See **Robinson Bay**. Dumas, 3; 1964 USGS Raquette River Quad. / **Robinson Road**: r., t. Macomb; s., v. Massena, n. Daniel Robinson. Dumas, 57. / **Robinson School**: no. 10, common school, t. Fowler. 1915 USGS Gouverneur Quad. / **Robinson Street**: s., v. Massena.

Robroy Island: see **Rob Roy Island**.

Rock: occurs both as a specific and a generic, n. usually found coupled with other forms, sometimes in pure compounds. In the United States, **Rock** is far more popular than is **Stone**, the preferred n. in England and other English-speaking countries. / **Rock, The**: t. Hammond, island in Chippewa Bay. *Quarterly*, 16 (1971), no. 3, p. 11. See **The Rock**. / **Rock Cut**: geographic feature on Route 37, v. Morristown. Bogardus, 156. / **Rock Hollow Road**: t. Hermon. Also **Rockhollow Road**. / **Rock Hollow School**: no. 11, common school, t. Hermon, n. for rocks that were close around the school building, which was built about 1850. 1915 USGS Gouverneur Quad. / **Rock Island**: t. Hammond. / **Rock Island Bridge**: t. Gouverneur, over Oswegatchie River on Rock Island Road. 1956 USGS Richville Quad. / **Rock Island Road**: r., t. Gouverneur. See *Quarterly*, 18 (1973), no. 2, p. 4. / **Rock Island Road School**: no. 13, common school, t. Gouverneur. 1915 USGS Gouverneur Quad **Rock Island School**. / **Rock Island Street**: s., v. Gouverneur. / **Rock Lake**: pond, t. Fine. *Quarterly*, 5 (1960), no. 1, npn. 1916 USGS Oswegatchie Quad. / **Rock Point**: t. Piercefield. 1860 Merrit. / **Rock Pond**: t. Clare. 1921 Stark Quad; t. Fine. *Quarterly*, 5 (1960), no. 1, npn; t. Hopkinton. 1858 Rogerson; 1860 Merrit; 1896

New; 1902 Blankman; 1920 USGS Childwold Quad; t. Parishville. 1865 **Round Pond** Beers; 1896 **Round Pond** New; 1898 **Round Pond** EGB map; 1902 **Round Pond** Blankman; 1908 USGS Potsdam Quad; 1912 Stoddard; 1964 USGS Rainbow Falls Quad.

Rockaway: origin n. unknown: **Rockaway Point**: on St. Lawrence River, t. Waddington. 1963 USGS Sparrow Quad. / **Rockaway Street**: s., v. Massena.

Rockby Pond: t. Parishville.

Rockhollow Road: r., t. Hermon. Also **Rock Hollow Road.**

Rockingham Place: home of Benjamin Nevins, t. Oswegatchie. *Quarterly*, 14 (1969), no. 4, p. 6.

Rocky Mountain: t. Clifton, alt. 1,700. 1911 USGS Cranberry Lake Quad.

Rodwell Mill Road; t., Parishville, n. mill, n. for John Rodwell.

Rogers Drive: s., v. Norfolk, n. Rogers family.

Rollway Bay: on south side of Black Lake, t. Morristown, "received its name from the 'Rollway,' a place between high rocks on one side and a ledge of rocks on the other, this being the only place near this section where it was possible for the early pioneer to roll the logs (cut to clear the land) into Black Lake, to be floated to the mouth of Fish Creek, thence to Pope's sawmill." India Murton, "Rollway Bay," *Quarterly*, 9 (1964), no. 1, p. 7. Also, **Roll-way**, *Quarterly*, 7 (962), no. 4, p. 14. 1961 USGS Pope Mills Quad. / **Rollway Road**: r., t. Macomb.

Rome, Watertown, & Ogdensburg Railroad: R. W. & O. R. R. serviced Massena and other stops, but only after connecting with the Ogdensburg and Lake Champlain Railroad (O. & L C. R. R.). Dumas, 61. Mott Meldrim, "North Country Railroading," *Quarterly*, 15 (1970), no. 1, p. 7.

Romeo Avenue: s., v. Massena, n. Romeo family.

Romoda: Joseph J. Romoda, an academic dean and vice president of St. Lawrence University: **Romoda Memorial Drive and Gateway**: s., v. Canton, street entering St. Lawrence University; also simply **Romoda Drive** **Ramoda** is a misprint.

Rooky Road: r., t. Waddington, n.

Rooky family.

Roosevelt Street: s., v. Massena, n. Theodore Roosevelt, 26th president of the U. S.

Rooseveltown: h., t. Massena, p. o. transferred from **Nyando** Nov. 1, 1933, William B. Milmoe, pm, existing, ZIP 13683; n. Franklin Delano Roosevelt, 32nd president of the U. S. 1964 USGS Hogansburg Quad.

Root Road: r., t. Potsdam, n. Root family.

Rose: n. either for a family or for the flower bush: **Rose Road**: r., t. Pitcairn, n. Rose family. / **Rose Brier Drive**: s., v. Massena, n. descriptive and promotional.

Rosenbarker Brook: t. Hopkinton, trib. Dan Wright Brook, n. Rosenbarker family. 1964 USGS Sylvan Falls Quad.

Roslyn Pond: t. Parishville.

Ross: surname used as a specific: **Ross Hall**: on Clarkson University campus, n. John Alexander Ross, who came to Clarkson in 1911 and served as a professor, administrator, and president. / **Ross Road**: r., t. Lisbon, n. Ross family.

Rosseel Street: s., c. Ogdensburg, n. Joseph Rosseel, from Ghent, Belgium, arrived in 1807 at the age of 25 as a land agent and evaluator for David Parish. He settled in Ogdensburg and became a merchant. He served as a village trustee for several terms and as village president. / **Rosseel Street North**: s., c. Ogdensburg; same as **North Rosseel Street**.

Rossie: t. southwestern border with Jefferson Co., n. "From Rossie Castle in Scotland, which was owned by the husband of David Parish's sister. Her name was Rossie, but she was usually called Rosa." Durant, 313. Formed Jan. 27, 1813, from Russell (Durant, 312). 1961 USGS Hammond Quad. / **Rossie**: h., t. Rossie, p. o. transferred from **Rossie Iron Works** Nov. 27, 1827, Stillman Fuller, pm. closed to become rural branch Dec. 31, 1960, reopened Jan. 1, 1961 from **Hammond**, ZIP 13646. Hough, 575, claims erroneously that p. o. est. May 6, 1816, Roswell Ryon, pm. Formerly, **Howard's Mill**, n. James Howard, who bought the land in 1817. Rossie was called the "Pittsburgh of the North." *Quarterly*, 1 (1956), n. 2, npn. 1961 USGS Hammond Quad. / **Rossie Iron Works**: p. o. est. Nov. 20, 1814, Francis Jourdain, pm, changed to **Rossie** Nov. 27, 1827. / **Rossie-Macomb Road**: r., t. Rossie, Macomb. / **Rossie-Oxbow Road**: r., t. Rossie. / **Rossie-Redwood Road**: r., t. Rossie. / **Rossie School**: no. 1, common school, t. Rossie. Also, **Rossie Village School**.

ROTC Building: on Clarkson University campus, houses the Military Science Department and the Reserve Officers Training Corps. This building, acquired in 1962, was formerly the Episcopal Rectory.

Roulston's Creek: t. Oswegatchie, n. Roulston family.

Round: shape-n. for any area that looks circular; occasionally a translation from an Amerindian word. **Round Hill**: t. Fine. 1916 USGS Oswegatchie Quad. / **Round Island**: in St. Lawrence River, t. Lisbon. 1906 Red Mills Quad. / **Round Lake**: pond, t. Fine, alt. 1,319 ft. 1916 USGS Oswegatchie Quad. / **Round Mountain**: t. Clifton, alt. 2,050 ft. 1896 New; 1902 Blankman. / **Round Pond**: see **Ormsbee Pond**. / **Round Pond**: t. Fine, alt. 1,233. *Quarterly*, 5 (1960), no. 1, npn. 1915 USGS Russell Quad / **Round Pond**: see **Rock Pond**, t. Parishville. / **Round Pond Road**: r., t. Parishville.

Roundtop Mountain: n. shape, t. Fine, alt. 2,300 ft. 1896 **Plains Mountain** New; 1902 **Plains Mountain** Blankman; 1919 USGS Cranberry Quad.

Rowen Road: r., t. Lisbon, n. Rowen family.

Rowley: surname used as specific: **Rowley Labs**: on Clarkson University campus, n. William J. Rowley, President of Swartout & Rowley, Inc., Clarkson trustee. / **Rowley Street**: s., v. Gouverneur, n. Aaron and Moses Rowley, surveyors, 1923. Cent. Souv., 45.

Roxburgh Settlement: See **Scotch Settlement**.

Royce School: no. 18, common school, t. Potsdam, n. Royce family.

Ruby Corner: t. Macomb. 1961 USGS Pope Mills Quad. Also, **Ruby Corners**. Origin of n. unknown.

Ruddy Road: r., t. Madrid, n. Ruddy family.

Rundell Road: r., t. DeKalb. Poss, n. George Rundell, barn builder. Cent. Souv., 21. See **Jeffers Road**.

Rushton: n. J. Henry Rushton, boat

builder, "very light boats for fishing and sporting purposes" and "Rob Roy" canoe. He began building in 1874. Durant, p. 217. The annual canoe race on the Grass(e) River in Canton is n. for Rushton. **Rushton Drive**: s., v. Canton. / **Rushton Falls**: in the Grass(e) River at the foot of the Grasse River Apartments, v. Canton; see "Naming of 'Rushton Falls' Not a Rush Job," *Watertown Daily Times*, Feb. 17, 1991, Sec. B, pp. 1, 7, cols. 1-5, 1-2.

Russell: t. southwest of center of county, tenth t. formed in St. Lawrence County, Mar. 27, 1807 (Durant, 426), n. Russell Attwater, who in 1798 purchased the land from Daniel McCormick, who wanted the place n. **Ballybean**, after his native place in Ireland. Durant, 426. Russell was called the "Hub of the North." *Quarterly*, 11 (1966), no. 4, p. 15; 5 (1960), no. 4, p. 9. 1964 USGS Pierrepont Quad. / **Russell**: h. in t. Russell, p. o. est. June 27, 1812, Pliny Goddard, pm (Hough, 575), existing, ZIP 13684. Also see Durant, 430. Settlers arrived, 1805. The arsenal was erected soon after the bill was passed, Feb. 24, 1809, authorizing Russell as site. See Durant, 431. In 1892 the baseball team was unimaginatively nicknamed **The Russells**. 1915 USGS Russell Quad. / **Russell Cemetery**: t. Russell. / **Knox Memorial High School**: t. Russell. Now consolidated as **Edwards-Knox Central School**. / **Russell-Martin Corners Road**: r., t. Canton, Russell. / **Russell- Pierrepont Road**: r., t. Russell, Pierrepont. / **Russell Pond**: t. Colton. 1908 USGS Potsdam Quad; 1912 Stoddard. / **Russell Road**: t. Piercefield; r., t. Hermon; s., v. Massena, n. John Russell. / **Russell School**: no. 1, common school, t. Russell. Also, **Russell Village School**. / **Russell Turnpike**: n. Russell "Long Falls" Attwater; inc. Apr. 5, 1810, designed to run from Carthage to Malone. Same as **St. Lawrence Turnpike**. / **Russell Turnpike Road**: r., t. Parishville.

Rutherford: family n.: **Rutherford Ridge**: t. Waddington, n. John and Thomas Rutherford, from Scotland. Same as **Scotch Ridge**. Tedford, 38-39. / **Rutherford Road**: r., t. Madrid; r., t. Potsdam.

Rutherville: settlement, t. Waddington, p. o. est. June 17, 1836, Thomas Rutherford, Jr., pm, closed July 30, 1904.

Rutman Road: r., t. Parishville, n. Rutman family; appears on some

Suspension foot bridge over the Grass(e) River in Russell.
Students crossed to Pestle St. School.

THE FORMER RUSSELL ARSENAL

When war threatened with Great Britain, the State Legislature passed the act to build several arsenals. Governor Thompson selected for one site a commanding hill above Russell village and the arsenal was built shortly after 1809. The walls were of native stone with the size of 30' b 50'. It was surrounded by a high stone wall, bristling with iron spikes. During the War of 181 a small company of soldiers was stationed there. In 1850 the arsenal was sold by the State together with 400 stand of arms. The building became the village school in 1860. It was town down after being ruined by fire in March of 1945.

maps as **Ratman Road** [misprint].

Ryan Road: r., t. Brasher, n. Ryan family.

S

Sabattis: h., t. Piercefield, n. Peter Sabattis, an Abenaki chief and longtime resident of St. Lawrence County, and a member of the 1812 surveying party. *Quarterly*, 13 (1968), no. 1, p. 6.

Sacred Heart School: v. Massena. 1964 USGS Massena Quad.

Sails School: Misprint for **Salls School**.

St. Henrys Cemetery: t. DeKalb, near DeKalb Junction. 1963 USGS Rensselaer Falls Quad.

St. Huberts Cemetery: t. Clifton.

St. James Cemetery: t. Gouverneur. 1956 USGS Gouverneur Quad.

St. Johns School: v. Morristown. 1963 USGS Morristown Quad.

St. Joseph Mine: t. Edwards, n. St. Joseph Lead Co.

St. Joseph Road: t. Edwards, n. mine.

St. Lawrence: Saint Laurentius (?-258), a martyr of Rome. He has become the most celebrated of those persecuted and executed by Valerian. He was born reportedly in Spain and came to Rome as a deacon of the Roman Catholic Church. When Valerian put to death Pope Sixtus II and most of the enemies of the Church, Laurentius appeared before him with the poor of the city, whereupon it was said he was sentenced to death by being broiled over a slow fire. French form: **St. Laurent**. See, also, **Hochelaga**. See Eugene Hatch, "Saint Lawrence," *Quarterly*, 17 (1972), no. 4, p. 3. Many names have derived from **St. Lawrence**: **St. Lawrence Academy**: Founded by Benjamin Raymond in 1816. Years later, this beginning, through many changes, became the Normal School and then SUC at Potsdam. See Lahey, **The Potsdam Tradition.** / **St. Lawrence Avenue**: n. St. Lawrence River, s., v. Hammond; s., c. Ogdensburg; s., v. Waddington. / **St. Lawrence Cemetery**: t. Lawrence; t. Louisville. 1964 USGS Louisville Quad. / **St. Lawrence Central School**: t. Lawrence. 1964 USGS Brasher Falls Quad. / **St. Lawrence County**: est. Mar. 3, 1802, n. the river; contains 2,880 sq. m., being the largest county in New York. Its northern boundary is the national line, in the channel of the St. Lawrence River between the United States and the Dominion of Canada. It is bounded on the south by Hamilton and Herkimer Counties, on the east by Franklin County, and on the west and southwest by Jefferson and Lewis Counties. "Largely unexplored in the 1700's, it was claimed by the Mohawks and Oneidas as a hunting ground. On old maps it is designated variously as Iroquoisia, deer hunting grounds of the Iroquois, or Coughsagage, beaver hunting country of the Six Nations." A map as late as 1798 shows no streams. "This country by reason of mountains, swamps and drowned lands is impassable and uninhabited." See Eugene Hatch, "The Ordeal of Sir John Johnson," *Quarterly*, 8 (1963), no. 2, p. 7. / **St. Lawrence County History Center**: The center for records and research into the history of the county, formerly housed in the county courthouse, now in a building behind the **Silas Wright House** in Canton. / **St. Lawrence International Campground Association**: organized in June 1874, 23 acres, to provide fine camping for GAR members and families, later called **Terrace Park**,, after the hotel, now a privately owned resort. / **St. Lawrence River**: Flows generally northeast from Lake Ontario to the Gulf of St. Lawrence, Atlantic Ocean. It was n. (1535) by Jacques Cartier on the saint's day, August 10. He applied the name to a harbor, but it spread to the gulf and river and finally the county. The river also forms part of the boundary between Canada and the United States. Nickname, **The River**. Iroquois n. **Kanawaga**, "rapid river," for the rapids. 1964 USGS Hogansburg Quad. Also, **Catarakui/ Cadarakui; Fleuve St. Laurant** (French). / **St. Lawrence Road**: r., v. Brasher Falls, Route 11. / **St. Lawrence Seaway**: The portion of the St. Lawrence River developed to make the river navigable for ocean-going ships from the Great Lakes to the Atlantic Ocean. / **St. Lawrence State Forest**: t. Brasher. 1964 USGS Hogansburg Quad. / **St. Lawrence State Hospital**: in Ogdensburg, received its first patients 7:00 p. m., Dec. 9, 1898, now **Psychiatric Center**. *Quarterly*, 11 (1966), no. 4, p. 3. 1963 USGS Ogdensburg East Quad. / **St. Lawrence State Park**: above Ogdensburg, on St. Lawrence River. / **St. Lawrence Summit**: see **County Line Mountain**. / **St. Lawrence Turnpike**: from Black River, through Russell, Pierrepont, Parishville, and Hopkinton, ending near Malone, constructed by direction of

Russell Attwater. *Quarterly*, 5 (1960), no. 4, p. 1. / **St. Lawrence University**: in Canton, chartered Apr. 3, 1856, "for the promotion of general education, and to cultivate and advance literature, science and the arts; and to maintain a theological school. . . ." Blankman, 76-79. / **St. Lawrence University Conference Centers**: t. Colton, at Catamount Lodge, 15 miles south of Canton; the other is on Upper Saranac Lake, outside the county.

St. Margarettes Island: in St. Lawrence River, t. Hammond. 1958 USGS Chippewa Quad.

St. Marys Cemetery: t. Canton. 1964 USGS Canton Quad; t. Oswegatchie. 1963 USGS Ogdensburg East Quad; t. Potsdam. 1943 USGS Potsdam Quad; t. Waddington. 1964 Waddington Quad.

St. Mary's School: v. Canton; v. Massena. 1964 USGS Massena Quad; v. Potsdam. Also **St. Marys School**.

St. Michaels Cemetery: t. Fine.

St. Patrick Cemetery: t. Brasher. 1964 USGS Brasher Falls Quad.

St. Patricks Cemetery: t. Clifton; t. Rossie, on Scotch Settlement Road beside Indian River. 1966 USGS Muskellunge Lake Quad.

St. Regis: n. Jean Francis Regis, a priest, who never visited the area and probably never knew that it had been n. for him. See also George L. Frear, Jr., "The Founding of St. Regis," *Quarterly*, 18 (1983), no. 4, pp. 3-10, who writes, "The oldest continuously occupied community in the North Country is the village of St. Regis, which actually lies within the Canadian border but the point of land juts out of the south shore of the St. Lawrence River just west of the mouth of the St. Regis River. Derived names include: **St. Regis Boulevard**: s., v. Massena, leads to St. Regis Reservation. / **St. Regis Mission: built in 1760 between mouth of Racquette and St. Regis Rivers. *Quarterly*, 9 (1964), no. 4, p. 15. / St. Regis Reservation**: see **Mohawk Reservation**. / **St. Regis River**: t. Brasher, flows northeast through northeastern part of St. Lawrence County into the St. Lawrence River, Huntingdon Co., Quebec, Canada. Amerindian name: **Akwesasne**, "where the partridge drums." Shown as **Eyensawyee River** on 1779 map. / **St. Regis Street**: s., v. Brasher Falls. 1964 Hogansburg Quad; 1873 Hamilton Child, p. 89.

Salisbury Marsh: swamp, t. Piercefield, n. Salisbury family. 1920 USGS Childwold Quad.

Salls School: no. 24, common school, t. Potsdam, n. Salls family.

Sallys Rock: t. Piercefield, in Big Tupper Lake on the St. Lawrence County side, a small, rocky island, "setting for the first wedding in the Town of Altamont. Sally Cole, daughter of Tupper's first settler, and 'Zibe' Westcott had decided to set up housekeeping together. There was no clergyman then (1850) within many miles, so when a timber cruiser who was also a justice of the peace in St. Lawrence County happened by, they seized the opportunity. The wedding party rowed out to the island – nearest point in St. Lawrence County – to tie the knot within the justice's jurisdiction." Clipping, ca 1974. Also spelled, **Sally's Rock**.

Saloon Hill: t. Edwards, h. Talcville. Freeman, 10.

Sam Buell Road: r., t. Brasher, n. Samuel Buell.

Sam Day Road: r., t. Hermon. n. Samuel G. Day, a twin son of John Day.

Sampson Pond: t. Colton, in Jamestown area, alt. 1,498, n. Sampson family. 1880 Ely; 1883 Ely-Wallace; 1896 New; 1902 Blankman; 1908 Adm; 1912 Stoddard; 1921 USGS Stark Quad.

Sand: n. desc. of a feature with loose particles of rocks or of a place located nearby: **Sand Banks**: t. Canton, on Grass(e) River; once a public swimming and boating area. *Quarterly*, 25 (1980), no. 4, p. 4. / **Sand Hill**: t. Pierrepont. / **Sand Hill School**: t. Pierrepont. Also, **Jenner School**, Dist. 1. / **Sand Road**: r., t. Lisbon. / **Sand Street**: r., t. Hammond, n. sandstone from various areas along the road that aided in the construction of many homes for the Scots who settled in the Brier Hill vicinity in 1838. / **Sand Street**: r., t. Lawrence. / s., h. Nicholville, same as r., t. Lawrence.

Sanderson Cemetery: t. Lisbon. / **Sanderson Road**: r., t. Lisbon. Both n. Moses Sanderson, early settler

Sandstone Drive: s., v. Potsdam, n. Potsdam sandstone, distinctive stone in color used throughout North America for public and private buildings.

Sanford Road: r., t. Fine, n. Sanford family.

Sanfordville: h. in t. Stockholm, n. Jonah Sanford (1790-1867), first settler. He served the county and his t. in many positions, including commissioner to find a site for a new courthouse, judge, assemblyman (1829-1830), U. S. Representative (1830-1831), and Stockholm t. supervisor for several terms. He also enlisted as a Union soldier at the age of 71. Durant, 391; Biondi, 95. Dorothy Squires, "Judge Jonah Sanford," *Quarterly*, 5 (1960), no. 1, npn. A claim is made that the place was n. for Benjamin Sanford. Nina W. Smithers and Mary H. Biondi, "From Podunk To Zip Code 13652," *Quarterly*, 10 (1965), no. 4, p. 8. 1964 USGS Potsdam Quad. / **Sanfordville Cemetery** / **Sanfordville School**: no. 7, common school, t. Stockholm.

Santamount Road: r., t. Hopkinton, n. Santamount family.

Santimaw Brook: t. Hopkinton, trib. West Branch St. Regis River. 1964 USGS Sylvan Falls Quad. Spelling and pronunciation variant of **Santamount**.

Sarahsburg: a survey township, now divided between t. Russell and Fine, n. daughter of Daniel McCormick, land speculator.

Sardine Pond: t. Colton, n. the fish, the pilchard (*Sardina pilchardus*), but perhaps here used facetiously. 1912 Stoddard; 1954 USGS Tupper Lake Quad.

Satterlee Hall: on SUC, Potsdam, campus, n. O. Ward Satterlee, a professor and dean of Education.

Sault School: no. 12, common school, t. Massena, n. rapids in St. Lawrence River.

Saunders Dam: t. Massena, in St. Lawrence River, n. Robert Saunders, hydro chief when the dam was built.

Savage Road: r., t. Lawrence, n. Savage family.

Sawmill Road: r., t. Macomb, n. for a local mill.

Sawyer Creek: t. Fowler, trib. Oswegatchie River, n. Sawyer family. 1956 USGS Gouverneur Quad. Also **Sawyer's Creek**.

Sayer Road: r., t. DeKalb, n. Samuel Sayer family.

Sayers Road: r., t. Macomb, n. Thomas, William Sr., James, and Fortunatus Sayers families.

Sayles Road: r., t. Potsdam, n. Nicholas Sayles family.

Schermerhorn Bay: original n. bay at Oak Point. / **Schermerhorn Landing**: t. Hammond, n. Schermerhorn family who own a boat and aquatic goods business on the St. Lawrence River. 1958 USGS Chippewa Quad. Also **Schemerhorn's Landing**.

Schoff School: no. 4, common school, t. Brasher, n. Schoff family.

School: both a specific and generic n.; occurs often for places where a school exists: **School Road**: r., t. Madrid; s., h. Star Lake. / **School Street**: s., h. Brier Hill; s., h. DeKalb Junction. "School Street was so named because of the high school, est. in the 1860s." Mabel Sheldon, "Early School Life in DeKalb Junction," *Quarterly*, 6 (1951), no. 1, p. 14; s., v. Gouverneur; s., h. Hannawa Falls; s., h. Madrid; s., v. Massena; r., t. Morristown; s., h. Parishville; s., v. Richville.

Schoolhouse Road: r., t. Potsdam.

Schuette Hall: in the Julia E. Crane Music Center on SUC, Potsdam, campus, n. Marie A. Schuette, former faculty member of the Crane School of Music.

Schuler Building: see **Andrew S. Schuler Building**.

Schuyler Road: r., t. Fine, n. Schuyler family.

Science Center: on Clarkson University campus, opened 1971 on the Hill Campus.

Scotch: adjectival n. Scots, here for emigrants from Scotland who settled under the sponsorship of David Parish: **Scotch Bush Road**: r., t. Morristown, from Black Lake to St. Lawrence River, n. Scotch Bush Grange which had a lodge on the Black Lake terminus of the road. / **Scotch Bush School**: no. 3, common school, t. Morristown. / **Scotch Cemetery**: t. Waddington. / **Scotch Ridge**: see **Rutherford Ridge**. Tedford, 39-40. / **Scotch Ridge Cemetery**: t. Potsdam. / **Scotch Settlement**: t. Rossie, formerly, **Roxburgh Settlement**, after Roxburghshire, Scotland. / **Scotch Settlement Cemetery**: on Scotch Settlement Road, t. Rossie. 1964 USGS Muskellunge Lake Quad. / **Scotch Settlement Road**: s., v. and r., t. Gouverneur; r., t. Rossie. 1949 USGS Hammond Quad. / **Scotch Settlement School**: no. 8, common school, t. Gouverneur; no. 2, common school, t. Rossie; no. 11, common school, at Chipman, t. Waddington.

Scotland: t. Edwards, area settled by Scots and Irish settlers. *Quarterly*, 10 (1965), no. 2, p. 5. For a list of names of the Scots who settled in 1819, see Eugene Hatch, "David J. Cleland: A Tribute," *Quarterly*, 14 (1969), no. 1, p. 4. / **Scotland School**: no. 9, common school, t. Edwards, Dist. 9. Freeman, 22. 1915 USGS Russell Quad.

Scott: many families with the n. live in St. Lawrence County, and their n. have become specifics in geo- graphical n. / **Scott Pond**: t. Colton, alt. 1,832, part of the 4-pond chain. 1896 New; 1902 Blankman; 1908 Adm; 1919 USGS Cranberry Lake Quad. / **Scott Road**: r., t. Fine; r., t. Lisbon, n. Charles Scott; r., t. Stockholm, n. either the Thomas or Ozias W. Scott family. / **Scott School**: no. 5, common school, t. Fine. / **Scott's Bridge**: settlement and bridge, t. Fine, over Oswegatchie River, n. Charles Scott, first settler. *Quarterly*, 7 (1962), no. 2, p. 13. Also, **Scotts Bridge**. / **Scott's Bridge School**: t. Fine, Dist. 5. Reynolds, 199. / **Scott's Bridge-Fine Road**: r., t. Fine. / **Scotts Corners**: t. Russell, n. Harry Scott (1797-1860). 1915 USGS Russell Quad.

Scouten Road: off Heuvelton Hill Road, n. George Scoughton. *Quarterly*, 16 (1971), no. 4, p. 7. Spelling reflects pronunciation.

Scovil Road: r., t. Colton, n. Scovil family.

Scow Island: in St. Lawrence River, t. Hammond. Scows were used to bring goods from mainland for larger ships to pick up. See **Ore Road**. 1958 USGS Chippewa Quad.

Scriba: t. Fine. A survey township, n. George Scriba. Durant, 446.

Scullen Road: r., t. Brasher, n. Bernard Scullen, whose family has owned land here since 1837.

Scuttle Hole: pond, t. Fine, prob. n. an incident, but still undetermined. 1916 USGS Oswegatchie Quad. / **Scuttle Hole Creek**: t. Fine, trib. Fish Creek, t. Diana (Lewis Co.). 1916 USGS Oswegatchie Quad.

Sealtest Road: r., t. Lawrence, n. milk company. Also **North Lawrence-Moira Road**.

Sealey Drive: s., v. Potsdam, n. Seeley family; spelling was changed. Also, **Sealy**.

Sears: a family name used as a specific: **Sears Island**: in Cranberry Lake, t. Clifton, n. Sears family. 1896 **Catamount Island** New; 1919 USGS Cranberry Quad. See

Catamount Island. / **Sears Island:** in St. Lawrence River, t. Lisbon, family name. 1906 USGS Red Mills Quad.

Seaverton: t. Brasher, p. o. est. May 27, 1902, n. Lyndon R. Seaver, pm, closed July 30, 1904.

Seavey: family n.: **Seavey Road:** r., t. Gouverneur, n. Seavey family, in particular Samuel Seavey and his son James E. Seavey. Samuel Seavey came to Gouverneur in 1834 and was married to Thankful Poole of Antwerp. Cent. Souv., 359. Also, **Seavy Road.** / **Seavey School:** no. 20, common school, t. DeKalb, n. Seavey family. 1915 USGS Gouverneur Quad.

Seaway: Short form, **The Seaway,** from **United States-Canadian St. Lawrence Seaway and Power Project.** / **Seaway Shopping Center:** c. Ogdensburg. 1963 USGS Ogdensburg East Quad.

Second: a number-n.: **Second Congregational Cemetery:** t. Massena. / **Second Pond:** see **Lows Lake.** / **Second Street:** s., v. Edwards; s., h. Norfolk; s., h. Wanakena.

Selleck Road: t., Pierrepont, n. Selleck family.

Sellecks: h. t. Colton, n. Guy Selleck. *Quarterly*, 22 (1977), no. 4, p. 6. / **Sellecks Corners.** t., Pierrepont. *Quarterly*, 17 (1972), no. 1, p. 7. / **Sellecks School:** t. Pierrepont, Dist. 11, n. Selleck family. Also, **Selleck School.**

Serra Drive: s., v. Massena, n. Miguel Jose Serra (1713-1784), Spanish Roman Catholic missionary to the Amerindians. The n. was given by the land developer of a housing project.

Setting Pole: t. Piercefield. According to information in a clipping, ca 1974, "The rapids on Raquette River below Underwood Bridge, between Tupper and Piercefield . . . The last stretch of white water for early travelers coming from Potsdam-way. They used long poles to push their boats through the rapids" by setting them in the river bed and pushing. The place is now the site of the dam which controls Tupper area water level.

Settlement of the Pines: see **Massena.**

Seventh Day Adventist School: v. Canton.

Sevey: settlement, corners, and cemetery, t. Colton; p. o. est. Feb. 5, 1886, John J. Sevey, pm, closed Dec.

31, 1907. 1880 Ely (Johnson T. Seavy and William Seavy were living in the area, some distance apart, 1860); 1896 New; 1912 Stoddard; 1920 USGS Childwold Quad. The cemetery is at the junction of Routes 3 and 56. / **Sevey Pond**: t. Colton, alt. 1,520 ft. See **Sevey**. 1920 USGS Childwold Quad. / **Sevey School**: no. 9, common school, t. Colton.

Seymour Street: s., c. Ogdensburg, n. George N. Seymour (1794-1859), who came to the area to work for the Rosseel and Lewis firm. He was a veteran of the War of 1812, an agent for David Parish, and later a merchant. In 1847 he was involved in the raising of funds for Irish relief.

Shady City: h. nine m. from Brasher Falls on Iron Works Road and across the Clark Bridge; n. the many shade trees on the site. *Quarterly*, 14 (1969), no. 4, p. 5. / **Shady City Brook**: t. Brasher. / **Shady City School**: no. 22, common school, t. Brasher.

Shallow River Lane: s., h. Louisville.

Shambo Island: in St. Lawrence River, t. Hammond. 1958 USGS Chippewa Quad. Origin of n. undetermined.

Shampine School: no. 6, common school, t. Brasher, n. Shampine family.

Shanty Bay: on Trout Lake, t. Hermon. *Quarterly*, 16 (1971), no. 1, p. 9; n. a temporary, crude building used to house workers, such as timber and lumber workers, or sometimes mine workers.

Shantyville Road: r., t. Fowler. / **Shantyville School**: no. 6, common school, t. Fowler. 1913 USGS Lake Bonaparte Quad.

Sharon Drive: s., v. Massena, n. coastal plain in ancient Palestine, more immediately, "Rose of Sharon," by a land developer of a housing project.

Sharp Road: r., t. Madrid, n. John Sharp family.

Sharp Top Mountain: part of County Line Mountain, t. Hopkinton, alt. 1,880 ft., n. shape. 1919 USGS Nicholville; 1964 USGS Lake Ozonia Quad.

Shaw Road: r., t. Edwards, n. Shaw family. See **Shawville**.

Shawville: h., t. Edwards, n. Elijah and Noah Shaw, settlers in 1825, Elijah being the first merchant. Leah Noble, "Edwards Pioneers," *Quarterly*, 7 (1962), no. 2, pp. 8-9, 15.

1873 **South Edwards** Hamilton Child, p. 113; 1915 USGS **South Edwards** Russell Quad; 1915 USGS Shawville. Now, **South Edwards.** / **Shawville Road**: r., t. Edwards. See **Shawville.** / **Shawville Road**: r., t. Stockholm, n.Calvin and Daniel Shaw families.

Sheads: Orra Shead, mill owner: **Sheads Corners**: now, **Edwards.** / **Sheads Mills.** Also, **Shead's Mills.** See **Edwards.**

Sheephead Point: on St. Lawrence River, t. Hammond, n. shape. 1958 USGS Chippewa Quad.

Sheepwalk: "The Kearney Tract was reduced by sales to Parish and Nicholas Low so that it finally was about one-fourth of a mile wide, and from its narrowness and length, the latter being about twenty miles, it probably became known as the 'Sheepwalk.'" Cent. Souv., 54. See **Kearney Road.**

Sheldon: a surname used as a specific: **Sheldon Mt.**: t. Hopkinton, n. J. Sheldon. 1858 Rogerson; 1896 New; 1902 Blankman; 1908 Adm. / **Sheldon Road**: r., t. Hopkinton, n. Abraham Sheldon family. / **Sheldon School**: no. 3, common school, t. Lisbon, n. Nehemiah Sheldon family

Shelton Crest; s., h. Star Lake, short s. leading off Katherine Street, n. Willis H. Shelton, former Star Lake resident.

Sherman Street: s. c., Ogdensburg, n. Socrates N. Sherman (1801-1873), physician

Sherwood: a survey township, now in t. Colton, n. Sherwood, Nottinghamshire, England; meaning "shire's wood (forest)." / Sherwood Drive: s., v. Massena, n. Sherwood family.

Shiells School: no. 7, common school, t. Hammond, n. Andrew Shiells, an early Scottish settler of Hammond, arriving in 1818. Hough, 315, gives the n. as Andrew Shields.

Shiner Pond: t. Pitcairn, n. minnows. 1951 USGS Harrisville Quad.

Shingle Creek: t. Fowler, trib. Matoon Creek, p. o. changed from **West Fowler** Feb. 6, 1828, James Bailey, pm, changed to **Keeneville** Dec. 16, 1878; n. place where wooden slats were made. Other pms were Daniel Wilcox, Alexander Wright, George F. Steele, Eben Gillett, A. M. Vedder, and L. G. Draper. Durant, 316. Durant does not list James Bailey. 1956 USGS Gouverneur Quad. See **Spragueville.** / **Shingle Pond**: t.

Clare, Fine, alt. 919 ft. 1915 Russell Quad.

Shinnock Road: r., t. Lawrence, n. Jeremiah Shinnock family.

Shoal, The: island in Chippewa Bay, t. Hammond. *Quarterly*, 16 (1971), no. 3, p. 11.

Shop Road: r., t. Stockholm, farm to market r., prob. n. shop, now disappeared.

Short Road: r., t. Madrid, n. Thomas Short family.

Shurtleff: h., t. Colton, n. Thomas Shurtleff family. 1920 USGS Childwold Quad.

Sibley Road: r., t. Fowler, n. Albert Sibley (1844-1934). / **Sibley Cemetery**: t. Fowler.

Sigourney School: no. 2, common school, t. Hammond, n. Charles M. Sigourney (1784-1852) and sons Anthony, Andrew, and Joseph W. Durant, 385.

Silas Wright House: home of the St. Lawrence County Historical Association, Canton, New York, formerly the home of Silas Wright (1795-1847), New York statesman, who served as both U. S. Representative and U. S. Senator. He was governor of New York (1844-46). / **Silas Wright Cemetery**: t. Canton, corner of West and Miner Streets. For an account, see Edward F. Heim, "Silas Wright Cemetery," *Quarterly*, 7 (1962), no. 1, pp. 10-11, 14-16.

Silver: generic n. for the metal or the color resembling the metal; very common and popular n. for places. / **Silver Brook**: stream, trib. Grass River Flow, t. Colton. 1896 New; 1912 Stoddard; 1954 USGS Tupper Lake Quad. / **Silver Hill**: t. Russell, n. for early silver mining frenzy; silver was reported as discovered there. / **Silver Hill Road**: t. Russell. / **Silver Hill School**: no. 17, common school, t. Russell. 1915 USGS Russell Quad. / **Silver Hill State Forest**, #35, t. Russell. / **Silver Lake**: pond across Route 3 from Cranberry Lake, t. Clifton, alt. 1,483 ft. *Quarterly*, 3 (1958), no. 4, p. [7]. 1865 **Norway Pond** Beers; 1880 **Silver Pond** (misplaced) Ely; 1883 **Deer Pond** Ely-Wallace; 1883 **Silver Pond** Ely-Wallace; 1896 **Silver Pond** New; 1898 EGB, p. 26; 1902 **Silver Pond** Blankman; 1908 Adm; 1912 Stoddard; 1919 USGS Cranberry Lake Quad. / **Silver Lake Mountain**: t. Colton, alt. 2,600. 1880 Ely; 1883

Ely-Wallace; 1896 New; 1912 Stoddard; 1954 USGS Tupper Lake Quad. / **Silver Leaf Pond**: t. Clifton. 1896 New; 1898 EGB, p. 26; 1902 Blankman; 1919 USGS Cranberry Lake Quad. / **Silver Pond**: see **Silver Lake**.

Silvia Lake: see **Sylvia Lake**.

Simmons Pond: t. Clifton. 1896 **Simons Pond** New; 1898 **Simons Pond** EGB, p. 28; 1902 **Simons Pond** Blankman; 1908 **Simons Pond** Adm; 1912 **Simons Pond** Stoddard; 1919 USGS Cranberry Lake Quad. Noted on 1988 Highway Map of St. Lawrence County as **Simmons Pond**.

Simpson: t. Hermon, p. o. at West Hermon, est. Dec. 24, 1897, Nancy Maybee, pm, closed Mar. 31, 1899, reopened Apr. 29, 1899. Elmer Grant, pm, closed Sept. 30, 1903; n. David Simpson, sawmill owner, from NH. / **Simpson Road**, r., t. Hermon. / **Simpson School**, no. 6, common school, t. Hermon. / **Simpson Street**: s. in Terrace Park. t. Morristown, n. a Methodist bishop.

Sinclair Corners: crossroads, t. Parishville, n. Henry Sinclair, migrant from Essex County, or William M. Sinclair, early settler from NH. 1964 USGS Potsdam Quad. / **Sinclair Road**: r., t. Parishville. See **Sinclair Corners**. Also spelled **Sinclare** and **Sinkler**.

Sisson: several places, with exception of **Sisson Hall**, n. George Sisson, miller, papermaker: **Sisson**: railroad crossing, t. Potsdam. 1964 USGS Potsdam Quad. / **Sisson Hall**: on SUC, Potsdam, campus, n. Charles Wing Sisson, president of a Potsdam corporation that petitioned the state of New York to keep the Crane School of Music in Potsdam as a part of the Potsdam State Normal School. / **Sisson Road**: r., t. Potsdam. / **Sisson Street**: s., v. Potsdam. / **Sissonville**: h., t. Potsdam. The Griswold & Sisson Sawmill was located here. / **Sissonville Road**: r., t. Potsdam / **Sissonville School**: no. 23, common school, t. Potsdam.

Sister Islands: several adjacent islands in St. Lawrence River, t. Hammond. 1958 USGS Chippewa Quad; 1963 USGS Morristown Quad.

Sitting Bull Camp: on Oswegatchie River, t. Fine. *Quarterly*, 11 (1966), no. 4, p. 15. Origin n. undetermined, but one source claims it was because of a "stubborn bovine." / **Sitting Bull Road**: r., t. Fine.

Sitts Bay: in Black Lake, t. Macomb, n.

Jacob Sitts family from Montgomery County. 1961 USGS Hammond Quad. See Bogardus, 35, for account of Mary Sitts.

Sixmile Creek: stream, trib. Cranberry Lake, t. Clifton. 1880 **South Creek** Ely; 1883 **South Creek** Ely-Wallace; 1896 **South Brook** New; 1902 **Six Mile Creek** Blankman; 1908 **Six Mile Creek** Adm; 1919 USGS Cranberry Lake Quad.

Sixth Street: s., h. Wanakena.

Skate Creek: t. Fine, Edwards, trib. Oswegatchie River, origin of n. unknown, but may have derived from the creek being used for skating when it was frozen over. 1916 USGS Oswegatchie Quad; 1919 USGS Cranberry Lake Quad. Mentioned in *Quarterly*, 7 (1962), no. 2, p. 15. / **Skate Creek Hill**: t. Fine.

Skimball Island: printing error for **Kimball Island**.

Skinnerville: h., t. Stockholm, n. either for Isaac W. Skinner or for the Skinner family. *Quarterly*, 10 (1965), no. 1, p. 14. 1964 USGS Brasher Falls Quad. / **Skinnerville Road**: r., t. Stockholm. / **Skinnerville School**: no. 8, common school, t. Stockholm.

Skunk Ridge: v., t. Massena, n. presence of the animal.

Slab City: h., t. Potsdam, n. for the "slab" wood cut by the sawmill. The **Old Slab Bridge** across the stream nearby was floored with slabs from the mill. Formerly, **Bailey's Mills**, n. Benjamin Bailey and his sons, Ancel and Nathan, who built a sawmill on the site in 1806. 1964 USGS West Potsdam Quad. / **Slab City**: h. East Norfolk. / **Slab City School**: no.13, common school, t. Norfolk.

Slash, The: near Childwold, an area hit by a tornado in 1845. See **Windfall.**

Slender Pond: t. Clifton, alt. 1,776 ft., n. shape. See **Chair Ponds**. 1882 Ely-Wallace; 1896 New; 1902 Blankman; 1908 Adm; 1912 Stoddard; 1919 USGS Cranberry Lake Quad.

Slick Street: r., t. Canton, n. slippery condition. Also **Morley-Woodbridge Corners Road**.

Slough Pond: t. Clare. 1896 New; 1902 Blankman; 1908 Adm; 1912 Stoddard; 1921 Stark Quad. Also appears as **Slouch Pond** [misprint]. / **Slough Pond**: t. Hopkinton, n. swamp-like area. 1964 USGS Sylvan Falls Quad.

Small Flats Road: r., t. Hermon, n. Jacob and Dorothy Small.

Small Road: r., t. Brasher, n. Joseph Small family.

Smith: the many Smith families are well represented in specific n. for places: **Smith Corners**: t. Madrid. 1964 USGS Chase Mills Quad. / **Smith Island**: t. Piercefield, in Racquette River. 1920 USGS Childwold Quad. / **Smith Lane**: s., v. Massena, n. Arad and Perez Smith. Dumas, 57. / **Smith Pond**: t. Edwards, alt. 791 ft. 1915 USGS Russell Quad. / **Smith Residence Hall**: on SUNY Canton College of Technology campus, n. Robert H. Smith, Professor of Farm Engineering and Mechanics. / **Smith Road**: r., t. Brasher; r., t. Fowler, n. Eliphalet Smith; r., t. Gouverneur, known also as **Redford Road** and **Natural Dam Road**, but see Dick Sterling, "Road Name Switch: Is it Smith Road or Redfield or Natural Dam? **Gouverneur Tribune-Press**, July 17, 1991; r. t., Potsdam, south off Rte. 56, Madrid Road, n. Smith family who owned land at the end of the road; r., t. Russell, n. Gerrit Smith from Peterboro, Madison County, early absentee landowner, and Rollin Smith, r. now an extension of Woods Bridge Road, local usage for both being **Lazy River Road**. / **Smith School**: no. 8, common school, t. Brasher; no. 6, common school, t. Hopkinton. / **Smith Street**: s., v. Gouverneur, n. probably for Samuel Smith (1789-1866), landowner, who also owned a house and lot in Gouverneur that extended from the Peck Hotel to Trinity Avenue. Cent. Souv., 361-362. A claim is also made for Harvey Douglas Smith (1789-1864), justice of the peace, state assemblyman, surrogate judge, supervisor of Gouverneur, and county judge. Durant, biographical sketch, between p. 350 and p. 351. / **Smiths Corners**: t. Potsdam, n. Gurdon Smith. Now, **West Potsdam**. Durant, 240. Also, **Smith's Corners**. / **Smiths Corners**: t. Russell. Also, **Smith's Corners**, n. Smith family. Clarke, 10. / **Smith-Trippany Road**: r., t. Massena.

Smithville: h. in t. Fine, n. William P. Smith, one of its earliest citizens; p. o. est. 1853, with Smith as first pm; date of closing unknown. Formerly, **Andersonville**, for Anderson family. Now, **Fine**.

Smoke Marsh: t. Clare and Colton.

Smuggle Hill: t. Brasher, reason for name undetermined. The only reference is as follows: "A man by the name of Foster, who lived above

Smuggle Hill" on northeast side of Brasher/Stockholm Depot. S. E. Chandler, "The Way it Was," *Quarterly*, 20 (1975), no. 1, p. 11.

Smuggler's Road: t. Morristown. See **Olds Mill Road**.

Snaith Lane: s., v. Massena, n. Snaith family.

Snake Island: In Schermerhorn Bay at Oak Point. t. Hammond. In Black Lake, t. DePeyster and Morristown; both n. sighting of snakes. 1961 USGS Pope Mills Quad; 1963 USGS Edwardsville Quad.

Snell: Prominent family n. in St. Lawrence County, especially in the t. Potsdam: Bertrand Hollis Snell (1870-1958), United States Representative, 1915-1939. Clarkson University trustee for 34 years. *Quarterly*, 14 (1969), no. 4, p. 5: **Snell Field**: on Clarkson University campus, built in 1916. / **Snell Hall**: on Clarkson University campus, now the Administration Building, formerly New York State Normal School. / **Snell Lock**: t. Massena, lock and spillway in the St. Lawrence River near Massena. / **Snell Road**: r., t. Colton, n. Snell family. / **Snell Music Theatre**: in the Julia E. Crane Music Center, SUC, Potsdam, campus, n. Sara Merrick Snell (1800-1964), wife of Bertrand Hollis Snell.

Snipe Island: in St. Lawrence River, t. Hammond, n. game bird (**Gallinagor**) found in marshy areas. 1958 USGS Chippewa Quad.

Snow: desc.; considering the area, few snow-n. occur: **Snow Bowl State Forest**: #34, t. Colton, n. for the St. Lawrence University ski area. / **Snow Street**: s., v. Gouverneur, n. Sumner Snow.

Snowshoe Island: n. shape, Oswegatchie River, t. DeKalb. 1956 USGS Richville Quad.

Snyder Lake: pond, t. Pitcairn, alt. 772 ft., n. Snyder family. 1916 USGS Oswegatchie Quad.

Sober Street: s., v. and r., t. Norfolk, origin n. unknown.

Sodom: n. ancient city destroyed for its sinfulness, Genesis, 18-19: former n. Nicholville. / **Sodom Forest**: county forest, t. Madrid. / **Sodom State Forest**, #25. t. Madrid.

Sols: origin n. unknown, poss. personal first n.: **Sols Island**: in Racquette River, t. Piercefield. 1860 Merrit;

1880 **Sol's Island** Ely; 1883 **Sol's Island** Ely-Wallace; 1902 Blankman; 1908 Adm; 1920 USGS Childwold Quad. / **Sols Rapids**: in Racquette River, t. Piercefield. 1920 USGS Childwold Quad.

Somerset: n. county in England: **Somerset Avenue**: s., v. Massena. / **Somerset Drive**: also **Somerset Street**, s., v. Potsdam. / **Somerset Street**: see **Somerset Drive**.

Somerville: h., in southern part of t. Rossie, n. Mr. and Mrs. John Somerville. Durant, 77; *Quarterly*, 6 (1961), no. 1, p. 7. A claim has also been made for Somerville, NJ, but the evidence is for the personal n. A p. o. est. May 2, 1828, Solomon Pratt, first pm (Hough 575, closed Dec. 31, 1903. 1961 USGS Natural Dam Quad. Derived names: **Somerville Cemetery**. / **Somerville Road**: r., t. Rossie. / **Somerville School**: no. 4, common school, t. Rossie. Sometimes appears as **Summerville**.

Soper Avenue: s., v. Hammond, n. Soper family, members of whom were mill owners, inventors (early "snow sleds,"), and early automobile engineers. Durant, 171, 513. Now **Mill Street**.

South: direction-n., contrasted with **North**, although a counterpart **North** may not exist. See **North**: **South Avenue**: s., v. Massena. / **South Bay**: in Cranberry Lake, t. Clifton. New; 1908 Adm. / **South Bay**: in Tupper Lake, t. Piercefield (St. Lawrence Co.), t. Altamont (Franklin Co.). 1896 New; 1908 Adm; 1954 USGS Tupper Lake Quad. / **South Branch Beaver Creek**: t. Dekalb, trib. Beaver Creek. 1956 USGS Richville Quad. / **South Branch Cold Brook**: t. Colton, with trib. Cold Brook. 1921 USGS Stark Quad. / **South Branch Creek**: t. Gouverneur. / **South Branch Grass(e) River**: t. Russell, trib. Grass(e) River. See **Grass(e) River**. 1915 USGS Russell Quad. / **South Branch Mountain Brook**: t. Piercefield, trib. Mountain Brook. 1896 **South Branch** [Mountain Brook] New. / **South Brasher Road**: r., t. Lawrence. See **Finnegan Road**. / **South Brook**: t. Clifton, trib. Pleasant Lake Stream. 1921 USGS Stark Quad. / **South Brook**: see **Sixmile Creek**. / **South Brother Pond**: t. Clifton. See **Brothers Ponds**. / **South Canton**: p. o. est. Feb. 13, 1838, James Livingston, pm, changed to **Craigs Mills** Sept. 17, 1849. See **Langdon Corners**. In 1892, the South Canton baseball team was nicknamed **The Eagles**. / **South Canton Road**: r., t. Potsdam.

/ **South Channel of the St. Lawrence River**: part of the Seaway, t. Massena, leads into the Moses-Saunders Power Dam. / **South Colton**: h. in t. Colton, five m. south h. Colton; p. o. est Nov. 14, 1854, Thomas McGarry, pm, closed Dec. 20, 1858, reopened Apr. 25, 1862, Garland L. Sweet, pm, existing, ZIP 13687. Formerly, **Three Falls**. *Quarterly*, 5 (1960), no. 2, p. 5. 1858 **Three Falls** Rogerson; 1908 USGS Potsdam Quad; 1964 UGS Colton Quad. / **South Colton Reservoir**: in Racquette River, t. Colton, alt. 974. 1964 USGS Colton Quad. / **South Colton School**: no. 2, common school, t. Colton. / **South Creek**: see **Sixmile Creek**. / **South Creek**: t. Clifton. / **South Creek**: t. Pitcairn, trib. West Branch Oswegatchie River. 1951 USGS Harrisville Quad. / **South Creek Lake**: t. Fine (St. Lawrence Co.) and t. Diana (Lewis Co.). 1916 USGS Oswegatchie Quad. / **South Edwards**: t. Edwards, p. o. est. Sept. 16, 1828, James C. Haile, pm (Hough, 575), closed Apr. 30, 1919. *Quarterly*, 7 (1962), no. 1, p. 13. Formerly, **Shawville**. / **South Edwards Cemetery** / **South Edwards School**: no. 4, common school, t. Edwards. Freeman, 16. / **South Grass River Road**: r., t. Massena. / **South Hammond**: t. Hammond, p. o. est. Jan. 10, 1833, Jonathan King, first pm, closed Apr. 21, 1852, reopened Sept. 22, 1884, Daniel D. Moyer, pm, closed Feb. 28, 1957. / **South Hammond Road**: r., t. Hammond, from Route 37; r., t. Hammond, from Robb Road. / **South Hammond School**: no. 5, common school, t. Hammond. / **South Hammond State Forest, #24**, t. Hammond. / **South Inlet**: see **Dead Creek Flow**. / **South Main Street**: s., v. Massena. Formerly, **Spring Street**. / **South Potsdam**: p. o. est. Mar. 30, 1855, Ira T. French, pm, closed Feb. 7, 1857. / **South Raquette Street**: also **South Racket Street**, also **River Road**. s., v. Massena, n. Racquette River. / **South Road**: r., t. Canton. / **South Russell**: h., t. Russell, Albert Law, first settler, before 1837; Will Howland family arrived March 17, 1837; p. o. est. May 27, 1890, Salem Town, pm, and the place took the name of South Russell, closed June 30, 1911, reopened Oct. 9, 1912, Perley J. Brundage, pm, closed Nov. 30, 1933. 1915 USGS Russell Quad. Derived names: **South Russell Cemetery**: also, **Boutwell Cemetery**. / **South Russell School**: no. 14, common school, t. Russell. / **South Shore Road**: r., t. Fine, at Wanakena. / **South State Street**: s., v. Rensselaer Falls, t. Canton, n. direction. / **South Street**: s., v. Gouverneur; s., v. Massena; s., h. Norfolk; s., c. Ogdensburg;

s., v. Potsdam. **Main Street** was formerly **South Street**, a separate street from the entry here; s., v. Rensselaer Falls, n. on south side of the cemetery. The street is seldom used now and has only one lane [Hartman]. / **South Street West**: s., c. Ogdensburg. / **South Woods**: the frontier land south of t. Russell, Clare, and Clifton. Clarke, 28. known also as **The Big Woods**, meaning "The Adirondacks." / **South Woods Road**: r., t. Macomb. / **South Woods School**: no. 2, common school, t. Macomb, southwest of Rte. 58. 1949 USGS Hammond Quad. See **Southwood School**.

Southville: corners, located on south line of t. Stockholm; p. o. est. May 6, 1825, Hosea Brooks, first pm (Hough, 575), closed July 30, 1904. 1964 USGS Parishville Quad. Only a road sign remains at the corners. Derived names: **Southville Cemetery**. / **Southville-Holmes Hill Road**: r., t. Stockholm. / **Southville School**: no. 14, common school, t. Stockholm. / **Southville State Forest**, #23, t. Stockholm. / **Southville-West Stockholm Road**: r., t. Stockholm.

Southwood: building at St. Lawrence State Hospital, now the Psychiatric Center, Ogdensburg. *Quarterly*, 11 (1966), no. 4, p. 19.

Southwoods School: t. Macomb. Also **South Woods School**.

Southworth Library: on SUNY Canton College of Technology campus, n. Lottie Southworth, former Assistant Director, Domestic Art Department.

Spangler Brook: t. Piercefield, trib. Jordan River. 1896 **Beaver Dam Brook** (?) New; 1920 USGS Childwold Quad. Origin n. unknown.

Sparrowhawk Point: on St. Lawrence River, t. Lisbon, n. George Sparrowhawk family. 1963 USGS Sparrow Quad.

Spawning Bed Mt.: t. Hopkinton, prob. n. fish spawning area. 1896 New; 1902 Blankman.

Spears Street: s., v. Canton, n. Spears family.

Spearville: n. used locally; one of the four wards of the city of Ogdensburg est. on Apr. 27, 1868; n. as the place where fishermen would spear fish.

Spectacle Ponds: two ponds, t. Clifton, n. because two ponds are connected by a stream, giving the appearance of spectacles. 1896

New; 1898 **Spectacle Pond** EGB, p. 28; 1902 **Spectacle Pond** Blankman; 1919 USGS Cranberry Lake Quad.

Spencer Street: s., v. Gouverneur, n. Benjamin Spencer, a physician who arrived in 1807. Cent. Souv., 52.

Spencer Walker Road: r., t. Gouverneur, n. Spencer family and Jacob Walker family.

Spicer Road: r., t. Russell, n. Philemon J. Spicer family.

Spider Pond: t. Fine, n. presence of spiders. *Quarterly*, 5 (1960), no. 1, npn. 1916 USGS Oswegatchie Quad.

Spile Bridge: t. Oswegatchie and De-Peyster, n. of bridge on Black Lake. Also, **Pile Bridge**. *Quarterly*, 10 (1965), no. 4, p. 14. About 1874 known as King Bridge; moved from Spring Street, Ogdensburg in 1914 to replace a crude spile bridge, one supported by posts ("a pile"), the name derived prob. from an Old English word meaning "stake." George King, founder of the King Bridge Co., was born at Kings Corners, now **Kokomo**, t. De-Peyster. / **Spile Bridge Road**: r., t. De Peyster. See **Spile Bridge**.

Spinks School: no. 8, common school, t. Colton, n. Levi Spinks family.

Spinner Street: one block long s., c. Ogdensburg, n. Francis Elias Spinner, army general, controller of New York State.

Split Rock Road: r., t. Rossie, Hammond, n. geological feature.

Spooner Flat: flatlands, t. DeKalb, n. Spooner family. 1956 USGS Richville Quad.

Sports Avenue: s., v. Norwood. Origin n. undetermined.

Spragueville: h., t. Rossie, railroad stop, n. Samuel B. Sprague; p. o. est. from **Keenesville** Jan 3, 1883, Lucius G. Draper, pm, closed Aug. 2, 1963, opened Aug. 3, 1963 as rural branch out of **Gouverneur** ZIP 13689, closed Dec. 5, 1975. First, **Sprague's Corners**; then, **Shingle Creek** (for p. o. moved to the area); then, **Keenesville**, for Hiram Keene. Since the latter was too close in spelling to **Keeseville**, the n. was changed to **Spragueville**. *Quarterly*, 6 (1961), no. 1, p. 6. 1961 USGS Natural Dam Quad. Derived names: **Spragueville Cemetery**. / **Spragueville-Fowler Road**: r., t. Fowler. Also, **Farm to Market Road / Spragueville Road**:

r., t. Rossie. / **Spragueville School**: no. 11, common school, t. Rossie.

Spring: a common generic and specific for places where water flows from ground: **Spring Pond**: t. Colton, alt. 1,787. 1896 New; 1908 Adm; 1912 Stoddard; 1919 USGS Cranberry Lake Quad; 1954 USGS Tupper Lake Quad. / **Spring Street**: r., t. Madrid and s., h. Madrid; s., v. Massena (see **South Main Street**, v. Massena); s., v. Norwood; s., c. Ogdensburg; s., v. Potsdam.

Spruce: the American evergreen tree or conifer (*canachites canadensis* of the genus *Picea*), a popular n. in spruce-growing areas: **Spruce Grouse Pond**: t. Clifton, alt. 1,735 ft., n. the game bird (family **Tetraonidae**) that can be found in dense tree growths. 1896 New; 1898 EGB, p. 28; 1902 Blankman; 1908 Adm; 1912 Stoddard; 1919 USGS Cranberry Lake Quad. / **Spruce Mountain**: t. Clifton, alt. 1,735 ft. 1919 USGS Cranberry Quad; 1921 USGS Stark Quad. / **Spruce Pond**: t. Clifton. 1896 New; 1898 EGB, p. 28; 1902 Blankman; 1908 Adm; 1912 Stoddard; 1921 USGS Stark Quad. / **Spruce Road**: r., t. Edwards, Hermon. / **Spruce Street**: s., v. Massena; s., v. Norwood; s., c. Ogdensburg.

Square Township: see **Lisbon**.

Squaw: n. occurs infrequently, but refers to an Amerindian woman. **Squaw Creek**: t. Lisbon, trib. Sucker Brook. 1963 USGS Sparrow Quad. / **Squaw Point**: *Quarterly*, 14 (1969), no. 3, p. 16. / **Squaw Point**: v. Potsdam, off Water Street, on Racquette River.

Squeak Brook: t. Stockholm, Brasher, trib. Racquette River, prob. n. noise. 1964 USGS Raquette River Quad.

Squires School: no. 7, common school, t. Louisville, n. Squires family.

Stacy's Island. n. Stacy family. See **Croil's Island**.

Stafford: a family n.: **Stafford Brook**: trib. Racquette River, t, Potsdam, n. Stafford family. 1964 USGS Potsdam Quad. / **Stafford Corners**: t. Potsdam, Parishville, n. Thomas S. Stafford, shoemaker. 1908 Adm; 1908 USGS Potsdam Quad; 1964 USGS Potsdam Quad.

Stalker Road: r., t. Russell, n. Stalker family.

Stalbird: Flavius A. Stalbird, resident and Civil War veteran, **Stalbird Corners**: t. Russell, p. o. est. Oct. 30, 1891, Lucy D. Stalbird, pm, after Flavius A. Stalbird not appointed, closed Jan. 31, 1905. The n. appears on the Blankman map. Jan Barnes, "The Stalbird Post Office," *Quarterly*, 12 (1967), no. 3, p. 3. 1915 USGS Russell Quad. / **Stalbird School**: no. 13, common school, t. Russell.

Stamford Pond: see **Lilypad Pond**, t. Parishville.

Stammer: a family n.: **Stammer Creek**: t. Edwards and Fine, trib. Oswegatchie River. The creek flows a corkscrew course and has had seven dams to enable log drives. 1915 USGS Russell Quad. / **Stammer Creek State Forest**, #43, t. Edwards. / **Stammer Road**: r., t. Gouverneur.

Stammerville: h. t. Russell, n. Warder W. Stammer of Edwards area. / **Stammerville Road**: r., t. Edwards, n. Stammer family. / **Stammerville School**: no. 20, common school, t. Russell, n. Stammer family. 1915 USGS Russell Quad.

Staplin Corners: crossroads, t. Gouverneur, n. Staplin family, in particular Monroe Staplin, farmer. 1956 USGS Richville Quad.

Star Lake: lake, t. Fine, alt. 1,450 ft. Around 1880, n. for the "star" shape of the lake. Other n.: **Big Lake, Pointed Lake, Point Lake, Harewood.** 1916 USGS Oswegatchie Quad: **Star Lake**: h., t. Fine, n. lake; p. o. est. as **Starlake** June 30, 1892, Frank J. Redway, pm, closed Oct. 31, 1893, reopened July 16, 1896, James C. Lee, pm, closed Jan. 12, 1899, reopened May 20, 1899, Edmund Pendleton, Jr., pm, changed to **Star Lake** Oct. 1, 1953, existing, ZIP 13690. 1916 USGS Oswegatchie Quad. / **Star Lake Campus**: SUC, Potsdam, campus for physical education and meeting facilities. / **Star Lake Road**: r., t. Clifton and s., h. Star Lake. / **Star Lake School**: no. 9, common school, t. Fine. Reynolds, 199. / **Star School**: see **Starr School**.

Starbuck Street: s., v. Gouverneur, n. Isaac Starbuck, engaged in lumber Business. Cent. Souv., 362.

Stark: a family n. that has been given to many places in St. Lawrence County: **Stark**: settlement, t. Colton, transfer n. from **Stark Falls**, p. o. est. from **Bog** May 12, 1884, Caroline A. Munger, first pm, closed May 18, 1933. 1896 New; 1903, J. N. Mathews, **New York**, Buffalo; 1908 Adm; 1912 Stoddard; 1921 USGS Stark Quad. / **Stark Falls**: t. Colton, n. Wilder Charles Stark, who drowned on May 30, 1839 when he fell 40 feet into the Racquette River. *Quarterly*, 14 (1969), no. 1, p. 15. 1858 **Starks Fall**; 1860 **Starks**

Falls Merrit; 1880 **Stark Falls** Ely; 1883 **Starks Falls** Ely-Wallace; 1896 **Starks Falls** New; 1902 Blankman; 1921 USGS Stark Quad. / **Stark Road**: r., t. Colton. / **Stark Road**: r., t. Norfolk. / **Stark School**: no. 10, common school, t. Colton. / **Stark School**: no. 6, common school, t. Macomb, on Rte. 58, n Morgan Stark family. 1949 USGS Hammond Quad. / **Stark School**: no. 12, common school, t. Parishville. / **Stark School Corner**: t. Macomb. 1961 USGS Pope Mills Quad.

Starr School: no. 17, common school, t. Pierrepont, n. Lovell Starr. Also, **Star School.**

State: Although a prosaic n., **State** carries with it the bureaucratic, honorific, legalistic, and commendatory connotations of the people: **State Highway 37, 56, 56A, 68, 345, 378, 420**: St. Lawrence County roads / **State Hospital Cemetery**: c. Ogdensburg. 1963 USGS Ogdensburg East Quad. / **State Normal and Training School**: successor of St. Lawrence Academy, now SUC, Potsdam. / **State Ranger School**: in Wanakena, t. Fine. / **State Ridge**: t. Clifton, alt. 1,950. 1919 Cranberry Lake Quad. / **State Street**: s., v. Canton; s., v. Heuvelton; s., c. Ogdensburg, formerly **Euphemia Street**, changed on May 27, 1824; s., v. Potsdam; s., v. Rensselaer Falls. / **State Wetlands Swamp**: t. Canton, DEC protected wildlife refuge.

Station Road: r., t. Piercefield to Conrail Line.

Stearns: a family name: **Stearns Cemetery: t. Louisville.** / **Stearns Street**: also **Stearnes Street**, s., v. Massena.

Steeles Corners: h. near Spragueville. Poss. n. George F. Steele. Durant, 316. Laura Gillett, "Spragueville Had a Busy Prosperous Past," *Quarterly*, 6 (1961), no. 1, p. 7.

Steep Bank Brook: t. Clare, trib. South Branch Grass(e) River, n. condition. 1915 Russell Quad.

Stellaville: h., t. DeKalb, n. Stella Mine Co., a pyrite mine. *Quarterly*, 11 (1966), no. 2, p. 19. Formerly **Stokesville**, also **Stokes Mills.** The pyrite mine was opened July 8, 1884. During World War I, the St. Lawrence Pyrite Co. employed a large force of men, refined pyrite being used for sulfuric acid manufacturing by DuPont Powder Works to make explosives. Stellaville was abandoned in 1925, houses sold to an Ogdensburg contractor who moved the property to Ogdensburg, leaving the refuse of the former hamlet. One of the pyrite shafts was 3,000 feet deep; one level several hundred feet underground followed a vein of ore 1/4 m. under the highway, railroad track, and creek. 1915 USGS Russell Quad.

Stephenville Street: s., v. Massena.

Sterling: Sterling Wick, resident in t. Parishville: **Sterling Pond**: t. Parishville, p. o. est. 1890, V. B. Laughlin, 1st pm. 1858 Rogerson; 1865 Beers; 1873 Hamilton Child; 1883 Ely-Wallace; 1896 New; 1898 EGB map; 1908 Adm; 1919 USGS Nicholville Quad; 1964 USGS Sylvan Falls Quad. Formerly, **Barkley Pond**. / **Sterling Pond Outlet**: t. Parishville, trib. Dead Creek, n. pond. 1919 USGS Nicholville Quad; 1964 USGS Sylvan Falls Quad / **Sterling Pond Road**: r., t. Parishville, n. pond. / **Sterling Street**: s., v. Gouverneur, poss. n. William E. Sterling, a prominent citizen and a director of the Potsdam-to-Watertown Railroad. See **Beckwith Street**.

Sterlingwick: p. o. est. Mar. 22, 1910, Maggie Wilson, pm, changed to **Joeindian** Aug. 10, 1920.

Sternberg: hotel on bank of Oswegatchie River at inlet crossing of Albany Road, n. for proprietor. *Quarterly*, 11 (1966), no. 4, p. 16. See **Inlet**. Also **Sternberg's Hotel**.

Stevens: family n.: **Stevens Road**: r., t. Gouverneur. / **Stevens Street**: r., t. Fine; s., v. Canton.

Stevenson Road: r., t. DeKalb, n. Robert Stevenson.

Stiles: a family n.: **Stiles Avenue**: s., v. Canton, n. Justus Stiles. Durant, 213. / **Stiles Road**: r., t. Canton, n. family of Justus Stiles. Durant, 213. / **Stiles School**: no. 7, common school, t. DeKalb, n. Stiles family, prob. for Daniel O. Stiles. b.1823, farmer, school trustee, church deacon. Durant, 359. / **Stiles School**: no. 10, common school, t. Russell, n. Ezra Stiles family. Ezra was a prosperous farmer. Durant, 435.

Stillman: a surname used as a specific: **Stillman Computing Center**: n. Alan H. Stillman, first director of Computer Services at SUC, Potsdam. / **Stillman Drive**: s., v. Canton, n. Cornelius Stillman family, Cornelius being President of the Board of Trustees of the v. in 1847. Durant, 160.

Stillwater: desc. of a placid, barely

moving expanse in a stream: **Stillwater**: Racquette River between Hedgehog Rapids and Smith Island, t. Piercefield. 1860 **Moose-head Still Water**; 1880 Ely; 1883 Ely-Wallace; 1896 **Moosehead Still Water** New. / **Stillwater, The**: in North Branch Grass(e) River, t. Clare. 1916 Russell Quad; 1919 Stark Quad. / **Stillwater Club**: t. Clare.

Stilwell: see **DePeyster**.

Stillwells Point: on St. Lawrence River, t. Oswegatchie, n. Stillwell family. 1963 USGS Ogden East Quad.

Stockholm: in northeastern interior of county, one of the ten original t., formed Feb. 21, 1806 (Durant, 390), n. Stockholm, Sweden. / **Stockholm**: h., t. Stockholm, p. o. est. Oct. 26, 1806, William Staples, pm, closed May 31, 1904. / **Stockholm Center**: h., t. Stockholm; p. o. est. as **Stockholm Centre** Mar 11, 1872. Henry W. Stearns, first pm, changed to **Stockholm Center** Dec. 1894 (day unknown), Ann E. Ainger, pm, closed Feb. 28, 1905. 1964 USGS Brasher Falls Quad. / **Stockholm Center School**: no. 2, common school, t. Stockholm. / **Stockholm Depot**: h. t. Stockholm, now **Winthrop**, p. o. est. Apr. 23, 1851, Jason W. Stearns, first pm (Hough, 575), closed Feb. 24, 1891. *Quarterly*, 10 (1965), no. 3, p. 16. / **Stockholm-Lawrence Road**: r., t. Stockholm, Lawrence. / **Stockholm Road**: r., t. Stockholm.

Stocking School: no. 16, common school, t. Lisbon, n. Billious S. Stocking family.

Stockwell Pond: t. Russell, n. Levi Stockwell. 1915 USGS Russell Quad.

Stokes Mills: t. Hermon, n. Alexander Stokes, sawmiller. See **Stellaville**.

Stone: Although **Rock** is the more popular n., **Stone** also has its followers; some may be personal n.: **Stone Church Cemetery**: t. Oswegatchie. n. The Stone Church, Second Presbyterian Church of Oswegatchie. / **Stone Church Road**: r., t. Oswegatchie; Black Lake to St. Lawrence River. / **Stone Dam**: on Deerskin Creek, t. Colton. / **Stone Road**: r., t. Fowler, probably n. Stone family. / **Stone School**: v. Edwards, built 1840. Freeman, [57]. / **Stone School House School**: no. 1, common school, t. Hopkinton; no. 4, common school, t. Norfolk; no. 16, common school, t. Pierrepont. 1915

USGS Russell Quad **Stone School**; no. 9, common school, South Hammond. / **Stone School-Waterman Hill Road**: r., t. Russell, Pierrepont.

Stony: desc. of terrain, many rocks; var. spelling, **Stoney**: **Stoney Brook**: see **Stony Brook**, t. Hopkinton. / **Stoney Creek**: t. Clare. / **Stony Brook**: t. Clifton, trib. Pleasant Lake Stream. 1921 USGS Stark Quad. / **Stony Brook**: t. Hopkinton, trib. West Branch St. Regis River. 1853 **Stoney Brook** HMC; 1858 **Stoney Brook** Rogerson; 1873 Hamilton Child; 1896 New; 1902 **Stoney Brook** Blankman; 1908 Adm; 1912 **Stoney Brook** Stoddard; 1919 USGS Nicholville Quad; 1964 USGS Sylvan Falls Quad. / **Stony Brook**: t. Piercefield, trib. Racquette River. 1896 New. / **Stony Brook**: t. Potsdam, trib. Trout Brook. 1964 USGS West Potsdam Quad. / **Stony Lonesome**: see **Crossover Island**.

Storie Road: r., t. Hammond, n. Storie family, in particular David Storie, who settled in Rossie, 1819. Durant, 314; r., t. Louisville, n. Storie family.

Stowe Bay Road: in Higley Flow area, r., t. Colton.

Stowe Road: r., t. Morristown, n. Stowe family.

Stowell: surname used as a specific: **Stowell Hall**: SUC, Potsdam, campus, n. Thomas B. Stowell, president of Potsdam Normal School. / **Stowell School**: no. 13, common school, t. Fowler, n. Willard Stowell family.

Straight Road, The: See **Parishville Turnpike**.

Strawberry Island: in St. Lawrence River, t. Louisville, n. wild strawberries.

Strawford Pond: see **Lilypad Pond**, t. Parishville.

Streeter: a common family n. in the county: **Streeter Lake**: t. Fine, n. Reuben Streeter, mill owner. 1916 USGS Oswegatchie Quad. / **Streeter Mountain**: t. Fine. 1916 USGS Oswegatchie Quad. / **Streeter Road**: r., t. DeKalb, n. Alonzo Streeter; r., t. Pierrepont, n. Jesse Streeter; r., t. Pitcairn, n. Amos Streeter.

Stroughton Avenue: s., v. Massena, n. Stroughton family.

Sturgeon Point: on St. Lawrence River, t. Hammond, n. fish. 1958 USGS Chippewa Quad.

Sturtevant Road: r., t. Pierrepont, n.

Sturtevant family.

Sucker: a fish of the family *Catostomidae* common in the bodies of fresh water in the county; **Sucker Brook**: t. Clifton, trib. Cranberry Lake. 1880 **Sucker Creek** Ely; 1883 **Sucker Creek** Ely-Wallace; 1896 New; 1902 Blankman; 1908 Adm; 1912 Stoddard; 1919 USGS Cranberry Lake Quad. See, also, *Quarterly*, 6 (1961), July, npn. / **Sucker Brook**: t. Colton. / **Sucker Brook**: t. Hopkinton, trib. Hopkinton Brook. 1865 **Stony Brook** Beers; 1919 USGS Nicholville Quad; 1964 USGS Nicholville Quad. / **Sucker Brook**: t. Waddington, trib. St. Lawrence River. 1964 USGS Waddington Quad. / **Sucker Brook**: settlement, t. Waddington, p. o. est. Apr. 1, 1892, Thomas L. Brown, pm, closed Oct. 14, 1893. / **Sucker Brook School**: no. 3, common school, t. Waddington. / **Sucker Creek**: see **Sucker Brook**. / **Sucker Creek**: t. Oswegatchie. / **Sucker Creek School**: no. 11, common school, t. Oswegatchie. / **Sucker Lake**: t. Fine. *Quarterly*, 5 (1960), no. missing, npn. / **Sucker Lake School**: t. Fine, Dist. 13. Reynolds, 199.

Sugar: usually for the presence of the sugar maple: **Sugar Creek**: trib. Trout Brook, t. Potsdam. 1964 USGS West Potsdam Quad. / **Sugar Grove Mountain**: t. Hopkinton, alt. 1,680. 1919 USGS Nicholville Quad; 1964 USGS Sylvan Falls Quad. / **Sugar Grove Pass**: pass (swamp), t. Hopkinton. 1919 USGS Nicholville Quad. / **Sugar Island/Dam**: island and dam in Racquette River, t. Potsdam. 1964 USGS Potsdam Quad. Also, see *Quarterly*, 20 (1975), no. 2, p. 3.

Sullivan: a popular family n. in the county: **Sullivan Road**: r., t. Edwards; r., t. Fine, n. John Sullivan; r., t. Fowler, n. Daniel and John Sullivan; r., t. Oswegatchie, n. Peter Sullivan; r., t. Potsdam, n. Morley Sullivan; r., t. Stockholm, n. James and Patrick Sullivan families.

Summerville: see **Somerville**.

Summit Avenue: s., h. Newton Falls.

Sunday Rock: t. Colton, outside the h. South Colton, a 43-ton glacial rock, located so as to require a sharp diversion of the original dirt road leading from the mouth of the Racquette River to the central Adirondacks. The rock has been relocated twice. Once, it seemed to mark the limit of formal civilization beyond which lay the region where only logging crews and hunters ventured.

Beyond this point, it was said that law and Sunday did not exist.

Sunny: n. commendatory, prob. n. during sunny weather: **Sunny Lake**: see **Sunny Pond**. / **Sunny Lake Road**: r., t. Fine. / **Sunny Pond**: t. Clifton, Fine, alt. 1,403 ft., descriptive and commendatory, a mood change in n. from **Lonesome Pond**. 1896 **Lonesome Pond** New; 1902 **Lonesome Pond** Blankman; 1919 USGS Cranberry Lake Quad. Also **Sunny Lake**.

Sunnyside Cemetery: Adjacent to Pine Hill Cemetery, v. Morristown. 1963 USGS Morristown Quad. Bogardus, 233; t. Massena, at Massena Springs.

Swamp Road: r., t. Lisbon, descriptive.

Swan Street: s., v. Potsdam, n. George B. Swan, local merchant.

Sweeney Road: r., t. Potsdam, n. either Patrick or Jeremiah Sweeney family.

Sweet: either for taste or family n.: **Sweet Pond**: t. Russell, possibly n. "sweet water." 1915 USGS Russell Quad. / **Sweet Road**: r., t. Madrid, n. Ezekiel Sweet family.

Swiss: usually pertaining to settlers from Switzerland: **Swiss Hill**: t. Fowler, n. for Gaudin family, from Switzerland. / **Swiss Point Road**: r., t. Fowler. / **Swiss Point Road**: s., h. Star Lake.

Swegatchie: See **Oswegatchie**.

Syakos Place: s., v. Massena, n. Syakos family.

Sykes: family n.: **Richard Eddy Sykes Residence**, St. Lawrence University campus, formerly residence hall for men, now renovated for four residence dormitories, n. Dr. Sykes, president of the then College (1919-1935). / **Sykes Road**: r., t. Canton, Potsdam, in Olin District, n. Edwin J. Sykes. Beers, p. 13. Others of the name lived in the area: H. Sykes, B. Sykes, and Heber Sykes, the latter an early settler of Canton, Lot 4, Range 3. Durant, p. 208. *Quarterly*, 25 (1972), no. 4, p. 21. / r., t. Fine, n. Sykes family. / **Sykes School**: no. 12, common school, t. Canton, n. Sykes family.

Sycamore Street: s., v. Massena, n. tree (*Platanus occidentalis*).

Sylvan Falls: falls, in West Branch St. Regis River, t. Parishville, n. romantically for **sylvan**, "forest." 1896 New; 1902 Blankman; 1908 Adm;

1912 **Sylvian Falls** [misprint] Stoddard; 1919 USGS Nicholville Quad; 1964 USGS Sylvan Falls Quad. / **Sylvan Falls Road**: r., t. Parishville, n. falls.

Sylvia Lake: t. Fowler, n. Sylvia Amelia DePau, betrothed of Theodosius O. Fowler. Mary Smallman and Nina Smithers, *Quarterly*, 10 (1965), no. 4, p. 8, "Another of Lafayette's officers accompanying him in 1777 was Major Gooden. His daughter Nancy married John D. Balmat, a Parisien, who later gave his name to the mining community of Balmat. Many French settled in the interior of the county including descendants of Count de Grasse. His daughter [Silvie] became the mother of Amelia DePau, who married Capt. Theodosius Fowler, all of whose names are still on the land of our county. Fowler's daughter later give her first name to rename Sylvia Lake which had originally been Lake Killarney from that part of Ireland from which Daniel McCormick came." See also Isabelle Hance, "Who was Sylvia?" *Quarterly*, 13 (1968), no. 3, p. 5. 1956 USGS Gouverneur Quad. / **Sylvia Lake Road**: r., t. Fowler, n. lake.

Sylvian Falls: see **Sylvan Falls**.

Symonds Square (Street): s., h. Colton.

T

Taft Island: in St. Lawrence River, t. Hammond. Origin n. unknown.

Taggart Road: r., t. Lisbon, n. Taggart family.

Tailings: land area, t. Fowler, n. "lead mine tailings," materials from mines and smelting. 1956 USGS Gouverneur Quad. / **Tailings Pond**: t. Edwards. 1956 USGS Edwards Quad.

Tait Road: r., t. Lisbon, probably for Robert Tate, surveyor. See **Rensselaer Falls**.

Talcott Street: s., v. Massena, n. Talcott family.

Talcville: h., t. Edwards, n. talc deposits, first ones found in the county; talc mill settlement, est. in 1870s, with p. o. est. Sept. 6, 1889, Thomas Whalen, first pm, closed Jan. 15, 1935. Formerly, **Freemansburgh**, n. Alfred Freeman, who built a blast furnace and forge on the site. *Quarterly*, 7 (1962), no. 2, p. 15. 1956 USGS Edwards Quad. / **Talcville Road**: r., t. Edwards, n. talc mines; r., t. Fowler, n. talc mines. / **Talcville School**: no. 10, common school, t. Edwards, Dist. 6. Freeman, 16.

Tallman Road: r., t. Oswegatchie, n. John E. Tallman family from Troy, NY.

Tamarack: the larch tree (*Larix laricina*), a species of the pine family. **Tamarack** is prob. of Amerindian origin, but the ety. is unknown. / **Tamarack Branch**: t. Clare, trib. Bullhead Pond. 1915 USGS Russell Quad. / **Tamarack Creek**: t. Fine, trib. Little River. 1916 USGS Oswegatchie Quad. / **Tamarack Point**: on Cranberry Lake, t. Clifton. 1896 New. / **Tamarack Pond**: t. Clifton, alt. 1,778 ft. 1902 Blankman; 1908 Adm; 1912 Stoddard; 1919 USGS Cranberry Lake Quad. See **Chair Ponds**. / **Tamarack Street**: s., v. Massena.

Tamblin Road: r., t. Gouverneur, n. John Tamblin (1915 Census).

Tanner: surname used as a specific: **Tanner Creek**: t. Hermon, outlet for Trout Lake, southwest corner of St. Lawrence County, n. Thomas Tanner, settled 1809. Tanner Creek becomes Harrison Creek through Canton. / **Tanner Road/Street**: r., t. DeKalb and s., h. DeKalb Junction, n. Thomas Tanner; r., t. Potsdam, n. Tanner family.

Tate Street: s., c. Ogdensburg, n. Thomas B. Tate, civil engineer and army officer. He was brought to the United States from England when he was three years old. His father, Robert Tate, was also a civil engineer who settled in Lisbon in 1817.

Tateville: h.,t. Canton, n. Robert Tate. Later **Canton Falls**, now v. **Rensselaer Falls**. *Quarterly*, 11 (1966), no. 1, p. 3.

Tavern Island: in Black lake, t. Morristown, n. by Daniel Church, who, with a boy as a guide, was looking for a mill site and was caught by nightfall and stayed on the island, enjoying a fish and a duck, good as staying at a tavern. Recounted by Trudie Calvert, "Tavern Island," *Quarterly*, 20 (1975), no. 3, p. 19. 1961 USGS Hammond Quad.

Taylor: a popular n. everywhere but especially so in the county, where many places honor it: **Taylor Creek**: trib. Van Rensselaer Creek, t. Pierrepont. 1915 USGS Russell Quad; 1964 USGS Pierrepont Quad. / **Taylor Creek State Forest**, #3, t. Pierrepont. / **Taylor House**: v. Waddington, n. Ira Taylor, host. Tedford, 80. / **Taylor Park**: public recreation park at **Taylors Rapids**, on Grass(e) River; also called **Woodcocks Rapids** on west side of river, t. Canton. *Quarterly*, 14 (1980), no. 4, p. 4. / **Taylor Road**: r., t. De Peyster; r., t. Louisville; r., t. Oswegatchie; r., t. Pierrepont; s., v. Massena, n. Ruel Taylor, hotel keeper. / **Taylors Corner**: crossroads, t. Lawrence. 1964 USGS North Lawrence Quad.

Tealls Road: r., t. Rossie, n. Joseph Teall, first settler, 1807. Durant, 312.

Temagami Islands: two islands, St. Lawrence River, t. Hammond, n. Amerindian, meaning unknown. 1958 USGS Chippewa Quad.

Temperance Tavern: see **Chamberlain House**.

Ten Towns: Formed 1787, of ten square miles each: Potsdam, Madrid, Canton, Lisbon, Cambray, Hague, Stockholm, Louisville, Oswegatchie, DeKalb (spelled De Kalb when formed). Only four retain their ten square miles. Cambray and Hague were renamed Gouverneur and Morristown to honor Gouverneur Morris. See Hough and Durant for full accounts.

Terrace Park: t. Morristown, camp ground for Ogdens- burg and Potsdam district of Methodist Episcopal Church, with depot in Morristown. Later, Civil War veterans assumed control of it. *Quarterly*, 2 (1957), no. 3, p. 3. Bogardus, 81-83. 1963 USGS Morristown Quad.

Terry Road: r., t. Russell. See **Grandy Road**.

Tewatenetarenies: see Potsdam.

Thacher: see **Thatcher Street.**

Thatcher: a surname used as a specific: **Thatcher Hall**: on campus of SUC, Potsdam, n. Hervey Dexter Thatcher (1852-1925), inventor, physician, pharmacist, and inventor. He is credited with inventing the milk bottle, with promoting paper containers for milk, and improving baking powder. Thatcher was also involved in many mercantile and advertising ventures with his H. D. Thatcher & Co., 1895-1924, in Potsdam. Dayton Dewey, "Dr. Hervey D. Thatcher: Inventor of the Glass Milk Bottle," *Quarterly*, 4 (1959), no. 3, pp. [4-5]; and Robert A. Wyant and Victoria Levitt, "The Thatcher Story," *Quarterly*, 32 (1987), no. 2, pp. 3-9. / **Thatcher Street**: s., v. Hermon, n. Dr. Edwin Thacher, but spelled **Thatcher** on some maps.

Thayer School: no. 5, common school, t. Gouverneur, n. Thayer family, possibly Thomas M. Thayer, cabinet maker, justice of the peace, and a deacon in the Baptist Church. Cent., Souv., 73.

The Bog: swamp, t. Hopkinton. 1919 USGS Nicholville Quad; 1964 USGS Sylvan Falls Quad.

The Bog Outlet: t. Hopkinton, trib. Long Pond Outlet. 1919 USGS Nicholville Quad; 1964 USGS Sylvan Quad.

The Cedars: see **Cedars, The**.

The Corduroy: see **Corduroy, The**.

The Fire Fall: t. Edwards.

The Gulf: pond, t. Pitcairn. See **Gulf, The**. 1916 USGS Oswegatchie Quad.

The Meadows: flatlands, t. Hopkinton (St. Lawrence Co.) and t. Waverly (Franklin Co.). 1964 USGS Lake Ozonia Quad.

The Plains: flatland, t. Fine. 1896 New; 1902 Blankman; 1908 Adm; 1912 Stoddard; 1919 USGS Cranberry Lake Quad. / **The Plains**: flatland, t. Parishville and Colton. 1853 HMC; 1858 Rogerson; 1921 USGS Stark Quad. / **Plains Road** (Beech Plains).

The River: shortened and affectionate n. **St. Lawrence River.**

The Rock: island, in St. Lawrence River, t. Hammond, descriptive. 1958 USGS Chippewa Quad.

Third: a number-n., in a series: **Third Brother Island**: in St. Lawrence River, t. Hammond. 1958 USGS Chippewa Quad. / **Third Pond**: t. Colton. See **Lows Lake**. / **Third Street**; s., h. Wanakena.

Thirty-five: a number-n.: **Thirty-Five Pond**: see **Thirty- five Pond. / Thirtyfive Outlet**: t. Hopkinton, trib. Jo(e) Indian Outlet. 1920 USGS Childwold Quad. / **Thirtyfive Pond**: t. Hopkinton, alt. 1,513. 1896 **Thirty Five Pond** New; 1902 **Thirty Five Brook** Blankman; 1908 **Thirty Five Brook** Adm; 1912 **Thirty-five Brook** Stoddard; 1920 USGS Childwold Quad. Origin n. undetermined.

Thomas: a popular family n. in the county; sometimes a given or first name: **Thomas Brook**: t. Clifton, trib. Oswegatchie River. 1896

Thomas Creek New; 1902 **Thomas Creek**; 1919 USGS Cranberry Lake Quad. / **Thomas Brook**: t. Hopkinton, trib. Stony Brook. 1964 USGS Sylvan Falls Quad. / **Thomas Creek**: see **Thomas Brook**. / **Thomas Hall**: on Clarkson University campus, n. James Shelby Thomas, president from 1933 to 1940. / **Thomas Ridge Road**: r., h. Louisville. / **Thomas School**: t. Macomb. / **Thomas School**: no. 14, common school, on Route 37, near Oak Point Road, t. Morristown. Bogardus, 60.

Thompson: a common and popular family n. in the county: **Thompson Bay**: in Cranberry Lake, t. Clifton, n. Albert Thompson (1854-1933), said to be Cranberry Lake's earliest settler, working as a farmer, carpenter, and guide. Reynolds, 189. 1896 New. / **Thompson Corners to Chipman Road**: r., t. Madrid. n. John Thomp-son family. / **Thompson Island**: in Black Lake, t. Morristown. 1961 USGS Pope Mills Quad. / **Thomp-son Ridge Road**: r., t. Louisville. / **Thompson Road**: r., t. Canton, n. William, Moses, and Gustavus Thompson families. / **Thompson School**: no. 27, common school, t. Potsdam. / **Thompsons Island**: in St. Lawrence River, t. Waddington. 1942 USGS Murphy Island Quad.

Three: a number-n.: **Three Falls**: in Racquette River, t. Colton. *Quarterly*, 5 (1960), no. 2, p. 5; 9 (1964), no. 4, p. 17. 1853 HMC. / **Three Falls Lane**: r., t. Colton. / **Three Pound Pond**: t. Colton, westernmost of the ponds, n. size of fish caught there. See **Hornet Ponds**. 1880 Ely; 1902 Blankman. Also, **3 Pound Pond**.

Three Falls: now, **South Colton**. *Quarterly*, 5 (1960), no. 2, p. 5; 9 (1964), no. 4, p. 17. / **Threemile Mountain**: t. Fine and Clifton. 1919 USGS Cranberry Lake Quad.

Tibbits Creek: t. Lisbon, trib. St. Lawrence River, n. John Tibbits family. 1963 USGS Ogden East Quad.

Tick Island: in St. Lawrence River, t. Lisbon, n. prob. for the prickly achenes of the bur-marigold (**bidens**) or beggar-ticks (**bidens frondosa**), a pervasive wet-ground waste-place weed. Also, sticktight, stick-metights. 1906 USGS Red Mills Quad.

Tiehonwinetha: See **Ogden Island**.

Tiernan: a family n.: **Tiernan Ridge**: t., Norfolk. formerly, **Douglas Ridge**, n. Thomas Tiernan family. *Quarterly*, 12 (1967), no. 1, p. 16. Also spelled **Tiernon Ridge**. **/Tier-**

nan Ridge School: no. 14, common school, t. Norfolk, n. ridge. / **Tiernan Road**: r., t. Waddington, n. Andrew Tiernan family.

Tierney Road: r., t. Rossie, Hammond, n. Lawrence Tierney family, but not otherwise identified; r., t. Oswegatchie, now **Monkey Hill Road**.

Tilden: h., t. Lisbon, n. Tilden family, p. o. est. Dec. 10, 1896, William J. McBath, pm, closed Nov. 15, 1902. 1906 USGS Red Mills Quad. / **Tilden School**: no. 11, common school, t. Lisbon, n. Tilden family.

Timerman Hall: on SUC, Potsdam, campus, n. C. Donald Timerman, a science teacher at Potsdam Normal. He was killed in action in World War II, 1945.

Tin Island: in Black Lake, t. Morristown. 1961 USGS Hammond Quad.

Tinkle Brook: in Paradise Valley. Noted on cover of *Quarterly*, 15 (1970), no. 1, n. poss. for noise.

Tiohionhoken: see **Brasher Falls**.

Toad: n. small amphibian of the genus *Bofo americanus*: **Toad Hollow**: section,t. Parishville. See **Toad Pond** for n., but "An old tale that Toad Hollow was named from the quantity of toads in this section is just hearsay." See *Sketches of Parishville*. / **Toad Pond**: t. Clifton. 1896 New; 1898 EGB, p. 28; 1902 **Tood Pond** (misprint) Blankman; 1908 Adm; 1912 Stoddard; 1919 USGS Cranberry Lake Quad.

Todd: William Todd, farmer, Durant, 415: **Todd Road**: r., t. Lisbon. / **Todd School**: no. 12, common school, t. Lisbon, n. Todd family. / **Todd's Corners**: t. Lisbon. *Quarterly*, 11 (1966), no. 2, p. 18.

Toland Road: See **Ore Road**.

Tollbridge: at Edwardsville, t. Morristown, Black Lake, ferry at crossing in 1851 using cables and flat-bottomed barge; tolls over bridge in 1922 discontinued 1931 when replaced by concrete causeway. Some people went across on the ice rather than pay the toll.

Tom Bean Cemetery: t. Hermon, at West Hermon, n. Thomas Bean, Englishman.

Tomlinson Road: r., t. Edwards, n. John Tomlinson family.

Ton Mountain: see **Hamilton Mountain**.

Tooley: family n.: **Tooley Pond**: t. Clare, Clifton, alt. 1,509 ft., n. Samuel Tooley family. 1858 Rogerson; 1865 Beers, p. 86; 1883 Ely-Wallace; 1896 Blankman; 1912 Stoddard; 1921 Stark Quad. / **Tooley Pond Mountain**: t. Clare, alt. 1,792 ft., n. pond. 1921 Stark Quad. / **Tooley Pond Outlet**: stream, trib. Oswegatchie River, t. Clifton, n. pond. 1919 USGS Cranberry Quad. / **Tooley Pond Road**: r., t. Clare, n. pond. / **Tooley Road**: r., t. Clifton, n. Tooley family.

Toothacher: a cluster of n. for Roswell Toothacher and family. **Toothacher District**: t. Pitcairn, *Quarterly*, 10 (1965), no. 4, p. 14. / **Toothacher School**: no. 4, common school, t. Pitcairn. / **Toothaker Pond**: t. Pitcairn, n. variant spelling of **Toothacher**. 1951 USGS Harrisville Quad. / **Toothaker Road**: r., t. Pitcairn, n. pond. / **Toothaker State Forest**, #16, t. Pitcairn.

Toothpick Island: a small, narrow island, in St. Lawrence River, t. Hammond. 1958 USGS Chippewa Quad.

Torrey Field: on St. Lawrence University campus, used for women's field hockey and women's lacrosse, n. Arthur S. Torrey, Chair of the Board of Trustees, 1968-1978.

Totten's and Crossfield's Purchase: The purchase consisted of approximately 800,000 acres of land from the Mohawk and Canajoharie tribes in July 1773 and included all the lands lying on the west side of the Hudson River (Hough, 235-236). The northern border of the purchase formed the southern boundary of Franklin and St. Lawrence Counties; n. Joseph Totten and Stephen Crossfield. R. E. Kerr, "Lumbering in the Adirondack Foothills," *Quarterly*, 9 (1964), no. 2, p. 12, gives the acreage as 1,150,000 and the date 1792. The boundary between Macomb's Purchase and T & C Purchase can still be seen in t. of Fine marked with the "copper bolt" noting the "great corner" of the T & C line. See Kerr for description.

Town: n. for boundaries, legal appellations, and other bureaucratic business, but occasionally a personal name: **Town Road**: r., t. Russell, n. Clark Town and family. Clarke, 20. Also, **Towne Road**. / **Town Line Pond**: t. Colton, Piercefield. 1880 Ely; 1883 Ely-Wallace; 1896 New; 1902 **Tow Line Pond** (misprint) Blankman; 1912 Stoddard; 1954 USGS Tupper Lake Quad. / **Town Line Road**: r., t. Canton, Russell; r., t. Madrid, Waddington; r., t. Potsdam; r., t. Waddington. / **Town**

Line School: no. 31, common school, t. Lisbon; no. 13, common school, t. Massena; no. 14, common school, t. Waddington; no. 10, common school. t. Louisville.

Townline School: h. Pyrites, t. Canton. Edward J. Austin, *Quarterly*, 10 (1965), no. 3, p. 13.

Towns Mills: t. Russell, n. Town family.

Tows Point: on Massawepie Lake, t. Piercefield, n. Ferris Tow, home owner. 1896 New.

Tracy: a popular and honored family n. in the county. / **Tracy Brook**: stream, trib. Little River, t. Canton, n. Festus Tracy, early, perhaps first, settler of t. Canton and surveyor of St. Lawrence and Franklin Counties. A claim can be made for Septimus Tracy, also an early settler in the Lisbon-Canton area. Durant, pp. 205, 298. 1963 Canton Quad. / **Tracy Crossroad**: t. Massena, on Long Sault Island. Dumas, 27. / **Tracy Pond**: t. Clare, alt. 1,376 ft. 1865 Beers, p. 86; 1896 New; 1902 Blankman; 1908 Adm 1908; 1912 Stoddard; 1921 Stark Quad. / **Tracy Road**: r., t. Lisbon. / **Tracy School**: no. 15, common school, t. Massena, on Long Sault Island. Also **Tracys School**. Dumas, 27. / **Tracy Street**: s., v. Massena, n. Samuel Tracy from Townsend, VT. / **Tracys Landing**: t. Massena, on south side of Long Sault Island, n. Samuel Tracy, arrived 1816. Dumas, 26. Also **Tracy's Landing**.

Traffic Circle Road: r., t. Massena, desc.

Train Pond: t. Hopkinton, n. Horace Train (1784-1880), settled 1804-1805 on Independence Hill. Also Robert Train settled in 1804.

Trask School: no. 9. common school, t. Hopkinton, n. Trask family.

Triangle: for geometrical shape: **Triangle Pond**: t. Colton, n. shape. 1880 Ely; 1883 Ely-Wallace 1896 New; 1902 Blankman; 1912 Stoddard; 1954 USGS Tupper Lake Quad. / **Triangle Road**: r., t. Hammond, sometimes called **Triangular Road**, was last of three important roads laid out to form a triangle consisting of Triangle Road, Chippewa Bay Road, and Route 37. *Quarterly*, 10 (1965), no. 4, p. 9.

Trim Road: r., t. Colton, prob. n. Trim family.

Trinity: n. church or a condition of threes: **Trinity Avenue**: s., v. Gouverneur, n. Trinity Church. / **Trinity Elm**: in Richville, t. DeKalb, a landmark, with three trees growing from one trunk; n. by Reverend Gorham Cross, 1840, who saved it by giving a woodchopper $10.00 not to cut it down. Also **Trinity Tree, Old Cross Elm.** *Quarterly*, 18 (1973), no. 4, p. 17. The elm is now gone.

Tripod Point: on St. Lawrence River. Caption on picture, "Tripod Point Camp, Gallop Rapids, St. Lawrence River, 1892," *Quarterly*, 18 (1973), no. 3, p. 12.

Trippanyville Road: r., t. Norfolk, n. Frank Trippany and wife, parents of 11 children.

Tromboli Road: r., t. Norfolk, n. Tromboli family.

Trout: a game fish of the genus *Salmo*, considered a culinary and gourmet delicacy, as well as an angler's delight, its n. adorns any stream in which even one trout has been caught, or so it seems: **Trout Brook**: several occur: t. Brasher, near Raymondville. *Quarterly*, 6 (1961), no. 1, p. 12, trib. Deer River. 1964 North Lawrence Quad; 1873 Hamilton Child, p. 89 / t. Hopkinton / t. Lawrence / t. Massena, in v., off West Hatfield Street / t. Norfolk, trib. Racquette River. 1964 USGS Norfolk Quad / t. Pierrepont; trib. West Branch St. Regis River / t. Stockholm. 1964 USGS Brasher Falls Quad. / **Trout Brook Forest**: county forest, t. Stockholm. / **Trout Brook Road East**: r., t. Madrid. / **Trout Brook Road West**; r., t. Madrid. / **Trout Brook School**: no. 29, common school, t. Potsdam. / **Trout Lake**: t. Hermon, alt. 746 ft. See Leah M. Noble, "The Trout Lake Story," *Quarterly*, 16 (1971), no. 1, p. 9. 1956 USGS Edwards Quad. / **Trout Lake**: see **Big Trout Pond.** / **Trout Lake**: see **Lake Ozonia.** / **Trout Lake Forest**: county forest, t. Hermon. / **Trout Lake Road**: r., t. Hermon. / **Trout Lake School**: no. 8, common school, t. Hermon. 1915 USGS Gouverneur Quad. / **Trout Lake State Forest**, #42, t. Edwards, Hermon. / **Trout Lake Street**: s., v. Edwards. / **Trout Pond**: see **Dog Pond**, t. Colton. / **Trout Pond**: t. Piercefield, formerly in t. Hopkinton before 1901, alt. 1,780. 1865 Beers, p. 86; 1873 Hamilton Child; 1880 Ely; 1883 **Big Trout Pond** Ely-Wallace; 1896 New; 1902 Blankman; 1908 **Big Trout Pond**; 1912 Stoddard; 1954 USGS Tupper lake Quad.

Trudell Road: r., t. Norfolk. n. H. E. Truesdell, before change in spelling. [Also appears as **Trubell**, a misprint]

Tryon Road: r., t. Stockholm, n. Benjamin Tryon family.

Tsiiakotennitserronttietha: see **Gallup Rapids**.

Tsiiakoontieta: See **Raymondville**.

Tsiiowenokwakarate: see **Croil's Island**.

Tsitkaniatareskowa: see **Tupper Lake**.

Tuck Road: r., t. Lisbon, n. Tuck family from Ireland.

Tucker: a popular family n. in the county: **Tucker Brook**: trib. West Branch St. Regis River, t. Stockholm. 1964 USGS Potsdam Quad. / **Tucker Road**: r., t. Louisville, n. Aubrey Tucker family; r., t. Pierrepont, n. Martin Tucker family. / **Tucker Terrace**: t. Louisville. 1963 USGS Massena Quad.

Tully Road: r., t. Canton, n. Tully family.

Tully Road: r., t. Macomb, n. Joseph Tulley family. Spelled **Tully** on maps.

Tunkethandle Hill: t. Clare, n. unclear but believed to mean "devil's elbow."

Tupper Lake: t. Piercefield, alt. 1,554. n. a Mr. Tupper, a surveyor for the great Macomb Purchase. Durant, 79. Amerindian names: **Arguna**, "green rocks"; **Paskuugemah** "lake going out from a river [Racquette]." **Tsitkaniatareskowa**, "biggest lake." 1853 **Tuppers Lake** HMC; 1858 **Tupper's Lake** Rogerson; 1860 **Tupper's Lake** Street, pp. 76, 177; 1873 **Tupper's Lake** Hamilton Child; 1880 Ely; 1882 Ely-Wallace; 1896 **Big Tupper Lake**; 1902 **Big Tupper Lake** Blankman; 1908 **Big Tupper Lake** Adm; 1912 Stoddard; 1954 USGS Tupper Lake Quad. Derived names include **Tupper Road**: s., v. Canton (road no longer exists). / **Tupper School**: no. 17, common school, t. Canton, n. D. M. Tupper family.

Turkey Hill: v. Potsdam, nickname for **Elm Street**, said to be so n. for the high class prostitutes ("turkeys") who lived in the area.

Turnbull: family n.: **Turnbull Road**: r., t. Rossie, n. Adam, Andrew Hunter, Michael, Thomas, and William Turnbull families who arrived from Scotland in 1820. (Durant, 314). Also **Turn Bull Road**. / **Turnbull Corner**: t. Madrid, n. Turnbull family. 1964 USGS Waddington Quad.

Turner Road: r., t. Macomb, n. Elisha Turner family.

Turnpike: any toll road. Earlier roads called turnpikes had tollgates: **Turnpike**: settlement, t. Potsdam; p. o. est. Nov. 25, 1896, Herbert J. Thompson, pm, closed Jan. 30, 1904. / **Turnpike, The**: see **Parishville Turnpike**. / **Turnpike Creek**: t. Fowler, trib. Oswegatchie River. 1956 USGS Gouverneur Quad. / **Turnpike School**: no. 7, common school, t. Potsdam.

Tuttle Pond: stream, trib. Jocks Pond Outlet, t. Colton, n. Tuttle family. 1920 USGS Childwold Quad.

Twilight Island: See **Dark Island**. 1958 USGS Chippewa Quad.

Twin: a popular name for a pair of something, or a feature joined with a similar one: **Twin Island**: t. Lisbon. 1906 USGS Red Mills Quad. / **Twin Lake**: t. Edwards. / **Twin Lake Road**: r., t. Fine. / **Twin Lake Stream**: t. Fine, trib. Little River. 1916 USGS Oswegatchie Quad. / **Twin Lakes**: t. Fine, alt. 1,356 and 1,361 ft. *Quarterly*, 5 (1960), no. 1, npn. 1916 USGS Oswegatchie Quad. Outlet flows into Little River, adjacent to Rte. 3. / **Twin Mountain**: t. Clifton, alt. 1,800 ft. 1919 USGS Cranberry lake Quad. / **Twin Ponds**: t. Hopkinton. 1898 New; 1902 Blankman; 1908 Adm; 1912 Stoddard; 1919 USGS Nicholville; 1964 USGS Sylvan Falls Quad. / **Twin Ponds**: t. Clare, Pierrepont. 1902 Blankman; 1921 Stark Quad. / **Twin Ponds**: t. Pitcairn. 1916 USGS Oswegatchie Quad; 1951 USGS Harrisville Quad. / **Twin Ponds Outlet**: t. Clifton, trib. South Branch Grass(e) River. 1921 USGS Stark Quad.

Tyler School: no. 12, common school, t. Hammond, n. Joel, James, John, and Moses Tyler families.

Tyo Road: r., t. Louisville, n. Tyo family of many children.

U

Under the Hill: a settlement in the valley along river at Nicholville. *Quarterly*, 16 (1971), no. 1, p. 14.

Underhill Drive: s., h. Hannawa Falls. Origin n. uncertain.

Underwood Road: r., t. Hermon, n. William Underwood family.

Union: also, see **Unionville** for names and comments. **Union** and its combinations are the most popular abstract names in the United States, commemorating the union of the states and the union of diverse groups and even geographical features. **Union Cemetery**: t. DeKalb. Same as **Risley Cemetery**. / t. Potsdam. / t. Stockholm, near Buckton. 1964 USGS Parishville Quad. / t. Waddington, near Handlin Road. 1963 USGS Sparrowhawk Point Quad. / **Union Free School**: v. Canton. / **Union Free School**, t. Hammond. /**Union Free School**: org. Oct. 31, 1874, v. Heuvelton, t. Oswegatchie, school district No. 5. Durant, 200. / **Union Free School**: v. Rensselaer Falls, about 1892, burned in 1903. / **Union Free School: h. Russell, inc. September, 1905; became Knox Memorial in 1912.** / **Union Point**: on Cranberry Lake, t. Clifton. 1896 New; 1919 USGS Cranberry Quad. / **Union School**: no. 6, common school, t. Potsdam. See **Union Street**. / **Union Settlement**: t. Potsdam; see **Unionville**. / **Union Street**: s., v. Brasher Falls; s., v. Potsdam, may have been n. for the group, "the union, that formed **Unionville**." It was the center of Potsdam in the early years. Benjamin Raymond erected the first building on what is now Union Street. The building housed a church and a school, the latter being the beginning of SUC many years later. Formerly, **Union Lane, Union Road**. The street is now very short and connects Main and Elm Streets. / **Union Street**: s., v. Heuvelton.

Unionville: t. Potsdam. In 1804, several farmers pooled their money and land and formed "The Union." In April or May 1807, "The Union" settlement was organized, an experiment in communal living. William Bullard was "King of the Union." The experiment came to an end in 1810, but the n. lives on. *Quarterly*, 5 (1960), no. 2, p. [1]. Other n. transferred from **Union** include **Union Graveyard**, **Union Schoolhouse**, **Union Road**, **Union Falls**, **Union Settlement**. 1064 USGS Potsdam Quad.

United States-Canadian St. Lawrence Seaway and Power Project, The: known as **The Seaway**, opened in 1959, allowing ocean-going ships to navigate between the Great Lakes and the Atlantic Ocean.

United States Highway 11, 11B, 11C. St. Lawrence County.

University Drive: also **University Avenue**, s., v. Canton, n. St. Lawrence University.

Upper: direction-n., contrasted with **Lower**, connotes either a higher level or a northerly direction: **Upper & Lower Lakes Wildlife Management Area**, t. Canton. / **Upper Big Bay**: in Black Lake, bay is located at the upper end near the town line, t. Morristown. 1963 USGS Edwardsville Quad. / **Upper Deep Bay**: in Black Lake, t. Morristown. 1961 USGS Pope Mills Quad. / **Upper Grasse School**: t. Russell. 1915 USGS Russell Quad **Upper District School**. See also Clarke, 26. / **Upper Indian Lake**: pond, expansion of Indian Creek, t. Canton. See **Indian Creek**. 1963 **Upper Lake** Rensselaer Falls Quad. / **Upper Lake**: See **Upper Indian Lake**. / **Upper Long Sault**: See **Croil's Island**. / **Upper Wick**: t. Parishville, section from Jo(e) Indian Pond to Stark Corner, later became known as **Blake**. See **Wick**.

Urban Drive: s., v. Massena, apparently n. Roman Catholic popes (Urban I-VII), by the land developer of a housing project. It is in a cluster of such names as **Serra**, **Sharon**, **Urban**, and **Madonna**.

V

Vaile Street: s., v. Gouverneur; poss. n. Cyrenus Vail, farmer, town assessor, commissioner of highways, and 19 years as a street commissioner, "although a Democrat." Cent. Souv., 368.

Valentine Hall: on St. Lawrence University campus, n. Joseph W. and Grace W. Valentine, benefactors.

Valley Drive: s., v. Gouverneur, descriptive.

Valley View Drive: s., h. Star Lake.

Van Buren Road: r., t. Gouverneur, n. Harmon and Thomas Harvey Van Buren families, who settled in 1817, and in particular their brother Peter V., who settled in 1820 and became a hotel keeper and the volunteer caretaker for the park. Cent. Souv., 26.

Van House Corners: t. Russell, n. Peter Van House. 1915 USGS Russell Quad.

Van Housen Hall: on SUC, Potsdam, campus, n. Bernice and Charles Van Housen, educators.

Van Kennen Road: r., t. Stockholm, n. Van Kennen family.

Van Note Hall: on Clarkson University campus, n. William Gardner Van Note, ninth president of Clarkson (1951- 1961).

Van Rensselaer: n. is commemorated in many features, here in the full namesake. See **Rensselaer** for other n.: **Van Rensselaer Creek**: trib. Little River, Pierrepont, n. Stephen and Henry Van Rensselaer. 1915 USGS Russell Quad; 1964 USGS Pierrepont Quad. / **Van Rensselaer Point**: on St. Lawrence River, c. Ogdensburg. / **Van Rensselaer Point Lighthouse**: landmark, on St. Lawrence River, city of Ogdensburg. / **Van Rensselaer Road**; r., t. Lisbon, Waddington; Earliest deeds from New York State are to Jeremiah Van Rensselaer (deed dated 1788) and Stephen (deeds dating 1798-1821); Jacob R. from 1821 (Seaway Trail Booklet).

Vaughan's Switch: on Carthage and Adirondack Railroad, n. Vaughan family. *Quarterly*, 11 (1966), no. 1, p. 16.

Vebber: n. family, p. o. est. Oct. 16, 1884, Fred E. Vebber, pm, closed May 10, 1888. / **Vebber Corners**: crossroads, t. Pierrepont. Same as **Vebber**. 1964 Colton Quad.

Vermont Settlement: t. Oswegatchie, between Heuvelton and Rensselaer Falls, n. settlers from Windsor Co., VT. Durant, 200.

Veterans Mountain Camp of American Legion, Department of New York State, Inc.: In the survey township of Atherton (Piercefield), about 1,000 acres of the Barbour Tract were sold by executors of William Barbour for $85,000, July 21, 1922. The acreage also included land under the water of Horseshoe Lake and Big Tupper Lake as well as the islands in the latter. In 1990 it was negotiated for permission to be subdivided and is now privately owned, no longer a health and recreation camp for veterans.

Vice Road; r., t. Brasher, between Bush and Sam Buell Roads, n. George Vice.

Victory Road: s., v. Massena, n. Mamre Victory. Dumas, 57.

View Street: s., v. Massena, desc. and promotional.

Village Beach: v. Norwood, on Racquette River.

Vista Street: s., v. Gouverneur, desc, for the view and promotional.

Volans School: no. 9, common school, t. Oswegatchie, n. Volans family. See **Oswegatchie School**.

Vollens Corners: n. Volans family.

See Persis Yates Boyesen, "Oswegatchie 1884," *Quarterly*, 10 (1965), no. 1, p. 13.

Vosburg Road: r., t. DeKalb, n. Jacob and Abram Vosburg families.

Vrooman: n. Elihu Vrooman family: **Vrooman Ridge**: t. Edwards and Fine. 1916 USGS Oswegatchie Quad. Variant: **Vroman.** / **Vrooman Ridge School**: t. Fine. Dist. 8, built in 1874. Also **Green School**. Reynolds, 199. Also **Vroman**. Also **Froman**, a misprint. / **Vrooman Road**: r., t. Pitcairn. Also **Vroman**.

W

Waddington: t. northern border on St. Lawrence River, n. Joshua Waddington, Mar. 3, 1818. In 1803, David A. and Thomas Ogden conveyed "the undivided third of their land to Waddington." On Nov. 22, 1859, the t. Madrid was divided in half forming the t. Waddington. Hough, 342, 344; *Quarterly*, 5 (1960),no. 4, p. 7. 1964 USGS Waddington Quad. / **Waddington**: v. in t. Waddington, p. o. est. from **Madrid** April 15, 1819, Alexander Richards, first pm (Hough, 575, has an erroneous date), existing, ZIP 13694. Formerly, **Kanateroken**, "wet village;" then **Hamilton**, in honor of Alexander Hamilton, Secretary of the Treasury during Washington's presidency and later killed in a duel with Aaron Burr. Hamilton was a business associate of David A. and Thomas Ogden and Joshua Waddington. 1964 USGS Waddington Quad. / **Waddington-Chamberlain Corners Road**: r., t. Waddington. / **Waddington School**: no. 1, common school, t. Waddington. Also, **Waddington Village School**. / Waddington Union Free School and Academy. 1989 Blankman.

Wadhams Hall: college for students preparing for the priesthood, n. first Bishop of Ogdensburg Diocese, The Very Reverend Edgar Philip Wadhams (1817-1891). He was appointed Feb. 15, 1872 by Pope Pius IX when the diocese was established. His remains are buried beneath the sanctuary of St. Mary's Cathedral. / **Wadhams Park**: map 1903 shows lots between Utica and Black River Railroad, Morristown to Ogdensburg. / **Wadhams Street**: s., c. Ogdensburg.

Wadleigh: r., t. Stockholm, n. Luther E. Wadleigh, attorney of Potsdam.

Wagner Road: r., t. Lisbon, probably n. Joseph Waggener family. Spelling has been changed. 1850 Census.

Wagners Corners: t. Waddington, n. Wagner family. 1964 USGS Waddington Quad.

Wagstaff Corner: crossroads, t. Lawrence, n. Henry Wagstaff and sons Henry, Robert, and John. 1964 USGS North Lawrence Quad.

Waid Street: s., v. Gouverneur, n. Josiah Waid, sheriff of the county (1847-1849).

Wait Road: r., t. Potsdam, n. Allen Wait family; sometimes spelled **Waite**.

Walker: surname used as a specific: **Walker Arena**: on Clarkson University campus, the hockey arena, n. Murray Walker, a Potsdam businessman and founder of Clarkson hockey. / **Walker Road**: r., t. Gouverneur, n. Walker family, in particular William Walker, merchant, postmaster, and farmer. / **Walker Road**: r., t. Madrid, n. William Walker family.

Wall Street: s., v. Gouverneur, n. James Wall, early settler.

Wallace Road; r., t. Louisville, n. Wallace Family.

Walnut: a tree of the genus *Juglans*, valued for its rich edible nuts, its n. for places, especially streets, is popular throughout the United States: **Walnut Street**: s., v. Massena / s., v. Norwood / s., v. Potsdam.

Walrath: family n.: **Walrath Road**: r., t. Canton, n. S. Z. Walrath, farmer and dairyman; / r., t. DeKalb, off Stevenson Road; / r., t. DeKalb, off Ritchie Road; / r., t. Morristown, n. Philip Walrath from Montgomery County. / **Walrath School**: no. 13, common school, t. Lisbon.

Walter F. Pratt Memorial Forest: picnic area t. Brasher in State Forest no. 1, n. first District Director of New York State Conservation Department. 1964 USGS North Lawrence Quad.

Wanakena: h., t. Fine, Amerindian n. unknown, but theories exist: (1) n. an Indian princess who jumped from a cliff as the result of a love affair; (2) Indian n. "beautiful waters"; (3) n. Pullman car; and (4) in Ojibway language, "a good place to live." It is doubtful that the original name and meaning can be recovered, which means that it can mean anything anyone wants it to mean. L. P. Plumley, "Wanakena," *Quarterly*, 7 (1962), no. 4, p. 13; p. o. est. Sept. 12, 1902, George H. Bullock, first pm, existing ZIP 13695.

1908 Adm; 1912 Stoddard; 1919 USGS Cranberry Lake Quad. / **Wanakena Road**; r., t. Fine. / **Wanakena School**: t. Fine, Dist. 11. Reynolds, 199.

Ward Road: r., t. Macomb, n. John and McClellan Ward families.

Wardell Road: r., t. DePeyster, n. Wardell family.

Wardwell's Bay: where the ferry **James S. Bean** burned (1876) in Black Lake, halfway between Heuvelton and Rossie. Bogardus, 123. Origin n. unknown.

Warm Brook: t. Colton, trib. Racquette River, temperature name contrasted with **Cold**. 1865 Beers, p. 27; 1878 Durant & Pierce; 1896 New; 1902 Blankman; 1908 Adm; 1908 USGS Potsdam Quad. / **Warm Brook Flow**: t. Colton, trib. Racquette River, n. brook. 1964 USDS Colton Quad.

Warren: a surname that is used as a specific n.: **Warren Point**: on Tupper Lake, t. Piercefield. 1954 USGS Tupper Lake Quad. / **Warren School**: no. 7, common school, t. DePeyster, n. Joel Warren family. / **Warren Street**: also **Warren** Avenue, s., v. Massena, n. Warren family; s., c. Ogdensburg, n. Joseph Warren, general in the Revolutionary War, killed at Bunker Hill.

Washburn Corners: t. Pierrepont, n. Washburn family. 1964 USGS Colton Quad.

Washburnville: h., t, Macomb, p. o., July 27, 1837, David Day, pm, changed to **Macomb** May 13, 1842; n. Rufus Washburn. *Quarterly*, 7 (1962), no. 4, p. 14. Later **Pierces Corners**.

Washington: for George Washington, lst president of the United States: **Washington School**: v. Massena. 1964 USGS Massena Quad. / **Washington Street**: s., v. Gouverneur; s., v. Hermon; s., v. Heuvelton; s., v. Massena; s., c. Ogdensburg; s., v. Potsdam.

Watch Island: in St. Lawrence River, t. Hammond. 1858 USGS Chippewa Quad. Origin n. unknown. / **Watch Island**: in Black Lake, t. Morristown. A century and a half ago, and from there back into antiquity, Watch Island was undoubtedly a favorite camping site of the Indians who journeyed every summer from tribal headquarters of the central part of the state to the great river. Relics of their work in the shape of stone arrows, spearheads, pipes, tomahawks, and broken pottery, have been found in considerable quality there. 1961 USGS Hammond Quad. Just why Watch Island was selected as an Indian summer residence may be conjectured, but it may be that it was because of its nearness to the mainland and to the hunting grounds a few miles Inland, and sufficiently for many to be a safeguard against attack by warriors of hostile tribe.

Water: n. presence of water, either a spring or near a body of water, but sometimes a surname: / **Water Road**: r., t. Lawrence. / **Water Street**: r., t. Stockholm; s., v. Canton, now Riverside Drive along the Grass(e) River; s., v. Gouverneur; s., v. Hermon, follows Elm Creek toward DeKalb Junction; s., v. Heuvelton, along Oswegatchie River; r., t. Lawrence; s., h. Louisville; s., v. Massena. Formerly, **Mill Street**. Dumas, x; s., v. Morristown, along the St. Lawrence River; s., c. Ogdensburg, along the Oswegatchie; s., h., Nicholville; s., v. Potsdam. / **Water Street Cemetery: near v., t. Edwards, n. Waters family. 1956 USGS Edwards Quad.** / **Water Street School**: no. 2, common school, t. Lawrence.

Watering Trough Hill: between Edwards and Fine, n. place where horses were watered. *Quarterly*, 12 (1967), no. 3, p. 4.

Waterman: Zuriel Waterman, resident: **Waterman Hill**: t. Pierrepont, alt. 700 ft., between Pierrepont Center and Canton. *Quarterly*, 12 (1967), no. 3, p. 8. 1964 USGS Pierrepont Quad. / **Waterman Hill Road**: r., t. Pierrepont, n. hill. / **Waterman Hill School**: no. 11, common school, t. Russell, n. hill.

Watson Road: r., t. Edwards, n. Samuel Watson family from Ireland. A claim is made for Robert Watson, who arrived from Scotland in 1818 or 1819. Durant, 442. / r., t. Morristown, n. Watson family.

Waugum Road: r., h. Helena, a backwoods settlement road to dismal swamps of Lawrence Brook (out of Helena).

Waverly Street: s., v. Potsdam, prob. n. Sir Walter Scott's novel, **Waverly**.

Wayne Hunter Road: r., t. Waddington, n. Wayne Hunter.

Wayside Cemetery: v. Richville, t. DeKalb, n. metaphorically for "death," along the way, "at the side of the way." 1956 USGS Richville Quad

Wayside Inn: place for a change of horses for the trip on the Concord coach from Massena to Norwood. Dumas, 61.

Weaver School: no. 15, common school, t. Morristown, n. Joseph Weaver family from Montgomery County. Bogardus, 60.

Webb: family n.: **Webb Creek**: trib. Blue Mountain Stream, t. Colton. 1921 USGS Stark Quad. / **Webb Road**: r., t. Russell, n. Webb family.

Webster Road: r., t. Hammond, n. Samuel Webster, who settled in the area in 1819. Previously known as **Militia Road**, constructed just before the War of 1812 to connect Sackett's Harbor and Hammond.

Weeks Field: on St. Lawrence University campus, tennis courts, track, and football, n. Lew Weeks.

Wegatchie: h., t. Rossie, p. o. est. Nov. 27, 1849, Artemus M. Church, first pm, closed June 15, 1911. See **Oswegatchie**. *Quarterly*, 17 (1971), no. 4, p. 8. 1961 USGS Natural Dam Quad. / **Wegatchie Cemetery** / **Wegatchie School**: no. 3, common school, t. Rossie.

Welch: a surname used as a specific: **Welch Brook**: t. Parishville, trib. Dead River. 1964 USGS Sylvan Falls Quad. / **Welch Creek**: t. Fine, trib. Oswegatchie River, J. Welch. 1916 USGS Oswegatchie Quad. / **Welch Road**: r., t. DeKalb, Gouverneur, n. Henry Welch who settled in 1808. Cent. Souv., 10. See also **Welsh.**

Weller: a surname, usually a family n., used as a specific: **Weller Mountain**: t. Hopkinton, alt. 2,075 ft., n. Weller, a trapper. 1896 New; 1902 Blankman; 1908 Adm; 1912 Stoddard; 1919 USGS Nicholville Quad; 1964 USGS Lake Ozonia Quad. / **Weller Pond**: t. Hopkinton. n. Weller family. 1896 New; 1902 Blankman; 1908 Adm; 1919 USGS Nicholville Quad; 1964 USGS Lake Ozonia Quad. / **Weller Pond Outlet**: t. Hopkinton, trib. Stony Brook, n. Weller family. 1919 USGS Nicholville Quad; 1964 USGS Lake Ozonia Quad.

Wellings Drive: s., v. Potsdam, n. Wellings family.

Wells: a surname, or family n.: / **Wells Road**: r., t. Stockholm; / **Wells School**: no. 11, common school, t. Louisville. / **Wells Street**: s., v. Canton, n. Abner Wells, early settler in Canton; s., v. Massena.

Welsh Road: r. v. Richville, n. Welsh settlers.

West: sometimes a family n., but usually directional, contrasted with **East**, which see. Seldom will a **West** and **East** appear together; for instance, **East DeKalb** is not balanced with a **West DeKalb. West Avenue**: also **West Street**, s., v. Massena. / **West Babcock Street**: s., v. Gouverneur. / **West Barney Street**: s., v. Gouverneur. / **West Branch [Oswegatchie River]**: t. Edwards, trib. Oswegatchie River. 1956 USGS Edwards Quad. / **West Branch St. Regis River**: trib. St. Regis River, t. Stockholm. 1964 USGS **West Branch** Brasher Falls Quad. / **West Branch** [of Squeak Brook]: t. Brasher, trib. Squeak Brook. 1964 Raquette River Quad. / **West Canton**: t. Canton. / **West Fowler**: t. Fowler, a farming community three miles west of **Little York**, p. o. est. from **Shingle Creek** Jan 25, 1826, James Bailey, pm, closed Feb. 6, 1828, reopened Jan. 15, 1850, Thomas Mitchell, pm (Hough, 575). closed Oct. 29, 1856. Durant, 380. 1956 USGS Gouverneur Quad. Derived n.: **West Fowler Cemetery**; t. Fowler / **West Fowler School**: no. 8, common school, t. Fowler. 1915 USGS Gouverneur Quad. / **West Front Street**: s., v. Rensselaer Falls, parallel to Front Street, only on the west side of the Oswegatchie River. [Hartman]. / **West Hannawa Road**: r., t. Potsdam, Colton. / **West Hatfield Street**: s., v. Massena. / **West High Street**: s., v. Norfolk. / **West Lake Road**: r., t. De Peyster. / **West Main Road School**: no. 4, common school, t. Gouverneur. / **West Main Street**: s., v. Gouverneur, formerly, "**Brooklyn**," or "the other side," "across the river." / **West Orvis Street**: s., v. Massena. / **West Orvis Street Cemetery**: v. Massena. / **West Parishville**: crossroads, t. Parishville; p. o. est. Apr. 7, 1879, Daniel Smith, pm, closed July 30, 1904. 1908 USGS Potsdam Quad; 1964 USGS Potsdam Quad. / **West Parishville Cemetery**. / **West Parishville School**: no. 5, common school, t. Parishville. / **West Parishville State Forest**, #28, t. Parishville. / **West Pierrepont**: h., t. Pierrepont; p. o. est. as **West Pierpont** July 5, 1876, Alvin Robinson, pm, closed Oct. 14, 1903. 1915 USGS Russell Quad. / **West Pierrepont School**: no. 5, common school, t. Pierrepont. 1056 USGS Gouverneur Quad. / **West Potsdam**: t. Potsdam, p. o. est. Sept. 22, 1847, William T. Galloway, pm (Hough, 575; Durant, 246), closed Oct. 14, 1903; originally **Smith's Corners**, after George Gurdon Smith, first settler, also an uncle to Joseph Smith, the famous Mormon leader. Also, **Pudding Hill**, because Amerindians raised corn here and made it into a corn pudding; another story is that during the cold winter of 1816-1817, the only food available was Johnny cake, a pudding made out of yellow corn saved from the harvest. 1964 USGS West Potsdam Quad. / **West Potsdam Cemetery.** / **West Potsdam Road**: r., t. Potsdam. / **West Potsdam School**: no. 16, common school, t. Potsdam. / **West River Street**: s., c. Ogdensburg. / **West Road**: r., t. Russell; r., t. De Peyster. / **West Russell**: See **Stalbird.** / **West South Street**: s., c. Ogdensburg. / **West Stockholm**: v. southwest corner t. Stockholm. Also, **Bickneyville**, a form of the name of Amos Bicknell, who built a grist mill on the site in 1811; p. o. est. Mar. 25, 1825, Joseph H. Sanford, first pm (Hough, 575), existing, ZIP 13696. Also, **Bicknelville**. Durant, 390; *Quarterly*, 10 (1965), no. 1, p. 14. 1964 USGS Potsdam Quad. / **West Stockholm Cemetery**: t. Stockholm. / **West Stockholm School**: no. 4, common school, t. Stockholm. / **West Street**: s., h. Balmat; s., v. Brasher Falls; s., v. Canton, n. West family. / **West Wall Street**: s., v. Gouverneur. See **Wall Street**.

Westaway Road: r., t. Madrid, n. Simon W. Westaway family from Scotland.

Westwood Drive: s., v. Massena.

Whalen: family n.: **Whalen Road**: r., t. Louisville. / **Whalen School**: no. 13, common school, t. Louisville. / no. 1, common school, t. Macomb.

Whaleback Island: in St. Lawrence River, t. Hammond, n. shape. 1963 USGS Morristown Quad. Usually **Whaleback Shoal.**

Wheeler: a popular n. in the county: **Wheeler Avenue**: s., v. Norfolk. / **Wheeler Marsh**: t. Parishville. 1908 USGS Potsdam Quad; 1919 USGS Nicholville Quad; 1964 USGS Rainbow Falls Quad. / **Wheeler Lane**: s., v. Norfolk. / **Wheeler Mountain**: t. Piercefield, alt. 2,205. 1896 New; 1902 Blankman; 1908 Adm; 1912 Stoddard; 1954 USGS Tupper Lake Quad. / **Wheeler Road**: r., t. Potsdam. See also **Camp Wheeler**. Also see **Camp Wheeler**.

Whippoorwill Corners: t. Russell. n. nocturnal bird of the genus *Caprimulgus vociferus*, with the onomato- poetic call. 1915 USGS Russell Quad. / **Whippoorwill Corners State Forest**, #41, t. Russell.

Whiskey Brook: t. Parishville, n. because "in the old days, when Parishville had a distillery, patrons used to stop to add a little volume to the fiery liquor by diluting it a bit with some clear sparkling water from this little brook. . ." and one day a man dropped his jug and broke it. Another came along, saw the broken jug, and called the stream Whiskey Brook. See *Sketches of Parishville*. / **Whiskey Flats**: t. Parishville. / **Whiskey Flats State Forest**, #2, t. Hopkinton.

Whitaker Falls: in West Branch St. Regis River, t. Parishville, n. Whitaker family. 1908 USGS Potsdam Quad.

White: perhaps the most popular color-n., it is also a common surname: **White Church Cemetery**: t. Lisbon. / **White Church School**: no. 4, common school, t. Lisbon. / **White Creek**: t. DeKalb, trib. Borland Creek. 1956 USGS Richville Quad. / **White Hill**: t. Hopkinton. *Quarterly*, 9 (1964), no. 4, p. 17; t. Hopkinton, alt. 1,420 ft. 1908 USGS Potsdam Quad; 1964 USGS Rainbow Falls Quad. Also **Whites Hill**. / **White Hill Road**: r., t. Hopkinton. / **White Hill School**: no. 11, common school, t. Hopkinton. / **White Road**: r., t. Colton, Higley Flow area; r., t. Russell, called **Grandy Road** in 1925, n. Judson C. Grandy, resident. / **White Road East**: r., t. Pierrepont. / **White Road West**: r., t. Clare, n. Osburn White. / **White School**: in Brasher Falls, painted white. *Quarterly*, 15 (1970), no. 4, p. 5. Not in 1896 common school listing; no. 4, common school, on White Road, t. Clare; no. 10, common school, t. Lawrence.

Whiteford Road: r., t. Fowler, n. Whiteford family.

Whitehouse Bay: in St. Lawrence River, t. Waddington. 1963 USGS Sparrow Quad.

Whitman Hall: on St. Lawrence University campus, n. Florence Lee Whitman, an 1882 graduate.

Whitney Pond: t. Hopkinton, alt, 1,516 ft., n. Whitney family. 1896 New; 1902 Blankman: 1908 Adm; 1912 Stoddard; 1920 USGS Childwold Quad.

Whitney: family n.: **Whitney Street**: s., v. Massena; s., v. Norwood.

Wick: surname. **Wick**: h, t. Parishville, n. Sterling Wick; p. o. est. July 27, 1893, Virgil B. Laflin, pm, changed to **Sterlingwick** Mar. 22, 1910. *Quarterly*, 9 (1964), no. 4, p. 17. 1898 New; 1902 Blankman; 1908 Adm; 1912 Stoddard. Also **Upper Wick** and **Lower**

Wick. / **Wick School**: no. 15, common school, t. Parishville. / **Wick**, h., became **Piercefield** in 1901. / **Wick**: a survey township, probably n. Wick, England; ety, OE **wic** "dairy farm."

Wicks Hall: on SUNY Canton College of Technology campus, n. Dr. Rollo Wicks, Professor of Division of General Education, 1944-1971.

Wilbur: a surname used as a specific: **Wilbur Hill**: t. Norfolk, n. Lewis Wilbur family from NH. 1964 USGS Norfolk Quad. / **Wilbur School**: no. 1, common school, t. Oswegatchie, n. Henry C. Wilbur.

Wildwood: corner, t. Colton, desc. and commendatory; p. o. est. Dec. 10, 1902, Frank B. Taylor, pm, never opened, terminated Jan. 29, 1903. 1964 USGS Colton Quad. / **Wildwood Road**: r., t. Colton, n. the wood.

Wiley-Dondero Ship Channel: t. Massena, in St. Lawrence Seaway; channel is ten miles long and includes Dwight D. Eisenhower and Bertrand H. Snell locks. It bypasses the St. Lawrence Power Project's principal structures. The bottom width is 442 ft., water surface width 550 ft., and navigation depth 27 ft.; n. Alexander Wiley (1884-1967), senator from Wisconsin, and George Anthony Dondero, (1883-1968), co-sponsors of the Seaway bill.

Wilkinson Road: r., t. Canton, Potsdam, n. Horatio C. Wilkinson.

Willard: family n.: **Willard Road**: r., t. Louisville. / **Willard School**: no. 4, common school, t. Louisville.

Willes Road: t. Potsdam, n. Sylvanus Willes. Durant, 456.

William: a personal n., usually a surname, used as a specific: **William Street**: s., v. Gouverneur; s., v. Morristown; s., c. Ogdensburg. / **Williams Road**: r., t. Macomb, n. Williams family. / **Williams Street**: s., v. Massena, n. Williams family. / **Williams Town**: see **Williamstown**.

Williamson School: no. 13, common school, t. Parishville, n. Williamson family.

Williamstown: "the capital of Judge Cooper's settlement," now, **DeKalb**. David B. Dill, Jr., "From Cambray to Ogdensburg in 36 Hours with Gouverneur Morris," *Quarterly*, 21, no. 2, p. 6.

Willis: a surname: **Willis Brook**: t. Hopkinton, trib. West Branch St.

Regis River, J. F. Willis. 1880 Ely; 1896 New; 1902 Blankman; 1912 Stoddard; 1920 USGS Childwold Quad; 1964 USGS Sylvan Falls Quad. / **Willis School**: no. 23, common school, t. Stockholm, Robert Willis family. / **Willis Schoolhouse-Wagstaff Road**: r., t. Lawrence.

Willisville: corner, in West Parishville, t. Parishville, n. Charles and John Willis. 1964 USGS Colton Quad. / **Willisville Cemetery**: t. Parishville. A shooting contest was arranged to raise money for the "purchase of land for a burying ground." The bounty money for killing a wolf was to be donated toward the purchase. Now **Riverview Cemetery**. See *Sketches of Parishville*. / **Willisville Road**: r., t. Parishville, n. J. F. Willis.

Willow Street: s., v. Massena. n. tree of the genus *Salix*, usually growing near water or wet land; s., v. Potsdam, n. tree.

Willy Island: in St. Lawrence River, t. Hammond. 1958 USGS Chippewa Quad. Origin n. unknown.

Wilsey: surname used as a specific: **Wilsey Avenue**: s., h. Newton Falls. / **Wilsey Circle**: s., h. Newton Falls.

Wilson: very popular family n. in the county, but none apparently n. Thomas Woodrow Wilson, 28th president of the United States: **Wilson Corners**: crossroads, t. Pierrepont. 1964 USGS Colton Quad. / **Wilson Hall**: on Clarkson University campus, n. Frederick C. Wilson (1875-1968), served from 1915 to 1950 in the Civil Engineering Department and as Dean of Engineering. / **Wilson Hill Island**: in St. Lawrence River, t. Louisville. 1964 USGS Louisville Quad. / **Wilson Hill Road**: r., t. Louisville. Also **Louisville-Wilson Hill Road**. / **Wilson Hill Wildlife Management Area**, t. Louisville. / **Wilson Lake**: pond, t. Hopkinton, n. Samuel Wilson, arrived 1808-9. 1920 USGS Childwold Quad. / **Wilson Mountain**: t. Clifton, alt. 1,850. 1921 USGS Stark Quad. / **Wilson Road**: r., t. Hopkinton; r., t. Pierrepont. / **Wilson School**: no. 18, common school, t. Oswegatchie. / **Wilson Street**: s., v. Massena; s., v. Gouverneur, n. Robert P. Wilson, first officer of first company enlisted in the Civil War (1861); s., v. Heuvelton.

Wilstrop Road: r., t. Canton, possibly n. Austin Wilstrop.

Wiltse Avenue: s., h. Star Lake, located in housing development near Newton Falls, n. Edwin S. Wiltse of New York

City, chairman of New Falls Paper Mill, 1926-1952.

Wind Mill Road: r., t. Colton.

Windfall: called "The Great Windfall" and "The Great Tornado of 1845," created an area where a tornado swept a path 1/2 mile wide through Colton, Hopkinton, and Piercefield and into Franklin Co., in 1845. See "The Great Windfall of 1845 in New York State" (reprinted from **Weatherwise**, no. 14, no. 4, Aug., 1961), *Quarterly*, 7 (1962), no. 1, pp. 8-9, 12. Also, **The Slash**. See Reynolds, 136-138 for pictures of Windfall, NY. / **Windfall Brook**: t. Colton, trib. Racquette River. 1920 USGS Childwold Quad. / **Windfall**: settlement. Colton, p. o. est. July 31, 1899, Charles F. Thomas, pm, closed Feb. 28, 1907. / **Windfall Brook**: t. Colton, trib. Dead Creek. 1921 USGS Stark Quad. / **Windfall Pond**: t. Piercefield. 1860 Merrit; 1880 Ely; 1883 Ely-Wallace; 1896 New; 1902 Blankman; 1908 Adm; 1912 Stoddard; 1920 USGS Childwold Quad. / **Windfall Ponds**: See **Windfall Brook**.

Windsor Road: s., v. Massena, n. Windsor family.

Winn Road: r., at North Lawrence, t. Lawrence, n. Orville E. Winn.

Winning Health Center: on St. Lawrence University campus, n. Stuart A. Winning, trustee emeritus and University physician, 1969-1978.

Winter: surname, but also referring sometimes to road used during inclement and snowy weather: **Winter Road**: r., t. DeKalb. Also **Poor Road**. / **Winter Street**: s., v. Massena.

Winthrop: h., t. Stockholm, n. Henry Wilkerson Winthrop, a descendant of Isaac Kelsey, first settler; p. o. est. Feb. 24, 1891, from **Stockholm Depot**, Eli M. Shaw, first pm, existing, ZIP 13697. Formerly, **Stockholm Depot**; changed to **Winthrop**, Apr. 1, 1891. Mrs. Maude Ellison, credited with the founding of Father's Day, was born in Winthrop. *Quarterly*, 7 (1962), no. 1, p. 8. 1964 USGS Brasher Falls Quad. / **Winthrop Cemetery**: near Winthrop. 1964 USGS Brasher Falls Quad.

Wires School: no. 6, common school, t. Stockholm, n. Wires family.

Witch Bay: in Cranberry Lake, t. Clifton. 1896 New. Reason n. unknown.

Witherbee: see **Ike Noble Drive**.

Wolf: the animal (*Canis lupus*) furnishes its n. to numerous features in the United States, but only a few in the county, since the animal no longer inhabits the area: **Wolf Hole**: pond, t. Clifton. 1921 USGS Stark Quad. / **Wolf Lake**: pond, t. Edwards. 1956 USGS Edwards Quad. / **Wolf Lake State Forest**, #30, t. Hermon and Edwards. / **Wolf Mountain**: t. Clifton, alt. 2,400 ft. 1896 New; 1902 Blankman; 1908 Adm; 1919 USGS Cranberry Quad. / **Wolf Pond**: t. Clifton. 1896 New; 1898 EGB, p. 28; 1902 Blankman; 1908 Adm; 1912 Stoddard; 1921 USGS Stark Quad. / **Wolf Pond Outlet**: t. Fine, trib. Oswegatchie River. 1919 USGS Cranberry Lake Quad. / **Wolf Ridge**: t. Colton, alt. 1,650. 1921 USGS Stark Quad.

Wood: n. presence of forested area or n. family: **Wood Avenue**: s., h. Piercefield. / **Wood Cemetery**: t. Hermon, n. John Wood. / **Wood Haven Drive**: s., h. Star Lake, commendatory. / **Wood Island**: in Black Lake, t. Morristown. 1961 USGS Pope Mills Quad; s., h. Raymondville. / **Wood Road**: r., t. Lisbon, n. Wood family.

Woodbridge Corners: t. Canton, n. George Woodbridge (ca 1810-1866), owner of a large farm and the Quarterway House (a tavern). *Quarterly*, 14 (1969), no. 2 p. 10. A claim is also made for his son Emery Woodbridge (?-1899). **Woodbridge Hill**: t. Canton. / **Woodbridge School**: no. 7, common school, t. Canton. 1963 Lisbon Quad.

Woodcocks Rapids: t. Canton, 4 mi. upstream on the east side of Grass(e) River; land and "to the center of the river" purchased by Daniel P. Woodcock from Henry and Elizabeth Van Rensselaer, Esq., in 1855. A cottage colony developed. Also, **Woodcock's.**

Woodland: desc. of wooded area: **Woodland Drive**: r., t. Louisville; r., t. Norfolk; s., h. Raymondville.

Woodlawn: desc. and promotional n.: **Woodlawn Avenue**: s., v. Massena. / **Woodlawn Cemetery**: t. Fine.

Woods: in the plural form, usually a family or personal n.: **Woods Bridge**: over Grass(e) River, t. Russell, now **Lazy River Bridge**. See **Woods Bridge Road.** / **Woods Bridge Road**: r., t. Hermon, Russell, n. Oliver Woods, merchant and farmer who lived adjacent. Also locally called **Lazy River Road.** / **Woods Cemetery**: t. Hermon, abandoned cemetery on Jonesville Road, n. John Wood and related families adjacent to the no. 4 Jonesville School. /

Woods Drive: s., v. Canton. / **Woods Road**: r., t. Hermon, n. John Wood family, early emigrants from England.

Woodstock Lodge: on Clarkson University campus, the family residence of Augustus L. Clarkson, built in 1827, now a student center.

Woodworth Cemetery: t. Macomb, near Ruby Corners, n. Woodworth family. 1961 USGS Pope Mills Quad.

Wooster Road: r., t. Hammond, n. Wooster family. Wooster. / **Wooster School**: see **Brick School House School**.

Worden: family n.: **Worden Pond**: t. Russell, n. John Worden, but a claim is made for Nathaniel Worden. Clarke, 20. 1915 USGS Russell Quad. / **Worden Road**: r., t. Morristown, n. Aaron Worden. Bogardus, 60. / **Worden School**: no. 13, common school, t. Morristown, n. Aaron Worden. Bogardus, 60.

World War II Memorial Field: on St. Lawrence University campus, baseball and soccer, n. 1965 in memory of military personnel killed in World War II.

Worthmore Park Road: r., t. Norfolk, perhaps an enhancement n.

Wright: surname used as a specific: **Wright Road**: r., t. Potsdam; r., t. Russell, south from Spicer Road in southeast corner of t., n. Silas Wright. / **Wright School**: no. 10, common school, t. Oswegatchie.

Wrightsburgh: t. Madrid, p. o. est. Mar. 31, 1841, Ralph Chamberlain, pm, closed Nov. 30, 1848. Poss. n. Silas Wright.

Wyandot Island: in Chippewa Bay. n. Wyandot Amerindians. *Quarterly*, 16 (1971), no. 3, p. 11.

Wyanoke Island: in St. Lawrence River, t. Hammond, possibly Amerindian n., meaning unknown. 1958 USGS Chippewa Quad.

Wyman Preserve: private forest and game preserve; see **Forest Commission Report**, 1893, p. 154.

Y

Yaleville: h., t. Norfolk. Moses Patterson made first settle- ment in 1806; n. Barnabas Yale and sons, Lloyd C. and John. Claim is also made for John Yale only, who is reported to have owned a house divided in half, with women residing in one half and the men in the other. Durant, 245-246. *Quarterly*, 17 (1972), no. 4, p. 5. 1964 USGS Norfolk Quad. / **Yaleville Road**: r., t. Norfolk.

Yankee Street: r., t. Morristown. Road named for the resident Hadlock brothers, Yankees, from Deerfield, MA. Also, spelled **Yankey**. *Quarterly*, 10 (1965), no. 4, p. 9.

Yellow: color-n.: **Yellow Creek**: trib. Big Creek, t. Pitcairn. 1865 Beers, p. 72, but shown as Portaferry Lake outlet; 1915 USGS Oswegatchie Quad. / **Yellow Creek State Forest**, #44, t. Rossie. / **Yellow Lake**: t. Rossie. "It derives its name from the circumstance of its being covered with the blossoms of the pond lily when first discovered." Durant, 316. Amerindian name: **Katsenekwar**, "lake covered with yellow lilies." 1961 USGS Natural Dam Quad. / **Yellow Lake Road**: r., t. Gouverneur.

York Street: s., v. Heuvelton, n. county in England, former home of the Backus family.

Youngs: possessive of **Young**, family n.: **Youngs Road**: r., t. Fine and s., h. Star Lake; r., t. Hopkinton.

Z

Z. C. A. Property Road: Zinc Corporation of America, r., t. Fowler.

Zophen Cemetery: incorrect listing of **Anshe Zophen**, "People of the North," Jewish congregation, on map of 1963 USGS Ogdensburg East Quad. See **Anshe Zophen**.

References

Barnett, Michael G. *Reminiscences of the early days of the Village of Potsdam*. Typed manuscript, given to K. B. Harder by G. B. North. No date. Barnett was born on April 30, 1874 and died on May 5, 1968. He attended Pine Street School, was graduated from Potsdam Normal School in 1900. He taught at the #17 Grade school from 1900 to 1913. He then owned a general insurance agency until his retirement in 1946.

Beers, S. N. & D. G. *New Topographic Atlas of St. Lawrence County, New York*. Philadelphia: L. H. Everts, 1865.

Brown, Henry A. L., and Richard J. Walton, with introduction by William G. McLoughlin. *John Brown's Tract: Lost Adirondack Empire*. Providence, RI: Rhode Island Historical Society, date not listed.

Blankman, Edgar G. *Geography of St. Lawrence County*. Canton: Plaindealer Presses, 1898.

Bogardus, Lorraine B. *River Reflections: A Short History of Morristown, New York*. Worcester, MA: Danbe Press, 1988. Key: Bogardus.

Child, Hamilton. *Gazetteer and Business Directory of St. Lawrence County*. Syracuse, NY, 1873.

Clarke, Susan, Compiler. *The Birth of Russell 1807-1975: History of Russell, South Russell, North Russell, Clare, DeGrasse*. Bicentennial booklet, 1976.

Corbin, Jay S. *Centennial Souvenir History of Gouverneur, Rossie, Fowler, Hammond, Edwards, DeKalb: Commemorating* "Old Home Week," *August 24-30, 1905. Watertown, NY*: The Hungerford-Holbrook Co., 1905. Key: Cent. Souv.

Costa, Edith L., and Mary H. Biondi. *Top O' The State*. Ogdensburg: Northern New York Publishing Company, 1967.

Dickinson, David, and Steven Crane, compilers. *A Short History and Reminiscences of the County Home, St. Lawrence County, New York. Canton*: Spokesmen of Citizens for Saving the County Home, 1976.

Dobbie, Jean, Louis Greenblatt, and Blanche Levine. *Before Us: Studies of Early Jewish Families in St. Lawrence County 1855-1920.* Potsdam: Privately printed, 1984.

Dumas, Eleanor L. and Nina E. *History of Massena: The Orphan Town.* Illus., Jane Ashley. Massena: Massena Printing, 1976. A Massena Bicentennial Production. Key: Dumas.

Durant, S. W., and H. B. Pierce. *History of St. Lawrence County, New York.* Philadelphia: L. H. Everts & Co., Press of J. B. Lippincott & co., 1878. Key: Durant.

Ekwall, Eilert. *The Concise Dictionary of English Place-Names*, 4th ed. Oxford: At the Clarendon Press, 1960.

Field, John. *Place Names of Great Britain and Ireland.* Totowa, NJ: Barnes & Noble Books, 1980.

Freeman, LaVerne H., chair of Bicentennial Committee. *Edwards on the Oswegatchie: Memories of Township #8 1812-1976.* Edwards: Published for America's Bicentennial 1776-1976, 1976. Key: Freman.

Harder, Kelsie B., ed. *Illustrated Dictionary of Place Names: United States and Canada.* New York: Van Nostrand and Reinhold, 1976.

Harder, Kelsie B., "Name Clusters in the North Country," *New York Folklore*, 3.1-4 (1977), 45-52.

Hough, Franklin B. *History of St. Lawrence and Franklin Counties, New York.* Albany, 1853. Reprinted, Baltimore: Regional Publishing Co., 1970. *Index of Place Names and Personal References in History of St. Lawrence & Franklin Counties*, prepared by Mary H. Biondi, Canton, NY, 1971. Key: Hough.

Hoyt, Van. *Hoyt's Index to Where it's at in St. Lawrence County.* unbound sheets, entries alphabetized, no date. Indexed by the Deputy County Historian for Mary Smallman, County Historian.

Key, John L., and Chester M. Smith, Jr. *New York Postal History: The Post Offices and First Postmasters from 1775 to 1980.* State College, PA: American Philatelic Society, 1982.

Lahey, W. Charles. *The Potsdam Tradition: A History and a Challenge.* New York: Appleton-Century-Crofts, 1966.

Mathews, J. N. *New York.* Buffalo: Hamilton Child, 1903.

Parishville Historical Association.

Sketches of Parishville. Parishville, NY: Parishville Historical Association, 1976.

Pennock, Kathleen. "A Historic Study of the Street Names in Potsdam, New York," unpublished paper, May 14, 1967.

Reynolds, Jeanne, and Bessie Decosse. *Two Towns . . .Two Centuries*. For the Clifton-Fine Bicentennial Committee. Gouveneur, NY: MRS Press, 1976.

Road and Street Guide for St. Lawrence County. West Stockholm, NY: Way-Mark Co., 1988.

St. Lawrence County 1988 Highway Map. County Superintendent of Highways, Canton, NY.

Sandburg, Susan & Mike. *Mormons: Return to Potsdam*. Potsdam, [1978].

Sanford, Carlton. *History of Hopkinton,* 1903.

Smithers, Courtland F. *History of Heuvelton and Vicinity*. Heuvelton, NY: Privately published, 1971.

Smithers, Nina W., and Mary H. Biondi. "From Podunk To Zip Code 13652," *New York Folklore*, 1963.

State of New York. *Annual Report of the Forest Commission For the Year 1893*, Vol. I. Albany: James B. Lyon, State Printer, 1894.

Stewart, George R. *American Place-Names*. New York: Oxford University Press, 1970. Key: Stewart.

Stewart, George R. "A Classification of Place Names," *Names*, 2 (1954), 1-13.

Swart, James M., and Jay A. Bloomfield, *Characteristics of New York State Lakes: Gazetteer of Lakes, Ponds and Reservoirs*, 2nd ed. Albany, NY: Lakes Assessment Section, Division of Water, New York State Department of Environmental Conservation, 1985.

Tedford, Pauline, and Tom Fife, compl. *Waddington, St. Lawrence County*, New York: A Look at Our Past. Ogdensburg, NY: Ryan Press, for the Town of Waddington, 1976. Key: Tedford.

United Publications. *Your Personal Maps of Ogdensburg City, Villages of Canton, Massena & Potsdam, St. Lawrence County, New York: Bicentennial Issue: 1776-1976*. Cincinnati OH 45206: United Publications, Inc., 2337 Victory Parkway, [1976].

United States Department of the Interior Geological Survey. *United States Geological Survey* map quadrangles: 1948 Alexandria Bay; 1911, reprinted 1947, Antwerp; 1951 Antwerp; 1942 Barnhart Island; 1956 Bigelow; 1964 Brasher Falls; 1906 Brier Hill, 1964 Brushton; 1964 Canton; 1920 Childwold; 1958 Chippewa Bay; 1919 Cranberry Lake; 1956 Edwards; 1963 Edwards; 1915, reprinted 1947, Gouverneur; 1956 Gouverneur; 1949 Hammond; 1961 Hammond; 1951 Harrisville; 1963 Heuvelton; 1964 Hogansburg; 1913 Lake Bonaparte; 1951 Lake Bonaparte; 1964 Lake Ozonia; 1963 Lisbon; 1964 Louisville; 1906 Massena; 1964 Massena; 1963 Morristown; 1942 Murphy Island; 1961 Muskellunge; 1961 Natural Dam; 1919 Nicholville; 1964 Nicholville; 1964 North Lawrence; 1904 Ogdensburg; 1963 Ogdensburg East; 1963 Ogdensburg West; 1916 Oswegatchie; 1964 Parishville; 1961 Pope Mills; 1943 Potsdam; 1964 Rainbow Falls; 1964 Raquette River; 1906, reprinted 1942, Red Mills; 1963 Red Mills; 1958 Redwood; 1963 Rensselaer Falls; 1956 Richville; 1915 Russell; 1964 Saint Regis Falls; 1963 Sparrowhawk Point; 1921 Stark; 1964 Sylvan Falls; 1954 Tupper Lake; 1964 Waddington.

Webster, Clarence J. *History of Gouverneur.* Reprinted from *The Tribune-Press* issues of Sept. 4, 1935 to June 24, 1936. Gouverneur, NY: The York Press Corporation, Printers and Publishers, 1936.

St. Lawrence County maps used: 1853 HMC; 1858 Rogerson; 1860 Merrit; 1873 Hamilton Child; 1878 Durant & Pierce; 1880 Ely; 1883 Ely-Wallace; 1896 New; 1898 EGB (E. G. Blankman) map; 1902 Blankman; 1908 Adm; 1912 Stoddard.

Informants

Blocher, Christopher (book design)
Burdick, Neal S. (St. Lawrence University buildings)
Mullens, Mike (Canton College of Technology buildings)
Hartman, Priscilla (streets in Rensselaer Falls)
Hurley, Robert (Edwards and Trout Lake)
Pennock, Kathleen (v. Potsdam streets)
Kutsko, Joseph (contributed forest names)
Pennock, Lee (contributed New York State forest names)
Perrin, Thomas (names from USGS maps)
St. Hilaire, Karen (Clarkson University buildings)

To all the county's historians who have furnished valuable information, we wish to acknowledge their help.

Afterword

Mountains of references and streams of folklore in story and print flowing across the editors' desks have not always been successful in plummeting the depths of truth about every place name. Nearly every rock has been overturned in the search, and many historians' files mined for the most elusive sources. Some have never been found – maybe never will be.

Among those who helped were the majority of official municipal historians of the city, towns, and villages. Perhaps this work will prompt those who hold the key to still unknowns to contact their own historians and share.

– MHS

ST. LAWRENCE COUNTY

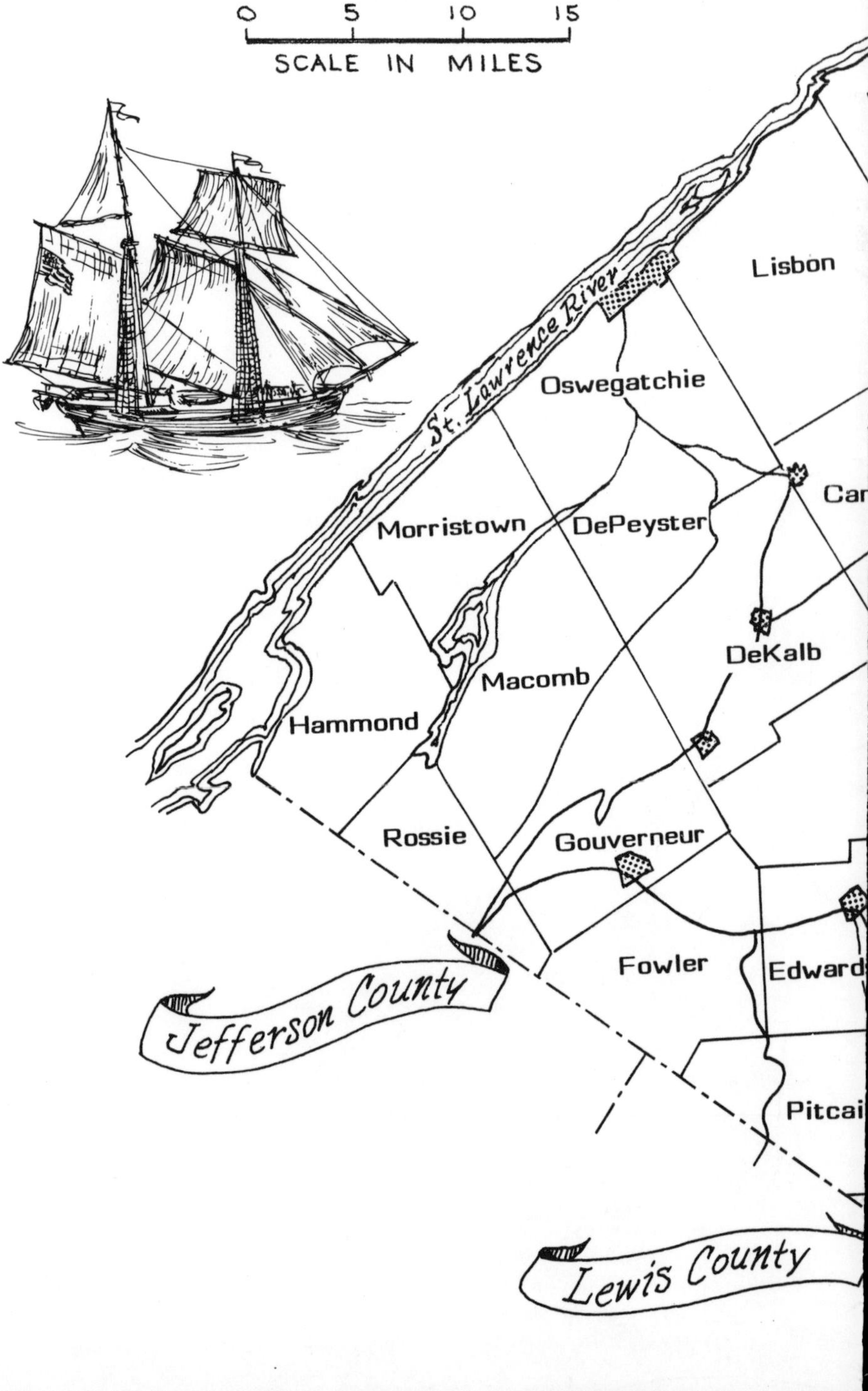